Family Matters

Family Matters focuses on research and clinical material which bridge the traditional gap between child and adult mental health. Rather than considering child and adult problems separately, the authors address the often complex interactions between the two, covering such topics as:

- the implications of childhood trauma in later life
- the impact of parental mental health problems on children
- how interactions within a family can affect the mental health of all individuals within the family

The authors review existing research and cover their own recent studies and practical experience, and put forward new theoretical models to underpin their recommendations for changes in practice, such as liaison initiatives between child and adult services and specialised services to treat adolescents, parenting breakdown and perinatal psychiatric illness.

The findings and recommendations in *Family Matters* have important implications for the organisation and funding of mental health and related services, and staff training, and should be read by all those in professions concerned with child and adult mental health, including psychiatrists, family therapists, psychotherapists, nurses, health visitors and social workers, and health service managers.

Peter Reder is a Consultant Child and Adolescent Psychiatrist at the Child and Family Consultation Centre in west London, and Honorary Senior Lecturer at Imperial College School of Medicine. **Mike McClure** is Consultant Child and Adolescent Psychiatrist in the Chelsea & Westminster Hospital, London, and Honorary Senior Lecturer at Imperial College. **Anthony Jolley** is a Consultant Psychiatrist at Charing Cross Hospital, London.

Family Matters

Interfaces between child and adult
mental health

Edited by Peter Reder, Mike McClure and Anthony Jolley

London and Philadelphia

First published 2000 by Routledge
11 New Fetter Lane, London EC4P 4EE

Simultaneously published in the USA and Canada
by Taylor & Francis Inc
325 Chestnut Street, 8th Floor, Philadelphia, PA 19106

Routledge is an imprint of the Taylor & Francis Group

Typeset in Times by RefineCatch Limited, Bungay, Suffolk
Printed and bound in Great Britain by
Biddles Ltd, www.biddles.co.uk

British Library Cataloguing in Publication Data
A catalogue record for this book is available from the British Library

Library of Congress Cataloging in Publication Data
Family matters: interfaces between child and adult mental health /
[edited by] Peter Reder, Mike McClure, and Anthony Jolley.
    p.   cm.
  Includes bibliographical references and index.
  ISBN 0–415–22217–6 (hbk.)—ISBN 0–415–22218–4 (pbk.)
  1. Psychic trauma—Patients—Family relationships. 2. Family—
Mental health. I. Reder, Peter, 1946– . II. McClure, Mike,
1948– . III. Jolley, Anthony, 1954– .
RC552.P67 F36 2000
616.89—dc21
                                                    00–023155

ISBN 0–415–22217–6 (hbk)
ISBN 0–415–22218–4 (pbk)

Contents

SECTION 3
Children of parents with mental health problems

SECTION 4
Service developments

SECTION 5
Future directions

Tables and figures

Tables

Figures

Contributors

Eia Asen Consultant Child and Adolescent Psychiatrist, Marlborough Family Service, 38 Marlborough Place, London NW8 0PJ; and Consultant Psychiatrist, Maudsley Hospital, London.

Mark Berelowitz Consultant Child and Adolescent Psychiatrist, Royal Free Hospital, Pond Street, London NW3 2QG.

D. Colin Drummond Reader in Addiction Psychiatry, Department of Addiction Behaviour and Psychological Medicine, St George's Hospital Medical School, Level 6, Hunter Wing, Cranmer Terrace, London SW17 0RE.

Sylvia Duncan Consultant Clinical Psychologist, Baker and Duncan Family Consultancy, Ashwood Centre, Stonemason's Court, Cemetery Pales, Brookwood, Woking, Surrey GU24 0BL.

Alicia Etchegoyen Consultant Child and Adolescent Psychiatrist, Chelsea and Westminster Hospital, Fulham Road, London SW10 9NH.

Liz Fellow-Smith Consultant Child and Adolescent Psychiatrist, Children and Families Consultation Service, Windmill Lodge, Uxbridge Road, Southall, Middlesex UB1 3EU.

Geraldine Fitzpatrick Consultant Child and Adolescent Psychiatrist, St George's Hospital, Lanesborough Wing, Blackshaw Road, London SW17 0QT.

Glenda Fredman Consultant Clinical Psychologist, South Kensington and Chelsea Mental Health Centre, Chelsea and Westminster Hospital, 1 Nightingale Place, London SW10 9NG; and Consultant Clinical Psychologist, Camden and Islington Community Trust.

Peter Fuggle Consultant Clinical Psychologist, Clinical Psychology Department, Hornsey Rise Health Centre, London N19 3YU.

M. Elena Garralda Professor of Child and Adolescent Psychiatry, Imperial

College School of Medicine, St Mary's Campus, Academic Unit of Child and Adolescent Psychiatry, Norfolk Place, London W2 1PG.

Martin Herbert   Professor, Psychology Department, Washington Singer Laboratory, Perry Road, Exeter University, Exeter EX4 4QG.

Matthew Hodes   Senior Lecturer in Child and Adolescent Psychiatry, Imperial College School of Medicine, St Mary's Campus, Academic Unit of Child and Adolescent Psychiatry, Norfolk Place, London W2 1PG.

Renuka Jeyarajah Dent   Chief Executive, The Bridge Child Care Development Service, First Floor, 34 Upper Street, London N1 0PN.

Anthony Jolley   Consultant Psychiatrist, Charing Cross Hospital, Fulham Palace Road, London W6 8RF.

Clare Lucey   Consultant Child and Adolescent Psychiatrist, Children and Families Consultation Service, Windmill Lodge, Uxbridge Road, Southall, Middlesex UB1 3EU.

Mike McClure   Consultant Child and Adolescent Psychiatrist, Department of Child and Adolescent Mental Health, Chelsea and Westminster Hospital, Fulham Road, London SW10 9NH.

Colleen McIntyre   Child Protection Coordinator, Riverside Community Trust, Parsons Green Centre, 5–7 Parsons Green, Fulham, London SW6 4UL.

Begum Maitra   Consultant Child and Adolescent Psychiatrist, Child and Family Consultation Centre, 1 Wolverton Gardens, London W6 7DY.

Peter Reder   Consultant Child and Adolescent Psychiatrist, Child and Family Consultation Centre, 1 Wolverton Gardens, London W6 7DY; and Director, Centre for Relationship Studies, Wolverton Gardens.

Juliet Singer   Specialist Registrar in Child and Adolescent Psychiatry, Child and Family Consultation Centre, 1 Wolverton Gardens, London W6 7DY.

Sylvia Tang   Specialist Registrar in Psychiatry, Royal Free Hospital, Pond Street, London NW3 2QG.

Brian Wells   Clinical Director, Farm Place UK, 5 Eaton House, 39/40 Upper Grosvenor Street, London W1X 9PF.

Alison Westman   Consultant Child and Adolescent Forensic Psychiatrist, Three Bridges Unit, Uxbridge Road, Southall, Middlesex UB1 3EU.

Harry Zeitlin   Professor of Child and Adolescent Psychiatry, University College Hospital, Child and Family Consultation Centre, Wych Elm House, Hamstel Road, Harlow CM20 1QR.

Preface

The idea for this book originated in a conference held in London in May 1998, called *'Interfaces between Child and Adult Mental Health'*. The conference aroused considerable interest, not only from participating mental health practitioners and academics but also from social workers, health visitors, managers and purchasers. An obvious development was to produce a book based on the proceedings, with additional chapters to cover topics that could not be represented on the day. The resulting volume has a clinical emphasis, although the authors have based their discussions on theoretical arguments, literature reviews and, in some cases, research projects. The book's aims are to acknowledge the mutual interaction between children and parents, to recognise the various ways that children's and adults' problems overlap and to consider the implications for service delivery.

The interfaces between children and adults have many dimensions and can be considered from the perspective of individual development, intergenerational influences over time, family relationship patterns, or mechanisms through which these processes interact together. Similarly, discussions about the interfaces between child and adult services might focus on liaison between teams to identify previously unrecognised problems in other family members, work with whole families, or preventive measures against intergenerational continuities of disorders. All these dimensions are represented in this volume.

The chapters have been divided into five sections. Section 1 is an introductory overview. Section 2 considers developmental and intergenerational links between children and adults. Section 3 addresses the effects of parental mental health problems on children. Section 4 contains discussions of the various ways that clinical services can address the interfaces between children's and adults' mental health. Section 5 offers theoretical and practical suggestions for future developments. This division is not a strict one, however, since most authors consider both the theoretical and practical aspects of their topic.

It is necessary also to acknowledge what the book does not include. We have intended the chapters to have a psycho-social emphasis and to cover those aspects of the interfaces that do not customarily receive much attention in the literature. We did not set out to compile a comprehensive textbook detailing all developmental models, intergenerational issues, or the impact of every parental psychiatric disorder on children. For example, there is no chapter specifically addressing genetic transmissions, although authors might make mention of them in order to provide balanced arguments. Our belief is that the theoretical and practical inferences drawn from those topics that are included should be generalisable to other areas of work.

We are very grateful to the authors, both those who spoke succinctly at the original conference and then agreed to rework their presentations into fuller papers, and those who had the equally demanding task of contributing additional chapters at the later stage. It is particularly gratifying that some of the co-authored chapters are the result of child and adult specialists coming together to address areas of common concern and interest.

It has been a privilege for us to work on this volume and to be able to blend together the wealth of knowledge and experience that the authors have reported in their respective chapters. We hope that this is reflected in the value that others derive from reading about, and then applying, the practical lessons that emerge.

Peter Reder, Mike McClure and Anthony Jolley

Section 1

Introduction

Chapter 1

Interfaces between child and adult mental health

*Peter Reder, Mike McClure and
Anthony Jolley*

Introduction

What do we mean by the 'interfaces between child and adult mental health'?
One way to illustrate this is through clinical vignettes which raise issues that
are probably echoed in services across the country. Consider the following.

> *A 7-year-old, only child of a single mother develops a sleep disturbance in
> which he resists going to bed and, once in his bedroom, cries for hours on
> end for his mother to comfort him. She regularly ends up sleeping in his bed
> with him as the only way to get him to go to sleep and to allow her to have
> any peace. She has a history of depressive episodes with suicidal thoughts
> which have required recurrent admissions to psychiatric wards and, in her
> more hopeless states of mind, she talks to her son about preparing for a life
> without her.*

Are the problems of parent and child connected and, if so, what interventions
might help resolve them? Could the impact of the mother's problems on her
child have been addressed before he developed symptoms?

> *A female patient is admitted to a psychiatric hospital under a Section of the
> Mental Health Act. The admitting psychiatrist asks about her current fam-
> ily and the patient volunteers that she has a daughter but she is 'all right'.
> That evening, social services are called about this child, who is sitting on the
> doorstep of her home, unable to gain admission because her mother is not
> there.*

Where does the responsibility lie to consider the welfare of the child – in the
mother; in the extended family; in the admitting psychiatrist; in social services; or in a process previously negotiated between the professional agencies
that caters for such circumstances?

> *A 39-year-old man with a long history of drug and alcohol misuse is*

*referred by the court for an expert psychiatric opinion about his capacity to
resume care of his two pre-adolescent children. Their mother has developed
a psychotic disorder and is considered unsuitable as a long-term carer. The
father spent time in the care of the local authority as a child because of
neglect by his parents, and his chronic substance misuse has led to numerous
concerns about his own health and his reliability as a parent. Even so, the
children say that they wish to live with him.*

What factors should the court take into account in determining the future
care of the two children? What types of assessments would assist the court in
its decision?

*A 17-year-old young person comes to the attention of the police because of
allegations that he has been involved in thefts, burglaries and arson. He is
from a broken home, having witnessed violence between his parents before
they separated, and had been referred five years previously to a child mental
health clinic because of aggressive behaviour at school. The family attended
the first assessment session but failed to attend all subsequent appointments
offered.*

What preventive work might have been possible to avoid this escalating anti-
social behaviour? Is it appropriate for mental health services to be involved in
his current management and, if so, should it be a team working with children
and adolescents or with adults?

*A 35-year-old female is admitted to a psychiatric hospital with depression.
In her history, she reveals that both her parents had recurrent depressive
episodes but she also hints that she experienced sexual and emotional abuse
in childhood, although she appears reluctant to talk further about it. Her
preoccupations include fears that her 5-year-old daughter has been
molested by a neighbour.*

What relevance should be given to the different elements of the mother's
history, and how important might it be for her mental health to encourage her
to recall further details of her childhood? Might there be a connection
between the mother's experiences and her concerns for her daughter?

These vignettes illustrate a significant overlap between the psychological
functioning of children and of their parents. Developmentally, the child will
become the adult and the effects of adverse experiences of childhood will be
carried through into adult life. These sequelae will interplay with genetic and
other biological factors, chronic stresses and adverse life events to determine
the adult's mental health. Interactionally, children and their parents (usually)
live in close contact with each other so that the mental health of one will
profoundly affect the mental health of the other. Even if they live apart

because of parenting or psychiatric breakdown, the meaning that each has for the other continues to affect their lives.

Interfaces between children and adults can therefore be considered from a number of different perspectives. First, there is individual development, in which childhood experiences lay the foundations for many facets of functioning in later life. Second, is the aspect of dyadic influence, through which parental behaviour and attitudes impact on the child's developmental processes and general well-being and, conversely, children affect the emotional life of their parents. Third, is the aspect of mutual group influence, in which processes of the whole family system impinge on all of its members, sometimes leading to distress experienced by all of them, at other times to disturbance in the one most vulnerable. The principal family influences may be found in its history or else in the members' current patterns of interaction.

In just the same way that the interfaces between the functioning of children and adults must be considered along different dimensions, so too must discussions about the interfaces between child and adult mental health services. It will be necessary to focus on liaison between different mental health teams, on collaboration between mental health and other welfare services, on interventions to reduce the impact of a parent's or a child's problems on other generations within the family, on work with whole families, or on strategies to prevent psychological dysfunction later in life.

Traditional barriers

The notion of interfaces between child and adult mental health, then, is both a theoretical and a practical one, in which acknowledgement of its many aspects opens up the possibility of modifying mental health services. Before being able to examine these various interface dimensions in detail in the chapters that follow, we shall first consider why mental health professionals have only recently begun to recognise and address such overlaps.

At least three related factors can be identified which have traditionally emphasised the differences between the age groups rather than their interrelationship and thereby acted as barriers to mental heath professionals working across the child–adult interfaces. These are: the theories and knowledge bases which have dominated the specialities; the organisational structures of services; and the ways that professionals are trained. These factors become apparent if we trace the different histories of adult mental health services and child and adolescent mental health services, which reveal parallel, rather than integrated, developments.

Development of the theory and practice of adult mental health services

There have been multiple domains of influence on modern psychiatry (see

Walmsley, 1988). These include the medical and neurological components (e.g. the contributions of Parkinson and Alzheimer), phenomenological description (e.g. by Jasper), the psychological approach (e.g. Freud's study of the unconscious), the sociological component (e.g. the work of Durkheim), and the teachings of eminent clinicians (e.g. Meyer, Lewis and Henderson).

For many years, asylum was the principal intervention available for disturbed people, through which the identified patient was separated from their family and from society and placed in an institutional culture (Jones, 1991; 1993). The asylum's Medical Superintendent position was one of considerable prestige and authority and, within a paternalistic milieu, occupation and physical forms of treatment were the mainstay of management. These treatments included: laxative cures; morphine injections; hydrotherapy; chloral hydrate sedation; bromine sedation; barbiturate-induced sleep therapy; convulsive therapy; and psychosurgery (Shorter, 1997). Freud's psychoanalytic theories and techniques began to be applied in some settings, primarily the voluntary outpatient services (Merskey, 1991; Pines, 1991).

The National Health Service Act of 1946 brought mental hospitals into the same administrative framework as acute hospitals, and general psychiatrists closer once again to neurologists and physicians, whom many still identified as their nearest professional partners. Psychotherapy gained a temporary increase in influence after the Second World War, with development of group therapy for war neuroses and the beginnings of day units and the therapeutic community movement, which emphasised the interrelationship between the patient and their milieu. The 1950s and 1960s witnessed the introduction of the major tranquillisers and anti-depressant medication, followed by the anxiolytics. This significant breakthrough in treatment, together with a change in public policy, led to the progressive closure of the Victorian asylums, with most patients discharged back into the community. Prescription of anxiolytic and anti-depressant medication increased rapidly to become the mainstay of outpatient psychiatric treatment, and only recently have the adverse consequences, such as dependency and cost, become apparent.

Meanwhile, clinical psychology can claim its own history that is both intertwined with the history of psychiatry and distinct from it (e.g. Hearnshaw, 1964; Miller, 1996). The Second World War, with the use of applied psychology in military settings, marked the consolidation of clinical psychology professionally. Initially, their work consisted mainly of psychometric and projective testing, but the introduction of behaviour therapy in the 1950s, followed by cognitive therapy in the 1970s, gave them distinct and specialist skills. Behaviourism also reasserted the role of a person's experiences in the genesis and resolution of mental health problems, while cognitive theories reintroduced the relevance of psychological meaning. However, areas of dissonance between the professions have meant that psychological principles have not been fully integrated into British psychiatric practice, which has remained primarily concerned with 'concepts of organic pathology, syndromal description and classification, and physically oriented treatments' (Parry-Jones, 1996).

This is well represented in Slater and Roth's introduction to the 1969 edition of their textbook *Clinical Psychiatry*, where they claimed that '[the psychiatrist's] special gifts and insights are derived from intimate familiarity with the phenomena of mental disorder and, while he will not wish to define these too rigidly, they should, if he is wise, provide for him the focus of interest' (p. 3). These influential authors expressed concern that 'psychiatry is in danger of losing its connexion with the body of medicine' (p. 1), which 'gives us information about individuals . . . [and] teaches us much about the causes of ill health' (p. 3), and they regarded 'our subject matter and our approach to it as essentially medical and our final concern as being with the health of individuals' (p. 6). Excessive interest in interpersonal relationships was dismissed as dangerous because 'Anatomical, physiological, biochemical, neurological and other modes of investigation are thereby excluded or regarded as of secondary importance' (p. 7). In short, they advocated that 'the primary concern of the psychiatrist is with morbid mental states' (p. 10).

These extreme views were clearly written as a counter-offensive against the anti-psychiatry movement of Laing, Cooper, Goffman and Szasz, and some psychiatrists' interest in psychoanalytic teachings, yet they represented a powerful body of thought at the time, which dominated the practice and training of psychiatrists and from which it has taken decades for the profession to begin to free itself. Historians of psychiatry are still writing that: 'Today, it is clear that when people experience a major mental illness, genetics and brain biology have as much to do with their problems as do stress and their early-childhood experiences' (Shorter, 1997, Preface). As we hope to demonstrate through the pages of this book, both biology *and* experience must be given due relevance when understanding the genesis of human suffering.

Development of the theory and practice of child and adolescent mental health services

Hersov (1986), Clarke and Clarke (1986), Wardle (1991) and Parry-Jones (1994; 1995; 1996) have written interesting accounts of the history of British child and adolescent psychiatry and psychology. Childhood disorders were recognised from the mid-nineteenth century, when a small number of young people were admitted to asylums. However, emergence of mental health services for children and adolescents was primarily within a social context and the result of social concerns for vagrant, destitute, brutalised or offending youngsters. The early years of the twentieth century witnessed the identification of children's educational needs and the emergence of educational psychology and remedial education. Since then, psychological theories of cognitive development and the process of learning have been particularly influential.

Of similar importance was psychoanalytic understanding about emotional development and an individual's vulnerability to psychological distress. Because the child was recognised as a developing being, the importance of experience and of relationships with others was accorded greater relevance to the understanding of psychological distress than was the case in adult psychiatry. Indeed, professionals in child and adolescent mental health services (CAMHS) usually had a much closer working alliance with educationalists or social welfare workers and, later, paediatricians than with adult psychiatrists.

Early child guidance was focused on work with delinquents but quickly broadened its focus to emotional and developmental problems and helping growing children adjust to their environment. According to Parry-Jones (1994, p. 806), the 'multidisciplinary speciality which took shape in the 1920s was a confluence of theories and expertise from paediatrics, asylum medicine, training and custodial care of the mentally retarded, psychoanalysis, psychology, psychiatric social work, remedial education and criminology'. The child guidance clinics that emerged were run by education departments of the local authority, and their teams primarily comprised a tripartite alliance between psychiatrist, psychologist and psychiatric social worker.

For many years, few outpatient hospital departments of child psychiatry existed. Change began in the 1950s as the new National Health Service (NHS) funded hospital services for children. It gathered momentum when asylum-based adult psychiatric services started to be replaced with departments in district general hospitals, since child mental health services were increasingly included within the same organisational structures as services for all other age groups. Identifiable services for adolescents started in the 1950s with the creation of inpatient adolescent units, often within the grounds of psychiatric hospitals. Whatever the setting for the multi-disciplinary groups of staff working with children and adolescents, they were primarily concerned with the interaction between individual developmental processes, family relationships and social experience, and offered treatments oriented towards the psychological therapies.

Training barriers

The training of doctors can be taken as a useful illustration of the way professionals have tended to be trained in a compartmentalised fashion, with insufficient emphasis on integrated learning. For most of the twentieth century, medical schools gave ambiguous messages about their primary aim. While they acknowledged that around half of their graduates would take up careers in general practice (see Davidson et al., 1998), the content of their courses tended to be highly specialised, with undue attention paid to complex and rare problems at the expense of the common ones and little attempt at coordination between the different specialties.

Thankfully, this has begun to change, with greater attention paid to such components as social medicine, psychiatry and the work of general practitioners. Furthermore, innovative methods are being devised to convey an integrative approach, such as allocating students to a family in the community so that they can observe their functioning and development and notice how social and physical factors interact.

It is at the postgraduate level that specialisation tends progressively to restrict practitioners' range of knowledge and interests. Psychiatrists decide early in their careers which age group or style of work they will pursue and this has meant that interfaces between, say, old-age psychiatry and psychotherapy, or substance misuse and adolescent services, have rarely been addressed.

Very recent changes to the training of general psychiatrists introduced by the Royal College of Psychiatrists have begun to redress this, with requirements that all trainees receive supervision in psychotherapy and undertake placements in CAMHS teams. The dilemma this has posed around service delivery within hard-pressed general psychiatry services, however, remains to be solved.

Equivalent issues of early postgraduate specialisation face the clinical psychology and psychotherapy professions, where practitioners must choose whether to focus on work with children or with adults. Often, it is only by deciding to undertake additional post-qualifying training in *family* therapy that these professionals can once again bridge the interfaces between child and adult issues.

In summary, it is evident that the theories, practices and services focusing on child and adolescent problems have a very different history from those concerned with adults. This has prevented areas of common concern from being recognised or addressed. The training of professionals has also exaggerated differences between specialties rather than areas of mutual interest. Fortunately, contemporary changes in knowledge, working practices and central policies have reversed this tendency, and we shall go on to explore these changes in greater detail.

Overcoming the barriers

There is undoubtedly a prevailing climate of interest in overcoming the traditional barriers between child and adult issues. A principal influence has come from academic research. Rutter and Quinton's (1984) landmark study and review about the adverse impact of adult psychiatric disorder on children has been the reference point for an expanding research literature (e.g. Reder and Lucey, 1995; Cassell and Coleman, 1995; Coleman and Cassell, 1995; Göpfert *et al.*, 1996; Falkov, 1997a; 1997b; 1998; Cleaver *et al.*, 1999). In recent years, academic conferences have been held around the UK to address the child protection implications (e.g. Michael Sieff Foundation, 1997), and local liaison initiatives have begun to emerge (e.g. Falkov and Davies, 1997).

Robins's (1966) early longitudinal research on continuities of childhood disorders into later life has been followed up by others (Zeitlin, 1986; Rutter, 1989; Robins and Rutter, 1990), which have clarified the importance of experience as well as genetic endowment in the genesis of psychopathology. A long-standing interest in developmental processes (e.g. Rutter, 1980) has included attention to intergenerational cycles of adversity, particularly parenting breakdown and child maltreatment (e.g. Rutter and Madge, 1976; Quinton and Rutter, 1988; Buchanan, 1996).

Academic pursuits such as these have been part of an interconnected web of influence. At an organisational level, recent changes in NHS structure have encouraged a levelling of hierarchy among sub-specialties, since the operational structures required to manage even the smallest services are the same as for the largest. In the field of mental health, concerns about children and adolescents had long been dominated by the financial and organisational implications of providing services for so many acutely and chronically disturbed adults. However, the new trusts have needed to recognise fully all sub-specialties in order to direct their financial, marketing and managerial affairs, so that they are now accorded appropriate status within the organisations.

Alongside being accorded this higher organisational profile, CAMHS staff have tended to move closer to their general psychiatry and psychology colleagues professionally. They have become less preoccupied with a strict focus on the inner world of individuals and more interested in the interplay between biological, developmental, cognitive, intrapsychic and relational aspects of children's lives. In addition, it must be relevant that those who specialise in children's services have always first trained in work with adults and so are attuned to the interrelational contributions to the total picture. Developmental processes continue to be part of the everyday thinking of child mental health professionals, which prompts curiosity about the transitional and intergenerational links between children and adults.

Within general psychiatry, greater emphasis on care in the community has heightened the significance of the social and family circumstances of patients. The Care Programme Approach enables practitioners to take a wider focus than previously, with its emphasis on a 'needs led', as opposed to 'service led', system. Clinicians are encouraged to identify the range of interventions that might be necessary to meet each patient's various needs and to declare the gaps in available provision. One repercussion of this way of thinking is that the individual's relationships with other family members become a relevant clinical focus. Closer working relationships between clinical psychologists and general psychiatrists in many services have further encouraged this wider perspective. In the sphere of psychiatric training, an important step is the recognition that general psychiatrists need to be conversant with 'the child in the adult', and the Royal College of Psychiatrists (1993) has recently increased the psychotherapy and child and adolescent experience necessary for trainees.

The family therapy movement has had a major influence both on those working with children and those working with adults. The theories that underpin family therapy have varyingly emphasised: intergenerational processes, through which experiences and beliefs rooted in a family's history influence its current functioning (e.g. Lieberman, 1979; Byng-Hall, 1995); contemporary interactional patterns, whereby boundaries between the parents and their children may be observed to be dysfunctional (e.g. Minuchin, 1974); and systemic dilemmas, where natural transitions in the family's life cycle remain unnegotiated (e.g. Selvini Palazzoli *et al.*, 1978). These foundations of the family therapy movement have been well summarised by Hoffman (1981) and it is evident that each of these models addresses one or more aspects of the interfaces between children and adults.

Many professionals in CAMHSs have undertaken family therapy training. At the same time, adult psychiatrists and psychologists have appreciated the relevance of using family approaches to improve their patients' recovery from major disorders (e.g. Leff and Vaughn, 1985; Falloon *et al.*, 1985). The focus on interpersonal phenomena that systemic approaches afford extends even beyond the assessment and treatment of whole families. Systemic thinking has allowed processes at inter-agency levels to be understood (e.g. Reder, 1986; Imber-Black, 1988; Reder and Duncan, 1990) so that the complexities of professional collaboration can be addressed and impediments overcome.

Clinical and academic experiences have rendered the nature–nurture debate progressively more sophisticated and less polarised, with valuable understandings about the interplay between genetic and environmental influences (e.g. Rutter, 1989; Silverman, 1989). Rutter succinctly summarises the integration:

> Knowing that there is a genetic contribution or an environmental contribution is of very little use in its own right. Virtually all forms of psychopathology involve both and it is necessary to move on to the question of which genes have which effect and which psychosocial risk factors are more important and, in both cases, how they operate and how they combine or interact with each other.
>
> (1999, p. 489)

This approach has, in turn, facilitated thinking about problems in a more holistic way. An example is work that shows that exposure of children to neglect or abuse in their formative years has anatomical and physiological consequences for their brain development, which are able to explain their violent, uncaring or overactive behaviour in later years. Perry (1997) described how the lower, more primitive parts of the brain (such as the brain stem, which regulates heart rate, blood pressure and temperature) are over-developed and overactive relative to the higher, more complex parts of the brain (such as the limbic or cortical areas, which are the seat of language and thought) in children who have experienced emotional neglect or been exposed to violence. The underdevelopment and decreased strength of the cortical and sub-cortical impulse-modulating capacity increase the child's arousal, reactivity, impulsivity, aggressivity and proneness to display violence. These children also show physiological hyperarousal, with increased muscle tone, temperature and heart rate and sleep disturbances. Haddad and Garralda (1992) presented five case examples of children with just such histories and clinical presentations that mimicked attention deficit hyperactivity disorder.

A further example of how the academic world has contributed to breaking down the barriers comes from research into Expressed Emotion (EE), which was originally confined to work with adults but is now of considerable interest to those treating young people. EE is a measure of one person's emotional attitude to another, negative features being their criticism, hostility or emotional overinvolvement. It has been demonstrated that high EE in relatives was a significant predictor of an adult patient's likelihood to relapse after recovery from schizophrenic breakdown. High EE was also shown to affect recovery from depression, bipolar affective disorder and obesity (Vaughn and Leff, 1976; Vaughn, 1989).

This work was originally confined to adult patients but has since been taken up in relation to children with physical and emotional problems. Parental overinvolvement has been linked with adolescents' diabetic control (Stevenson et al., 1991) and childhood epilepsy (Hodes et al., 1999). Maternal criticism has been associated with children's asthma (Hermanns et al., 1989), conduct disorder (Vostanis et al., 1994) and continuing symptoms in anorectic adolescents (Le Grange et al., 1992). Following discharge from inpatient treatment for depressive disorders, children returning to high EE homes were found by Asarnow et al. (1993) to have a significantly poorer outcome. Furthermore, changes in EE have been demonstrated in the course of systemic family therapy (Vostanis et al., 1992).

Three studies are of particular significance to the interfaces between child and adult mental health. Schwartz et al. (1990) found an inter-correlation between the critical component of maternal EE, maternal depression, and depression, conduct disorder or substance misuse in their children. Hibbs et al. (1991) concluded that parental psychiatric diagnosis and high EE (even among those parents in remission from their disorder) were linked to children's disruptive behaviour and obsessive compulsive disorder. Hirshfeld et al. (1997) demonstrated an association between criticism shown by mothers with anxiety disorders and the occurrence of psychiatric disorders in their children.

This momentum generated in clinical and academic circles has been maintained by concerns about child abuse and adolescents' problems which have gained public attention and become priorities for central government. With regard to child maltreatment, the Department of Health noticed in case reports submitted to them an association between parental mental health problems and severe or fatal abuse. A study by Falkov (1996) confirmed this link and dissemination of his report has led to numerous initiatives by local authorities and Area Child Protection Committees to address the problem. Around the same time, the government issued guidance that emphasised the need for those working with adults to participate in child protection procedures (Department of Health *et al.*, 1994; Department of Health and Welsh Office, 1995). Debates within trusts about confidentiality have kept children's concerns on the agenda (Reder, 1996a; 1996b).

The 1989 Children Act provided a further impetus to bridging the child/parent interfaces. The Act introduced the notion of 'significant harm' to describe the impact of adverse experiences on children. It required evidence to be placed before courts in child care cases about whether the child had suffered significant harm as a result of the parenting they had received (or were likely to receive in the future). Practitioners therefore needed to pay closer attention to describing the quality of a parent's care of their child and factors that might be impeding it (Reder and Lucey, 1995). The Act also emphasised that the parent's potential to change as the result of therapeutic interventions should be assessed and this has generated considerable interest in the development and validation of parenting skills programmes.

Furthermore, issues of clinical governance (Department of Health, 1998), through which trusts will be held accountable for harm to patients arising out of errors in clinical practice, have stimulated trusts to formalise measures for appraising risk. Many have taken the opportunity to include risk of the patient harming children as one of the factors considered, alongside risk of violence to other adults or to themselves. The Department of Health has continued its interest in the children of parents with mental health problems by sponsoring further literature reviews (Cleaver *et al.*, 1999) and research work (Reder and Duncan, 1999a; Glaser and Prior, 1997) and the development of teaching aids (Falkov, 1998).

Attention to adolescents' problems has tended to be patchy (Parry-Jones, 1995) because this age group has fallen in the gap between child and adult services. However, in Britain, central government has recognised and tried to overcome this, leading to publications by the NHS Health Advisory Service on adolescent mental health services generally (1986), and on substance misuse services for young people specifically (1996). In the area of youth justice, the creation of Youth Offending Teams as a result of the 1998 Crime and Disorder Act brings together professionals from mental health, the police and social services in an attempt to divert young people away from criminal activities. These multi-agency teams are intended to refer young offenders at an early stage to appropriate treatment resources in order to prevent further anti-social behaviour. Thus, adolescent issues continue to enter the public domain and compel health services to address them.

Conclusions

We have arrived at a stage in the development of mental health practice where it is possible to leave behind traditionally polarised divisions between bio-logical and environmental influences, physical and psychological forms of treatment, and child and adult concerns. The vignettes with which we opened this chapter pose questions that mental health and other helping profes-sionals are able to consider and have the potential to resolve. However, des-pite a gathering interest in the issues by many practitioners and policy makers, considerable work remains to be done to interest *all* relevant personnel in the overlapping concerns of children and adults.

One further personal history can be cited to encapsulate why mental health professionals should consider the many interfaces between child and adult mental health.

> *Norma Mortensen had probably been an unwanted child, born to a pro-miscuous mother and an unknown father, and was placed with a professional foster family from the age of 2 weeks, only seeing her mother occasionally thereafter. At the age of 7, her mother was hospitalised with an unremitting psychotic depression and through the rest of her childhood Norma was moved between numerous foster homes and children's homes, where she was sexually abused on more than one occasion. The nature of the abuse is uncertain but it is clear that her disclosures were not believed. She married first at the age of 16 and had two further failed marriages, one of which contained domestic violence. She engaged in countless sexual liaisons, which appeared to be driven by complex motives of mutual exploitation and a desire for physical affection. She was desperate to have children but lost at least three pregnancies. During her adult life, she became dangerously dependent on sleeping tablets and other drugs and drank excessively, suffer-ing recurrent episodes of anxiety and depression which were often linked to blows to her self-esteem or the loss of a close confidante. She resorted to self-harming behaviour and required a number of hospital admissions. She died from an overdose of prescribed medication at the age of 36.*

As a 20-year-old, Norma Mortensen had changed her name to Marilyn Monroe (Summers, 1985; Spoto, 1993; Reder and Duncan, 1999b).

References

Asarnow, J.R., Goldstein, M.J., Tompson, M. and Guthrie, D. (1993) One-year out-comes of depressive disorders in child psychiatric in-patients: evaluation of the prognostic power of a brief measure of expressed emotion. *Journal of Child Psychology and Psychiatry*, 34, 129–137.

Buchanan, A. (1996) *Cycles of Child Maltreatment: Facts, Fallacies and Interventions*. Chichester: Wiley.

Byng-Hall, J. (1995) *Rewriting Family Scripts: Improvisation and System Change*. New York: Guilford.

Cassell, D. and Coleman, R. (1995) Parents with psychiatric problems. In: P. Reder and C. Lucey (eds) *Assessment of Parenting: Psychiatric and Psychological Contributions*. London: Routledge.

Clarke, A.M. and Clarke, A.D.B. (1986) Thirty years of child psychology: a selective review. *Journal of Child Psychology and Psychiatry*, 27, 719–759.

Cleaver, H., Unell, I. and Aldgate, J. (1999) *Children's Needs – Parenting Capacity: The Impact of Parental Mental Illness, Problem Alcohol and Drug Use, and Domestic Violence on Children's Development*. London: The Stationery Office.

Coleman, R. and Cassell, D. (1995) Parents who misuse drugs and alcohol. In: P. Reder and C. Lucey (eds) *Assessment of Parenting: Psychiatric and Psychological Contributions*. London: Routledge.

Davidson, J.M., Lambert, T.W. and Goldacre, M.J. (1998) Career pathways and destination 18 years on among doctors who qualified in the United Kingdom in 1977: postal questionnaire survey. *British Medical Journal*, 317, 1425–1428.

Department of Health (1998) *A First Class Service: Quality in the New NHS*. Department of Health.

Department of Health and Welsh Office (1995) *Child Protection: Clarification of Arrangements between the NHS and Other Agencies*. Department of Health.

Department of Health, British Medical Association and Conference of Medical Royal Colleges (1994) *Child Protection: Medical Responsibilities*. London: HMSO.

Falkov, A. (1996) *Study of Working Together 'Part 8' Reports. Fatal Child Abuse and Parental Psychiatric Disorder: An Analysis of 100 Area Child Protection Committee Case Reviews Conducted under the Terms of Part 8 of Working Together under the Children Act 1989*. Department of Health.

Falkov, A. (1997a) Parental psychiatric disorder and child maltreatment. Part I: Context and historical overview. National Children's Bureau Highlight No. 148.

Falkov, A. (1997b) Parental psychiatric disorder and child maltreatment. Part II: Extent and the nature of the association. National Children's Bureau Highlight No. 149.

Falkov, A. (ed.) (1998) *Crossing Bridges: Training Resources for Working with Mentally Ill Parents and their Children*. Department of Health.

Falkov, A. and Davies, N. (1997) Solutions on the ground: a family mental health service? In: *Report of the 12th Annual Michael Sieff Foundation Conference 'Keeping Children in Mind: Balancing Children's Needs with Parents' Mental Health'*. Michael Sieff Foundation.

Falloon, I.R.H., Boyd, J.L., McGill, C.W., Williamson, M., Razani, J., Moss, H.B., Gildreman, A.M. and Simpson, G.M. (1985) Family management in the prevention of morbidity of schizophrenia. *Archives of General Psychiatry*, 42, 887–896.

Glaser, D. and Prior, V. (1997) Is the term child protection applicable to emotional abuse? *Child Abuse Review*, 6, 315–329.

Göpfert, M., Webster, J. and Seeman, M.V. (eds) (1996) *Parental Psychiatric Disorder: Distressed Parents and their Families*. Cambridge: Cambridge University Press.

Haddad, P.M. and Garralda, M.E. (1992) Hyperkinetic syndrome and disruptive early experiences. *British Journal of Psychiatry*, 161, 700–703.

Hearnshaw, L.S. (1964) *A Short History of British Psychology: 1840–1940*. London: Methuen.

Hermanns, J., Florin, I., Dietrich, M., Rieger, C. and Hahlweg, K. (1989) Maternal criticism, mother–child interaction, and bronchial asthma. *Journal of Psychosomatic Research*, 33, 469–476.

Hersov, L. (1986) Child psychiatry in Britain – the last 30 years. *Journal of Child Psychology and Psychiatry*, 27, 781–801.

Hibbs, E.D., Hamburger, S.D., Lenane, M., Rapoport, J.L., Kruesi, M.J.P., Keysor, C.S. and Goldstein, M.J. (1991) Determinants of expressed emotion in families of disturbed and normal children. *Journal of Child Psychology and Psychiatry*, 32, 757–770.

Hirshfeld, D.R., Biederman, J., Brody, L., Faraone, S.V. and Rosenbaum, J.F. (1997) Expressed emotion toward children with behavioural inhibition: association with maternal anxiety disorder. *Journal of the American Academy of Child and Adolescent Psychiatry*, 36, 910–917.

Hodes, M., Garralda, M.E., Rose, G. and Schwartz, R. (1999) Maternal expressed emotion and adjustment in children with epilepsy. *Journal of Child Psychology and Psychiatry*, 40, 1083–1093.

Hoffman, L. (1981) *Foundations of Family Therapy: A Conceptual Framework for Systems Change.* New York: Basic Books.

Imber-Black, E. (1988) *Families and Larger Systems: A Family Therapist's Guide Through the Labyrinth.* New York: Guilford.

Jones, K. (1991) The culture of the mental hospital. In: G.E. Berrios and H. Freeman (eds) *150 Years of British Psychiatry: 1841–1991.* London: Gaskell/Royal College of Psychiatrists.

Jones, K. (1993) *Asylums and After. A Revised History of the Mental Health Services: From the Early 18th Century to the 1990s.* London: Athlone.

Leff, J. and Vaughn, C. (1985) *Expressed Emotion in Families: Its Significance for Mental Illness.* New York: Guilford.

Le Grange, D., Eisler, I., Dare, C. and Hodes, M. (1992) Family criticism and self-starvation: a study of expressed emotion. *Journal of Family Therapy*, 14, 177–192.

Lieberman, S. (1979) *Transgenerational Family Therapy.* London: Croom Helm.

Merskey, H. (1991) Shell-shock. In: G.E. Berrios and H. Freeman (eds) *150 Years of British Psychiatry: 1841–1991.* London: Gaskell/Royal College of Psychiatrists.

Michael Sieff Foundation (1997) *Report of the 12th Annual Michael Sieff Foundation Conference 'Keeping Children in Mind: Balancing Children's Needs with Parents' Mental Health'.*

Miller, E. (1996) Twentieth century British clinical psychology and psychiatry: their historical relationship. In: H. Freeman and G.E. Berrios (eds) *150 Years of British Psychiatry: Volume II: The Aftermath.* London: Athlone.

Minuchin, S. (1974) *Families and Family Therapy.* London: Tavistock.

NHS Health Advisory Service (1986) *Bridges over Troubled Waters: A Report on Services for Disturbed Adolescents.* London: HMSO.

NHS Health Advisory Service (1996) *Children and Young People: Substance Misuse Services. The Substance of Young Needs: Commissioning and Providing Services for Children and Young People Who Use and Misuse Substances.* London: HMSO.

Parry-Jones, W.L. (1994) History of child and adolescent psychiatry. In: M. Rutter, E. Taylor and L. Hersov (eds) *Child and Adolescent Psychiatry: Modern Approaches*, 3rd edn. Oxford: Blackwell.

Parry-Jones, W.L. (1995) The future of adolescent psychiatry. *British Journal of Psychiatry*, 166, 299–305.

Parry-Jones, W.L. (1996) The heritage of modern child and adolescent psychiatry. In: J. Harris-Hendricks and M. Black (eds) *Child and Adolescent Psychiatry: A New Century*. Occasional Paper OP 33. London: Royal College of Psychiatrists.

Perry, B.D. (1997) Incubated in terror: neurodevelopmental factors in the 'cycle of violence'. In: J.D. Osofsky (ed.) *Children in a Violent Society*. New York: Guilford.

Pines, M. (1991) The development of the psychodynamic movement. In: G.E. Berrios and H. Freeman (eds) *150 Years of British Psychiatry: 1841–1991*. London: Gaskell/Royal College of Psychiatrists.

Quinton, D. and Rutter, M. (1988) *Parenting Breakdown: The Making and Breaking of Intergenerational Links*. Aldershot: Gower.

Reder, P. (1986) Multi-agency family systems. *Journal of Family Therapy*, 8, 139–152.

Reder, P. (1996a) Revised child protection arrangements for the health service. *Child Abuse Review*, 5, 128–132.

Reder, P. (1996b) Child protection: medical responsibilities. *Child Abuse Review*, 5, 64–66.

Reder, P. and Duncan, S. (1990) On meeting systems. *Human Systems*, 1, 153–162.

Reder, P. and Duncan, S. (1999a) *Lost Innocents: A Follow-Up Study of Fatal Child Abuse*. London: Routledge.

Reder, P. and Duncan, S. (1999b) Conflictual relationships and risks of child abuse. *Journal of Child Centred Practice*, 6, 127–145.

Reder, P. and Lucey, C. (eds) (1995) *Assessment of Parenting: Psychiatric and Psychological Contributions*. London: Routledge.

Robins, L.N. (1966) *Deviant Children Grown Up*. Baltimore: Williams & Wilkins.

Robins, L. and Rutter, M. (eds) (1990) *Straight and Devious Pathways from Childhood to Adulthood*. Cambridge: Cambridge University Press.

Royal College of Psychiatrists (1993) Guidelines for psychotherapy training as part of general professional psychiatric training. *Psychiatric Bulletin*, 17, 695–698.

Rutter, M. (ed.) (1980) *Scientific Foundations of Developmental Psychiatry*. London: Heinemann.

Rutter, M. (1989) Pathways from childhood to adult life. *Journal of Child Psychology and Psychiatry*, 30, 23–51.

Rutter, M.L. (1999) Psychosocial adversity and child psychopathology. *British Journal of Psychiatry*, 174, 480–493.

Rutter, M. and Madge, N. (1976) *Cycles of Disadvantage*. London: Heinemann.

Rutter, M. and Quinton, D. (1984) Parental psychiatric disorder: effects on children. *Psychological Medicine*, 14, 853–880.

Schwartz, C.E., Dorer, D.J., Beardslee, W.R., Lavori, P.W. and Keller, M.B. (1990) Maternal expressed emotion and parental affective disorder: risk for childhood depressive disorder, substance abuse, or conduct disorder. *Journal of Psychiatric Research*, 24, 231–250.

Selvini Palazzoli, M., Cecchin, G., Prata, G. and Boscolo, L. (1978) *Paradox and Counterparadox: A New Model in the Therapy of the Family in Schizophrenic Transaction*. New York: Jason Aronson.

Shorter, E. (1997) *A History of Psychiatry: From the Era of the Asylum to the Age of Prozac*. New York: John Wiley & Sons.

Silverman, M.M. (1989) Children of psychiatrically ill parents: a prevention perspective. *Hospital and Community Psychiatry*, 40, 1257–1265.

Slater, E. and Roth, M. (1969) *Mayer-Gross Slater and Roth: Clinical Psychiatry*, 3rd edn. London: Baillière, Tindall & Cassell.

Spoto, D. (1993) *Marilyn Monroe: The Biography*. London: Chatto & Windus.

Stevenson, K., Sensky, T. and Petty, R. (1991) Glycaemic control in adolescents with Type 1 diabetes and parental expressed emotion. *Psychotherapy and Psychosomatics*, 55, 170–175.

Summers, A. (1985) *Goddess: The Secret Lives of Marilyn Monroe*. London: Victor Gollancz.

Vaughn, C.E. (1989) Expressed emotion in family relationships. *Journal of Child Psychology and Psychiatry*, 30, 13–22.

Vaughn, C.E. and Leff, J.P. (1976) The influence of family and social factors on the course of psychiatric illness: a comparison of schizophrenic and neurotic patients. *British Journal of Psychiatry*, 129, 125–137.

Vostanis, P., Burnham, J. and Harris, Q. (1992) Changes of expressed emotion in systemic family therapy. *Journal of Family Therapy*, 14, 15–27.

Vostanis, P., Nicholls, J. and Harrington, R. (1994) Maternal expressed emotion in conduct and emotional disorders of childhood. *Journal of Child Psychology and Psychiatry*, 35, 365–376.

Walmsley, T. (1988) Historical introduction. In: R.E. Kendell and A.K. Zealley (eds) *Companion to Psychiatric Studies*, 4th edn. Edinburgh: Churchill Livingstone.

Wardle, C.J. (1991) Twentieth-century influences on the development in Britain of services for child and adolescent psychiatry. *British Journal of Psychiatry*, 159, 53–68.

Zeitlin, H. (1986) *The Natural History of Psychiatric Disorder in Children*. Institute of Psychiatry/Maudsley Monograph No. 29. Oxford: Oxford University Press.

Section 2

Developmental dimensions

Chapter 2

Continuities of childhood disorders into adulthood

Harry Zeitlin

Introduction

Implicit in any treatment programme is the question, 'What will happen to this child if nothing is done?' If the clinician does not ask that question most likely the child's parents will. There are two aspects to outcome. First, will the child's condition improve, and second, does the childhood disorder, untreated or treated, have any implication for adult mental health? With the enormous cost of adult mental health services more attention is being turned to prevention and early intervention. Psychiatric disorder in adulthood is often not preceded by childhood disturbance and much of the research therefore focuses on childhood environmental factors. However, depending on the population, up to 15 per cent of children will show significant disturbance (Rutter *et al.*, 1970; Rutter, 1973) and it is essential to have some idea as to the long-term outcome in terms of risk for adult morbidity.

To examine links between childhood and adult disorder what is required is reliable contemporaneous data at two points in the life of individuals selected from an identifiable population. Retrospective data is unreliable and prospective studies take a lifetime to complete. Computer databases are now helping but the time span needs to be twenty years or longer and that is only just becoming available. Some studies have attempted to follow up a childhood cohort (e.g. Farrington and West, 1990). The classical study of Robins, some thirty years ago (1966), made use of contemporary records that were detailed and systematic to re-evaluate the same individuals in adult life. Other studies have made use of case records where there is such two-time-point data available (Zeitlin, 1986).

Longitudinal research suffers from many technical difficulties. Harrington and Vostanis (1995) listed some of the methodological problems for long-term research for depressive disorders, but the issues apply as much to most conditions explored. They listed the problems as follows: developmental changes, e.g. symptom manifestation may differ according to development; heterogeneity of mood disorders, e.g. outlook for bipolar disorder is different; differences in definitions of depression; varying definitions of 'relapse';

varying definitions of 'recovery'; differing sensitivity and specificity of assessment tools; sample differences, e.g. clinic v. community; duration of follow-up (i.e. relatively few into adult life); period effects, e.g. changes in precipitants and treatment over time. An additional problem is that many conditions, such as schizophrenia, remain defined by the adult disorder so that 'rarity' in childhood is difficult to interpret.

None the less over the last three decades there has been an accumulation of information about the links between childhood psychiatric disorder and adult mental health (Robins, 1966; Zeitlin, 1986; Rutter, 1989; Thomsen, 1996). Thomsen's more recent study in Denmark confirms the high risk for adult disorder in children referred for behavioural and emotional problems. There has also been greater emphasis on the importance of a developmental perspective to understanding psychopathological processes, and Rutter (1989) pointed out the need to look at developmental discontinuities as well as continuities. More recently, interest has begun to focus on the significance of conditions that appear to occur together, comorbid disorder, particularly with regard to whether the comorbid conditions are phenomenologically different according to the associations.

Research on child–adult continuities sheds light on the classification of disorder but also highlights some of the shortcomings. Most diagnostic groups are operationally defined based on behaviours that tend to occur together. The behaviours themselves are 'epiphenomena' to the underlying process of disorder and as such are rarely specific to any one process, just as a cough and breathlessness are not specific to any one lung disease. Phenomenology of childhood psychiatric disorder is at a relatively primitive stage so that there are no guidelines to distinguish, for example, different types of repetitive behaviour or impaired concentration. In part that is because psychological phenomena are far more diffuse in character in the young, gradually changing with maturity. Thus it is probable that diagnostic groups are mixtures of different underlying pathologies and that in some circumstances individual behaviours are in themselves mixtures of different phenomena.

Child–adult continuities are more stable and clearer for individual behavioural phenomena than for diagnostic groupings, lending weight to the impurity of diagnostic groups. That can be true whether or not behaviours are single or grouped phenomena. The evidence from comorbidity also supports this, as persistence of comorbid conditions appears to vary according to the behaviours that they accompany. There is also supporting evidence for the heterogeneity of the behavioural phenomena themselves. Thus Attention Deficit Disorder (ADHD) in the presence of conduct disorder has a different long-term outcome, particularly with regard to a lack of continuity, to typical ADHD. The continuity suggests more that the phenomenon is one of impaired frustration tolerance. Similar findings are emerging for Obsessive Compulsive Behaviour (OCB). When there is comorbidity with Tourette's syndrome the OCB is different to that in otherwise uncomplicated Obsessive Compulsive Disorder (OCD) (Cath *et al.*, 1992; Eapen *et al.*, 1997).

For the clinician the import is that clinical judgement is still needed to note the particular character of behavioural phenomena, the behavioural associations, the course over time and, above all, to keep an open mind about the possible underlying mechanism. This chapter will try to collate some of the available data on links between child and adult disorder and relate that to the implications for clinical practice.

Childhood major depression

There had been fierce debate in the 1960s as to whether depression did occur in children, some saying that it was rare and others that it was common but usually masked by other symptoms, especially abdominal pain (Cytryn and McKnew, 1972; Frommer and Cottom, 1970; Drotar, 1974).

Depression was originally very much seen as a disorder of adults and until the late 1960s there was no category for childhood depression in the ICD classification (World Health Organization, 1992). Many conditions have been ascribed to depression in childhood but more systematic attempts were made to define depressive disorders in children (Pearce, 1977; Kashani *et al.*, 1981; Puig-Antich and Gittleman, 1982; Kovacs *et al.*, 1984a). The central criteria for major depression in childhood include: depressed mood, anhedonia, tearfulness, irritability and loss of concentration. There should be a change from a former state, the mood alteration should be sustained and there should be evidence of dysfunction.

Once the occurrence of childhood depression became well established (Angold, 1988) attention could turn to identifying outcome. Systematic data concerning prevalence became available and, for example, Asarnow *et al.* (1988) found a relapse rate for hospitalised children of 45 per cent within two years. Kovacs *et al.* (1984b) found at follow-up of children aged 8 to 13 with major depression according to DSM-III (American Psychiatric Association, 1994) the following relapse rate during childhood and adolescence: 26 per cent at 1 year, 40 per cent at 2 years and 72 per cent at 5 years.

It became clear that not only did depression occur during childhood but that the prognosis was far from good, at least during adolescence. The evidence for long-term outcome for childhood depression into adult life remained relatively thin. Using the case records at the Maudsley Hospital it was possible to identify individuals who had attended a clinic both in childhood and in adult life and to compare them with control groups with adult-only records and with childhood-only records (Zeitlin, 1986). Whilst the study was not specifically designed to look at depressive disorders it did reveal valuable data: 81 per cent of children with depressed mood showed depressed mood in adult life, compared with 51 per cent of non-depressed children. Depressive disorder was also predicted but less strongly. The association found does not indicate whether there is a raised risk of becoming ill in adult life, only that there is continuity if the person does become ill. Comorbid disorder was common and some of the poorer association for clinical diagnosis appeared to be due to the clinician rating the comorbid disorder as the main diagnosis rather than identifying the depressive symptoms. When only the depressive symptoms were considered, irrespective of the comorbid conditions, then a strong relationship between childhood and adult depressive syndromes became apparent.

The data also indicated that depressed mood was essential for the continuity. So-called depressive equivalents, such as somatic symptoms, in the absence of evidence for mood disturbance did not show the same correlation with adult depression. Further evidence for the continuity came from the age-related incidence in the sample. During childhood the age-related incidence showed a typical U-shaped curve, lowest at about age 6 to 7. The age of childhood onset for all depressed adults irrespective of the actual childhood symptoms was very similar.

The evidence so far had indicated two things: first that there was a tendency to relapse during childhood and adolescence, and second that if adult disorder occurred for any reason then depressive symptoms would recur in the adult disorder.

Evidence as to whether depressed children are in any case at greater risk for becoming unwell as adults was still lacking but other research began to confirm links with adult disorder (Ryan et al., 1987), possibly co-existing with other disorders (McGee and Williams, 1988). Harrington et al. (1991; 1994) reported a series of studies of outcome for a group of 68 children with major depression. They found that depression in childhood was a strong predictor of suicidal behaviour in adults and that the adult suicidal behaviour was largely related to the presence of adult depression. Other studies have similarly shown increased risk for adult suicidality (Rao et al., 1993), so that evidence is accumulating that childhood depression actually increases the risk for adult disorder.

The last decade has shown better evidence consolidating the picture that childhood depression has very important implications for adult health. There is added information about the persistence and associations of teenage depression. Charman (1994), investigating 268 teenage schoolchildren, using the Children's Depression Inventory (CDI) and a depression self-rating scale, found that depressed mood was relatively stable over time. Lewishon et al. (1994), investigating risk factors for adolescent suicide in 1,508 14–18-year-olds, found further support for the continuity of depression and suicidality into early adult life. Both shared several risk factors, such as being of low self-esteem, having a friend who has attempted suicide, and being born to teenage mothers, fitting well with the evidence linking childhood depression with adult suicidality.

Genetic predisposition was thought mainly to apply to bipolar disorder but there is evidence that relatives of depressed children are more likely to be depressed (Harrington *et al.*, 1993), suggesting a genetic predisposition for the wider range of major depression. Several authors (Angold and Costello, 1993; Fleming *et al.*, 1993) have confirmed a high comorbidity for other conditions, particularly anxiety. The high comorbidity seems likely to be one of the main reasons for the earlier lack of recognition that depression has its own continuity.

There has thus been a major change in the way that depression in childhood is perceived, from being uncommon with no implication for adult health, to being a common childhood disorder that carries significant risk for continuity into adult life and possibly a cycle of transmission through the impact of parental depression on children.

Schizophrenia

Typical schizophrenia as diagnosed in adults on DSM or ICD criteria is rare in early teens and childhood (Watkins *et al.*, 1988; Thomsen, 1996). Inclusion criteria for schizophrenia in adults are still subject to debate and those suffering from the disorder are heterogeneous in many ways. Disagreement over the concepts of 'nuclear disorder', subgroups and spectrum disorder complicates the search for child–adult continuities (Kendell, 1986). Typical psychotic phenomena are in any case harder to identify in children, having a more diffuse nature than in adults.

When schizophrenia is manifest there is a high rate of relapse of psychotic symptoms. Zeitlin (1986) found that over 70 per cent of children with an identified psychotic disorder re-attended the adult department of the same hospital in adult life with a psychotic disorder. Eggers (1978) was a little more optimistic for all cases but particularly for those with schizoaffective disorder for whom the remission rate at a mean 16-year follow-up was about 33 per cent.

About half of all adults with schizophrenia will have presented to clinical services during childhood, though without the adult disorder being anticipated. As the lifetime incidence of schizophrenia is about 1 per cent of the whole population, about 0.5 per cent of children will be seen in clinics. Evidently the majority will not have shown typical symptomatology. The symptoms commonly found in such children include emotional problems such as anxiety and withdrawal, anti-social behaviours including aggression, peer relationship problems and odd, bizarre or unpredictable behaviour (Watkins *et al.*, 1988; Zeitlin, 1986). Many of these children will have evidence of specific developmental delay or neurological dysfunction (Hendren *et al.*, 1995). A 40-year follow-up of boys from the Glueck delinquency study (Hartmann *et al.*, 1984) yielded factors, largely connected with affective appropriateness and social relationships, that gave 88 per cent correct assignment to schizophrenic and non-schizophrenic outcome. However, the authors noted methodological difficulties and they may have been identifying poor outcome in general rather than specifically schizophrenia.

Children who later show a schizophrenic illness seem to be 'different' in a way that does not fit with identifiable phenomena. In Zeitlin's (1986) study almost 60 per cent of such children were described as showing 'odd' or bizarre behaviour, compared with approximately 10 per cent in children destined to remain psychiatrically well or to develop non-psychotic adult disorders. It is likely that this reflects the appearance of thought disorder in children and raises the question as to whether the childhood disturbance is a 'prodrome' or schizophrenia with developmentally determined different manifestations.

This constellation of behaviours fits badly into the available diagnostic categories. Disinhibited behaviour often appears as anti-social behaviour and, for some, the diagnostic category used is conduct disorder. However, it is increasingly likely that the childhood disorder in many such children will be labelled as Asperger's syndrome or Attention Deficit Hyperactivity Disorder, or both.

Of those with such symptoms about half are likely to develop typical evidence for schizophrenia. The others are more probably said to show personality disorder. A different aspect of outcome concerns social competence irrespective of diagnostic symptomatology. Those adults with early onset schizophrenia appear far less socially competent than those with onset in adult life (Zeitlin, 1986). The significance of this is considered separately below.

Quite how to consider the implication of this severe childhood disorder is a matter for debate. It may be argued that these childhood manifestations represent an antecedent or predisposition to psychosis, or the childhood manifestations of schizophrenic disorder itself. As such children may be said to show Asperger's syndrome, another perspective would be that psychosis is one possible adult outcome for that condition. It should not be ruled out that such children could have a neuro-developmental disorder, separate and distinct from either Asperger's or schizophrenia. Unfortunately there is as yet very little long-term outcome data for children showing Asperger's syndrome and no specific independent measures for schizophrenic illness.

Whilst diagnosable schizophrenia is uncommon in childhood, it is difficult to escape a conclusion that a significant proportion of those who later develop schizophrenia are seen in children's services but that the nature of the illness is not recognised. Many of the children concerned present as being very dysfunctional and, whatever the label put on their disorder, they may appear resistant to treatment. Although the symptom complex that they show is not specific to an outcome of schizophrenia, the risk is high. The presence of such disorder throughout childhood and adolescence is also associated with greater social dysfunction in adult life. Whilst there remains uncertainty about the efficacy of antipsychotic medication for recognisable early-onset schizophrenia, some antipsychotic medication is thought to be helpful. For those children who are highly dysfunctional and failing to improve, consideration should be given to recommending a trial of anti-psychotic medication.

Affective psychosis

Major depression does occur in children but the presence of psychotic features is uncommon. For the most part bipolar disorder does not present until after puberty. In teenagers the greatest difficulty is not the distinction from other affective disorders but the differentiation from schizophrenia. Difficulty in diagnostic differentiation between schizophrenic illness and affective psychosis at first presentation in childhood has long been recognised (Zeitlin, 1986; Werry and Taylor, 1994). Longitudinal studies can shed some light. Onset after puberty with a predominant affective component is a more common presentation of affective psychosis (Zeitlin, 1986), but can be followed by more typical schizophrenia. As schizophrenia is the more common disorder, the presence of an affective component at presentation does not distinguish between the two. For some the course appears to be different and they may be better considered to have a schizoaffective disorder (Eggers, 1978; Freeman *et al.*, 1985). Eggers and Freeman *et al.* suggested that such children have a better long-term outlook in terms of a higher rate of remission and lower family morbidity for schizophrenia.

In practice the major implication relates to therapy maintenance and prevention. As the long-term medication for the two main groups of psychosis differs, given the difficulty in diagnostic distinction, it is better to use short-term treatment until the overall pattern becomes clearer.

Conduct disorder

Conduct disorder represents one of the commonest childhood behavioural problems. The behaviours involved include stealing, lying, promiscuity, truanting, etc. Although about half of all children showing such disturbance will make a satisfactory adjustment in adult life, the long-term prospect is for chronicity (Werry, 1997; Storm-Mathisen and Vaglum, 1994) and for impaired social functioning (Zeitlin, 1986; Zoccolillo *et al.*, 1992). Zoccolillo's study of children who had been in residential care found that childhood conduct disorder had a profound effect on adult social functioning even in those who did not receive a diagnosis of personality disorder. The areas included work, relationships and offending behaviour.

Pervasiveness and comorbidity, particularly for substance misuse, are probably the keys to identifying those with the worst prognosis (Myers *et al.*, 1998). Pervasiveness refers to the range of behaviours, the range of locations under which the behaviour is manifest and the duration or length of time over

which the disturbance has been manifest. Earlier age of onset is also associated with a higher rate of continuity (Werry, 1997; Myers *et al.*, 1998). In
Myers *et al.*'s four-year longitudinal study of 137 adolescents with substance
misuse, 61 per cent of those with a childhood diagnosis of conduct disorder
met DSM-III-R criteria for anti-social personality disorder four years later.
Continuity to adult anti-social disorder was predicted by conduct disorder
before age 10, a greater diversity of deviant behaviour, and more extensive
drug use. The Cambridge longitudinal study (Farrington and West, 1990) has
shown that the longer anti-social behaviours had been present, the more
they were likely to continue in the future.

There is some difference of opinion with regard to the significance of
aggression and violence, but for the most part aggression in childhood predicts similar behaviour in adult life (Olweus, 1979; Lundy *et al.*, 1993), and
indeed predicts a greater likelihood of adult anti-social behaviour. Lundy
found that, of 138 pre-adolescent male children who showed violence, 17 per
cent had adult prison records at follow-up in adult life. The converse also
seems to be mainly true, in that the absence of childhood violence predicts its
absence in adult life (Robins, 1978), although there are almost certainly
exceptions to that (Zeitlin, 1986).

Substance misuse

Childhood and teenage substance misuse is now a serious and very common
problem (Miller and Plant, 1996). There are some extremely important
aspects for child–adult continuities. Persistent adult substance misuse is
strongly related to early induction in childhood and adolescence (Robins *et
al.*, 1986; Swadi, 1992). The earlier the age of induction, the greater the likelihood of adult use, the greater the likelihood of addictive behaviour and the
greater the likelihood of progression on to harder and more addictive drugs.
In this respect parental and family factors are of the utmost importance.
Parental substance misuse, particularly alcohol, increases the risk of the children also having persistent alcohol or substance misuse. The converse is also
true. Good parenting with satisfactory relationships and a clear family ethos
against substance misuse are protective, reducing the chance of children
becoming influenced by anti-social peer groups (Garmezy, 1987; Farrington
and West, 1990).

Prognosis for substance misuse is also very much linked with the presence
and nature of comorbid disorder. The relationship between substance misuse
and comorbid disorder is complex and is reviewed elsewhere (Zeitlin, 1999).
In general the comorbid disorder has its own continuity into adult life but the
presence of both gives an overall worse prognosis, whether it is depression,
psychosis or attention deficit disorder. For many associated behavioural problems there is controversy as to whether substance misuse is a consequence of
a pre-existing disorder or whether the disorder arises as a result of substance

misuse. There is evidence that both mechanisms operate but that, in many, the circumstances – both genetically and environmentally – that increase vulnerability to one also do the same for the other.

The major implication is that if anything is to be done to tackle adult substance misuse it should be applied during childhood. At present there are very scant resources available for working with substance-misusing children and, whilst many users do not attend child mental health clinics, clinics tend not to recognise the presence of substance misuse in their clientele.

Obsessive compulsive disorder (OCD)

Emotional disorders as a whole are less clear in their child–adult continuities, with the notable exception of obsessive compulsive disorder and behaviour (OCD and OCB). Until relatively recently OCD was thought to be an uncommon condition with a poor outlook. Earlier studies indicated that prospectively from childhood the prognosis is poor, with a majority having further obsessional episodes during either childhood or adult life (Hollingworth *et al.*, 1980; Zeitlin, 1986). Estimates of the childhood onset for the disorder in adults vary between 20 per cent and over 60 per cent. Flament *et al.* (1990) followed 27 patients for 2 to 7 years. At follow-up 68 per cent still had obsessive compulsive disorder and 48 per cent had another psychiatric disorder, most commonly anxiety and/or depression.

There are two factors that bring this rather gloomy outlook into question. First, Rapoport *et al.* (1992) reviewed childhood obsessive compulsive disorders and proposed that the condition is under-reported with a true community prevalence of up to 5 per cent. Second, OCB is frequently associated with other disorders, including anxiety, depression, Tourette's syndrome, anorexia, conduct disorder, various neurological disorders, particularly temporal lobe epilepsy, and, also, though less often, with schizophrenia (Hollingworth *et al.*, 1980; Zeitlin, 1986; Rapoport *et al.*, 1992). The associated conditions themselves have varying prognostic significance and some of the poor prognosis found may relate to the high comorbidity in referred children. More recent studies have confirmed the presence of OCB in the community and in a follow-up study Thomsen (1995) found that duration of childhood symptoms was the main predictor of later presence in adult life. Those who did continue into adult life showed quite marked social impairment, compared with other psychiatric patients, being more socially isolated and more dependent on parents.

Attention deficit/hyperactivity disorder (ADHD)

ADHD has only recently been subjected to long-term follow-up studies, the majority of outcome research having followed young children into adolescence. However, these are important stepping stones in considering the continuity into adult life. Barkley *et al.* (1990), following 123 hyperactive children into adolescence, found high rates for anti-social behaviour and substance misuse and poorer academic record when compared with controls. They concluded that this pattern was stable. Given that anti-social behaviour tends to persist, it is not surprising that subsequent research has tended to confirm this (Wilson and Marcotte, 1996; Biederman *et al.*, 1996; Greene *et al.*, 1997). Wilson and Marcotte (1996) studied older teenagers who had previously been diagnosed as having ADHD and found that the presence of that condition was related to lower academic performance and poorer social, emotional, and adaptive functioning. Those with conduct disorder fared even worse on the same measures. Level of social dysfunction appears to be a general prognostic factor. In Greene *et al.*'s (1997) four-year follow-up study, children with ADHD who also had social disability had higher rates of mood, anxiety, disruptive, and substance use disorders, compared with non-socially disabled boys with ADHD. Over the four years the social disability was found to be a predictor of later conduct disorder and substance misuse.

Biederman *et al.* (1996), following children aged 4 or over into and through adolescence, found that ADHD symptoms remitted in only 15 per cent, of whom half remitted in childhood and half in adolescence. Predictors of persistence were family history of ADHD, psycho-social adversity, and comorbidity with conduct, mood, and anxiety disorders. A different mechanism for the persistence is suggested by Barkley *et al.* (1991). From observations of mother–adolescent interactions at eight-year follow-up, they found that where the child was hyperactive parent–child interactions displayed more negative and controlling behaviours and less positive and facilitating behaviours towards each other, compared with dyads where the child was not hyperactive. They felt that it was this interaction that maintained the oppositional behaviour.

Longer follow-up studies are beginning to confirm the pattern persisting into adult life. Mannuzza *et al.* (1993; 1998) followed children diagnosed as having ADHD at a mean age of 7.3 years into early adult life (mean age of 24.1 years). They had significantly greater rates than their comparison group for anti-social personality disorder (12 per cent and 3 per cent respectively) and non-alcohol substance misuse (12 per cent and 4 per cent respectively). Mannuzza and colleagues did not find any greater rate in adult life for attention deficit disorder.

Not all of the evidence is so consistent. In a Chinese study, Yan (1996) followed 197 children over 15 years finding that 70 per cent of the probands continued to have typical symptoms. They completed less formal schooling, and were less often employed in higher-level professions. Yan did not find that they exhibited significantly more conduct problems. These findings are the reverse of Mannuzza's and they could almost be different children, and indeed may be so. ADHD that is comorbid for conduct disorder may be nosologically different from other ADHD because of its long-term association with personality disorder, overall raised incidence of psychopathology and substance misuse. The findings of Faraone *et al.* (1998) are similar to those of Mannuzza's group and they suggest that ADHD in the absence of conduct disorder tends to breed true into adult life, but when comorbid for conduct disorder it is different and part of the comorbid condition rather than a separate entity.

Autistic spectrum disorders

There are few studies reporting the long-term outcome for Asperger's syndrome. The long-term course of autistic disorders is somewhat better researched and a recent study confirms the expected path. Nordin and Gillberg (1998) found that the majority of those with autism show deviance and socially or psychiatrically handicapping conditions throughout life. Those with 'high-functioning' autism and Asperger's syndrome improved enough to live an independent adult life. The level of cognitive functioning and other comorbid conditions (e.g. epilepsy) were factors determining outcome. An IQ below 50 and absence of communicative speech at 5–6 years of age were indicative of a poorer long-term overall outcome. Larsen and Mouridsen (1997) reported on 18 children, 9 with autism and 9 with a diagnosis of Asperger's syndrome, followed for 30 years. In adulthood the autistic patients had a poorer outcome than children with Asperger's syndrome as regards education, employment, autonomy, marriage, reproduction and the need for continuing medical and institutional care.

General factors relating to long-term outcome

Long-term outcome studies show some consistent patterns across different diagnostic groups. One of the most important is the significance of comorbid disorder. Long-term outcome is related to comorbid disorder for a number of conditions including depression, conduct disorder, OCB, substance misuse, ADHD, Asperger's and autism.

The nature of impact of comorbid disorder depends to some extent on the conditions concerned. For nearly all, comorbid disorder means a worse prognosis. For some conditions, phenomena seem to differ in nature according to comorbidity: for example, OCB appears to have different characteristics when associated with Tourette's syndrome (Eapen *et al.*, 1997). A general effect on outcome is seen when conduct disorder co-exists with substance misuse, with overall greater social incompetence and a higher risk of continuing with the substance misuse. Although each has fairly independent continuities into adult life, the co-existence of depression and conduct disorder introduces two specific effects: increased suicidal risk and higher rates of substance misuse (Rowe *et al.*, 1996; Myers *et al.*, 1998).

Comorbidity for attention deficit disorder and substance misuse is well reported (Biederman *et al.*, 1996; Mannuzza *et al.*, 1993), but the relationship is complex. The association has been found to predict greater adult use of substances (Carroll and Rounsaville, 1993). Biederman's group found that co-existence of ADHD and substance misuse was related to longitudinal persistence, particularly in males when conduct disorder was also comorbid (Milberger *et al.*, 1997), but it is possible that the ADHD associated with conduct disorder is in any case different from that in its absence (Faraone *et al.*, 1997). Some of the associations vary also according to the age of the child (Grilo *et al.*, 1996).

A second general finding that appears to apply across diagnostic groups is that of impaired adult social functioning (Zeitlin, 1986; Zoccolillo *et al.*, 1992). Zeitlin's (1986) longitudinal study found that, whilst in adult life the inclusion criteria for each diagnosis were identical, those commencing in childhood had evidence for greater social impairment. For adult schizophrenia, for example, it was apparent that for those who had shown childhood disorder there was evidence for greater social impairment on a variety of criteria, including relationship problems and socio-economic status, compared with their own parents, and with those with adult onset disorder. Mannuzza *et al.* (1997) made similar observations for ADHD. Children with ADHD followed into adult life had less often completed their education and had lower ranking occupations than controls.

There are several suggested mechanisms. At least for schizophrenia there is some evidence that those commencing in childhood have greater evidence for neurological dysfunction, and that this could apply to other, though not all, diagnostic groups. Persistence of dysfunction through developmental years is likely to have an adverse impact on the process of development. There is some evidence that difficult behaviours have secondary effects by impairing parent–child relationships, as for ADHD and conduct disorder. It is most likely that all such mechanisms operate to some extent.

The findings of longitudinal research suggest that at least some adult psychiatric morbidity could be prevented by treatment of childhood disorder, and point towards the advisability of investment in child and adolescent mental health services as a preventive measure. If early treatment can be confirmed as effective, it will be acting both to alleviate suffering in childhood and disorder later in life, with enormous implications for service costs.

References

American Psychiatric Association (1994) *Diagnostic and Statistical Manual of Mental Disorders*, 4th edn. (DSM-IV.) Washington: American Psychiatric Association.
Angold, A. (1988) Childhood and adolescent depression. I. Epidemiological and aetiological aspects. *British Journal of Psychiatry*, 152, 601–617.
Angold, A. and Costello E.J. (1993) Depressive comorbidity in children and adolescents: empirical, theoretical and methodological issues. *American Journal of Psychiatry*, 150, 1779–1791.

Asarnow, J.R., Goldstein, M.J., Thomson, M. and Guthrie, D. (1988) Childhood-onset depressive disorders. A follow up study of rates of rehospitalisation and out of home placement among child psychiatric inpatients. *Journal of Affective Disorders*, 15, 245–253.

Barkley, R.A., Fischer, M., Edelbrock, C.S. and Smallish, L. (1990) The adolescent outcome of hyperactive children diagnosed by research criteria: I. An 8-year prospective follow-up study. *Journal of the American Academy of Child and Adolescent Psychiatry*, 29, 546–557.

Barkley, R.A., Fischer, M., Edelbrock, C., Smallish, L. (1991) The adolescent outcome of hyperactive children diagnosed by research criteria: III. Mother–child interactions, family conflicts and maternal psychopathology. *Journal of Child Psychology and Psychiatry*, 32, 233–255.

Biederman, J., Faraone, S., Milberger, S., Curtis, S., Chen, L., Marrs, A., Ouellette, C., Moore, P. and Spencer, T. (1996) Predictors of persistence and remission of ADHD into adolescence: results from a four-year prospective follow-up study. *Journal of the American Academy of Child and Adolescent Psychiatry* 35, 343–351.

Carroll, K.M. and Rounsaville, B.J. (1993) History and significance of childhood attention deficit disorder in treatment-seeking cocaine abusers. *Comprehensive Psychiatry*, 34, 75–82.

Cath, D.C., van de Wettering, J.M., van Woerkom, T.C.A.M., Hoogduin, C.A.L., Roos, R.A.C. and Rooijman, H.G.M. (1992) Mental play in Gilles de la Tourette's Syndrome and obsessive-compulsive disorder. *British Journal of Psychiatry*, 161, 542–545.

Charman, T. (1994) The stability of depressed mood in young adolescents: a school based survey. *Journal of Affective Disorders*, 30, 109–116.

Cytryn, L. and McKnew, D.H. (1972) Proposed classification of childhood depression. *American Journal of Psychiatry*, 129, 149–155.

Drotar, D. (1974) Concern over the categorisation of depression in children. *Journal of Pediatrics*, 85, 290–293.

Eapen, V., Robertson, M.M., Alsobrook, J.P. and Pauls, D. (1997) Obsessive compulsive symptoms in Gilles de la Tourette Syndrome and obsessive compulsive disorder. *American Journal of Medical Genetics (Neuropsychiatric Genetics)*, 74, 432–438.

Eggers, C. (1978) Course and prognosis of childhood schizophrenia. *Journal of Autism and Childhood Schizophrenia*, 8, 21–36.

Faraone, S.V., Biederman, J., Jetton, J.G. and Tsuang, M.T. (1997) Attention deficit disorder and conduct disorder: longitudinal evidence for a familial subtype. *Psychological Medicine*, 27, 291–300.

Faraone, S.V., Biederman, J., Mennin, D., Russell, R. and Tsuang, M.T. (1998) Familial subtypes of attention deficit hyperactivity disorder: a 4-year follow-up study of children from antisocial-ADHD families. *Journal of Child Psychology and Psychiatry*, 39, 1045–1053.

Farrington, D.P. and West, D.J. (1990) The Cambridge study in delinquent development: a long-term follow-up of 411 London males. In: H.-J. Kerner and G. Kaiser (eds) *Criminality: Personality, Behaviour, and Life History*. Berlin: Springer-Verlag.

Flament, M.F., Koby, E., Rapoport, J.L., Berg, C.J., Zalin, T., Cox, C., Denckla, M.

and Lenane, M. (1990) Childhood obsessive-compulsive disorder: a prospective follow-up study. *Journal of Child Psychology and Psychiatry*, 31, 363–380.

Fleming, J.E., Boyle, M.H. and Offord, D.R. (1993) The outcome of adolescent depression in the Ontario Child Health Study follow up. *Journal of the American Academy of Child and Adolescent Psychiatry*, 32, 28–33.

Freeman, L.A., Poznanski, E.O., Grossman, J.A., Buschbaum, Y.Y. and Banegas, M.E. (1985) Psychotic and depressed children: a new entity. *Journal of the American Academy of Child Psychiatry*, 24, 95–102.

Frommer, E.A. and Cottom, D. (1970) Undiagnosed abdominal pain. *British Medical Journal*, 4, 113.

Garmezy, N. (1987) Stress, competence and development: continuities in the study of schizophrenic adults, children vulnerable to psychopathology, and the search for stress-resistant children. *American Journal of Orthopsychiatry*, 57, 159–174.

Greene, R.W., Biederman, J., Faraone, S.V., Sienna, M. and Garcia-Jetton, J. (1997) Adolescent outcome of boys with attention-deficit/hyperactivity disorder and social disability: results from a 4-year longitudinal follow-up study. *Journal of Consulting and Clinical Psychology*, 65, 758–767.

Grilo, C.M., Becker, D.F., Fehon, D.C., Edell, W.S. and McGlashan, T.H. (1996) Conduct disorder, substance use disorders, and coexisting conduct and substance use disorders in adolescents. *American Journal of Psychiatry*, 153 (suppl.), 914–920.

Harrington, R. and Vostanis, P. (1995) Longitudinal perspectives and affective disorder. In: I. M. Goodyer (ed.) *The Depressed Child and Adolescent: Developmental and Clinical Perspectives*. Cambridge: Cambridge University Press.

Harrington, R., Fudge, H., Rutter, M., Pickles, A. and Hill, J. (1991) Adult outcomes of childhood and adolescent depression. II. Links with antisocial disorders. *Journal of the American Academy of Child and Adolescent Psychiatry*, 30, 434–439.

Harrington, R., Fudge, H., Rutter, M., Bredenkamp, D., Groothues, C. and Pridham, J. (1993) Child and adult depression: a test of continuities with data from a family study. *British Journal of Psychiatry*, 162, 627–633.

Harrington, R., Bredenkamp, D., Groothues, C., Rutter, M., Fudge, H. and Pickles, A. (1994) Adult outcomes of childhood and adolescent depression. III. Links with suicidal behaviours. *Journal of Child Psychology and Psychiatry*, 35, 1309–1319.

Hartmann, E., Milofsky, E., Vaillant, G., Oldfield, M., Falke, R. and Ducey, C. (1984) Vulnerability to schizophrenia: prediction of adult schizophrenia using childhood information. *Archives of General Psychiatry*, 41, 1050–1056.

Hendren, R.L., Hodde Vargas, J., Yeo, R.A., Vargas, L.A., Brooks, W.M. and Ford, C. (1995) Neuropsychophysiological study of children at risk for schizophrenia: a preliminary report. *Journal of the American Academy of Child and Adolescent Psychiatry*, 34, 1284–1291.

Hollingworth, C.E., Tanguay, P.E., Grossman, L. and Pabst, P. (1980) Long term outcome of obsessive-compulsive disorder in childhood. *Journal of the American Academy of Child Psychiatry*, 19, 134–144.

Kandel, D.B. and Davies, M. (1986) Adult sequelae of adolescent depressive symptoms. *Archives of General Psychiatry*, 43, 255–262.

Kashani, J.H., Husain, A., Shekim, W.O., Hodges, K.K., Cytryn, L. and McKnew, D.H. (1981) Current perspectives in childhood depression: an overview. *American Journal of Psychiatry*, 138, 143–153.

Kendell, R.E. (1986) The classification and phenomenology of schizophrenia:

overview. In: A. Kerr and P. Snaith (eds) *Contemporary Issues in Schizophrenia.* London: Gaskell/Royal College of Psychiatrists.

Kovacs, M., Feinberg, T.L., Crouse-Novak, M.A., Paulauskas, S.L. and Finklestein, R. (1984a). Depressive disorders in childhood. I. A longitudinal prospective study of characteristics and recovery. *Archives of General Psychiatry*, 41, 229–237.

Kovacs, M., Feinberg, T.L., Crouse-Novak, M.A., Paulauskas, S.L., Pollock, M. and Finklestein, R. (1984b). Depressive disorders in childhood. II. A longitudinal study of the risk for a subsequent major depression. *Archives of General Psychiatry*, 41, 643–649.

Larsen, F.W. and Mouridsen, S.E. (1997) The outcome in children with childhood autism and Asperger syndrome originally diagnosed as psychotic. A 30-year follow-up study of subjects hospitalized as children. *European Child and Adolescent Psychiatry*, 6, 181–190.

Lewishon, P.M., Rhode, P. and Seely, J.R. (1994) Psychosocial risk factors for future suicide attempts. *Journal of Consulting and Clinical Psychology*, 62, 297–305.

Lundy, M.S., Pfohl, B.M. and Kuperman, S. (1993) Adult criminality among formerly hospitalized child psychiatric patients. *Journal of the American Academy of Child and Adolescent Psychiatry*, 32, 568–576.

McGee, R. and Williams, S. (1988) A longitudinal study of depression in 9 year old children. *Journal of the American Academy of Child and Adolescent Psychiatry*, 27, 342–348.

Mannuzza, S., Klein, R.G., Bessler, A., Malloy, P. and LaPadula, M. (1993) Adult outcome of hyperactive boys. Educational achievement, occupational rank, and psychiatric status. *Archives of General Psychiatry*, 50, 565–576.

Mannuzza, S., Klein, R.G., Bessler, A., Malloy, P. and Hynes, M.E. (1997) Educational and occupational outcome of hyperactive boys grown up. *Journal of the American Academy of Child and Adolescent Psychiatry*, 36, 1222–1227.

Mannuzza, S., Klein, R.G., Bessler, A., Malloy, P. and LaPadula, M. (1998) Adult psychiatric status of hyperactive boys grown up. *American Journal of Psychiatry*, 155, 493–498.

Milberger, S., Biederman, J., Faraone, S.V., Wilens, T. and Chu, M.P. (1997) Associations between ADHD and psychoactive substance use disorders. Findings from a longitudinal study of high-risk siblings of ADHD children. *American Journal of Addiction*, 6, 318–329.

Miller, P.M. and Plant, M. (1996) Drinking, smoking and illicit drug use among 15 and 16 year olds in the United Kingdom. *British Medical Journal*, 313, 394–397.

Myers, M.G., Stewart, D.G. and Brown, S.A. (1998) Progression from conduct disorder to antisocial personality disorder following treatment for adolescent substance abuse. *American Journal of Psychiatry*, 155, 479–485.

Nordin, V. and Gillberg, C. (1998) The long-term course of autistic disorders: update on follow-up studies. *Acta Psychiatrica Scandinavica*, 97, 99–108.

Olweus, D. (1979) Stability of aggressive reaction patterns in males: a review. *Psychological Bulletin*, 86, 852–875.

Pearce, J. (1977) Depressive disorder in childhood. Annotation. *Journal of Child Psychology and Psychiatry*, 18, 79–83.

Puig-Antich, J. and Gittelman, R. (1982) Depression in childhood and adolescence. In: E. S. Paykel (ed.) *Handbook of Affective Disorders*. Edinburgh: Churchill Livingstone.

Rao, U., Weissman, M.M. and Hammond, R.W. (1993) Childhood depression and risk of suicidality: a preliminary report of a longitudinal study. *Journal of the American Academy of Child and Adolescent Psychiatry*, 32, 21–27.

Rapoport, J.L., Swedo, S.E. and Leonard, H.L. (1992) Childhood obsessive compulsive disorder. *Journal of Clinical Psychiatry*, 53 (suppl.), 11–16.

Renouf, A.G. and Kovacs, M. (1994) Concordance between mother's report and children's self reports of depressive symptoms: a longitudinal study. *Journal of the American Academy of Child and Adolescent Psychiatry*, 33, 208–216.

Robins, L. (1966) *Deviant Children Grown Up*. Baltimore: Williams & Wilkins.

Robins, L. (1978) Sturdy predictors of adult antisocial behaviour. Replication of longitudinal studies. *Psychological Medicine*, 8, 611–622.

Robins, L.N., Helzer, J.E. and Pryzbeck, T. (1986) Substance abuse in the general population. In: J.E. Barrett and R.M. Rose (eds) *Mental Disorder in the Community: Progress and Challenge*. New York: Guilford.

Rowe, J.B., Sullivan, P.F., Mulder, R.T. and Joyce, P.R. (1996) The effect of a history of conduct disorder in adult major depression. *Journal of Affective Disorder*, 37, 51–63.

Rutter, M. (1973) Why are London children so disturbed? *Proceedings of the Royal Society of Medicine*, 66, 1221–1225.

Rutter, M. (1989) Pathways from childhood to adult life. *Journal of Child Psychology and Psychiatry*, 30, 23–51.

Rutter, M., Tizard, J. and Whitmore, K. (1970) *Education, Health and Behaviour*. London: Longman.

Ryan, N.D., Puig-Antich, J., Ambrosini, P., Rabinovitch, H., Robinson, D., Nelson, B., Iyengar, S. and Twomey, J. (1987) The clinical picture of major depression in children and adolescents. *Archives of General Psychiatry*, 44, 854–861.

Storm-Mathisen, A. and Vaglum, P. (1994) Conduct disorder patients 20 years later: a personal follow-up study. *Acta Psychiatrica Scandinavica*, 89, 416–420.

Swadi, H. (1992) A longitudinal perspective on adolescent substance abuse. *European Child and Adolescent Psychiatry*, 1, 156–169.

Thomsen, P.H. (1995) Obsessive-compulsive disorder in children and adolescents: predictors in childhood for long-term phenomenological course. *Acta Psychiatrica Scandinavica*, 92, 255–259.

Thomsen, P.H. (1996) Schizophrenia with childhood and adolescent onset – a nationwide register-based study. *Acta Psychiatrica Scandinavica*, 94, 187–193.

Watkins, J.M., Asarnow, R.F. and Tanquay, P.E. (1988) Symptom development in childhood schizophrenia. *Journal of Child Psychology and Psychiatry*, 29, 865–878.

Werry, J.S. (1997) Severe conduct disorder – some key issues. *Canadian Journal of Psychiatry*, 42, 577–583.

Werry, J.S. and Taylor, E. (1994) Schizophrenia and allied disorders. In: M. Rutter, E. Taylor and L. Hersov (eds) *Child and Adolescent Psychiatry. Modern Approaches*, 3rd edn. Oxford: Blackwell.

Wilson, J.M. and Marcotte, A.C. (1996) Psychosocial adjustment and educational outcome in adolescents with a childhood diagnosis of attention deficit disorder. *Journal of the American Academy of Child and Adolescent Psychiatry*, 35, 579–587.

World Health Organization (1992) *The ICD 10 Classification of Mental and Behavioural Disorders*. Geneva: World Health Organization.

Yan, W. (1996) An investigation of adult outcome of hyperactive children in Shanghai. *Chinese Medical Journal (English)*, 109, 877–880.

Zeitlin, H. (1986) *The Natural History of Psychiatric Disorder in Children*. Maudsley Monograph No. 29. Oxford: Oxford University Press.

Zeitlin, H. (1999) Psychiatric comorbidity with substance misuse in children and teenagers. *Drug and Alcohol Dependence*, 55, 225–234.

Zoccolillo, M., Pickles, A., Quinton, D. and Rutter, M. (1992) The outcome of childhood conduct disorder: implications for defining adult personality disorder and conduct disorder. *Psychological Medicine*, 22, 971–986.

Chapter 3

Abuse then and now

Peter Reder and Sylvia Duncan

Maltreatment by parents can have a profound impact on children's psychological development, with consequences that intrude into many aspects of their functioning in adult life. Greater sensitivity by those working with children to the prevalence of child abuse is leading to an increased awareness by all mental health practitioners of the pervasive impact of maltreatment during the formative years. This chapter addresses the significance of childhood abuse in a number of related areas. First, we consider its impact on the emotional life and development of children, and factors that afford children some degree of resilience. Next, we consider the long-term effects that persist into adult life, including risk of psychiatric breakdown, and the degree to which mental health professionals take account of such histories. We also address whether 'memories' of childhood abuse can be recovered many years later. Then, we discuss the intergenerational repetition of abuse and factors that afford resilience to such continuities.

Each of these topics is huge in its own right, with a considerable literature devoted to it. Our purpose is to summarise current knowledge about the issues in order to demonstrate their interrelationship and to highlight the implications for mental health practitioners. We shall only cite representative publications in order to indicate the significant trends in the literature, pointing to more comprehensive reviews where available.

Problems of definition can make comparisons of reports extremely difficult (Sheldrick, 1991). For example, researchers use varying parameters for what constitutes abusive behaviour and many do not clarify such important factors as the age at which the maltreatment occurred. Some do not distinguish between neglect and physical, sexual or emotional abuse, nor do they consider their overlap, since many children suffer from combinations of maltreatment. Furthermore, different criteria may be used as the measure of later psychological or psychiatric disturbance. None the less, certain patterns do appear in the literature with sufficient regularity to permit practical inferences to be drawn.

Impact of abuse on children

Current knowledge about the short- and long-term effects of childhood abuse has been brought together by Browne and Finkelhor (1986), Wolfe (1987), Sheldrick (1991), Briere (1992), Beitchman *et al.* (1992), Kendall-Tackett *et al.* (1993), Mullen *et al.* (1993) and Corby (1993), amongst others. Although the bodily assaults associated with physical and sexual abuse of children are undoubtedly traumatic, it is widely believed that the accompanying psychological injuries associated with all forms of abuse have the most profound effects (e.g. Claussen and Crittenden, 1991; Gibbons *et al.*, 1995). The violation and exploitation of the child, together with powerlessness and fear engendered, are major assaults on the child's sense of self and capacity to trust and to tolerate closeness with others, which may scar them psychologically for life.

Sylvia Duncan and Tony Baker (unpublished) consider that the impact of abuse on children is best understood within a developmental framework which recognises that their repertoire of emotional responses to trauma increases with progressive cognitive maturity. Although each child has their individual rate of cognitive development, in general, young children of pre-school age have limited ability to understand their experiences, and their principal responses to abuse are anxiety and confusion. They are still dependent on their parents, so that their anxieties include fear of abandonment. From approximately school age, children's cognitions become more ego-centric and they develop a greater capacity for guilt and shame, believing themselves to be the cause of the trauma. Later, children think more in terms of personal rights and social justice and their responses tend to be dominated by anger and a sense of unfairness. By their teens, young people are able to think abstractly and construct hypotheses, so that they can compare what is with what might have been and so experience grief and a sense of loss.

Therefore, the impact of maltreatment on a child not only depends on the nature and severity of the abuse, but also the age of the child when it occurred and the personal and interpersonal supports available at the time to help them make sense of their experiences. If there was insufficient containment to allow the child both to acknowledge the hurt and to believe they can survive it, they resort to defences which leave the conflicts unresolved and liable to re-emerge in later life as psychological or psychiatric disturbance. In addition, the meaning that children attribute to the events is modified through progressive cognitive development as they grow up, giving rise to changing emotional attitudes to the memories.

This model is consistent with research findings about the factors that shield children from the harshest sequelae of adversity, such as abuse.

Resilience

It is suggested that between one-quarter and one-third of those exposed to childhood abuse will not develop problems of personal adjustment (Finkelhor, 1990; Lynskey and Fergusson, 1997).

Rutter (1985) argued that protection arises as the result of an interaction between personal qualities and experiences. Adversity sets in motion a chain of events and their meaning varies according to the young person's temperament and stage of development, while different people will expose themselves to different experiences. The key elements in determining the outcome throughout are the person's sense of self-esteem and self-efficacy. The availability of another close, affectionate and supportive person, whether it be a non-abusing parent or mentor outside the family, is crucial in providing this self-esteem. This, in turn, increases the possibility of the individual forming a satisfying adult partnership later in life, which is itself another protective factor. Experience of success in any other area of life as a child, such as at school, contributes to the sense of self-efficacy and an internal locus of control, leading on to a propensity to act positively. A sense of helplessness and being a victim of circumstance, on the other hand, will increase the likelihood that one adversity will lead to another, and so on.

The positive factors that repeatedly emerge from studies of resilience are support from the non-offending parent (e.g. Conte and Schuerman, 1987; Spaccarelli and Kim, 1995) and a supportive family atmosphere (e.g. Kendall-Tackett *et al.*, 1993; Romans *et al.*, 1995). It is argued that these both confirm the reality that abuse did occur and minimise the child's self-blame (Wyatt and Mickey, 1988). Furthermore, Himelein and McElrath (1996) concluded that successful resolution of child sexual abuse involves some component of cognitively confronting and reflecting on one's experience. Scholastic and sporting success emerged as important mediating factors in Romans *et al.*'s study (1995). Clinical experience suggested to Gorell Barnes (1996) that children are protected from traumatising family relationships if they also have experiences which are developmentally appropriate and consistent with a child's world, such as is provided by play, sport, social life and other supportive adults.

Effects of childhood abuse in adult life

Although some children show resilience to the psychological trauma of abuse, many suffer emotional problems that persist into adult life. Briere (1992) has discussed the common effects of childhood abuse on the emotional and relationship functioning of adults, which include:

- *post-traumatic effects*, including the typical post-traumatic stress disorder symptoms of flashbacks and intrusive thoughts;

- *negative self-perceptions*, such as guilt and self-blame, impoverished self-esteem and learned helplessness;
- *impoverished sense of self*, for instance, identity problems, attachment difficulties, feelings of emptiness and boundary confusion;
- *altered emotional states*, especially depression, anxiety and somatisation;
- *dissociation*, including amnesia, numbing, depersonalisation and multiple personality disorder;
- *impaired interpersonal relationships*, such as ambivalence about intimacy, disturbances of sexual behaviour or problems with aggression or control;
- *avoidance behaviour*, for example, self-destructive actions, substance misuse and impulsivity.

Childhood abuse and psychiatric disorder in adult life

Clearly, many of the problems identified by Briere are liable to present to mental health services and there is now an extensive literature showing a link between childhood abuse and adult psychiatric and psychological disorder (see reviews by Browne and Finkelhor, 1986; Malinosky-Rummell and Hansen, 1993; Arellano, 1996; Read, 1997). Some of the studies sought to identify the extent of psychological problems in the community linked to a history of childhood abuse (e.g. Bifulco *et al.*, 1991; Mullen *et al.*, 1993; Fergusson *et al.*, 1996), or were interested in the effects of experiencing assaults at any time in the patients' lives (e.g. Carmen *et al.*, 1984; Jacobson and Richardson, 1987). We have restricted our focus here to investigations of clinical populations, in other words those psychiatric patients whose histories contained experiences of maltreatment during childhood.

The figures from our review need to be set against estimates for the prevalence of abusive experiences during childhood in the general population. Bifulco and Moran (1998) brought together results from a community study of inner-city women, 18 per cent of whom disclosed 'marked' or 'moderate' physical abuse as a child, 17 per cent 'marked' or 'moderate' neglect, with considerable overlap between these two forms of abuse, and 9 per cent sexual abuse involving contact. By contrast, Baker and Duncan (1985) found that 6 per cent of women admitted to contact sexual abuse.

Table 3.1 collates the available reports and demonstrates considerable variation in the findings. Among general psychiatric populations, prevalences ranging from 22 per cent to 76 per cent have been found, with an average between the studies of 48 per cent. Reported prevalences for patients with specific psychiatric disorders have ranged between 16 per cent and 90 per cent, with an average across the studies of 46 per cent. It is unclear whether these variations are the result of methodological discrepancies, such as many studies focusing only on female patients and histories of sexual abuse, or whether they stem from differences in definition. It is even possible that some of these figures are underestimates, since a proportion of patients withdrew

Table 3.1 Childhood abuse in the histories of psychiatric patients

Reference	Study group	Type of abuse	% abused	Further details
General psychiatric patients				
Rosenfeld, 1979	18 female outpatients	sexual, as child	33%	
Bryer et al., 1987	66 female inpatients	sexual and physical, <16 yrs	59%	sexual 21%, physical 15%, both 23%
Briere and Runtz, 1987	152 female crisis centre patients	sexual, <15 yrs	44%	
Craine et al., 1988	105 female inpatients	sexual, <18 yrs	51%	substance misuse 88%, schizophrenia 49%, affective disorder 48%, personality disorder 35%, neurosis 17%
Chu and Dill, 1990	98 female inpatients	sexual and physical, <16 yrs	63%	sexual 12%, physical 28%, both 23%
Jacobson and Herald, 1990	100 inpatients	sexual, <16 yrs	40%	females 54%, males 26%
Metcalfe et al., 1990	100 male patients	sexual, <16 yrs	23%	
Margo and McLees, 1991	38 female inpatients	sexual and physical, <16 yrs	76%	physical 18%, sexual 10%, both 47%
Walker and James, 1992	51 female emergency clinic patients	sexual and physical, <16 yrs	64%	sexual 49%, physical 48%
Palmer et al., 1992	115 female inpatients and outpatients	sexual, <16 yrs	50%	personality disorder 58%, manic-depression 50%, neurosis 50%, schizophrenia 40%
Wurr and Partridge, 1996	120 inpatients	sexual, <16 yrs	56%	males 39%, females 52%, personality disorder 60%, affective disorder 56%, substance misuse 47%, schizophrenia 38%, neurotic disorder 37%
Read, 1998	100 inpatients	sexual and physical, as child	22%	sexual 17%, physical 12%
Specific groups of psychiatric patients				
Sheldon, 1988	115 female psychotherapy patients	sexual, as child	17%	
Sarwer and Durlak, 1996	359 female sex therapy patients	sexual, <15 yrs	20%	
Beck and van der Kolk, 1987	26 female inpatients with psychosis resistant to treatment	sexual, as child	46%	

Study	Abuse type, age	%	Notes
Rohsenow et al., 1988	sexual, <17 yrs	74%	
	42 female inpatients for substance misuse		
Schaeffer et al., 1988	sexual, <17 yrs	18%	
	94 male inpatients for substance misuse	physical, as child	31%	
Windle et al., 1995	100 male inpatients for alcoholism	sexual and physical, <18 yrs	41%	
Teets, 1995	802 inpatients for alcoholism	sexual, <18 yrs	68%	sexual, 15%, physical 14%, both 12%
	60 female inpatients for chemical dependency			
Gil-Rivas et al., 1996	sexual, <12 yrs	22%	
	330 drug programme patients	physical, <12 yrs	25%	
Palmer et al., 1990	158 female patients with eating disorders	sexual, <16 yrs	31%	females 31%, males 10% females 21%, males 29%
Waller, 1991	67 female patients with eating disorders	sexual, <16 yrs	37%	
McClelland et al., 1991	50 female patients with eating disorders	sexual, <17 yrs	30%	anorexia 21%, bulimia 20%, mixed 58%
Walker et al., 1988	25 females with chronic pelvic pain	sexual, <15 yrs	64%	
Morrison, 1989	60 female patients with somatising disorder	sexual, <18 yrs	55%	
	31 female patients with affective disorder	sexual, <18 yrs	16%	
Zlotnick et al., 1995	37 female patients with depression	sexual and physical, <16 yrs	46%	
Ogata et al., 1990	18 inpatients with depression	sexual, as child	22%	
		physical, as child	33%	
	24 inpatients with borderline personality disorder	sexual, as child	71%	
		physical, as child	42%	
Shearer et al., 1990	40 female inpatients with borderline personality disorder	sexual, <15 yrs	40%	
		physical, <15 yrs	25%	
Putnam et al., 1986	100 patients with multiple personality disorder	sexual, as child	83%	
		physical, as child	75%	
Ross et al., 1990	102 patients with multiple personality disorder	sexual, as child	90%	
		physical, as child	82%	

from some studies once they were aware of its nature (e.g. Chu and Dill, 1990; Palmer *et al.*, 1992), or severely disturbed patients were not included in others (see Read, 1997).

Despite these limitations, there is support for the proposition that histories of abuse are linked to a range of psychiatric disorders, including the psychoses, and that there is a high association with personality disorders and substance misuse.

A number of the reports listed in Table 3.1 have particular clinical interest. Walker and James (1992) interviewed 51 women attending an emergency/walk-in psychiatric clinic and found a history of childhood physical or sexual abuse in 64 per cent. Fifteen of the 25 who had been sexually abused, and 15 of the 24 who had been physically abused, felt that the abuse had relevance for their present difficulties. Although only 16 per cent of the sexually abused inpatients questioned by Wurr and Partridge (1996) saw a definite connection between this and their mental health problems, a further 40 per cent replied that they were not sure.

There is evidence that abusive histories are associated with more serious symptoms and a worse prognosis. For example, Bryer *et al.* (1987) found a direct association between severity of disorder and history of abuse, and Read (1998) reports that sexually abused women and physically abused men spent significantly longer in psychiatric hospital on each admission. These two studies are typical of the many that point to a link between suicidal behaviour and childhood abuse. Margo and McLees (1991) concluded that women with histories of abuse had entered the mental health system at a younger age, and had higher depression scores, than psychiatric patients without such a history. Zlotnick *et al.* (1995) calculated that women with a history of physical or sexual abuse were 3.7 times more likely not to have recovered from a manic-depressive episode within 12 months than those women without such a history.

The more detailed research by Beck and van der Kolk (1987) is particularly salutary because it was prompted by curiosity about a group of institutionalised, treatment-resistant, psychotic women who were prone to confusion, agitation and violence and also kept approaching staff to engage in affect-laden conversations. Although many had already volunteered histories of sexual abuse to staff, the sexual content of their communications had been considered delusional.

The link with somatising disorders is worthy of note by physicians and surgeons as well as psychiatrists. Roy (1998) has provided impressive evidence from the literature and from his own clinical experience that psychogenic pain can have its origins in childhood abuse. Graphic illustrations were also offered by Arnold *et al.* (1990), who described 7 psychiatric patients with histories of childhood sexual abuse who had a mean of 18 contacts with medical and surgical teams and a mean of 8 operations with a 66–70 per cent rate of normal findings.

A striking finding of many of the reports is that the psychiatric patients might disclose their childhood abuse at any stage of their contact with clinicians or researchers. This especially applied to their experiences of sexual abuse. Half of Rosenfeld's (1979) psychotherapy patients revealed their history of abuse during therapy rather than at the outset of treatment. Four of the 32 women with eating disorders studied by Waller (1991) voluntarily disclosed prior sexual abuse later in their therapy, after the research was completed, and always during the process of examining the basis of automatic thoughts associated with low self-esteem. Jacobson and Herald (1990) noted that 56 per cent of patients who had experienced serious childhood sexual abuse and had been in therapy previously had not revealed their experiences to their therapists.

Furthermore, few clinicians appear to make enquiry about this aspect of their patients' upbringing or, if they do so, do not accord it much significance. Most of the clinical staff involved with the 51 per cent of patients who disclosed sexual abuse during childhood or adolescence to Craine et al. (1988) were unaware of these histories. Only 28 per cent of the female emergency clinic patients interviewed by Walker and James (1992) who admitted to sexual abuse histories during the study had disclosed this at initial clinical interview. A history of childhood sexual abuse was elicited by Wurr and Partridge (1996) from 56 per cent of patients questioned but from only 14 per cent of their notes. Introduction of routine inquiry about childhood sexual abuse at intake interview raised the disclosure rate amongst female substance misuse patients from 20 per cent to 74 per cent (Rohsenow et al., 1988). A random review of case notes by Goater and Meehan (1998) revealed that reference to enquiry about sexual abuse in childhood was only contained in 17 per cent and a positive history noted in under 5 per cent.

Macpherson and Babiker (1994) surveyed mental health professionals, wondering whether they included questions about childhood sexual abuse in their initial assessments: of 32 respondents, just 3 replied that they routinely asked male patients about this and only 5 asked female patients. Therefore, it is understandable that 31 per cent of general psychiatrists surveyed by Haeger and Dalton (1988) claimed never to have come across a case of an adult who had been sexually abused as a child. This is brought home by the reflections of the 24 sexual abuse victims who had previously seen a psychiatrist who were contacted by Pribor and Dinwiddie (1992): 21 had not found the psychiatrist helpful and most had neither volunteered their abusive history nor been asked about it.

Fergusson et al. (1996) placed research findings into perspective, inferring from their own community study that exposure to sexual abuse in childhood accounted for approximately 10 per cent to 20 per cent of the risk of psychiatric disorder in young adults. They suggest that abuse is:

one of a large class of adverse childhood factors spanning social disadvantage, family dysfunction, and childhood adverse life events which individually make relatively small contributions to the risk of disorder but which in combination may have a large impact on individual adjustment.

(Fergusson *et al.*, 1996, p. 1373)

Adult memories of childhood abuse

Our inference that many adult psychiatric patients would include relevant information about abusive experiences in childhood *if asked* should not be mistaken for the presumption held by a few practitioners that earlier sexual abuse is the central cause of all adult psychopathology and patients should be actively encouraged to 'recall' their forgotten memories of it. Indeed, a controversy remains unresolved about whether adults can recover through counselling valid memories of childhood abuse of which they were previously unaware. The issue has become plagued by dogma, vested interests and social pressures (e.g. Ofshe and Watters, 1995; Brandon *et al.*, 1998) and it is not possible to rehearse all the arguments here. Instead we shall briefly summarise the two sides of the debate.

On the one hand, it is clear from the previous sections that many adults do not volunteer information about abuse they did experience, and also that dissociation is a common feature of those who were once abused. For example, Terr (1991) has proposed that children remember well a single severely traumatic event but protect themselves with denial, repression and dissociation following long-standing or repeated exposure to trauma. Bowlby (1988) gave an important reminder that parents may disconfirm children's sense of reality by overtly warning them not to remember traumatic experiences. In particular, fathers often bewilder the child whom they are sexually abusing by behaving as though the abusive events have never occurred and also telling the child that they would never be believed if they were to disclose to someone else.

On the other hand, it is suggested that individuals do not fully forget memories of trauma, whether it was a single event or repeated, so that 'recovery' through counselling cannot be valid (e.g. Pope, 1998). Pope *et al.* (1998) reviewed recent studies on memory for traumatic events, including childhood abuse, and concluded that there is insufficient evidence for dissociative amnesia. Brandon *et al.*'s literature review (1998) led them to similar inferences, including the clarification that memory of traumatic events is not repressed but the associated affect may be suppressed.

Brewin (1996) tried to find areas of consensus and reported that most independent commentators agree that memories may be recovered from total amnesia that are essentially accurate but, equally, such 'memories' may sometimes be inaccurate in whole or in part. Dale and Allen (1998) also attempted to bridge the polarised theoretical debate. Their qualitative study suggested that the majority of adults abused as children have a continuous knowledge that they had been abused, although awareness may be kept from the fore-front of their minds or additional details of the experiences may emerge over time. However, a minority of abused individuals do recover unexpected memories from a state of no apparent prior awareness of the abuse.

Although Leavitt (1997) found that suggestibility was not a feature of those who had claimed recovered memories of abuse, the whole problem has been compounded by a small but vociferous group of counsellors who are not neutral to the issue and actively seek evidence from the client of child-hood abuse that they are convinced occurred. They fail to realise that their therapeutic interpretations are only hypotheses that may be invalid, and this has led the Royal College of Psychiatrists (1997) to issue warnings to its members on overzealous pursuit of presumed hidden memories of abuse. As Jones (1998) observed, the treatment community needs to tread a delicate middle way between caution and facilitation.

The transgenerational repetition of abuse

As the result of prospective studies, there is now reasonable consensus that approximately one-third of abused children will go on to become abusers of their own offspring (Kaufman and Zigler, 1987; 1989; Buchanan, 1996). The high rate of 70 per cent intergenerational continuity found by Egeland *et al.* (1987) included 42 per cent of parents who were providing 'borderline' care and were 'suspected of maltreating' their children. Oliver (1993) suggested that, while one-third of abused parents will abuse their child, a further one-third remain vulnerable to repeating abusive care, depending on extrafamilial pressure. Egeland *et al.* (1987) also concluded that the more severe the ori-ginal abuse, whatever its nature, the greater was the likelihood of the mother continuing an abusive parenting pattern.

Rutter (1989) offered a model within which to understand intergenera-tional continuities of abuse, arguing once again that there is a cumulative risk of serious parenting breakdown over a person's life cycle, which stems from a long chain of indirect connections. Each adverse experience creates a set of circumstances that makes it more likely that another adverse experience will occur. For instance, a hostile family environment may lead to family break-down and an inability to plan in life, so that partners are chosen who them-selves have personal problems, and these relationships are unstable and unsupportive, early pregnancies occur, and so on.

Fonagy *et al.* (1994) considered that aversive experiences of an extreme kind could lead to a defensive inhibition of particular mental functions, espe-cially the capacity for self-reflection. They argued that, if mothers are unable to reflect on their infant's mental state, the infant would become insecurely attached. The notion of internal working models associated with attachment theory was also used by Egeland *et al.* (1988), Zeanah and Zeanah (1989) and

Morton and Browne (1998) as the linking paradigm, in which the early infant–caregiver attachment relationship provides the prototype for later relationships. In particular, the child evolves expectations of the availability of others in time of need and a complementary model of the self as worthy, or unworthy, of care.

Egeland and Susman-Stillman (1996) have provided support for the hypothesis that dissociative processes are involved in the transmission of abuse across generations. They found that mothers who were abused as a child and then abused their own children recalled their own childhood history in an inconsistent, fragmented, disconnected or idealised fashion and showed high levels of dissociative symptoms.

Resilience

There is a consistent pattern to the main factors that have been found to mitigate against a transgenerational repetition of abuse and which are remarkably similar to those described as affording children resilience generally to adverse experiences. Egeland *et al.* (1988) reported that 'exception' mothers significantly differed from 'continuity' ones in: having had an emotionally supportive adult available during childhood; having undergone therapy (of over one year's duration) at any time in their lives; and in describing their relationship with their partner as stable, satisfying and supportive.

Rutter (1989) found that success in school was a significant protective factor for girls who had experienced institutional care and he considered that this gave them a sense of control over events and an ability to plan their lives.

Hunter and Kilstrom's study (1979) pointed to the protection afforded by mothers being able to acknowledge the details of their earlier abuse and to summon the appropriate affect. This was supported by Main and Goldwyn's (1984) findings that mothers were less likely to re-enact their own history of parental rejection if they had an awareness of their past abuse, were able to gain a perspective on it and integrate it into their view of themselves. They were able to recognise the possible effects of their experiences on their own parenting abilities and were able to 'forgive' the abusing parent. Similar observations have been made by Egeland *et al.* (1987) and Grossman *et al.* (1988).

Emde (1988) was particularly impressed that such findings indicated how a third relationship had intervened between the initial parent–child relationship and the parenting relationship one generation on. This third relationship might be with a non-abusing parent during childhood, a therapist, and/or a current supportive partner and it allowed the mothers to become reflective and to objectify their early experiences, rather than deny them or idealise their parents.

Conclusions

This review has sought to bring together a number of related themes concerning the impact of childhood abuse over time. It leads to the following conclusions.

- The consequences of maltreatment in the formative years can be severe, pervasive and persistent, although not invariably so.
- While statistical associations should not lead to assumptions about causality, the number of adult psychiatric patients who reveal childhood abuse, when asked, is noteworthy. In addition, it appears that experiences of such abuse have relevance for the severity of psychiatric disorders and the process of recovery from them.
- Histories taken by mental health professionals should include enquiry about their patients' care when they were children. Professional training should enable practitioners to be comfortable asking about this and dealing with the answers.
- Memories of childhood abuse are available to the majority of adults who have experienced it but dissociation and repression can impair awareness for a minority.
- Therapeutic resources within psychiatric services may well need to be enhanced in order to help patients resolve the consequences of adverse parenting.
- Practitioners working with children should be alert to the possibility that the child's parent/s might have experienced abuse in their formative years which has impacted adversely on their psychological functioning and may require referral to adult mental health services.
- Practitioners working with adults who report a history of childhood abuse should remain aware that they present an increased risk of maltreating their child and that liaison with child services may be necessary.
- Professionals undertaking parenting assessments in child care cases should enquire about factors known to afford resilience to the transgenerational continuities of abuse.

References

Arellano, C.M. (1996) Child maltreatment and substance use: a review of the literature. *Substance Use and Misuse*, 31, 927–935.

Arnold, R.P., Rogers, D. and Cook, D.A.G. (1990) Medical problems of adults who were sexually abused in childhood. *British Medical Journal*, 300, 705–708.

Baker, A.W. and Duncan, S.P. (1985) Child sexual abuse: a study of prevalence in Great Britain. *Child Abuse and Neglect*, 9, 457–467.

Beck, J. and van der Kolk, B. (1987) Reports of childhood incest and current behaviour of chronically hospitalised psychotic women. *American Journal of Psychiatry*, 144, 1474–1476.

Beitchman, J.H., Zucker, K.J., Hood, J.E., daCosta, G.A., Akman, D. and Cassavia, E. (1992) A review of the long-term effects of child sexual abuse. *Child Abuse and Neglect*, 16, 101–118.

Bifulco, A. and Moran, A. (1998) *Wednesday's Child: Research into Women's Experience of Neglect and Abuse, and Adult Depression.* London: Routledge.

Bifulco, A., Brown, G.W. and Adler, Z. (1991) Early sexual abuse and clinical depression in adult life. *British Journal of Psychiatry*, 159, 115–122.

Bowlby, J. (1988) On knowing what you are not supposed to know and feeling what you are not supposed to feel. In: *A Secure Base: Clinical Applications of Attachment Theory.* London: Routledge.

Brandon, S., Boakes, J., Glaser, D. and Green, R. (1998) Recovered memories of childhood sexual abuse: implications for clinical practice. *British Journal of Psychiatry*, 172, 296–307.

Brewin, C.R. (1996) Scientific status of recovered memories. *British Journal of Psychiatry*, 169, 131–134.

Briere, J.N. (1992) *Child Abuse Trauma: Theory and Treatment of the Lasting Effects.* Newbury Park, Calif.: Sage.

Briere, J. and Runtz, M. (1987) Post sexual abuse trauma: data and implications for clinical practice. *Journal of Interpersonal Violence*, 2, 367–379.

Browne, A. and Finkelhor, D. (1986) Impact of child sexual abuse: a review of the research. *Psychological Bulletin*, 99, 66–77.

Bryer, J.B., Nelson, B.A., Miller, J.B. and Krol, P.A. (1987) Childhood sexual and physical abuse as factors in adult psychiatric illness. *American Journal of Psychiatry*, 144, 1426–1430.

Buchanan, A. (1996) *Cycles of Child Maltreatment: Facts, Fallacies and Interventions.* Chichester: John Wiley & Sons.

Carmen, E., Reiker, P.P. and Mills, T. (1984) Victims of violence and psychiatric illness. *American Journal of Psychiatry*, 141, 378–383.

Chu, J.A. and Dill, D.L. (1990) Dissociative symptoms in relation to childhood physical and sexual abuse. *American Journal of Psychiatry*, 147, 887–892.

Claussen, A.H. and Crittenden, P.M. (1991) Physical and psychological maltreatment: relations among types of maltreatment. *Child Abuse and Neglect*, 15, 5–18.

Conte, J.R. and Schuerman, J.R. (1987) Factors associated with an increased impact of child sexual abuse. *Child Abuse and Neglect*, 11, 201–211.

Corby, B. (1993) *Child Abuse: Towards a Knowledge Base.* Buckingham: Open University Press.

Craine, L.S., Henson, C.E., Colliver, J.A. and MacLean, D.G. (1988) Prevalence of a history of sexual abuse among female psychiatric patients in a state hospital system. *Hospital and Community Psychiatry*, 39, 300–304.

Dale, P. and Allen, J. (1998) On memories of childhood abuse: a phenomenological study. *Child Abuse and Neglect*, 22, 799–812.

Egeland, B. and Susman-Stillman, A. (1996) Dissociation as a mediator of child abuse across generations. *Child Abuse and Neglect*, 20, 1123–1132.

Egeland, B., Jacobvitz, D. and Papatola, K. (1987) Intergenerational continuity of abuse. In: R.J. Gelles and J.B. Lancaster (eds) *Child Abuse and Neglect: Biosocial Dimensions.* New York: Aldine de Gruyter.

Egeland, B., Jacobvitz, D. and Sroufe, L.A. (1988) Breaking the cycle of abuse. *Child Development*, 59, 1080–1088.

Emde, R.N. (1988) The effect of relationships on relationships: a developmental approach to clinical intervention. In: R.A. Hinde and J. Stevenson-Hinde (eds) *Relationships within Families: Mutual Influences.* Oxford: Clarendon.

Fergusson, D.M., Horwood, L.J. and Lynskey, M.T. (1996) Childhood sexual abuse and psychiatric disorder in young adulthood: II. Psychiatric outcomes of childhood sexual abuse. *Journal of the American Academy of Child and Adolescent Psychiatry*, 34, 1365–1374.

Finkelhor, D. (1990) Early and long-term effects of child sexual abuse: an update. *Professional Psychology: Research and Practice*, 21, 325–330.

Fonagy, P., Steele, M., Steele, H., Higgitt, A. and Target, M. (1994) The theory and practice of resilience. *Journal of Child Psychology and Psychiatry*, 35, 231–257.

Gibbons, J., Gallagher, B., Bell, C. and Gordon, D. (1995) *Development after Physical Abuse in Early Childhood: A Follow-up Study of Children on Protection Registers.* London: HMSO.

Gil-Rivas, V., Fiorentine, R. and Anglin, M.D. (1996) Sexual abuse, physical abuse, and posttraumatic stress disorder among women participating in outpatient drug abuse treatment. *Journal of Psychoactive Drugs*, 28, 95–102.

Goater, N. and Meehan, K. (1998) Detection and awareness of child sexual abuse in adult psychiatry. *Psychiatric Bulletin*, 22, 211–213.

Gorell Barnes, G. (1996) The mentally ill parent and the family system. In: M. Göpfert, J. Webster and M.V. Seeman (eds) *Parental Psychiatric Disorder: Distressed Parents and their Families.* Cambridge: Cambridge University Press.

Grossman, K., Fremmer-Bombik, E., Rudolph, J. and Grossman, K.E. (1988) Maternal attachment representations as related to patterns of infant–mother attachment and maternal care during the first year. In: R.A. Hinde and J. Stevenson-Hinde (eds) *Relationships within Families: Mutual Influences.* Oxford: Clarendon.

Haeger, B. and Dalton, J. (1988) Attitudes of general psychiatrists to child sexual abuse. *Bulletin of the Royal College of Psychiatrists*, 12, 271–272.

Himelein, M.J. and McElrath, J.A.V. (1996) Resilient child sexual abuse survivors: cognitive coping and illusion. *Child Abuse and Neglect*, 20, 747–758.

Hunter, R.S. and Kilstrom, N. (1979) Breaking the cycle in abusive families. *American Journal of Psychiatry*, 136, 1320–1322.

Jacobson, A. and Herald, C. (1990) The relevance of childhood sexual abuse to adult psychiatric inpatient care. *Hospital and Community Psychiatry*, 41, 154–158.

Jacobson, A. and Richardson, B. (1987) Assault evidence of 100 psychiatric inpatients: evidence of the need for routine inquiry. *American Journal of Psychiatry*, 144, 908–913.

Jones, D.P.H. (1998) Editorial: memories of childhood abuse. *Child Abuse and Neglect*, 22, 797–798.

Kaufman, J. and Zigler, E. (1987) Do abused children become abusive parents? *American Journal of Orthopsychiatry*, 57, 186–192.

Kaufman, J. and Zigler, E. (1989) The intergenerational transmission of child abuse. In: D. Cicchetti and V. Carlson (eds) *Child Maltreatment: Theory and Research on the Causes and Consequences of Child Abuse and Neglect.* Cambridge: Cambridge University Press.

Kendall-Tackett, K.A., Williams, L.M. and Finkelhor, D. (1993) Impact of sexual abuse on children: a review and synthesis of recent empirical studies. *Psychological Bulletin*, 113, 164–180.

Leavitt, F. (1997) False attribution of suggestibility to explain recovered memory of childhood sexual abuse following extended amnesia. *Child Abuse and Neglect*, 21, 265–272.

Lynskey, M.T. and Fergusson, D.M. (1997) Factors protecting against the development of adjustment difficulties in young adults exposed to childhood sexual abuse. *Child Abuse and Neglect*, 21, 1177–1190.

McClelland, L., Mynors-Wallis, L., Fahy, T. and Treasure, J. (1991) Sexual abuse, disordered personality and eating disorders. *British Journal of Psychiatry*, 158 (suppl. 10), 63–68.

Macpherson, R. and Babiker, I. (1994) Who works with adult victims of childhood sexual abuse? *Psychiatric Bulletin*, 18, 70–72.

Main, M. and Goldwyn, R. (1984) Predicting rejection of her infant from mother's representation of her own experiences: implications for the abused–abusing intergenerational cycle. *Child Abuse and Neglect*, 8, 203–217.

Malinosky-Rummell, R. and Hansen, D.J. (1993) Long-term consequences of childhood physical abuse. *Psychological Bulletin*, 114, 68–79.

Margo, G.M. and McLees, E.M. (1991) Further evidence for the significance of a childhood abuse history in psychiatric inpatients. *Comprehensive Psychiatry*, 32, 362–366.

Metcalfe, M., Oppenheimer, R., Dignon, A. and Palmer, R.L. (1990) Childhood sexual experiences reported by male psychiatric patients. *Psychological Medicine*, 20, 925–929.

Morrison, J. (1989) Childhood sexual histories of women with somatising disorder. *American Journal of Psychiatry*, 146, 239–241.

Morton, N. and Browne, K.D. (1998) Theory and observation of attachment and its relation to child maltreatment: a review. *Child Abuse and Neglect*, 22, 1093–1104.

Mullen, P.E., Martin, J.L., Anderson, J.C., Romans, S.E. and Herbison, G.P. (1993) Childhood sexual abuse and mental health in adult life. *British Journal of Psychiatry*, 163, 721–732.

Ofshe, R. and Watters, E. (1995) *Making Monsters: False Memories, Psychotherapy, and Sexual Hysteria*. London: André Deutsch.

Ogata, S.N., Silk, K.R., Goodrich, S., Lohr, N.E., Westen, D. and Hill, E.M. (1990) Childhood sexual and physical abuse in adult patients with borderline personality disorder. *American Journal of Psychiatry*, 147, 1008–1013.

Oliver, J.E. (1993) Intergenerational transmission of child abuse: rates, research, and clinical implications. *American Journal of Psychiatry*, 150, 1315–1324.

Palmer, R.L., Oppenheimer, R., Dignon, A., Chaloner, D.A. and Howells, K. (1990) Childhood sexual experiences with adults reported by women with eating disorders: an extended series. *British Journal of Psychiatry*, 156, 699–703.

Palmer, R.L., Chaloner, D.A. and Oppenheimer, R. (1992) Childhood sexual experiences with adults reported by female psychiatric patients. *British Journal of Psychiatry*, 160, 261–265.

Pope, H.G. (1998) Recovered memories of childhood sexual abuse. *British Medical Journal*, 316, 488–489.

Pope, H.G., Hudson, J.I., Bodkin, J.A. and Oliva, P. (1998) Questionable validity of 'dissociative amnesia' in trauma victims: evidence from prospective studies. *British Journal of Psychiatry*, 172, 210–215.

Pribor, E.F. and Dinwiddie, S.H. (1992) Psychiatric correlates of incest in childhood. *American Journal of Psychiatry*, 149, 52–56.

Putman, F.W., Guroff, J.J., Silberman, E.K., Barban, L. and Post, R.M. (1986) The clinical phenomenology of multiple personality disorder: a review of 100 recent cases. *Journal of Clinical Psychiatry*, 47, 285–293.

Read, J. (1997) Child abuse and psychosis: a literature review and implications for professional practice. *Professional Psychology: Research and Practice*, 28, 448–456.

Read, J. (1998) Child abuse and severity of disturbance among adult psychiatric inpatients. *Child Abuse and Neglect*, 22, 359–368.

Rohsenow, D.J., Corbett, R. and Devine, D. (1988) Molested as children: a hidden contribution to substance abuse? *Journal of Substance Abuse Treatment*, 5, 13–18.

Romans, S.E., Martin, J.L., Anderson, J.C., O'Shea, M.L. and Mullen, P.E. (1995) Factors that mediate between child sexual abuse and adult psychological outcome. *Psychological Medicine*, 25, 127–142.

Rosenfeld, A. (1979) Incidence of a history of incest among 18 female psychiatric patients. *American Journal of Psychiatry*, 136, 791–795.

Ross, C.A., Miller, S.D., Reagor, P., Bjornson, L., Fraser, G.A. and Anderson, G. (1990) Structured interview data on 102 cases of multiple personality disorder from four centers. *American Journal of Psychiatry*, 147, 596–601.

Roy, R. (1998) *Childhood Abuse and Chronic Pain: A Curious Relationship?* Toronto: University of Toronto Press.

Royal College of Psychiatrists (1997) Reported recovered memories of childhood sexual abuse: recommendations for good practice and implications for training, continuing professional development and research. *Psychiatric Bulletin*, 21, 663–665.

Rutter, M. (1985) Resilience in the face of adversity: protective factors and resistance to psychiatric disorder. *British Journal of Psychiatry*, 147, 598–611.

Rutter, M. (1989) Intergenerational continuities and discontinuities in serious parenting difficulties. In: D. Cicchetti and V. Carlson (eds) *Child Maltreatment: Theory and Research on the Causes and Consequences of Child Abuse and Neglect*. Cambridge: Cambridge University Press.

Sarwer, D.B. and Durlak, J.A. (1996) Childhood sexual abuse as a predictor of adult female sexual dysfunction: a study of couples seeking sex therapy. *Child Abuse and Neglect*, 20, 963–972.

Schaeffer, M.R., Sobieraj, K. and Hollyfield, R.L. (1988) Prevalence of childhood physical abuse in adult male veteran alcoholics. *Child Abuse and Neglect*, 12, 141–149.

Shearer, S.L., Peters, C.P., Quaytman, M.S. and Ogden, R.L. (1990) Frequency and correlates of childhood sexual and physical abuse histories in adult female borderline inpatients. *American Journal of Psychiatry*, 147, 214–216.

Sheldon, H. (1988) Childhood sexual abuse in adult female psychotherapy referrals: incidence and implications for treatment. *British Journal of Psychiatry*, 152, 107–111.

Sheldrick, C. (1991) Adult sequelae of child sexual abuse. *British Journal of Psychiatry*, 158 (suppl. 10), 55–62.

Spaccarelli, S. and Kim, S. (1995) Resilience criteria and factors associated with resilience in sexually abused girls. *Child Abuse and Neglect*, 19, 1171–1182.

Teets, J.M. (1995) Childhood sexual trauma of chemically dependent women. *Journal of Psychoactive Drugs*, 27, 231–238.

Terr, L.C (1991) Childhood traumas: an outline and overview. *American Journal of Psychiatry*, 148, 10–20.

Walker, E., Katon, W., Harrop-Griffiths, J., Holm, L., Russo, J. and Hickock, L.R. (1988) Relationship of chronic pelvic pain to psychiatric diagnoses and childhood sexual abuse. *American Journal of Psychiatry*, 145, 75–80.

Walker, S. and James, H. (1992) Childhood physical and sexual abuse in women: report from a psychiatric emergency clinic. *Psychiatry in Practice*, Spring, 15–18.

Waller, G. (1991) Sexual abuse as a factor in eating disorders. *British Journal of Psychiatry*, 159, 664–671.

Windle, M., Windle, R.C., Scheidt, D.M. and Miller, G.B. (1995) Physical and sexual abuse and associated mental disorders among alcoholic inpatients. *American Journal of Psychiatry*, 152, 1322–1328.

Wolfe, D.A. (1987) *Child Abuse: Implications for Child Development and Psychopathology*. Newbury Park, Calif.: Sage.

Wurr, C.J. and Partridge, I.M. (1996) The prevalence of a history of childhood sexual abuse in an acute adult inpatient population. *Child Abuse and Neglect*, 20, 867–872.

Wyatt, G.E. and Mickey, M.R. (1988) The support by parents and others as it mediates the effects of child sexual abuse: an exploratory study. In: G.E. Wyatt and G.J. Powell (eds) *Lasting Effects of Child Sexual Abuse*. Newbury Park, Calif.: Sage.

Zeanah, C.H. and Zeanah, P.D. (1989) Intergenerational transmission of maltreatment: insights from attachment theory and research. *Psychiatry*, 52, 177–196.

Zlotnick, C., Ryan, C.E., Miller, I.W. and Keitner, G.I. (1995) Childhood abuse and recovery from major depression. *Child Abuse and Neglect*, 19, 1513–1516.

Chapter 4

The impact of children on their parents

Peter Reder and Clare Lucey

Insanity is hereditary: you get it from your children.
(Anon)

Parenting is best understood as a two-way process, a mutual interaction between adult and child. Parental factors commonly described as influencing children's welfare include divorce and separation, single-parent status, social isolation, and personal and cultural styles of child care. It is also evident from other contributions to this volume that parental mental health problems can significantly affect children's emotional life, development and well-being. In this chapter, we shall focus on the other component of the parent–child relationship, that is the influence of children on their parents and how children's problems may affect their parents' functioning and mental health. We shall outline the theoretical framework that underlies our thinking about family relationships and indicate how this model also points to the importance of children's influence on their parents. We shall suggest that stressful interactions with their children may be one component of the total picture when adults present to mental health teams and we shall offer clinical vignettes as illustrations.

Clearly, relationship phenomena do not fully explain mental health problems and genetic, neurological or biochemical disorders can lie at the heart of many psychiatric problems. However, psychological and interactional processes, some of which involve a child, may precipitate or perpetuate the course of a parent's disorder (e.g. Scheflen, 1981; Moltz, 1993). As an example, a depressed parent might be unable to use effective strategies to contain their child, who continues to be difficult to manage. This is experienced by the parent as an assault on their self-esteem and provokes self-blame so that the depression deepens.

An interactional framework

Our theoretical framework is based on the following premises:

1   Human beings are social animals and exist in relationship to each other.
2   They customarily engage in regular patterns of interaction with significant others in their lives.
3   As individuals develop, their psychological functioning evolves and their expectations of others change.
4   Some developmental changes are harder to adjust to than others, so that sufficient personal and relational flexibility is necessary for psychological health.

The concept of a family life cycle brings these themes together (Carter and McGoldrick, 1989). Children are brought up in family units, where they participate in formative relationships which significantly shape how they live their lives. This family unit evolves and changes as individuals join, grow up, leave or negotiate important experiences. When individuals move away from the unit, they forge relationships with others in a variety of settings and usually create new family units within which to bring up their own young. Each of the myriad of relationships that is part of this evolving process entails a mutual interaction between participants, in which one influences the behaviour of another and vice versa. As Hinde (1980) succinctly described it: 'the family consists of a network of relationships: the behaviour of one individual to another is affected by the relationships of each with others' (p. 48).

Family life cycle transitions are represented diagrammatically in Figure 4.1, which depicts a child living and developing in relationship with members of the nuclear family. The child brings its own innate characteristics to these relationships, such as appearance, temperament and abilities, while parental influences include their personality, attitudes, personal experiences and family history. The family exists in the context of the external world and interacts with social agencies, such as schools or churches, and with social structures, such as the prevailing culture and the law. All elements of these systems are in continual and mutual interaction, although with different intensity at different times. These relationships evolve over time as individuals develop and negotiate new phases in their lives. 'Slices' through the diagram taken at earlier phases in the family's history would reveal different interactional patterns, depending on who were members of the family unit at the time, their ages, which transitional events were most significant, and so on.

Certain transitional events can be considered as particularly important because they affect all members of the family system and require them to make significant adjustments to their view of themselves and their relationships with others. These include the birth or death of a family member, marriage or separation, an external trauma such as the loss of a job or the

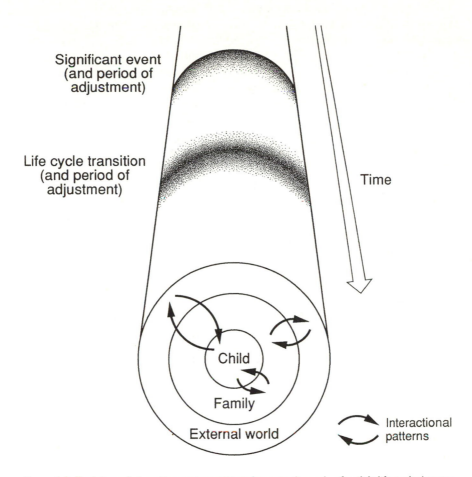

Significant event
(and period of
adjustment)

Life cycle transition
(and period of
adjustment)

Time

Child

Family

External world

Interactional
patterns

Figure 4.1 Evolving relationships and transitional events through a family's life cycle (repro-
duced with permission from Reder *et al.*, 1993)

onset of a severe illness, or phases of psychological transformation such as
onset of adolescence or leaving home. Some families negotiate these transitions without much difficulty but, for others, the adjustment can be prolonged or stressful because their established patterns of functioning are too
inflexible to cope with the new psychological demands. It is often when transitional change is required that problems in previous adjustments or the
enduring impact of past trauma or 'stuck' attitudes become apparent and
this leads to relationship tensions and psychological symptoms. Many mental
health problems are believed to be precipitated by transitional 'life events' in
the family life cycle.

As a result of the influence of history on current relationships, children often carry a psychological meaning for their parents that can be traced back to unresolved conflicts with family of origin (Reder and Duncan, 1995). For instance, some children are invested with the hope that they might redress past hurts in their parents' lives. The same John Lennon whose childhood felt that *'As soon as you're born they make you feel small, by giving you no time instead of it all, till the pain is so big you feel nothing at all'* (Lennon, 1970), could invite his first son to *'dream sweet dreams for me, dream sweet dreams for you'* (Lennon and McCartney, 1968), and reassure his second that *'every day, in every way, it's getting better and better'* (Lennon, 1980).

As well as family life being understood in terms of historical influences, it can also be examined through current interactional patterns – the contemporary 'slice' through the diagram in Figure 4.1. These patterns have been well described by Minuchin (1974) and include children becoming 'parentified' as caretakers of their parents or younger siblings, or 'triangulated' between competing demands for loyalty by parents unable to resolve their marital disharmony, or colluding with 'alliances' invited by one parent against the other.

Discussions about families often read as though the parents are considered to be the most powerful influence on the interactional patterns. It is customary to focus attention on how parents carry beliefs, attitudes and unresolved issues from their own history into current relationships and how parents may have difficulty adjusting to developmental changes in their children (e.g. Byng-Hall, 1995). Most authors also discuss the adverse effects on children when their parents embroil them in current dysfunctional relationship patterns. Indeed, parents often believe that they will be blamed for causing their child's difficulties when the whole family is invited to a child mental health service. Refocusing on the mutuality in relationships enables the influence that children can have on parental functioning and on family life also to be highlighted. A useful way to consider this further is to trace it through progressive phases in the family life cycle.

Child–parent influences during the family life cycle

Childbirth

It is reported that some 5 per cent of all women delivered will suffer from a depressive illness of such severity as to warrant psychiatric intervention and that psycho-social factors are at least as important as biological ones in its causation (Oates, 1996). The first pregnancy is a transitional point in a mother's female identity and also in her relationship with her family of origin. In particular, she must move from a primary sense of herself as a daughter to her mother to a realisation that she is herself a mother to her child. In this way, motherhood reawakens the original mother–daughter relationship so that earlier childhood identifications with the mother are measured against the reality of the new mother's relationship with her own child (Pines, 1972). It could be said that childbirth is a three-generational issue in which the baby is innocently responsible for reviving issues in the relationship between its mother and grandmother.

This aspect of children's influence, together with the risks to the welfare of child and mother, is probably the most recognised by mental health professionals, and Etchegoyen (Chapter 18) discusses in greater detail its implications for psychiatric services. However, less attention has been paid to the effect of childbirth on fathers. There are reports of men developing psychotic disorders after the birth of their first child (see LaCoursiere, 1972; Fedele *et al.*, 1988), and LaCoursiere has suggested that the mother's maternal preoccupations and focus on her baby can provoke a sense of deprivation in the man, leading to his depression or other serious psychological problems. The child's arrival can be seen as generating reverberations throughout the family system and there is accumulating evidence that domestic violence can start or escalate in the perinatal period (e.g. Hillard, 1985; Mezey and Bewley, 1997).

> *A 30-year-old professional man was referred for psychiatric assessment as part of child care proceedings. Neither he nor his wife had any previous history of psychological disorder. However, when their first child was 6 weeks old, the father had begun to show evidence of increasing aggression, including violence to his wife, and professionals were concerned that the domestic violence might extend to include the child. Assessment revealed a link between the father's own history of emotional deprivation by his mother and his current envy and rage at the attention his wife was bestowing on their child instead of him. These problems were resolved through marital and individual psychotherapy.*

More generally, the advent of parenthood requires both men and women to reorganise their lives in many ways and this may be a point of personal crisis for them. Cohler *et al.* (1996) considered that the dilemma faced by some women in choosing between motherhood and career, personal wishes and societal expectations may produce a sense of crisis which is re-evoked with the birth of each succeeding child. They suggest that, when women suffer from a psychiatric illness in mid-life, issues of parenting are often intertwined in the conflict leading to that episode. While this may be partially true, we shall go on to discuss other factors that are also liable to play a part.

Infancy

One of the commonest child-to-parent influences occurs when developmental transitions for the child reactivate unresolved conflicts for the parent, associated with that same phase of their own development. This, in turn, triggers psychological distress or psychiatric breakdown in the parent. Examples might be when the infant becomes a toddler and begins to develop an identity of their own and show greater autonomy. They might become oppositional, test out limits, or simply explore more areas of the home in order to satisfy curiosity. For a parent who has suffered overpunitive limit-setting or invasion of their psychological or personal boundaries in childhood, this can escalate into a crisis generating symptoms such as anxiety or depression.

Children starting to attend nursery school or school at the age of 4 or 5 years is a crucial phase of separation from parent/s and involvement with the outside world. This transition may similarly reawaken dormant conflicts for a parent whose own history is of disordered attachment, again manifesting as anxiety or agoraphobia symptoms.

> *Seeman (1996) presented a case in which a mother with schizophrenia interpreted her child's growing independence as a betrayal. The mother developed schizophrenia in early life and became a parent at the age of 18 years. Recovery from her psychiatric condition and her capacities as a mother were satisfactory during the son's infancy but, as the time approached for the child to begin school, her symptoms increased and she seemed to become less capable as a mother.*

Middle childhood

In middle childhood, a particularly important reawakening of past conflict may occur in mothers of sexually abused girls who were themselves similarly abused as children, and the child's disclosure prompts the mother's memories of her own sexual abuse. If the mother has never previously divulged this to anyone, the 'double-disclosure' becomes a crisis for her personally, as well as a crisis in her functioning as a parent. The mother can become overwhelmed with anxiety as emotional residues of the childhood trauma flood her mind, so that she becomes preoccupied by her own psychological state and is less able to dwell on the child's needs. While serious psychological symptoms in parents after their child discloses abuse are well recognised (e.g. Newberger *et al.*, 1993; Manion *et al.*, 1996), there have been only a few reports about the relevance of the parent's own history of sexual abuse and its impact on their capacity to support the child after disclosure (Courtois and Sprei, 1988; Deblinger *et al.*, 1994; Hiebert-Murphy, 1998). Smith (1995) noted that the non-abusing parent's capacity to protect may be limited in the short term when they, too, were abused as a child, since they are dealing with both disturbing episodes of sexual abuse. However, if they find help for themselves, resolution of their own issues may have positive outcomes for the child. Clearly, it is important in such circumstances to refer the mother for individual therapeutic help in her own right, as well as treating the child. At a later stage, conjoint sessions may further assist recovery of the mother–child relationship.

Adolescence

Later phases of children's development that might reverberate around the family's unresolved issues include puberty and early adolescence. The young person becomes aware of their own sexuality, aggression and power and, once again, this can be a crisis for the parent whose own experiences in these areas were traumatic. Adolescence is also the opportunity for young people to work again at issues of closeness and independence with their family of origin, and conflict between adolescent and parent can create psychological distress in either generation.

> *Reder and Fitzpatrick (1998) presented a case in which the mother of a 13-year-old school non-attender had strong pacifist ideals. She would not assert authority over her daughter, who continued to languish in bed all day and refused to attend meetings with the child mental health team. Treatment reached an impasse until the mother presented to a general psychiatry service having taken an overdose of tablets.*

The process of older adolescents leaving home may precipitate a crisis in the family if it threatens to uncover covert relationship tensions. The crisis can manifest as either parental psychiatric disorder or breakdown for the young person. Haley (1980) has argued that parents may be faced with having to relate to each other again after years of communicating through their child. When the adolescent tries to leave, they are unable to function as a viable organisation and may consider divorce or develop depression or other symptoms as a response to the threatened organisational change. Haley went on to describe how the young person may remain in the triangle and stabilise the family by failing to become autonomous, including returning home having failed at higher education, started to take drugs or developed a psychotic disorder.

> It might be mentioned in passing that the decision about which family member is institutionalised can seem arbitrary. In some cases it is one of the parents, or other adults, at this stage of family development. When a therapist enters a family in crisis, he can think that any one of the members is behaving strangely enough to need action. Usually, the young person is chosen for custody, and at that point the parents and other family members look more normal.
>
> (Haley, 1980, p. 80)

Children's involvement in on-going family disharmony

The above dilemmas illustrate how children's involvement in family disharmony may first become apparent at a transitional point in their lives, even though the relationship conflicts were long-standing. Tension can reverberate around the family system and be manifest in different members at different times.

> *A 15-year-old girl was seen with her family for assessment after she had taken an overdose of tablets. The interview revealed that a hostile and distant relationship had existed between the parents for many years and they virtually never spoke to each other. As a teenager, the daughter had become triangulated between her parents, acting as a conduit for their communications, and her act of deliberate self-harm could be understood as a message that she wanted them to change the atmosphere at home so that she could be freed from this intolerable conflict (see Reder et al., 1991), or else she would prefer to die. A second interview was arranged but, before this could take place, the mother took an overdose of tablets herself, as if to seek a further alliance with her daughter.*

Interactional circularity in families containing an alcoholic has been described by Janzen (1983): 'The alcohol abuser's behavior affects the family, whether that behavior is increased or reduced drinking, and the family members' response in turn affects the alcoholic, either to promote or to reduce the drinking behavior' (p. 56). For example, the spouse may at first collude with denial of the problem, then acknowledge it but excuse it as a response to stress, going on to try to moderate the severity by drinking with the alcoholic or limiting availability. In response, the alcoholic resists the partner's attempts at control, so that they enact cycles of control/out of control behaviour. Janzen recognised that children can easily participate in this circularity, by siding with the whole family's denial or with one parent against the other. The spouse may try to elicit children's help to control and moderate the drinking problem, or else the child assumes a parentified role and, in this sense, the child also helps maintain the problem. The spouse and children need to be freed from guilt and responsibility for the alcoholic's behaviour so that treatment can have a greater chance of success.

Christensen's (1997) interviews with children of alcoholic parents endorsed these observations: the study showed that the parents falsely imagined that their children did not know about their alcohol abuse, even though the children had tried to intervene by telling them to stop drinking.

There is now an abundant literature on high Expressed Emotion in families adversely affecting patients' recovery from schizophrenia and other major psychiatric disorders (e.g. Leff and Vaughn, 1985). However, studies appear to focus on adult partners or parents as the sources of high criticism levels and it is unclear whether investigators have considered children's contributions. A belief in the circularity of family interaction would point to this being a potentially fruitful area for research.

Caretaker children

Any discussion of children's impact on parental mental health must also recognise the positive benefit to parents of their children's behaviour. Some depressed parents regard their children as the only reason to keep going and, although this places an immense burden on the child from which they need to be freed, it can provide a route in to treatment that might not otherwise be effective. The following example illustrates two related themes: the significance of a son as a reason for his mother to continue living, and how this created an anxious attachment between them that was enacted in separation problems at night.

> *A single mother suffered from severe recurrent depressions, during which she contemplated suicide, and she required compulsory admission to hospital on a number of occasions. She was offered medication, psychotherapy and social work support but she did not regularly attend her appointments, so that her pessimism remained and her affective state continued to fluctuate. She then asked for referral to a child mental health team because of her young son's bedtime rituals, in which he would not let her leave him alone at night. On joint interview, it was evident that the son felt a considerable weight of responsibility for his mother and was anxious that she periodically spoke to him as though to prepare him for life without her. A behavioural programme was started to break the night-time cycle, together with interviews exploring the mother's background history of maltreatment and its impact on the mother–son relationship now. These discussions also linked the mother's rejection by her parents with her tendency to reject offers of professional help in adult life (see Reder and Fredman, 1996). The mother successfully returned to her psychotherapist and her mood improved considerably and she allowed her son gradually to become independent. During this time, she acknowledged that her son's existence and welfare had been the only thing that had prevented her believing she had nothing to live for.*

It is not uncommon for children to take on the role of caretaker to their ailing parent; Edwards and Smith (1997) estimated that there are some 10,000 young carers of a mentally ill parent in Great Britain. On the positive side, the child's support for their ill parent can help the psychiatric condition remain more stable so that hospitalisations are avoided. Some even claim that, in this way, the children develop a sense of fulfilment and self-esteem (see Pound,

1996). However, the more concerning aspect of this role reversal is that the children usually sacrifice many of their own childhood entitlements in order to shoulder the burden of an inappropriately parentified or protective role.

> *This was well illustrated by a patient of Bowlby (1988), whose mother had had a traumatic childhood and she remained apprehensive that, if reminded of it, she would become depressed. During his upbringing, the patient was required always to appear happy and avoid any expression of sorrow or anger and it was only through later therapy that he realised he had been extremely lonely but was never allowed to know it.*

The difficult-to-parent child

Children show substantial individual differences in such attributes as activity level, sociability, adaptability and 'ease' of mood (Thomas *et al.*, 1968; Thomas and Chess, 1977; Berger, 1985). These characteristics engender different feelings in peers, parents and other adults and therefore influence aspects of how they relate together. There are some children whose temperament makes them much more difficult to parent than others (e.g. Prior, 1992). They may be aggressive and provocative with little apparent concern for others and this does not appear to be explained by earlier adverse caring experiences. Or they may be fractious and irritable and always crying, despite all attempts by the parents to console them. The temperamentally frustrating child can become an assault to their parents' self-esteem and Wolkind and de Salis (1982) recorded that mothers of such difficult children may suffer from prolonged mental health problems such as depression.

Looked-after children can react to parental rejection or repeated temporary placements by making themselves unlovable. Their behaviour may be so provoking, challenging or destructive that potentially loving responses from others are submerged by feelings of dislike. In this way, they both test out any new potential caretakers and protect themselves against the risk of further rejection by ensuring that no one gets close to them (Boston and Szur, 1983). However, their caretakers find themselves at their wits' end as all overtures of concern are rebuffed, and this can be extremely stressful for the adults.

By far the greatest literature about child-to-parent influence concerns children with chronic physical disorders or learning disability (Eiser, 1993; Wallander and Varni, 1998). Caring for children with chronic disease has the potential to disrupt and destroy the parents' relationship, as well as serve to unite them. There is evidence that the mothers can experience clinical anxiety and depression, sufficient to warrant medication, while fathers tend to be less affected. However, their role as support to the mother is crucial in buffering the effects of the child's condition on her and, not surprisingly, the parents' mental health consequences are dependent on the quality of their relationship as a couple.

Parents of children with learning disability have been described as needing to mourn the 'normal' child that they had anticipated and some may suffer prolonged periods of guilt, depression or other psychiatric symptoms (Romans-Clarkson *et al.*, 1986). The families are often struggling because of inadequate knowledge, resources and support and, at its most extreme, this results in family fragmentation and breakdown (Turk, 1996). It is likely that similar issues about self-blame, feelings of failure and a sense of helplessness apply to parents caring for young people with chronic mental health problems, such as psychosis. At a less severe level of disorder, there is good evidence that parenting stress levels can be high among families of children with disorders of attention (e.g. Anastopoulos *et al.*, 1992), although this may not be at the level that would usually present to mental health services.

Implications

It is evident that children can play an important role in the onset, course and outcome of their parents' mental health problems. Therefore, considering the wider family system could enhance general psychiatrists' and psychologists' assessments and intervention strategies. An understandable first reaction to this suggestion might be concern about the time and resource implications, with yet another issue to address for a busy and demanding clinic. However, we believe that appreciating the children's relationship to the presenting problem can give an important dimension to the history and a greater understanding of the patient's disorder.

In practice, a history can be taken that includes mention of the children and information about the family structure can be organised and summarised through drawing a simple genogram (McGoldrick and Gerson, 1985; Reder *et al.*, 1993). By adding a small number of questions about the history of family relationships to the standard interview, the nature of the adult's condition might be more fully understood within its wider context. Then, effective treatment strategies can be devised that take into account these interactional and developmental influences.

References

Anastopoulos, A.D., Guevremont, D.C., Shelton, T.L. and DuPaul, G.J. (1992) Parenting stress among families of children with attention deficit hyperactivity disorder. *Journal of Abnormal Child Psychology*, 20, 503–520.

Berger, M. (1985) Temperament and individual differences. In: M. Rutter and L. Hersov (eds) *Child and Adolescent Psychiatry: Modern Approaches*, 2nd edn. Oxford: Blackwell.

Boston, M. and Szur, R. (eds) (1983) *Psychotherapy with Severely Deprived Children*. London: Routledge & Kegan Paul.

Bowlby, J. (1988) On knowing what you are not supposed to know and feeling what you are not supposed to feel. In: *A Secure Base: Clinical Applications of Attachment Theory.* London: Routledge.

Byng-Hall, J. (1995) *Rewriting Family Scripts: Improvisation and Systems Change.* New York: Guilford.

Carter, B. and McGoldrick, M. (eds) (1989) *The Changing Family Life Cycle: A Framework for Family Therapy*, 2nd edn. Boston, Mass.: Allyn & Bacon.

Christensen, E. (1997) Aspects of a preventive approach to support children of alcoholics. *Child Abuse Review*, 6, 24–34.

Cohler, B.J., Stott, F.M. and Musick, J.S. (1996) Distressed parents and their young children: interventions for families at risk. In: M. Göpfert, J. Webster and M.V. Seeman (eds) *Parental Psychiatric Disorder: Distressed Parents and their Families.* Cambridge: Cambridge University Press.

Courtois, C.A and Sprei, J.E. (1988) Retrospective incest therapy for women. In: E. Walker (ed.) *Handbook of Sexual Abuse of Children.* New York: Springer.

Deblinger, E., Stauffer, L. and Landsberger, C. (1994) The impact of a history of child sexual abuse on maternal response to allegations of sexual abuse concerning her child. *Journal of Child Sexual Abuse*, 3, 67–75.

Edwards, A. and Smith, P. (1997) Young carers and their parents with long term psychiatric disorders. In: *Report of the 12th Annual Michael Sieff Foundation Conference 'Keeping Children in Mind: Balancing Children's Needs with Parents' Mental Health'.* Michael Sieff Foundation.

Eiser, C. (1993) *Growing Up with a Chronic Disease: The Impact on Children and their Families.* London: Jessica Kingsley.

Fedele, N.M., Golding, E.R., Grossman, F.K. and Pollack, W.S. (1988) Psychological issues in adjustment to first parenthood. In: G.Y. Michaels and W.A. Goldberg (eds) *The Transition to Parenthood: Current Theory and Research.* Cambridge: Cambridge University Press.

Haley, J. (1980) *Leaving Home: The Therapy of Disturbed Young People.* New York: McGraw-Hill.

Hiebert-Murphy, D. (1998) Emotional distress among mothers whose children have been sexually abused: the role of a history of child sexual abuse, social support, and coping. *Child Abuse and Neglect*, 22, 423–435.

Hillard, P.J.A. (1985) Physical abuse in pregnancy. *Obstetrics and Gynecology*, 66, 185–190.

Hinde, R.A. (1980) Family influences. In: M. Rutter (ed.) *Developmental Psychiatry.* Washington, DC: American Psychiatric Press.

Janzen, C. (1983) Alcoholism. In: M.R. Textor (ed.) *Helping Families with Special Problems.* New York: Jason Aronson.

LaCoursiere, R. (1972) Fatherhood and mental illness: a review and new material. *Psychiatric Quarterly*, 46, 109–124.

Leff, J. and Vaughn, C. (1985) *Expressed Emotion in Families: Its Significance for Mental Illness.* New York: Guilford.

Lennon, J. (1970) *Working Class Hero.* Northern Songs.

Lennon, J. (1980) *Beautiful Boy (Darling Boy).* Lenono Music/BMG Music Publishing Ltd.

Lennon, J. and McCartney, P. (1968) *Goodnight.* Northern Songs.

McGoldrick, M. and Gerson, R. (1985) *Genograms in Family Assessment.* New York: W.W. Norton.

Manion, I.G., McIntyre, J., Firestone, P., Ligezinska, M., Ensom, R. and Wells, G. (1996) Secondary traumatization in parents following the disclosure of extra-familial child sexual abuse: initial effects. *Child Abuse and Neglect*, 20, 1095–1109.

Mezey, G.C. and Bewley, S. (1997) Domestic violence and pregnancy. *British Medical Journal*, 314, 1295.

Minuchin, S. (1974) *Families and Family Therapy.* London: Tavistock.

Moltz, D.A. (1993) Bipolar disorder and the family: an integrative approach. *Family Process*, 32, 409–423.

Newberger, C.M., Gremy, I.M., Waternaux, C.M. and Newberger, E.H. (1993) Mothers of sexually abused children: trauma and repair in longitudinal perspective. *American Journal of Orthopsychiatry*, 63, 92–102.

Oates, M. (1996) Post-natal mental illness: its importance and management. In: M. Göpfert, J. Webster and M.V. Seeman (eds) *Parental Psychiatric Disorder: Distressed Parents and their Families.* Cambridge: Cambridge University Press.

Pines, D. (1972) Pregnancy and motherhood: interaction between fantasy and reality. *British Journal of Medical Psychology*, 45, 333–343.

Pound, A. (1996) Parental affective disorder and childhood disturbance. In: M. Göpfert, J. Webster and M.V. Seeman (eds) *Parental Psychiatric Disorder: Distressed Parents and their Families.* Cambridge: Cambridge University Press.

Prior, M. (1992) Childhood temperament. *Journal of Child Psychology and Psychiatry*, 33, 249–279.

Reder, P. and Duncan, S. (1995) The meaning of the child. In: P. Reder and C. Lucey (eds) *Assessment of Parenting: Psychiatric and Psychological Contributions.* London: Routledge.

Reder, P. and Fitzpatrick, G. (1998) What is sufficient understanding? *Clinical Child Psychology and Psychiatry*, 3, 103–113.

Reder, P. and Fredman, G. (1996) The relationship to help: interacting beliefs about the treatment process. *Clinical Child Psychology and Psychiatry*, 1, 457–467.

Reder, P., Lucey, C. and Fredman, G. (1991) The challenge of deliberate self-harm by young adolescents. *Journal of Adolescence*, 14, 135–148.

Reder, P., Duncan, S. and Gray, M. (1993) *Beyond Blame: Child Abuse Tragedies Revisited.* London: Routledge.

Romans-Clarkson, S.E., Clarkson, J.E., Dittmer, I.D., Flett, R., Linsell, C., Mullen, P.E. and Mullin, B. (1986) Impact of a handicapped child on mental health of parents. *British Medical Journal*, 293, 1395–1397.

Scheflen, A.E. (1981) *Levels of Schizophrenia.* New York: Brunner/Mazel.

Seeman, M.V. (1996) The mother with schizophrenia. In: M. Göpfert, J. Webster and M.V. Seeman (eds) *Parental Psychiatric Disorder: Distressed Parents and their Families.* Cambridge: Cambridge University Press.

Smith, G. (1995) Assessing protectiveness in cases of child sexual abuse. In: P. Reder and C. Lucey (eds) *Assessment of Parenting: Psychiatric and Psychological Contributions.* London: Routledge.

Thomas, A. and Chess, S. (1977) *Temperament and Development.* New York: Brunner/Mazel.

Thomas, A., Chess, S. and Birch, H.G. (1968) *Temperament and Behavior Disorders in Children.* London: London University Press.

Turk, J. (1996) Working with parents of children who have severe learning disabilities. *Clinical Child Psychology and Psychiatry*, 1, 581–596.

Wallander, J.L. and Varni, J.W. (1998) Effects of pediatric chronic physical adjustment disorders on child and family adjustment. *Journal of Child Psychology and Psychiatry*, 39, 29–46.

Wolkind, S.N. and de Salis, W. (1982) Infant temperament, maternal mental state and child behaviour problems. In: R. Porter and G.M. Collins (eds) *Temperamental Differences in Infants and Young Children*. Ciba Foundation Symposium 89. London: Pitman.

Chapter 5

Adolescence – the transition from childhood to adulthood

Mike McClure

Adolescence is an opportunity to consider the interface between child and adult mental health from developmental and systemic perspectives. In adolescence, young people exhibit features of both the child and the maturing adult. The problems encountered in adolescence may be related to persisting childhood disorder or to the stress of adolescence, or in later adolescence they may be part of an emerging adult picture. Adolescence may be understood using an integrative systemic model, with interactions between biological, psychological, social and environmental factors (Cairns and Cairns, 1994). Development occurs in the context of a systemic interaction with parents, other family members, peers, neighbourhood, school and the wider society. Adolescence is characterised by change, but it need not be tumultuous and problematic unless social conditions prompt it (Jessor, 1993; Petersen and Leffert, 1995).

The developmental transitions of adolescence

Adolescence is the transitional phase between childhood and adulthood, but may also be regarded as a phase of life, lasting approximately from the age of 10 years to 20 years (Petersen and Leffert, 1995). Early adolescence, from approximately 10 to 13 years, is dominated by puberty; middle adolescence, from roughly 14 to 16 years, involves the transition to a distinct youth identity; and late adolescence, from approximately 17 to 20 years, involves the completion of the transition to adulthood. In fact, there is considerable variation in timing of these phases, and achievement of full adult maturity may be much later, or may never be fully attained.

The developmental transitions of adolescence include a biological (pubertal) transition, a cognitive transition, an emotional transition, an identity transition, and a social transition, within the context of the environment. These developmental transitions occur through the interaction of physical maturation, the development of personal values and goals, and cultural influences which vary with gender, class, culture and historical period. Social structure influences and is influenced by parent–child relationships and parenting goals and practices. Adolescents shape their own developmental transitions as they act on and are acted upon by the social and physical environment (Gottlieb, 1991). The developmental transitions of adolescence are characterised by both continuity of childhood influences and discontinuity as the individual matures (Schulenberg *et al.*, 1997). They form part of a pathway or trajectory from childhood into adulthood, with the possibility of turning points during significant periods.

Biological development

Parental genetic influences on the biological changes during puberty and subsequent adolescence are genetically pre-programmed, although the timing, course and expression may be affected by environmental factors (Brooks-Gunn and Reiter, 1990). Hormonal changes bring about the growth spurt and development of secondary sexual characteristics and contribute to sexual behaviour and aggression. Genetically inherited personality characteristics and traits are carried over from childhood or may be fully expressed in adolescence. Illnesses, including schizophrenia and affective disorders, may be expressed for the first time in adolescence (Angold and Rutter, 1992). Brain growth with proliferation in support cells and myelination with selective pruning of synapses is associated with cognitive development (Graber and Petersen, 1991).

Cognitive development

Cognitive change during adolescence involves increased capacity for abstract reasoning. There is questioning of abstract concepts such as 'justice' and a burst of artistic creativity in music, painting and language. These new abilities may be challenging or confusing for the young person. Adolescents develop a more psychological conception of the self, recognising personal and interpersonal characteristics, emotions and beliefs (Crockett and Petersen, 1993). Associated with cognitive development, the adolescent conforms less to parental opinion. Initially, there is increased conformity to peer opinion, though this declines during middle and late adolescence as the individual becomes more self-reliant and develops the capacity for independent decision making (Crockett and Petersen, 1993).

Emotional development

The emotional development of the young person is related to their genetic predisposition, to cognitive development and to social circumstances. Although adolescents experience sadness, tearfulness, anxiety and self-deprecation, the majority do not show emotional disorder. Most young people referred to adolescent mental health services, however, have emotional disorders where parental, family and social influences are prominent (Steinberg, 1991). Emotional disorders may present as anxiety states, affective disorders, obsessive compulsive disorders, school refusal and phobias. Adolescent presentations also include a relatively high proportion of psychosomatic conditions, illness behaviour and pretence of illness in which familial factors are important (Steinberg, 1994). Severe depressive conditions, which are usually associated with biological, psychological and social factors, may lead to suicidal behaviour in adolescence (McClure, 1984; 1994). Suicidal behaviour increases from adolescence into mid-adult life, associated with depression, substance misuse, and social isolation (McClure, 1986; 2000).

Identity development

Identity formation takes place in relation to social roles, ideology, sexuality and occupation (Bosma, 1992). During adolescence, there is an increased ability for self-awareness, which is associated with cognitive development. Young people are able to experiment with different self-images which they select from peers and culture, including the media, and blend with their own developing personality. As part of identity development, the young person's sexual identity becomes more important, and is influenced by biological factors, childhood and adolescent experience and social expectations. There is a gradual change of self-image, although, with the increased self-awareness, the young person may experience hyper-sensitivity and shyness. Adolescents may defend themselves by vagueness and diffidence or may experience identity confusion.

As part of their developing identity, young people become more conscious of their physical appearance and shape which changes in association with puberty. This may lead to dieting or eating disorders such as bulimia or anorexia nervosa. McClure et al. (1995) describe the complex interaction of biological, psychological and social factors contributing to the development of eating disorder. Young people may become involved in their mother's eating disorder; the most intractable cases of anorexia nervosa in adolescents involve daughters of mothers who themselves have anorexia nervosa (Hall, 1996).

Social development

Adolescents develop increased capacity to form meaningful relationships with both same-sex and opposite-sex peers (Savin-Williams and Berndt, 1990). At the same time, family relationships change, though this is not necessarily stressful (Steinberg, 1990). The social context of the developing adolescent includes parents, the family, peer group, neighbourhood, school and society (Feldman and Elliott, 1990). During adolescence both the young person and the parents are changing. Parents are likely to be in middle age and some will be in the process of separating or divorcing. Family structure has changed considerably, with increasing divorce rates in most industrialised countries, increasing the number of adolescents who grow up in single-parent families and reconstituted families (Hess, 1995). Parental divorce and the death of a parent are disruptive for adolescent development (Hetherington, 1991), with boys more likely to be affected by disruption in childhood and girls by disruption during adolescence. Adolescents develop more success-fully in two-parent families, though the effects of single parenting may be related to antecedent problems and socio-economic factors (Barber and Eccles, 1992).

The young person gradually emancipates from the parents (sometimes with difficulty on both sides) and becomes more interested and involved with their peer group. Generally there is development from single-sex 'gangs' to combined-sex groups, to groups of informal couples, and then to pairs of boys and girls, with a minority showing homosexual preference. Peer groups develop their own culture which excludes others and may require initiation. With increasing involvement with the peer group, minor disagreements with parents are common, though most adolescents consider pleasing parents and learning at school to be more important than peer group approval.

Problems may arise due to the dependence/independence conflict with parents, exacerbated by conflict in the family, loss and separations, and adverse life events. Whilst largely positive developments are taking place in the majority of individuals, a subgroup engages in seriously destructive behaviour involving substance misuse, delinquency and risky sexual activity (Elliott, 1993; Caspi et al., 1993). These young people may be involved in a rebellious anti-social peer group subculture where there is stealing, violence, vandalism, truanting and running away. Moffitt (1993) has suggested the need to differentiate between early onset anti-social behaviour (often associ-ated with hyperactivity and poor peer relations) and adolescent onset anti-social behaviour. The former is more likely to persist into adult life whereas adolescent onset anti-social behaviour is often transient. The link between adolescent disorder and adult disorder becomes apparent in later adolescence as the individual embarks upon early adulthood on a trajectory which is set during the transitional phase. Farrington (1991; 1993) suggests that there is an anti-social personality that arises in childhood, continues through ado-lescence and persists into adulthood. These anti-social adults then tend to produce another anti-social child (Farrington, 1995). Risk factors include high impulsivity, low intelligence, parental influences, family influences, peer influences, socio-economic factors and situational influences.

Young people develop friendships and love relationships where they often idealise the other party. They are immature in their social judgement and may become dependent upon a boyfriend or girlfriend whilst they reject support previously offered by their parents. Non-fatal deliberate self-harm is commonest in adolescence and young adulthood and is associated with failed experimentation with adult relationships and roles (McClure 1988; 1994). The formation of insecure relationships and anti-social behaviour, which might have been correctable, may become a permanent part of the individual's adult personality.

Environmental context

Within an integrative systemic model, the developmental transitions of adolescence occur in the context of the environment. This is an environment largely shaped by adults in previous generations, just as the maturing adolescent will contribute to developing society for future generations in a dynamic process. The environment extends from the immediate environment of the home to the school, neighbourhood, wider society and culture. At home, the teenager may be intellectually mature, yet still dependent upon parents. At school, the young person experiences increasing pressure for academic success. For those who fail, there may be feelings of inadequacy, compounded by increased difficulty in finding subsequent employment, with limitations of career prospects or unemployment. Economic factors and political decisions will also have consequences for family life, education and future prospects.

Legal aspects

As part of the environmental context, the legal status of the young person changes. The Children Act 1989 states that parental responsibility includes rights, duties, powers, responsibility and authority in relation to a child. It stops completely at the age of 18 years, but up to that age it considerably diminishes in law as youngsters are able to make more of their own decisions. Under the age of 16 years parental right is not absolute and young people may consent to treatment if they can demonstrate sufficient intellectual capacity to understand relevant advice (Reder and Fitzpatrick, 1998). Young people of 16 and 17 years have considerable responsibility for their own actions and wishes and may give consent to treatment without parental consent. After the age of 18 years the individual is legally regarded as an adult, with implications for their role in society and the legal system as it applies to adults. It is therefore a complex task for professionals to get a balance between diminishing parental authority and responsibility and increasing autonomy and responsibility for the young person's own actions during the transition between childhood and adulthood. When assessing a young person, it is essential to include an assessment of their emotional maturity and intellectual competence, truthfulness and needs and wishes, including those relating to family problems. Treatment programmes can then take account of issues such as competence to give consent, confidentiality and child protection.

Parenting of adolescents

Parenting of adolescents has its own particular issues and difficulties. Authoritative parenting tends to promote good academic performance but there may be lack of warmth within the family. Indulgent parents, on the other hand, express love but do not set boundaries for behaviour. Indifferent parents are deficient in all areas and youngsters with such parents have the worst outcomes (Steinberg, 1990; Steinberg *et al.*, 1992). Parenting problems may increase as the parents struggle with a more powerful and demanding young person. There is a natural emancipation as the young person stakes out his or her identity, which may involve choosing a lifestyle and values which are in opposition to those of the parent. Alternatively, the young person may model both good and bad aspects of parental adult behaviour. This is problematical when it involves maladaptive behaviour such as substance misuse, violence and crime, which may be the norm for the family. Where abuse exists within a family, the abused child may become the abuser in adolescence.

Poor parental supervision, erratic or harsh parental discipline, marital disharmony, parental rejection of the child and low parental involvement and interest in education are all predictors of juvenile conduct problems and delinquency (Farrington, 1992). Criminal, anti-social and alcoholic parents also tend to have delinquent sons (Robins, 1979; Farrington, 1992). A convicted parent is a strong predictor of anti-social behaviour and bullying in adolescence, and subsequent anti-social behaviour in adulthood (Farrington, 1994). Furthermore, substance use by parents predicts substance use by children (Johnson and Pandina, 1991).

Particular problems arise in adolescence when there is a psychiatrically ill parent. It is difficult to separate the direct emotional effects on the young person from the indirect effects of the illness, such as marital disharmony, separations due to hospital admissions, unemployment or social disadvantage (Hill, 1996). In some cases, an adolescent may present with a psychiatric illness which is already present in a parent or close relative. This may be very distressing for the family and young person. An adolescent who is very close to and identified with a parent may present with a shared delusional state such as *folie à deux* (McClure and Hart, 1989).

Prevention of adolescent problems and the subsequent negative trajectory into adult life requires alteration of parental child-rearing practices (Nash and Hay, 1993) by parent training before the teenage years (Patterson *et al.*, 1992).

Adolescent parents

One particular example of the interface between child and adult mental health is when the young person is also the parent – as in teenage pregnancy. Here the young person is not only part-child herself, but is also more likely to be a disturbed child with less than adequate parental support. Teenage pregnancy may alter the life trajectory for the young person (Rutter and Rutter, 1993), and may be considered a negative turning point. It is related to the girl's characteristics and circumstances, which are themselves related to her genetic constitution and upbringing by her own parents. Following the birth of a child, there is an interaction between the young mother, parental and partner support (or lack of it), and secondary educational and economic problems. The net effect is that there is likely to be considerable disadvantage to the child growing up in these circumstances. Teenage pregnancy is there-fore an event which may have implications for three generations, and indeed a pattern may be established for further generations. Werner and Smith (1992) have shown that teenage motherhood tends to lead to a negative trajectory. For the young mother, there is an increase in the school drop-out rate, leading to poor educational attainments with lowered work opportunities and finan-cial security. Monash and Rucker (1989) found that teenage child-bearing in a single-parent, female-headed household is conducive to later offending. Mar-riage to the father, who is often also young and from a disadvantaged back-ground, is more likely to lead to marital discord and divorce. Furthermore, the discord is more likely to persist into a second marriage, which is itself more likely to end in divorce. Teenage mothers are also more likely to have further unplanned births.

Clinical presentations

Adolescent disorder involves the need to address the child and adult embodied in the same individual. Furthermore, this young person not only is affected by the family, but in turn affects the family. The following are some examples to highlight the wide variety of clinical presentations that may occur in adolescence and the range of issues that need consideration when plans are made for management and treatment.

Case example I

> Joan was a 16-year-old girl who presented following an overdose. She was emo-tionally distraught because she had broken up with her boyfriend and it was difficult to engage with her. Biologically she was an adult, but psychologically and socially she was still a child. She was found to be pregnant and subsequently had the baby, though it proved difficult for her to care for it. The baby was left more and more with the grandmother who became the main carer. A significant part of Joan's history was that her mother gave birth to her at the age of 17 years. Following arguments, Joan's father left after five years and there was then a succession of stepfathers. Joan's mother was considered inadequate, and had been diagnosed as having recurrent depressive epi-sodes. Joan had been involved in previous substance misuse, delinquency and truanting since the age of 14 years.

Management consisted of crisis intervention following the overdose. Attempts were made to counsel Joan, but she found it hard to trust adults and insisted that she knew best when it came to herself and having the baby. Social Services were then involved and, because Joan's mother agreed to cooperate, it was decided that she could care for the baby. Follow-up by social services revealed early difficulties with the baby, but not so severe as to warrant removal of the child.

Ideal management would have been earlier support from adult services for Joan's mother in relation to her depression. Family work would have provided more stability at home and might have averted the early break-up of the parental relationship. Professional help should have been available to Joan and her mother when substance misuse, delinquency and truanting first became evident and Joan should also have had better sex education. Although there is monitoring of the development of the new baby, early intervention is required to prevent repetition of the cycle.

Case example 2

John was a 16-year-old boy who presented with a first acute psychotic episode. He had paranoid symptoms and was considered to be a danger to others. John came from an intact family, although his father had a history of schizophrenia which had responded well to treatment. Over the past year John had experienced deteriorating school achievement and preoccupation with his appearance and loss of friendships.

Management involved emergency referral by the GP to the casualty department. He was then referred to the child and adolescent mental health team for immediate assessment. Attempts at referral to an Adolescent Unit were made but several units were unable to take acute admissions and others were full. There then ensued a long wait in the casualty department with the casualty consultant pressing for transfer. Referral was made to the Adult Psychiatry ward but he was considered too young. A discussion with the bed manager ensued and eventually he was admitted to an adult ward after a distressing wait for John and his parents. The adult ward was considered unsuitable, and indeed upsetting for John and his parents; it was two weeks later before he was admitted to an Adolescent Unit.

Ideally, earlier involvement with the family, when John's father had been treated for his schizophrenia would have been helpful. Monitoring of John's progress would have revealed the significant deterioration in his condition prior to the presentation of psychosis. Earlier contact with adolescent services might have averted the acute crisis when he was referred as an emergency. Ideal management would have included a clear definition of responsibility for acute adolescent inpatient admissions. Prior planning would have provided an adolescent unit with an acute admission facility so that John could have been admitted directly to a facility with expertise in managing young people.

Services for adolescents

With the complex mixture of child and adult that we see in adolescence, there is a requirement for skills in the assessment and management of problems of childhood and adulthood within the same individual. Services for adolescents often fall between those which are available for children and those which are available for adults, with poor coordination and patchy provision of services (NHS Health Advisory Service, 1986; 1995). At the moment there are very few dedicated adolescent outpatient services as they are usually part of the child and family services. With complex problems in youngsters with adult-type disorders such as psychosis or affective disorder, however, child and family services may be inadequate. Acute admission facilities may be hard to access, as demarcation issues arise. The child and family service may say that they have inadequate resources to deal with the highly disturbed adolescent with adult-type problems. The adult service, on the other hand, may say that they are not trained to care for youngsters, and, in any case, it would be detrimental for the young person to mix with highly disturbed chronic adult patients. There are then coordination problems when both child and adult services try to work together. There may be lack of clarity concerning which service should take the lead, and communication problems between the two services, which may be based on different sites.

Joint planning of adolescent services is necessary to overcome these problems instead of *ad hoc* arrangements as and when problems arise. There needs to be improved coordination through regular meetings involving health, social services, youth services, education, the judicial/forensic service and the voluntary sector. Purchasers must recognise that adolescents may require the expertise and resources of specialised adolescent services in addition to child and family services and adult services. In the tiered organisation of service advocated by the Health Advisory Service, there is a requirement for outreach and community services at Tier 1, adolescent outpatient services at Tiers 2 and 3, and a range of adolescent day-patient and inpatient services at Tier 4 (NHS Health Advisory Service, 1995).

The wide range of presenting problems and the wide age span (from 10 years to 20 years) make it difficult for a single adolescent unit to offer services for all problems and conditions in adolescence at all age periods. Inpatient facilities should include acute admission facilities, general adolescent units, specialised units for youngsters with substance misuse and learning disability, and long-term residential units including therapeutic communities (Steinberg, 1994). Inpatient adolescent facilities must adapt to allow the acute admission of disturbed youngsters who would otherwise be admitted, eventually, to a temporary adult bed. Ideally, adolescent units should have a separate reception area of variable numbers of beds to receive disturbed youngsters without upsetting the general unit milieu. When the young person calms down, they may then gradually be introduced to the main unit.

Adolescents are a very special group of individuals requiring highly specialised skills. Professionals must understand the special needs of adolescents who are in the transition between childhood and adulthood, and are affected by and in turn affect their family. One cannot deal with them as children, or as adults, and they are not fully members of the family as they undergo the process of emancipation from the family. They are unique in that they are partly all of the above, yet none of them completely. Dedicated adolescent services, drawing upon the expertise of child and adolescent and adult mental health services, will be able to address these complex and potentially conflicting developmental issues.

References

Angold, A. and Rutter, M. (1992) Effects of age and pubertal status on depression in a large clinical sample. *Development and Psychopathology*, 4, 5–28.

Barber, B.L and Eccles, J.S. (1992) Long term influence of divorce and single parenting on adolescent family and work related values, behaviours and aspirations. *Psychological Bulletin*, 11, 108–126.

Bosma, H.A. (1992) Identity in adolescence: managing commitments. In: G.R. Adams, T. Gullotta and R. Montemayor (eds) *Identity Formation during Adolescence*. Newbury Park, Calif.: Sage.

Brooks-Gunn, J. and Reiter, E.O. (1990) The role of pubertal process. In: S.S. Feldman and G.R. Elliott (eds) *At the Threshold: The Developing Adolescent*. Cambridge, Mass.: Harvard University Press.

Cairns, R.B. and Cairns, B.D. (1994) *Lifelines and Risks: Pathways of Youth in Our Time*. New York: Cambridge University Press.

Caspi, A., Lynam, D., Moffitt, T.E. and Silva, P.A. (1993) Unravelling girls' delinquency: biological, dispositional, and contextual contributions to adolescent misbehaviour. *Developmental Psychology*, 29, 19–30.

Crockett, L.J. and Petersen, A.C. (1993) Adolescent development: health risks and opportunities for health promotion. In: S.G. Millstein, A.C. Petersen and E.O. Nightingale (eds) *Promoting the Health of Adolescents: New Directions for the Twenty-First Century*. New York: Oxford University Press.

Elliott, D.S. (1993) Health enhancing and health compromising lifestyles. In: S.G. Millstein, A.C. Petersen and E.O. Nightingale (eds) *Promoting the Health of Adolescents: New Directions for the Twenty-First Century*. New York: Oxford University Press.

Farrington, D. (1991) Antisocial personality from childhood to adulthood. *The Psychologist*, 4, 389–394.

Farrington, D. (1992) Juvenile delinquency. In: J.C. Coleman (ed.) *The School Years*, 2nd edn. London: Routledge.

Farrington, D. (1993) Childhood origins of teenage antisocial behaviour and adult social dysfunction. *Journal of the Royal Society of Medicine*, 86, 13–17.

Farrington, D. (1994) Childhood, adolescent and adult features of violent males. In: L.R. Huemann (ed.) *Aggressive Behaviour: Current Perspectives.* New York: Plenum.

Farrington, D. (1995) The challenge of teenage antisocial behaviour. In: M. Rutter (ed.) *Psychosocial Disturbances in Young People: Challenges for Prevention.* Cambridge: Cambridge University Press.

Feldman, S.S. and Elliott, G.R. (eds) (1990*)* *At the Threshold: The Developing Adolescent.* Cambridge, Mass.: Harvard University Press.

Gottlieb, G. (1991) Experimental canalisation of behavioural development: theory. *Developmental Psychology*, 274–313.

Graber, J.A. and Petersen, A.C. (1991) Cognitive changes at adolescence: biological perspectives. In: K.R. Gibsen and A.C. Petersen (eds) *Brain Maturation and Cognitive Development: Comparative and Cross-Cultural Perspectives.* New York: Aldine De Gryter.

Hall, A. (1996) Maternal eating disorders. In: M. Göpfert, J. Webster and M. Seeman (eds) *Parental Psychiatric Disorder: Distressed Parents and their Families.* Cambridge: Cambridge University Press.

Hess, L.E. (1995) Changing family patterns in Europe: opportunity and risk factors for adolescent development. In: M. Rutter and D. Smith (eds) *Psychosocial Disorders in Young People: Time Trends and their Origins.* Chichester: John Wiley & Sons.

Hetherington, E.M. (1991) Presidential address: Families, lies and videotapes. *Journal of Research on Adolescence*, 1, 323–348.

Hill, J. (1996) Parental psychiatric disorder and the attachment relationship. In: M. Göpfert, J. Webster and M. Seeman (eds) *Parental Psychiatric Disorder: Distressed Parents and their Families.* Cambridge: Cambridge University Press.

Jessor, R. (1993) Successful adolescent development among youth in high risk settings. *American Psychologist*, 48, 117–126.

Johnson, V. and Pandina, R.J. (1991) Effects of the family environment on adolescent substance use, delinquency and coping styles. *American Journal of Drug and Alcohol Abuse*, 17, 71–88.

McClure, G.M. (1984) Recent trends in suicide among the young. *British Journal of Psychiatry*, 144, 134–138.

McClure, G.M. (1986) Recent changes in suicide among adolescents in England and Wales. *Journal of Adolescence*, 9, 135–143.

McClure, G.M. (1988) Suicide in children in England and Wales. *Journal of Child Psychology and Psychiatry*, 29, 345–349.

McClure, G.M. (1994) Suicide in children and adolescents in England and Wales 1960–1990. *British Journal of Psychiatry*, 165, 510–514.

McClure, G.M. (2000) Suicide in England and Wales 1960–1997. *British Journal of Psychiatry*, 176, 64–67.

McClure, G.M. and Hart, J. (1989) Folie à deux and Capgras Syndrome in mother and child. *British Journal of Psychiatry*, 154, 552–554.

McClure, G.M., Timini, S. and Westman, A. (1995) Anorexia nervosa in early adolescence following illness – the importance of the sick role. *Journal of Adolescence*, 18, 359–369.

Moffitt, T.E. (1993) Adolescence – limited and life-course persistent antisocial behaviour: a developmental taxonomy. *Psychological Review*, 100, 674–701.

Monash, M. and Rucker, L. (1989) An exploratory study of the connection of mother's age at childbearing to her children's delinquency. *Crime and Delinquency*, 35, 45–93.

Nash, A. and Hay, D.F. (1993) Relationships in infancy as precursors and causes of later relationships and psychopathology. In: D.F. Hay and A. Angold (eds) *Precursors and Causes in Development and Psychopathology*. Chichester: Wiley.

NHS Health Advisory Service (1986) *Bridges over Troubled Waters*. London: Department of Health.

NHS Health Advisory Service (1995) *Together We Stand*. London: HMSO.

Patterson, G.R., Reid, J.B. and Dishion, T.J. (1992) *Antisocial Boys*. Eugene, Oreg.: Castalia.

Petersen, A.C. and Leffert, N. (1995) What is special about adolescence? In: M. Rutter (ed.) *Psychosocial Disturbances in Young People: Challenges for Prevention*. Cambridge: Cambridge University Press.

Reder, P. and Fitzpatrick, G. (1998) What is sufficient understanding? *Clinical Child Psychology and Psychiatry*, 3, 103–113.

Robins, L.N. (1979) Sturdy childhood predictors of adult outcomes: replications from longitudinal studies. In: J.E. Barrett, R.M. Rose and G.L. Kloman (eds) *Stress and Mental Disorder*. New York: Raven Press.

Rutter, M. and Rutter, M. (1993) *Developing Minds: Challenges and Continuity across the Lifespan*. Harmondsworth: Penguin.

Savin-Williams, R.C. and Berndt, T.J. (1990) Friendship and peer relations. In: S.S. Feldman and G.R. Elliott (eds) *At the Threshold: The Developing Adolescent*. Cambridge, Mass.: Harvard University Press.

Schulenberg, J., Maggs, L.L. and Hurrelmann, K. (1997) Negotiating developmental transitions during adolescence and young adulthood: health risks and opportunities. In: J. Schulenberg, J. Maggs and K. Hurrelmann (eds) *Health Risks and Developmental Transitions during Adolescence*. Cambridge: Cambridge University Press.

Steinberg, D. (1991) The concept of adolescent psychiatry. In: A. Seva (ed.) *The European Handbook of Psychiatry and Mental Health*, vol. II. Barcelona: Anthropos.

Steinberg, D. (1994) Adolescent services. In: M. Rutter, E. Taylor and L. Hersov (eds) *Child and Adolescent Psychiatry: Modern Approaches*, 3rd edn. Oxford: Blackwell.

Steinberg, L.D. (1990) Autonomy, conflict and harmony in the family relationship. In: S.S. Feldman and G.R. Elliott (eds) *At the Threshold: The Developing Adolescent*. Cambridge, Mass.: Harvard University Press.

Steinberg, L.D., Dornbusch, S. and Brown, B.B. (1992) Ethnic differences in adolescent achievement: an ecological perspective. *American Psychologist*, 47, 723–729.

Werner, E.E. and Smith, R.S. (1992) *Overcoming the Odds: High Risk Children from Birth to Adulthood*. Ithaca, NY: Cornell University Press.

Children of parents with mental health problems

Chapter 6

Children's experience of major psychiatric disorder in their parent

An overview

Sylvia Duncan and Peter Reder

When considering the impact of external stress on children, it is important to do so from the child's perspective. Only in this way is it possible to understand how the influence is shaped by their sense of vulnerability, their developmental phase and their way of thinking. This particularly applies to stresses that might overtake the caretaking relationship (Fitzpatrick *et al.*, 1995), including development of a major psychiatric disorder in the parent.

This overview is intended as an introduction to the chapters that follow in this section, and it focuses on how a child is likely to experience their parent's disturbance. The parental disorders that we shall use as illustrations are depression and schizophrenia. We shall particularly emphasise that, although there are important differences in their nature and course as seen from the point of view of the adult, they tend to be experienced by children in the family in similar ways and it is for this reason that they can be discussed together.

As general psychiatrists find ever higher proportions of their caseloads to be patients with severe disturbances, the impact of these major disorders on children in the family assumes even greater importance. Oppenheimer (1981) reported that 13 per cent of adults admitted to an urban psychiatric hospital were caring for a child under 5 years, and 28 per cent were caring for a child under 16 years. More recently, Oates (1997) quoted studies which show that 25 per cent of all new female psychiatric referrals now have a child under 5 years, and that 26 per cent of adults with schizophrenia living in the community are in households with a child under 16 years. Furthermore, Oates reports that in Lambeth, in south London, 25 per cent of women with a serious chronic mental illness have children under the age of 5 years, and 60 per cent have children under 16 years. The current national policy of care in the community means that these parents and their children spend more time together than might have occurred in the past.

In New York State, 22 per cent of all patients in intensive case management programmes because of serious and persistent mental illness were reported to have children, and 45 per cent of the female patients under the age of 35 were mothers (Blanch *et al.*, 1994).

Interest has grown progressively about the effects of major psychiatric disorders on children within the family, although research focusing on the impact of parental (usually the mother's) depression on children's development and functioning far exceeds that concerned with parental psychosis, especially in recent years. This literature has been brought together through a series of reviews (e.g. Beardslee *et al.*, 1983; Rutter and Quinton, 1984; Rutter and Cox, 1985; Puckering, 1989; Downey and Coyne, 1990; Cummings and Davies, 1994; Cassell and Coleman, 1995; Hall, 1996; Pound, 1996; Oates, 1997; Falkov, 1998; Cleaver *et al.*, 1999). It is not our purpose to reprise details of all the studies cited in these reviews, but to distil out their principal messages so that practitioners can recognise the effects on children and respond to their needs. Links between parental psychiatric disorder and child physical abuse will not be addressed specifically, as they are the focus of another chapter in this volume (see Reder and Duncan, Chapter 12).

Components of 'good-enough' parenting

In order to appreciate the impact of major psychiatric disorders in parents on their children, it is first necessary to consider the basic needs of children that must be satisfied by their caretakers and, by extension, the core components of 'good-enough' parenting. Some of these components will vary in different cultures because of the interplay between biological process and societal expectations and beliefs that shape children's experiences and development. Here, we shall summarise the components that are commonly agreed for western cultures.

Kelmer Pringle (1986) identified the four major psycho-social needs of children as the need for: love and security; new experiences; praise and recognition; and responsibility. Reder and Lucey (1995) built on these principles in suggesting that the task of good-enough parenting is to facilitate age-appropriate development within a safe environment. Therefore, the child's needs that must be satisfied are physical, behavioural and emotional, as shown in Table 6.1. There is, of course, reciprocity between these requirements, so that, for example, parents who support their child in their early steps are simultaneously encouraging their physical maturation, social exploration and learning, as well as facilitating development of their self-esteem, personal identity and sense of safety.

A crucial developmental need for children is facilitation of the attachment dynamic (see Holmes, 1993; Rutter, 1995; Hill, 1996; Morton and Browne, 1998), in which the parent initially provides a secure and reliable base for the infant to explore from and return to, and gradually encourages the child to develop a sense of autonomy and self-assurance. The parent's role is to respond consistently, sensitively, appropriately and with commitment to proximity-seeking cues of the child. In the formative years, the child's sense of security can be considered to be facilitated by familiar persons, routines

Table 6.1 Essential needs of children that must be satisfied by 'good-enough' parenting

Physical needs	Behavioural needs	Emotional needs
Nutrition	Stimulation/interaction	Affection/empathy
Warmth/shelter	Exploration/learning	Availability
Health/cleanliness	Socialisation/role model	Consistency
Safety	Limit-setting	Reality testing
Contact/comfort	Rest	Building of self-esteem
		Attachment/autonomy
		Individual identity
		Advocacy

and places. In the early months, attachment is not person-specific but is allied to the provision of consistent routine, in which the caretaker(s) reliably anticipates and meets the child's needs. From around 6 months of age, the child depends more on the availability of identifiable persons to satisfy their needs, again with routine and consistency. Familiarity of place, such as the home, its surroundings and the child's belongings, reinforce this attachment process. In this way, the child develops a belief that others can be relied upon and, in the future, that they are worthy of receiving support and affection when wanted.

The first three years of life are the most sensitive period for development of secure attachment, with the initial twelve months especially critical. However, the attachment dynamic continues to shape the child's personality and emotional life in the years that follow, albeit moderated by their cognitive development which enables them increasingly to comprehend adverse experiences. In particular, attachment relationships will be reactivated at times of threat or trauma, when the availability of familiar persons, places and routines once again becomes essential.

Some of these facets of caretaking are especially vulnerable to major psychiatric disorder in parents. This notably applies to those in the emotional dimension, although the adult's behaviour towards, and physical relationship with, the child may also become distorted by the disturbance. As we shall go on to elaborate, the child is affected both by the primary manifestations of their parental disturbance and by the secondary psycho-social consequences of the disorder.

Effects of major psychiatric disorders on parents and their parenting

The major psychiatric disorders of depression and schizophrenia have certain features in common. They have a genetic component and tend to be recurrent but each onset may be precipitated by external stressors. The episodes are usually severe, affecting the individual's capacity for independent and responsible living. The person may feel psychically out of control and also behave in an irrational and uncontrolled manner, manifesting behaviour such as violence or suicidal attempts, or they may become withdrawn and self-preoccupied. Interventions may only be possible in hospital and, if admission is against their wishes, it may need to be enforced. Treatments for the acute episodes are effective but the person's functioning during remission may show residues of the acute problem. The disorders can be frightening to the person and to those living with them.

The primary symptoms intrude directly into the individual's parenting role through, for example, increased irritability or aggressiveness, unresponsiveness, critical attitudes, unrealistic expectations and difficulty planning ahead for everyday needs. Attempts at limit-setting are more liable to be ineffective because the parent has a smaller repertoire of strategies and tends to behave in all-or-none extremes. These problems may then become circular, so that the adult believes they are failing as a parent, which reduces their self-esteem and optimism, leading to poorer child care, and so on. Cox et al. (1987, p. 927) concluded that: 'while maternal depression may contribute to the start of difficulties in the relationship between mother and child, these difficulties may gather their own momentum and persist even when circumstances improve.'

Hospital admissions during the acute phases of the illness further disrupt the caretaking relationship. In a survey of consecutive psychiatric admissions in London, 26 patients who were mothers were caring for 53 children, 12 of whom had to move homes to be looked after for the duration of their mother's admission (Hawes and Cottrell, 1999). Similarly, a study in New York (Shachnow, 1987) found that 22 recently admitted patients had been caring for 36 children, only 8 of whom had a readily available surrogate caretaker who could be called upon; the others depended on makeshift arrangements or were left alone.

The primary symptoms also have secondary effects on the emotional atmosphere, living standards and lifestyle of the family, with higher risks of deterioration in social circumstances and family breakdown. Rutter and Cox (1985) highlighted these psycho-social factors as being particularly influential on the development of problems in the children, emphasising the link between psychiatric disorder in one parent and disruptive marital discord and the presence of psychiatric disorder in the other parent as well. Rutter and Quinton (1984, p. 877) concluded that: 'family discord and hostility constitute the chief mediating variable in the association between parental mental disorder and psychiatric disturbance in the children.'

Effects on children

It must be recognised that many parents with a major psychiatric disorder can parent their children adequately, especially between the recurring episodes of disturbance. However, for other children, the impact is significant. In a four-year follow-up study of children of psychiatric patients, Rutter and Quinton (1984) concluded that one-third showed no emotional or behavioural disturbance, one-third showed transient problems and one-third exhibited persistent disorders.

In terms of general psychopathology, children of depressed parents have a significantly higher than expected likelihood of developing psychological or cognitive problems. Psychiatric diagnoses have been found in around 40 per cent of children of parents with an affective disorder (Beardslee *et al.*, 1983) and it is estimated that children of depressed parents are up to five times more likely to develop behaviour problems than other children (Cummings and Davies, 1994).

A spectrum of difficulties has been described in children of depressed parents and Pound summarised our present knowledge as follows:

> children of depressed parents, and particularly depressed mothers, are at high risk of developing psychiatric disorder either currently or in the future, have poor interpersonal skills and few friends, and suffer either from dysfunctional levels of guilt, poor self esteem and clinical depression or from detachment, aggression and conduct disorder. Cognitive impairments and attention deficits interfere with learning skills such as reading.
>
> (1996, p. 209)

There is less literature on the impact of parental psychosis on children and that which is available tends to be preoccupied with identifying the genetic contribution to aetiology. The later studies (e.g. Shachnow, 1987) confirm earlier findings by Landau *et al.* (1972) that, when compared with controls, children of psychotic parents have significantly more psychopathological diagnoses. More specifically, Landau *et al.* found the following to be significantly increased: delay in speech development and toilet training; enuresis; eating and sleeping problems; undisciplined and aggressive behaviour; difficulties relating to peers; psychosomatic complaints; anxiety; depressive tendencies; insecurity; and obsessive symptoms, which they relate to the daily stress of having to adapt to their parent's bizarre behaviour and thoughts and not having someone with whom to identify.

Links between parental behaviour and effects on children

In Rutter and Quinton's (1984) study, the effects on the child were independent of the parent's diagnosis and related more to the social and interactional consequences of their problems, especially hostility and marital disharmony. These findings have led us to propose that the most useful way to consider how children experience their parent's mental health problem is to focus on the impact of the parental *behaviour* rather than their *diagnosis*. The consequences of the parent's behaviour need to be considered from the child's perspective and Table 6.2 summarises a range of behaviours that can accompany psychosis and depression in adults, together with their likely impact on children who are exposed to them. In most instances, the effect is on the child's emotional well-being or relationships; however, problems of attachment in the child are a possible consequence of all of the parental behaviours described (e.g. Radke-Yarrow, 1991).

There is not an automatic relationship between the parental behaviours and the impacts on a child as listed in the table. However, some patterns are commonly found. Parental withdrawal into self-preoccupation means that they are not available either emotionally or physically to others and this is likely to leave children anxious or depressed, liable to be neglected or exposed to physical danger, or to behave in an uncontrolled manner. The child might resort to self-reliance and pseudo-maturity as a defence against this neglect and isolation. Repeated hospitalisations, perhaps precipitated by a dramatic crisis or an attempt at suicide, often leave the child anxious and perplexed, as well as liable to neglect if adequate alternative caretakers are not found. However, some children are also exposed to repeated threats of abandonment by irritated parents, through such comments as 'You'll be the death of me' or 'I've had enough of you and if you don't do that I'll put you into care', which are even more emotionally damaging.

Table 6.2 Potential impact on child of primary and secondary behaviours associated with parental psychiatric disorder

Parental behaviour	Potential impact on child (in addition to attachment problems)
Self-preoccupation	Neglected
Emotional unavailability	Depressed, anxious, neglected
Practical unavailability	Out-of-control, self-reliant, neglected, exposed to danger
Frequent separations	Anxious, perplexed, angry, neglected
Threats of abandonment	Anxious, inhibited, self-blame
Unpredictable/chaotic planning	Anxious, inhibited, neglected
Irritability/over-reactions	Inhibited, physically abused
Distorted expressions of reality	Anxious, confused
Strange behaviour/beliefs	Embroiled in behaviour, shame, perplexed, physically abused
Dependency	Caretaker role
Pessimism/blames self	Caretaker role, depressed, low self-esteem
Blames child	Emotionally abused, physically abused, guilt
Unsuccessful limit-setting	Behaviour problem
Marital discord and hostility	Behaviour problem, anxiety, self-blame
Social deterioration	Neglect, shame

A common feature of severe parental psychiatric disorder is unpredictable behaviour and chaotic planning, with an inability to anticipate the child's needs. This interferes with the attachment process generally and also affects young children who need to be picked up from school or to have food bought for them. Their reaction can be anxiety or confusion or, in older children, self-reliance. Inhibition and timidity are a frequent response of children whose parent is irritable or unpredictable, because they fear provoking another eruption of frightening behaviour. Psychotic ideation, with distorted expressions of reality and strange beliefs, is usually frightening and confusing to children, or else they can feel ashamed of their family. However, some children who are exposed to psychotic beliefs find it increasingly difficult to distinguish reality from distortions and come to share their parent's ideas. Even young children who witness their parent's distress are liable to assume a caretaker role, worrying about their parent's welfare and trying to find ways to support them.

The important secondary effects of disturbed parental behaviour include unsuccessful limit-setting, marital discord and deterioration in social circumstances, which are liable to lead to behaviour problems, anxiety, shame and neglectful care of the child.

Children's sensitivity to their parent's disturbed behaviour

Clearly, the nature and severity of the parent's disturbed behaviour are important factors determining the effect on children in the family. As Rutter (1966) demonstrated, the children will manifest more problems if they are involved in their parent's symptoms, whether it be through delusional ideas, neglect or hostility, while exposure to hostility showed the strongest association to 'child mental status' in Cox et al.'s (1987) study.

A child's vulnerability will also depend on their age and whether the parent's breakdown coincides with sensitive periods in their own development. For instance, a 5-year-old who is about to start school will be less able to understand and tolerate the parent's first emergency admission to hospital than an adolescent who has developed a degree of self-reliance as the result of similar episodes during their upbringing and can make greater sense of the experiences. Again, parental depression during the child's first year will have a much greater impact on the attachment dynamic than if it occurs later in life. Another influence will be the support and sensitivity of other adults, both within the family and among the professional network, to the child's dilemmas. We have discussed this contribution to children's resilience in Chapter 3. Especially relevant is the child's own capacity to make sense of what they see and hear happening around them, which we shall go on to consider in greater detail.

Children's capacity to make sense of their parent's behaviour

In a discussion about the ability of children to give informed consent to medical interventions or plans about their future care, Reder and Fitzpatrick (1998) argued that children's understanding about important matters in their lives is related to: (a) the complexity of the issue; (b) the clarity of communications with them about it; (c) their stage of cognitive development; (d) their emotional state; and (e) any personal and interpersonal conflicts associated with the issue. Similar considerations apply to children's capacity to make sense of their parent's disturbed behaviour.

Complexity

The working of the mind is very difficult for children to comprehend and for many it remains a mysterious and frightening aspect of human functioning. Evidence of abnormal mental functioning, with the bizarre behaviour and alarming ideas that it produces, and even professionals' difficulty to explain them adequately, complicates their already meagre understanding.

> *A 6-year-old struggled to explain to an interviewer that her depressed mother had 'problems in her head . . . but it wasn't problems you could put a bandage on . . . she wasn't well but hadn't had a bang on the head . . . she didn't go to bed for it . . . she had tablets for it but didn't have a headache.'*

Communication

It is not unusual for adults to try to 'protect' children from the harsh realities of their experiences with a disturbed parent by minimising its severity or even lying about it. For family members, this may be because of their own uncertainty or distress at the course of events. Children who are told that their hospitalised parent has 'gone away' could believe that they have been abandoned. Even when the child is informed truthfully, the words or concepts used may be beyond their comprehension. For example, the expression 'losing their mind' could be taken literally.

> *Children who had heard from an adjacent room their psychotic father murder their mother had been told by a relative that their mother had gone shopping and that their father was in hospital.*

Cognitive development

Children's capacity for abstract thinking takes many years to develop, during which they may, for example, relate every issue to themselves and so believe that they caused their parent's breakdown. Young children also have a rudimentary concept of time and so fail to understand that what is happening currently may be different in the future, while their ability to reality-test is more vulnerable to distortions imposed by their parents. Older children might well have an understanding of inheritance and so fear that the same breakdown will happen to them.

> *A 7-year-old boy retained rudimentary memories of his psychotic mother trying to smother him when he was a toddler. Even after many relatively settled years in a foster home, he believed that his badness had been responsible for his mother's attack on him and for the family break-up. At Christmas time, he constructed an elaborate story that Father Christmas had failed to bring him any sweets or to leave him a card, unlike for other children in the household, because they were good and he was bad.*

Emotional state

Because the acutely disturbed, out-of-control behaviour that they witness is usually so alarming, children's anxiety levels rise considerably and this impairs their capacity to understand explanations given to them. They fear for both their parent and for themselves, and Anthony (1986) has demonstrated that post-traumatic stress disorder may continue for months or years afterwards. The anxieties may well include fear of abandonment, if previous episodes have led to admission to hospital, and might extend to a fear that their parent will go into hospital and never come out again.

> *A father arrived in an irrational state for a contact visit with his daughter, who was now living in a foster home because of his severe alcohol dependency and the mother's unavailability. The more uncontrollably he behaved, the more tense and frozen she became, so that she was inaccessible to the social worker's attempts to reassure her or to explain her father's problems.*

Conflicts

Finally, children's capacity to make sense of what is happening will be affected by their personal conflicts about it, or interpersonal conflicts that they have become embroiled in. For instance, the caretaker child, who has been drawn in to a parentified role to watch over their ill parent's welfare, might consider themselves a failure, while the child whose parent has previously told them that they were the cause of their parent's illness would find alternative explanations more difficult to accept.

> *A mother had jumped off a bridge into the Thames with her two children whilst in a depressed state. Despite treatment, she remained intermittently*

suicidal or threatened to leave the father and he had progressively displayed anxiety and depression himself. Both children were preoccupied about their parents' welfare, as well as their own, and had become inhibited, reluctant to discuss their circumstances with teachers or counsellors, and had developed multiple psychosomatic complaints. It required months of psychotherapy, combined with social work monitoring and appropriate help for the parents, to help the children acknowledge the reality of what had happened and their feelings about it.

Concerns about child maltreatment

Parental irritability, rigidity in limit-setting or thought disorder involving the child do have the potential to culminate in physical abuse and it is important that professionals caring for the parent are aware of that risk, however small, and monitor for it. A more general concern is whether the threats of abandonment, exposure to hostility, suicidal attempts or unrealistic expectations are emotionally abusive to the child. In our experience, unlike other instances of emotional abuse in which the parent's hostility is part of an on-going rejection of the child, parents with depressive or psychotic disorders are predominantly concerned for their children and distressed at their own inability to tolerate closeness with them. They usually are willing to seek help with their parenting role alongside treatment for their own psychiatric disorder.

None the less, there will be a minority of cases in which the parent's capacity to continue or resume care of their child requires detailed assessment for the purposes of court proceedings. The capacity of parents with a major psychiatric disorder to care for their child depends on a number of inter-related factors, including the nature of their disorder, the way it manifests in behaviour generally and parenting behaviour in particular, its short- and long-term prognosis, its relevance for future behaviour, its effect on the child *as experienced from the child's perspective*, and its likely future impact, again *from the child's perspective*.

In recognition of these various dimensions of parenting assessments, Poole (1996, p. 5) believed that 'general adult psychiatrists cannot give a truly expert opinion on parenting skills'. Unfortunately, some general or forensic psychiatrists approach the cases solely from the adult's perspective and base their recommendations about the child's future care entirely on the prognosis of their parent's psychiatric condition. Grünbaum and Gammeltoft (1993) regarded this as a failure to differentiate between the mother's needs as a patient, her needs as a parent and the child's needs. While the psychiatric prognosis is clearly one significant issue, it is only part of the necessary picture, and needs to be integrated with a detailed appraisal of the child's experiences of their parent's behaviour. Thus, complementary assessments are required by different experts who address the separate issues, out of which a coherent opinion can emerge.

From time to time, such cases raise difficulties in professional networks about conflicts of interests and confidentiality. The Department of Health, British Medical Association and Conference of Medical Royal Colleges (1994) agreed the common principle that 'the needs of the child must always be regarded as of first importance', yet their guidance to doctors responsible for child welfare was worded as 'the patient's interests are paramount and will *usually* [our italics] require a doctor to disclose information to an appropriate . . . statutory agency'. This has left an area of ambiguity for some adult mental health professionals, who believe it is their responsibility to guard their patient's confidentiality, even if this compromises a child's safety (Reder, 1996). We do not believe that this was the intention behind the joint guidance and we consider that it is a principle of good practice to prioritise children's welfare, even if this means breaking confidentiality and not appearing fully to support the parent's interests. In our experience, parents often appreciate professional concern for their children and do not experience protective interventions as an assault on their own civil liberties or psychological health.

Helping affected children

As in many other spheres, early intervention can facilitate resolution before the problems become too severe, entrenched or disturbing to development. For example, the impact of maternal postnatal depression on infant attachment points to the importance of having perinatal services available to recognise and treat such disorders. For older children, the effect on them of their parent's disorder needs to be considered at the point of referral. If admission is required, this should include a review of whether appropriate arrangements have been made for their immediate care. Thus, liaison may be necessary with social workers, either placed in the mental health teams or available in the community, with health visitors, or else a child welfare role might be created for community psychiatric nurses. Issues about the children's understanding of their parent's disorder can also be addressed at planned family interviews later in their treatment. Regular liaison from child mental health workers can facilitate this. The essential point is that the relevance for other members of the family should be considered by the adult mental health team. All of these measures are discussed more fully by other contributors to this volume.

Regrettably, it is still more common for concerns about the children to surface later in the course of the parent's disorder, when they are showing symptoms or when assessments of parenting are deemed necessary. As we have argued, when such assessments are required, they should focus on the experience of the child, as seen from their perspective, so that placement and/or treatment can be planned that suit their needs. In most instances, services will need to be commissioned that enhance the relationship between the parent and child. Only very occasionally will there appear to be a conflict of interests between needs of the parent and those of the child. In such circumstances, it is evident that the welfare of the child should take precedence.

References

Anthony, E.J. (1986) Terrorising attacks on children by psychotic parents. *Journal of the American Academy of Child Psychiatry*, 25, 326–335.

Beardslee, W.R., Bemporad, J., Keller, M.B. and Klerman, G.L. (1983) Children of parents with major affective disorder: a review. *American Journal of Psychiatry*, 140, 825–832.

Blanch, A.K., Nicholson, J. and Purcell, J. (1994) Parents with severe mental illness and their children: the need for human services integration. *The Journal of Mental Health Administration*, 21, 388–396.

Cassell, D. and Coleman, R. (1995) Parents with psychiatric problems. In: P. Reder and C. Lucey (eds) *Assessment of Parenting: Psychiatric and Psychological Contributions*. London: Routledge.

Cleaver, H., Unell, I. and Aldgate, J. (1999) *Children's Needs – Parenting Capacity: the Impact of Parental Mental Illness, Problem Alcohol and Drug Use, and Domestic Violence on Children's Development*. London: The Stationery Office.

Cox, A.D., Puckering, C., Pound, A. and Mills, M. (1987) The impact of maternal depression on young children. *Journal of Child Psychology and Psychiatry*, 28, 917–928.

Cummings, E.M. and Davies, P.T. (1994) Maternal depression and child development. *Journal of Child Psychology and Psychiatry*, 35, 73–112.

Department of Health, British Medical Association and Conference of Medical Royal Colleges (1994) *Child Protection: Medical Responsibilities*. London: HMSO.

Downey, G. and Coyne, J.C. (1990) Children of depressed parents: an integrative review. *Psychological Bulletin*, 108, 50–76.

Falkov, A. (1998) *Crossing Bridges: Training Resources for Working with Mentally Ill Parents and their Children*. Department of Health.

Fitzpatrick, G., Reder, P. and Lucey, C. (1995) The child's perspective. In: P. Reder and C. Lucey (eds) *Assessment of Parenting: Psychiatric and Psychological Contributions*. London: Routledge.

Grünbaum, L. and Gammeltoft, M. (1993) Young children of schizophrenic mothers: difficulties of intervention. *American Journal of Orthopsychiatry*, 63, 16–27.

Hall, A. (1996) Parental psychiatric disorder and the developing child. In: M. Göpfert, J. Webster and M.V. Seeman (eds) *Parental Psychiatric Disorder: Distressed Parents and their Families*. Cambridge: Cambridge University Press.

Hawes, V. and Cottrell, D. (1999) Disruption of children's lives by maternal psychiatric admission. *Psychiatric Bulletin*, 23, 153–156.

Hill, J. (1996) Parental psychiatric disorder and the attachment relationship. In: M. Göpfert, J. Webster, and M.V. Seeman (eds) *Parental Psychiatric Disorder: Distressed Parents and their Families*. Cambridge: Cambridge University Press.

Holmes, J. (1993) *John Bowlby and Attachment Theory*. London: Routledge.

Kelmer Pringle, M. (1986) *The Needs of Children: A Personal Perspective*. London: Routledge.

Landau, R., Harth, P., Othnay, N. and Sharfhertz, C. (1972) The influence of psychotic parents on their children's development. *American Journal of Psychiatry*, 129, 70–75.

Morton, N. and Browne, K.D. (1998) Theory and observation of attachment and its relation to child maltreatment: a review. *Child Abuse and Neglect*, 22, 1093–1104.

Murray, L. (1992) The impact of postnatal depression on infant development. *Journal of Child Psychology and Psychiatry*, 33, 543–561.

Oates, M. (1997) Patients as parents: the risk to children. *British Journal of Psychiatry*, 170 (suppl. 32), 22–27.

Oppenheimer, R. (1981) At risk: children of female psychiatric patients. *Child Abuse and Neglect*, 5, 117–122.

Poole, R. (1996) General adult psychiatrists and their patients' children. In: M. Göpfert, J. Webster and M.V. Seeman (eds) *Parental Psychiatric Disorder: Distressed Parents and their Families*. Cambridge: Cambridge University Press.

Pound, A. (1996) Parental affective disorder and childhood disturbance. In: M. Göpfert, J. Webster and M.V. Seeman (eds) *Parental Psychiatric Disorder: Distressed Parents and their Families*. Cambridge: Cambridge University Press.

Puckering, C. (1989) Maternal depression. *Journal of Child Psychology and Psychiatry*, 30, 807–817.

Radke-Yarrow, M. (1991) Attachment patterns in children of depressed mothers. In: C. Murray Parkes, J. Stevenson-Hinde and P. Marris (eds) *Attachment Across the Life Cycle*. London: Routledge.

Reder, P. (1996) Child protection: medical responsibilities. *Child Abuse Review*, 5, 64–66.

Reder, P. and Fitzpatrick, G. (1998) What is sufficient understanding? *Clinical Child Psychology and Psychiatry*, 3, 103–113.

Reder, P. and Lucey, C. (1995) Significant issues in the assessment of parenting. In: P. Reder and C. Lucey (eds) *Assessment of Parenting: Psychiatric and Psychological Contributions*. London: Routledge.

Rutter, M. (1966) *Children of Sick Parents: An Environmental and Psychiatric Study*. Institute of Psychiatry, Maudsley Monographs No. 16. London: Oxford University Press.

Rutter, M. (1995) Clinical implications of attachment concepts: retrospect and prospect. *Journal of Child Psychology and Psychiatry*, 36, 549–571.

Rutter, M. and Cox, A. (1985) Other family influences. In: M. Rutter and L. Hersov (eds) *Child and Adolescent Psychiatry: Modern Approaches*, 2nd edn. Oxford: Blackwell.

Rutter, M. and Quinton, D. (1984) Parental psychiatric disorder: effects on children. *Psychological Medicine*, 14, 853–880.

Shachnow, J. (1987) Preventive intervention with children of hospitalised psychiatric patients. *American Journal of Orthopsychiatry*, 57, 66–77.

Chapter 7

Impact of parental anxiety disorder on children

Liz Fellow-Smith

Parenting and family relationships are important factors shaping a child's developmental progress. The style and quality of the parent–child interaction are in themselves influenced by many factors, of which parental mental health is one. In this chapter, consideration will be given to one particular aspect: the impact of parental anxiety disorders. An overview of the literature is provided and issues are highlighted by case examples.

Parental anxiety disorders

Adult disorders classified within the neurotic disorder spectrum of ICD-10 (World Health Organization, 1992) are included in this chapter. This covers the phobic anxiety disorders F40 (for example, agoraphobia and social phobia), other anxiety disorders F41 (for example, panic disorder and generalised anxiety disorder), obsessive compulsive disorder F42, and dissociative disorders F44.

Impact on children

Studies and literature regarding the impact on children of parental anxiety disorders are limited. There is, however, evidence to suggest that these children are at increased risk of psychopathology. This includes domains such as increased behavioural inhibition in unfamiliar situations (Rosenbaum *et al.*, 1991; Manassis *et al.*, 1995), less perceived control over risks (Capps *et al.*, 1996), the use of avoidant strategies in response to stressful or problematic situations (Barrett *et al.*, 1996), increased worry and fearfulness (Capps *et al.*, 1996; Turner *et al.*, 1987), separation anxiety (Weissman *et al.*, 1984; Mufson *et al.*, 1994), school difficulties and more somatic complaints (Turner *et al.*, 1987).

Furthermore, these children are at increased risk of developing childhood anxiety disorders. Turner *et al.* (1987), for example, found children of anxiety disorder parents to be more than seven times as likely to meet criteria for an anxiety disorder as children of control parents, and twice as likely to meet anxiety disorder criteria as children of parents with depressed mood (dysthymia).

Studies of children of *agoraphobic* parents indicate they are vulnerable to childhood psychiatric disturbance and to separation anxiety in particular (Mufson *et al.*, 1994). Weissman *et al.* (1984), comparing family history data of children of mothers with major depression plus panic disorder or agoraphobia with that of children of controls and mothers with major depression only, demonstrated that the presence of anxiety disorder in the parents conferred on the children additional risk of anxiety disorder. Parents with panic disorder conferred more than a threefold risk of childhood separation anxiety. Capps *et al.* (1996), comparing children of agoraphobic parents with children of parents with no history of psychopathology, demonstrated that the majority (68 per cent) of children of agoraphobic parents met DSM-III-R (American Psychiatric Association, 1987) diagnostic criteria, the most common diagnosis being anxiety disorder.

The picture regarding *obsessive compulsive disorder* is not so clear. In their study of the children of patients with either obsessive compulsive disorder or agoraphobia, Turner *et al.* (1987) demonstrated them to be seven times more likely to meet DSM-III-R criteria for an anxiety disorder when compared with children of control group parents. However, a community study of adolescent offspring (aged 10–18) of parents who are members of an Obsessive-Compulsive Neurosis Support Group, suggests that these children do not have more problems than other adolescents in the community (Sawyer *et al.*, 1992). It may be, however, that this self-identified group is biased towards the less severe end of the disorder, with the Turner *et al.* study of a clinic population being biased towards the more severe end, with there being a corresponding range of impact on the children.

With regard to parental diagnosis of *social phobia*, a pilot study (Mancini *et al.*, 1996) indicates that half of the children (aged between 4 and 18) had at least one lifetime diagnosis of an anxiety disorder. This included childhood diagnoses of overanxious disorder (30 per cent), social phobia (23 per cent) and separation anxiety disorder (19 per cent). This suggests that children of parents with social phobic disorder may have increased rates of psychiatric disorder, which needs further study with a comparison control group.

Transmission of risk

Whilst it is evident that parental anxiety disorder does act as a risk factor for childhood psychiatric disorder, how such risk is mediated remains unclear. Whilst genetics play a role (Weissman, 1993), factors associated with the impact of the disorder on the tasks of parenting, the impact on attachment and the parent–child relationship, modelling of behaviours and the indirect factors of the overall circumstances of the family, comorbid parental personality disorder, and individual variances of the child, are also likely to be involved.

Impact on parenting

The behavioural and psycho-social sequelae of anxiety disorder may impact directly on the tasks of parenting. A parent with agoraphobia may not, for example, be able to escort a child to school, may not be able to take a toddler to playgroups or be able to provide other age-appropriate opportunities for socialisation. The parent may be preoccupied with their own distress and worries to such a degree that their capacity to identify and meet the needs of the child is impaired. They may respond to the child on the basis of their own fears and psychopathology, not from an understanding of the child's individual needs and development. Being preoccupied, they may be detached, non-responsive or inconsistent in relation to the child, behaving in ways that are perceived by the child as rejecting. It has been suggested that, in turn, such rejecting, inconsistent, detached parenting impedes the child's developing sense of security, so that they become anxious and defensively detached from the parent (Mann and Sanders, 1994).

This is an important area of assessment and focus of treatment for an adult patient. It is suggested that parent and child adaptation are intertwined and intervention for one individual is likely to affect functioning in the other. Therefore parental interventions aimed at improving social functioning may decrease the risk of disorder and dysfunction in the children (Mufson *et al.*, 1994).

Impact on attachment

Bowlby's attachment theory (Bowlby, 1969) proposes that the child's early relationships with its parents are internalised as 'working models' for later relationships. The attachment relationships are characterised by proximity-seeking behaviours at times when the infant is stressed: that is they seek the safety and comfort of those to whom they are attached. As the infant develops, they explore the world from this 'secure base' of a parent, exploring when the perceived threat or stress is low, returning to the parent when the level of threat increases – for example, when confronted by a stranger. The quality of this early attachment relationship and pattern of the infant's attachment behaviours are influenced by the response from the parent at times of stress: consistent and warm responses from the parent facilitate secure attachment; unreliable, remote, detached responses from the parent are more likely to lead to insecure attachment. The attachment relationship and pattern of attachment behaviour that a child develops are important building blocks for the child's developing emotional, behavioural and social well-being.

The developing pattern of attachment appears to bear relationship with the parent's own attachment style (Fonagy *et al.*, 1991). The adult's style of behaviour and interaction with the child influence the quality and nature of the secure base that they can provide. In addition to the impact of their own early childhood experiences and lifelong relationships, the presence of anxiety disorder will impact on the parent's interaction with and sensitiveness to the child. The parent's preoccupation with the distress and symptoms of an anxiety disorder and engagement in consequent avoidant or compulsive behaviours, will interfere with the parent's primary task of absolute commitment to and preoccupation with the care of the young child. It is likely, for example, that a mother with obsessive compulsive disorder who is preoccupied with the need to hand-wash and unable to attend immediately to the cries and needs of her baby, will be experienced by the baby as unavailable and unresponsive. The baby's developing pattern of attachment behaviours is more likely to be insecure avoidant or insecure ambivalent than secure. Whilst there is limited research in this area, one study has shown the rate of insecure attachment in the children of parents with anxiety disorders to be as high as 80 per cent (Manassis *et al.*, 1995). This is of particular interest as pregnancy and the post-partum period are times of risk for the development and exacerbation of anxiety disorders (Neziroglu *et al.*, 1992; Sichel *et al.*, 1993; Cohen *et al.*, 1994; Northcott and Stein, 1994). Hence, new mothers may be faced with the distress and impact of an anxiety disorder at the time when their preoccupation and energy need to be directed towards the child in order to facilitate the development of a warm, secure, responsive relationship.

Modelling

Through their own patterns of behaviour and responses to stress, parents with anxiety disorders may model and reinforce maladaptive behaviour and coping strategies in their children. It has been suggested that exposure to a parent with an anxiety disorder may predispose a child to develop an anxious stance by modelling caution and fearfulness (Rosenbaum *et al.*, 1988; 1991). Agoraphobic mothers, for example, self-reported more separation anxiety than did comparison mothers, maternal separation anxiety being negatively correlated with the child's perceived control of risk (Capps *et al.*, 1996). This suggests that the mother's fears regarding separation and managing risk provide a model of fearful approach for the child. Furthermore, there is some evidence from a study by Barrett *et al.* (1996) that family processes may be anxiety enhancing. In this study, groups of anxious, oppositional and non-clinic children were asked to interpret and provide plans of action to ambiguous scenarios. The child was asked to discuss the scenarios with their family and to return with a final answer. Anxious and oppositional children were more likely to interpret the ambiguous scenarios in a threatening manner. The anxious children chose avoidant solutions, the oppositional children chose aggressive solutions. After family discussion, the anxious children's avoidant plans of action increased, suggesting family enhancement of the avoidant responses.

Indirect factors

Personality disorder

Impact on children may be mediated through factors associated with anxiety disorders. Concurrent with a diagnosis of anxiety disorder may be evidence of personality disorder. Attendant functional problems such as unemployment, social isolation, relationship difficulties, aggression, irritability, hostility, and exposure to alcohol, drugs and offending behaviour, will influence both the style and quality of parenting and the socialisation of the child. The early study by Rutter and Quinton (1984) demonstrated, for example, that the psychiatric risk to the children was greatest in the case of personality disorders associated with high levels of exposure to hostile behaviour, as compared with the risks associated with parental depression and psychosis.

Marital discord and family disturbance

Similarly, marital discord and family disturbance may be present and impact on the experiences, care and parenting of the child (Rutter and Quinton, 1984). Such discord may be secondary to the anxiety disorder itself or be a function of associated personality difficulties. Rutter and Quinton postulated that this may be the most important mediating risk factor for the child's adjustment and mental health.

The child

In addition to the factors that the parent contributes to the parenting relationship, the child brings along their individual variances. A child with a difficult temperament may, for example, pose more management difficulties. Should a parent's capacity to respond appropriately and sensitively already be compromised by mental ill-health, there is greater risk of a dysfunctional pattern of interaction developing. A spiral of problems may be set in motion, the stress of parenting exacerbating the parent's difficulties, this in turn negatively impacting on the child's behaviour. There is evidence to suggest that temperamentally difficult boys are most vulnerable to the ill-effects associated with parental mental disorder (Rutter and Quinton, 1984). Conversely, secure attachment, confiding relationships and other protective factors will mean that some children are less affected by parental ill-health than others.

In addition, the child may be worried about the parent. This can lead to stress, preoccupation and emotional disturbance, with negative impact on the child's social, emotional and educational functioning. Alternatively, the child may be parentified, needing to care for the parent or other siblings, so that their own dependency and developmental needs are not adequately met.

Case examples

The following case histories illustrate the impact of parental anxiety disorders on family relationships, the task of parenting and the well-being of children. In order to illustrate this impact and how parenting is vulnerable, cases at the extreme end of the spectrum have been chosen. The cases also illustrate the complexity of and interaction between the direct and indirect factors of transmission (as detailed above) in such cases, the impact of comorbid personality disorder and the importance of overall family functioning.

Case 1

Two children, age 9 and 6, were referred by a social worker for assessment to the child and adolescent mental health service. The presenting history was of poor school attendance, educational delays and irregular attendance at medical appointments. Both children had been placed on the Child Protection Register, under the category of neglect. The question posed for assessment was whether child mental health input could improve family functioning such that the children could remain at home with their mother. If not, it was anticipated they would be placed in alternative care.

The children lived at home with their single mother, three older siblings having left home to live independently. The maternal grandmother, who had lived for many years with the family and had supported the care of the children, had died some eighteen months earlier.

At interview the mother described her own emotionally deprived childhood. Her father had abused alcohol, gambled, been physically violent towards his wife and children and had spent long periods of time away from home. The maternal grandmother had been depressed, exhausted and emotionally unavailable to her children. There had been insufficient money in the household to provide food and clothing.

In her adulthood, the mother had sought emotional support from violent men, entering a series of abusive relationships. There was concern within the professional network that the younger children may have been abused by a convicted sex offender with whom the mother had had a relationship.

In addition to these many areas of concern and evident worries about her capacity to provide for the children's emotional and safety needs, it became evident during assessment that the mother also suffered from agoraphobia. She experienced marked anxiety when away from home and was housebound unless accompanied. She was unable to take the children for medical appointments, health checks or immunisations. She could not ensure the children's attendance at school and had great difficulty attending school meetings. She was unable to provide adequate supervision or social stimulation for the children. She did not take them out, and the older child played outdoors unsupervised whilst the younger child spent time indoors with adults. The mother looked to her children to run errands, do the shopping and take on age-inappropriate responsibilities.

In addition to educational concerns, the 6-year-old displayed impaired peer relationships, interacting in a somewhat precocious, adult manner. The 9-year-old harboured many fears about school and was fearful of travelling on public transport. Both children were concerned about their mother's well-being and safety. They did not like to leave her alone.

In this case, identification of the mother's anxiety disorder made a significant difference to the overall management and planning for the children. The mother was referred to adult mental health services and engaged in behavioural therapy. With the needs of the children in mind, the treatment goals centred on taking the children to school and age-appropriate social activities. This was supported by a youth worker who befriended the older child, introduced him to clubs and helped the mother attend with him. The overall emotional well-being of both children improved. The additional concerns regarding the mother's relationships remained but, with the overall improvement in the family functioning and care of the children, the social worker was willing to support and monitor the family situation.

Case 2

In this second case, two children from one family were separately referred to the child and adolescent mental health service. The eldest son of the family, Anthony, had been convicted at the age of 11 of sexually assaulting his younger sister, Sandra. He had been living away from the family for three years. When previously assessed following disclosure of the abuse, Anthony had revealed that his mother was overly worried about tidiness and that his parents would not allow friends to visit the home. There was no evidence of physical or sexual abuse.

The first mental health referral concerned the sister, Sandra, for whom the parents were seeking individual therapy post-abuse. The second referral, made some months later by the education department, concerned another sister, Mandy, who at the age of 7 was not attending school. Assessment revealed a severe anxiety disorder and consequent refusal to attend school.

It was not until some time into family therapy and individual psychotherapy for Sandra that it came to light via the father that the mother had suffered from an obsessive-compulsive disorder since Anthony's birth. She had been traumatised by earlier neonatal deaths and had experienced many painful losses during her childhood. Her core fear was of contamination and she sought to protect the children from the harm of infection. She experienced marked anxiety symptoms and compulsively engaged in rituals and behaviours to avoid contamination of the house and family. This meant that she scrubbed anything new coming into the house. Soft toys that could not be adequately scrubbed were thrown away, as were toys, cups, cutlery, etc. that touched the carpet. On entering the house each person was undressed and washed thoroughly. To minimise the time involved in the rituals the children stayed upstairs all weekend, often being left unsupervised whilst the parents went out shopping. The rituals were so time-consuming that the children were often late for school or did not attend. In order to prevent contamination and to keep the family lifestyle secret, friends were not allowed to visit.

The father, whilst trying to limit the impact on the family, did not challenge his wife's beliefs or rituals and family life came to revolve around her disorder. It was in the context of poor supervision and 'imprisonment' upstairs on weekends that the sexual abuse took place between the children. It was evidently difficult for the mother to separate her own worries and fears from those of the children. She was unable to help Mandy overcome her fears about school, her responses serving to reinforce rather than alleviate the worries.

Family and individual child therapy continued, while the mother was encouraged and supported to accept help from the adult mental health services. She reluctantly engaged in a course of cognitive-behavioural treatment and made some progress. The overall family functioning improved but significant concern remained about the potential for future deterioration and on-going impact on the children.

Case 3

In this third case, the mother of a 2-year-old child was diagnosed as suffering from an obsessive-compulsive disorder, the child having initially presented to the paediatric service with failure to thrive.

The mother, a 21-year-old single woman, had for some four years experienced an increasing fear of mess and dirt. Prior to the birth of the baby, she had compulsively washed her hands but had otherwise maintained adequate daily functioning and activities. The arrival of the baby presented a significant challenge. She was unable to tolerate the mess and smell associated with changing the baby's nappies. The baby was left unchanged for up to twelve hours at a time. The mess associated with mealtimes caused her considerable anxiety. She attempted to contain the problem by continuing to spoon-feed, by withholding sloppy, messy foods and later by avoiding mealtimes. Similarly she dealt with the messiness of the child's play by restricting her activities and locking play equipment and toys in cupboards.

As a result the child was found on assessment to be timid, quiet, underfed and undernourished. Her self-feeding and motor skills were delayed. She sat quietly demonstrating limited interest in her surroundings and restricted exploratory play. The relationship with her mother was tense, the mother anxiously trying to anticipate the child's behaviour to prevent mess and accidents.

In this case the maternal anxiety disorder impacted on the tasks of parenting. Hygiene and physical care of the child were impaired. Adequate age-appropriate stimulation was not provided. The child was exposed to a constantly tense atmosphere. The child's development was adversely affected.

Having identified the mother's anxiety disorder, referral was made to adult mental health services. Unfortunately the mother found it difficult to engage in treatment and little progress was made. Care proceedings were instigated by the local authority.

Conclusion

Children of mentally ill parents are not alike in their responses to maternal disorder and functioning. Parent and child adaptation appear intertwined. It is important to recognise parental disorder both as clinicians working with adults, since parental disorder may have an impact on the children, and as clinicians working with children, in order to identify vulnerability and risk factors. Intervention in one is likely to affect functioning in the other. Addressing parental disorder and improving overall functioning, particularly in areas that impact on relationships and the tasks of parenting, may well improve the overall well-being and functioning of the children. Interventions to address parental social functioning may decrease the risk for disorder and dysfunction in children (Mufson *et al.*, 1994).

The case histories detailed above, while at the extreme end of parental disorder, illustrate the need to consider and constantly review the impact on the children. Issues of significant harm must be considered. The case histories demonstrate that a child's welfare and well-being are at particular risk when they become embroiled directly in a parent's strange behaviour without the moderating influence of a healthy other parent, or when the psycho-social functioning of the family deteriorates as a result of the parent's disorder. In these situations, it may become necessary to involve social services in order that the welfare and safety of the children can be assessed. With careful planning and good communication, comprehensive inter-agency treatment packages involving child mental health, adult mental health, social services and the education department may be sufficient to protect and support the children while change is brought about to decrease the level of detrimental impact on the child. In some cases, however, if treatability is low and significant parental disorder persists, separation of the child from the parent may, on balance, be in the best interests of the child. In practice, most cases are less severe than those detailed above and improvement is achieved with good liaison between child and adult mental health services.

References

American Psychiatric Association (1987) *DSM-III-R Classification*. Washington, DC: American Psychiatric Association.

Barrett, P.M., Rapee, R.M., Dadds, M.M. and Ryan, S.M. (1996) Family enhancement of cognitive style in anxious and aggressive children. *Journal of Abnormal Child Psychology*, 24, 187–203.

Bowlby, J. (1969) *Attachment and Loss: Attachment*. New York: Basic Books.

Capps, L., Sigman, M., Sena, R., Henker, B. and Whalen, C. (1996) Fear, anxiety and perceived control of agoraphobic parents. *Journal of Child Psychology and Psychiatry*, 37, 445–452.

Cohen, L.S., Sichel, D.A., Dimmock, J.A. and Rosenbaum, J.F. (1994) Postpartum course in women with preexisting panic disorder. *Journal of Clinical Psychiatry*, 55, 289–292.

Fonagy, P., Steele, H. and Steele, M. (1991) Maternal representations of attachment during pregnancy predict the organisation of infant–mother attachment at one year of age. *Child Development*, 62, 891–905.

Manassis, K., Bradley, S., Goldberg, S., Hood, J. and Swinson, R.P. (1995) Behavioural inhibition, attachment and anxiety in children of mothers with anxiety disorders. *Canadian Journal of Psychiatry*, 40, 87–92.

Mancini, C., van-Ameringen, M., Szatmari, P., Fugere, C. and Boyle, M. (1996) A high-risk pilot study of the children of adults with social phobia. *Journal of the American Academy of Child and Adolescent Psychiatry*, 35, 1511–1517.

Mann, B.J. and Sanders, S. (1994) Child dissociation and the family context. *Journal of Abnormal Child Psychology*, 22, 373–388.

Mufson, L., Aidala, A. and Warner, V. (1994) Social dysfunction and psychiatric disorder in mothers and their children. *Journal of the American Academy of Child and Adolescent Psychiatry*, 33, 1256–1264.

Neziroglu, F., Anemone, R. and Yaryura-Tobias, J.A. (1992) Onset of obsessive-compulsive disorder in pregnancy. *American Journal of Psychiatry*, 149, 947–950.

Northcott, C.J. and Stein, M.B. (1994) Panic disorder in pregnancy. *Journal of Clinical Psychiatry*, 55, 539–542.

Rosenbaum, J.F., Bierderman, J., Gersten, M., Hirshfeld, D.R., Meminger, S., Herman, J.B., Kagan, J., Reznick, S. and Snidman, N. (1988) Behavioural inhibition in children of parents with panic disorder and agoraphobia. *Archives of General Psychiatry*, 45, 463–470.

Rosenbaum, J.F., Bierderman, J., Hirshfeld, D.R., Bolduc, E.A., Faraone, S.V., Kagan, J., Snidman, N. and Reznick, S.J. (1991) Further evidence of an association between behavioural inhibition and anxiety disorders: results from a family study of children from a non-clinical sample. *Journal of Psychiatric Research*, 25, 49–65.

Rutter, M. and Quinton, D. (1984) Parental psychiatric disorder: effects on children. *Psychological Medicine*, 14, 853–880.

Sawyer, M.G., Slocombe, C., Kosky, R., Clark, J., Mathias, J., Burfield, S., Faranda, I., Hambly, H., Mahar, A., Tang, B.N. *et al.* (1992) The psychological adjustment of offspring of adults with obsessive-compulsive disorder: a brief report. *Australian and New Zealand Journal of Psychiatry*, 26, 479–484.

Sichel, D.A., Cohen, L.S., Dimmock, J.A. and Rosenbaum, J.F. (1993) Postpartum obsessive-compulsive disorder: a case series. *Journal of Clinical Psychiatry*, 54, 156–159.

Turner, S.M., Beidel, D.C. and Costello, A. (1987) Psychopathology in the offspring of anxiety disorder patients. *Journal of Consulting and Clinical Psychology*, 55, 229–235.

Weissman, M.M. (1993) Family genetic studies of panic disorder. *Journal of Psychiatric Research*, 27 (suppl. 1), 69–78.

Weissman, M.M., Leckman, J.F., Merikangas, K.R., Gammon, G.D. and Prusoff, B.A. (1984) Depression and anxiety disorders in parents and children. *Archives of General Psychiatry*, 41, 845–852.

World Health Organization (1992) *The ICD-10 Classification of Mental and Behavioural Disorders*. Geneva: World Health Organization.

Chapter 8

The children of mothers with eating disorders

Matthew Hodes

Introduction

In recent years there has been increasing interest in the effects of maternal eating disorders on children's adjustment and development. Research studies have suggested that these children are at increased risk of abnormal growth and psychiatric disorders, and frequently experience difficult family relationships. The implications for clinical practice and intervention are only starting to be investigated. The aim of this chapter is to provide a summary of some key research issues and findings regarding the effects of maternal eating disorders on children. The clinical relevance will be discussed by considering the possibility of screening for problems in the children.

Defining eating disorders

The defining criteria for anorexia nervosa and bulimia nervosa according to the American psychiatric classificatory system DSM-IV (American Psychiatric Association, 1994) are more precise than those of ICD-10 (World Health Organization, 1992) and are more frequently used in research. The DSM-IV features are described in Table 8.1.

Although anorexia nervosa and bulimia nervosa are regarded as distinct disorders, it can be seen that there is substantial overlap between their defining features. Partial syndromes of both disorders are recognised by ICD-10 when one of the defining features is not present. However, according to DSM-IV, partial syndromes of anorexia nervosa and bulimia nervosa are classified together as 'eating disorders not otherwise specified'.

Both anorexia nervosa and bulimia nervosa are associated with significant levels of comorbidity, most frequently depression (Cooper, 1995). Other relevant comorbid disorders are alcohol and substance misuse and obsessive compulsive disorder (Garfinkel, 1992; Fairburn and Wilson, 1993). Personality disorders also occur, with 'borderline' and anti-social type personality disorder associated with bulimia nervosa and obsessive compulsive personality disorder with anorexia nervosa (Wonderlich, 1995).

Table 8.1 DSM-IV diagnostic criteria for anorexia nervosa and bulimia nervosa (main criteria, summarised)

Anorexia nervosa	Bulimia nervosa
A. Refusal to maintain body weight at or above a minimally normal weight for age and height (e.g. weight loss leading to maintenance of body weight less than 85% of that expected). B. Intense fear of gaining weight or becoming fat, even though underweight. C. Disturbance in the way in which one's body weight or shape is experienced, undue influence of body weight or shape on self-evaluation, or denial of the seriousness of the current low body weight. D. In postmenarchal females, amenorrhoea, i.e. the absence of at least three consecutive menstrual cycles.	A. Recurrent episodes of binge-eating. An episode of binge-eating is characterised by both of the following: 1 eating, in a discrete period of time (e.g. within any two-hour period), an amount of food that is definitely larger than most people would eat during a similar period of time and under similar circumstances. 2 a sense of lack of control over eating during the episode (e.g. a feeling that one cannot stop eating or control what or how much one is eating). B. Recurrent inappropriate compensatory behaviour in order to prevent weight gain, such as self-induced vomiting; misuse of laxatives, diuretics, enemas, or other medications; fasting; or excessive exercise. C. The binge-eating and inappropriate compensatory behaviours both occur, on average, at least twice a week for three months. D. Self-evaluation is unduly influenced by body shape and weight. E. The disturbance does not occur exclusively during episodes of anorexia nervosa.
Specify type: *Restricting type:* during the current episode the person has not regularly engaged in binge-eating or purging behaviour (i.e. self-inducing vomiting or the misuse of laxatives, diuretics, or enemas). *Binge-eating/purging type:* during the current episode of anorexia nervosa, the person has regularly engaged in binge-eating or purging behaviour (i.e. self-induced vomiting or the misuse of laxatives, diuretics, or enemas).	Specify type: *Purging type:* during the current episode of bulimia nervosa, the person has regularly engaged in self-induced vomiting or the misuse of laxatives, diuretics, or enemas. *Nonpurging type:* during the current episode of bulimia nervosa, the person has used other inappropriate compensatory behaviours, such as fasting or excessive exercise, but has not regularly engaged in self-induced vomiting or the misuse of laxatives, diuretics, or enemas.

This outline of psychopathology has been included because it specifies the range of abnormal behaviours that children of mothers with eating disorders may witness, and the abnormal cognitions and affect that their mothers will have while they endeavour to care for their children. It also indicates that the children's difficulties may sometimes be due not to the eating problem *per se* but to the associated disorders (Garmezy and Masten, 1994; Kumar and Hipwell, 1994).

The significant overlap in core psychopathology between anorexia nervosa and bulimia nervosa, occasional change of one disorder into the other in some individuals, and frequent comorbidity of both anorexia and bulimia, especially with depression, are reasons why the children of mothers with the different eating disorders can be considered together. An additional reason is that many studies have investigated children with anorexia nervosa, bulimia nervosa, and partial syndromes. There is also a relatively small amount of research in this field.

Methodological issues

There are a number of methodological issues and limitations that should be considered in relation to the existing literature. First, there are limitations in the way that study samples have been ascertained. Many studies and reports have come from specialist adult eating disorder services (Lacey and Smith, 1987; Fahy and Treasure, 1989; Woodside and Shekter-Wolfson, 1990; Hodes *et al.*, 1997; Russell *et al.*, 1998). These services typically do not serve defined catchment areas and may be more likely to treat sufferers with particular characteristics and considerable difficulties. Occasional reports have come from paediatric services (van Wezel-Meijler and Wit, 1989). The samples in all studies may be unrepresentative of community populations of mothers with eating disorders as none has been exclusively based on community samples, although the studies of Stein's group (Stein *et al.*, 1994; 1996) were largely made up of mothers recruited from a community group.

Most studies are limited by their design. Many reports have multiple single case study designs (Fahy and Treasure, 1989; Lunt *et al.*, 1989; Stein and Fairburn, 1989; Woodside and Shekter-Wolfson, 1990; Russell *et al.*, 1998). Some take the form of surveys (Brinch *et al.*, 1988; Hodes *et al.*, 1997). Only the studies by Stein and his group (Stein *et al.*, 1994; 1996) have control groups which can compare the children of mothers with eating disorders with the children of mothers without.

There are also limitations of the instruments used. A number of studies have been concerned with children's adjustment and difficult family relationships but these aspects of functioning have usually not been investigated with standardised instruments. This sometimes makes the reports hard to interpret, especially regarding child behavioural deviance, as the maternal accounts may be influenced by the mother's own psychopathology.

Difficulties of growth, psychopathology and relationships

Children's difficulties have been described in three domains of functioning. First, there are many reports of inadequate weight gain and growth in infancy and childhood. Even in pregnancy there is a consistent finding that the weight gain of the developing foetus of anorexia nervosa sufferers is likely to be inadequate (Stewart *et al.*, 1987; Brinch *et al.*, 1988; Treasure and Russell, 1988), and this can also occur when mothers have bulimia nervosa (Franko and Walton, 1993). The infants may show low weight gain, sometimes severe enough to be regarded as non-organic failure to thrive (Brinch *et al.*, 1988; Stein *et al.*, 1994). Low weight gain may occur in middle childhood and be associated with growth retardation or wasting (van Wezel-Meijler and Wit, 1989; Stein and Fairburn, 1989; Fahy and Treasure, 1989; Hodes *et al.*, 1997; Russell *et al.*, 1998). Low weight gain may be more common when mothers have anorexia nervosa than bulimia nervosa (Hodes *et al.*, 1997). Poor weight gain in adolescence can occur in female offspring of anorexia nervosa sufferers who themselves develop that disorder (Griffiths *et al.*, 1995; Hodes *et al.*, 1997). A different weight control problem that has been identified in the children of bulimia nervosa sufferers is obesity (Stein and Fairburn, 1989; Hodes *et al.*, 1997).

The second area of difficulties is risk for psychiatric disorders and poor adjustment. Most studies have found high rates of eating disorders in the offspring of mothers with eating disorders (Woodside and Shekter-Wolfson, 1990; Griffiths *et al.*, 1995; Strober, 1995; Hodes *et al.*, 1997). Only the study by Hodes *et al.* (1997) has used standardised child psychiatric interviews or questionnaires. It found that 50 per cent of children aged 3–26 years of mothers who attended an eating disorder service had various psychiatric disorders (see below). The finding of internalising and externalising disorders and developmental problems is consistent with other reports (Stein and Fairburn; 1989; Fahy and Treasure, 1989; Woodside and Shekter-Wolfson, 1990).

The third area of difficulties is poor relationships with spouses and children. These include critical, coercive speech style, low levels of warmth and involvement with the children, and ineffectual strategies for containing children and setting limits. Mothers may have difficulties in providing meals for and eating with their children (Stein *et al.*, 1994). The parents' relationship may be strained or avoidant, and parental separation is frequent (Woodside and Shekter-Wolfson, 1990; Hodes *et al.*, 1997). Some mothers feel that they are unable to meet the needs of their children for brief periods, and alternative carers, perhaps other family members, are involved. In extreme situations the children, sometimes as infants, are abandoned and require long-term alternative carers.

The children of mothers attending one eating disorder clinic

To provide an overview of the difficulties of children whose mothers have eating disorders, a survey of one clinic will be described in more detail (Hodes *et al.*, 1997). The survey aimed to assess the growth and psychiatric disorders of children of all mothers attending the Peter Dally Eating Disorders Clinic in London. The study attempted to overcome two of the problems mentioned previously regarding sampling bias in case selection and absence of standard research instruments to assess psychiatric disorder of the children.

There were 294 cases on the clinic database, of whom 17 were female and identified as having at least one child. Twelve mothers, 4 with anorexia nervosa and 8 with bulimia nervosa, agreed to participate in the study. In addition, one other mother was included who was attending a specialist eating disorder service for children in the locality because of parenting problems. Assessment included maternal interview regarding the sufferer's own eating disorder and psycho-social adjustment (Morgan and Hayward, 1988; Morgan and Russell, 1975) and also her offspring's adjustment. Questionnaires were completed by mothers regarding the children, using the Rutter A scale (Rutter *et al.*, 1970) for children aged 5–17 years and the behaviour checklist (Richman *et al.*, 1982) for the children aged 3–4 years. The children were weighed and had their height measured during the assessment. Where possible children completed questionnaires regarding their eating attitudes (Eating Attitudes Test, Maloney *et al.*, 1989) and self-esteem (Harter, 1985).

It was found that the mothers had a mean age of 35 years (Standard Deviation 6.4), and mean illness duration of 13.9 years (Standard Deviation 9.3). The body mass index (defined as weight in kilograms divided by height in metres squared; healthy range 20–25) of the five mothers with anorexia nervosa was 17.5 (Standard Deviation 1.8), and for the bulimia nervosa sufferers it was 22.5 (Standard Deviation 3.4). Seven of the mothers were single, and six married. Eight were regarded as having good family relationships, and five had poor relationships. There were 26 children, aged between 9 months and 25 years.

With regard to psychopathology, 11 (50 per cent) of the 22 children aged 3–26 years had psychiatric disorders. The type of disorder was varied but included anorexia nervosa, obsessive compulsive disorder, oppositional defiant disorder, emotional disorder and enuresis. Eight (32 per cent) of the children had abnormal weight, and this group consisted of six children with wasting (weight for height, corrected for age, less than 85 per cent expected), including two with anorexia nervosa, and two boys with obesity. Mothers rarely had concerns about their children being underweight. Five mothers had concerns about giving the children too much food but these were not the mothers of the boys with obesity. These findings may underestimate the rates of disturbance because the five mothers who did not participate may have had more severe eating disorders and this would place their children at increased risk for problems (Beglin and Fairburn, 1992).

The following case vignette illustrates the diversity of difficulties the children and families may have (Hodes *et al.*, 1997).

Case A

Ms A, who was 29 years, was seen together with her two children at her mother's home where the children had been living for the previous few weeks. Ms A had a ten-year history of bulimia nervosa which had recently become severe, with binge eating and self-induced vomiting occurring several times per day. She had been living as a single parent trying to look after her two children but said that over the previous year the demands of parenting had overwhelmed her. She had been unable to cook regularly for the children as she had been too preoccupied with trying to control her bulimic symptoms, and became frightened of having food in the house. Eventually she asked her mother to care for the children, who moved into their maternal grandmother's home. The mother visited the children once or twice per week.

Ms A's daughter, 9 years old, was very quiet and compliant throughout the interview. Ms A described her as a worrier. When asked about her eating she said her daughter 'goes on binges then sort of goes off her food'. She also mentioned that her daughter seemed pre-occupied with her looks. On the modified Eating Attitudes Test scale she scored 16, less than the threshold of 20 for disorder, and her score on the Rutter A scale was 12, just below the threshold for indicating high risk of disorder. Her global score on the Harter self-esteem questionnaire was 2.68, considerably below the mean scores for community peers. Her subscale scores were particularly low regarding athletic competence (1.48), scholastic performance (2.32) and physical appearance (2.32) (Hoare et al., 1993).

Ms A's son was 5 years old, and behaved in a very attention-seeking way throughout the interview. He was keen to ask questions, do drawings on request, and showed no anxiety or shyness in attempts to interest the interviewer. He was described by Ms A as 'hyperactive, always on the go'. With regard to his eating habits, Ms A said he 'eats everything, he's preoccupied with food'. His weight for height was 69 per cent, in the wasting range. He scored 10 on the modified Eating Attitudes Test scale. His Rutter A score was 30, well above the threshold of 13, indicating high risk for psychiatric disorder, and the subscales indicated both anti-social and hyperactive symptoms.

Mechanisms for the development of problems

Five broad mechanisms can be described by which parents' eating disorders affect their children (Stein and Woolley, 1996; Woolley *et al.*, 1998). First, maternal attitudes to eating, food and body shape are important. Inadequate maternal diet resulting from fear of fatness during pregnancy may result in poor foetal growth and low birth-weight infants. Mothers may fear that their children are fat or will become overweight (van Wezel-Meijler and Wit, 1989; Hodes *et al.*, 1997; Russell *et al.*, 1998) and provide an inadequate diet or become critical during feeding and mealtimes (Stein *et al.*, 1994). This could result in the children's starvation and sometimes inadequate growth (van Wezel-Meijler and Wit, 1989; Hodes *et al.*, 1997; Russell *et al.*, 1998). This situation can be regarded as a form of child maltreatment.

Second, parents' disturbed eating behaviour may serve as a role model. This refers to the process by which children might witness abnormal behaviour, such as self-induced vomiting, as well as be exposed to unhealthy attitudes to eating and body shape, and so learn those behaviours and attitudes. Evidence for this comes from studies of children of severely affected mothers. There are also some research reports that show that in community populations maternal abnormal eating attitudes are associated with abnormal eating attitudes in daughters (Hill *et al.*, 1990; Pike and Rodin, 1991).

The third mechanism is an indirect influence of the maternal eating disorder and concerns the lack of sensitivity to the child's needs because of the maternal eating psychopathology or depression. As with depressed mothers, less warmth and more irritability may be shown to the children. Parental criticism and hostility are often associated with high levels of distress and conflict, and are risk factors for the development of childhood psychiatric disorder (Rutter and Quinton, 1984).

Fourth, eating disorders may be associated with generally disrupted relationships, including high rates of marital discord and separation (Hodes *et al.*, 1997; Woodside and Shekter-Wolfson, 1990). There may also be difficulties in the relationships between mothers and their children. Sufferers with severe eating disorders, who occasionally have associated personality disorders and substance misuse problems, may have generally more critical, intrusive and inconsistent relationship styles towards their offspring (Stein *et al.*, 1994; Woodside and Shekter-Wolfson, 1990). The severely impaired mothers might be unable to care for their children, and the fathers or other relatives become the main carers (Russell *et al.*, 1998; Woodside and Shekter-Wolfson, 1990).

Fifth, there are genetic factors which have been shown to be relevant for the transmission of eating disorders, especially anorexia nervosa and, to a lesser extent, bulimia nervosa (Treasure and Holland, 1990; Strober, 1992; 1995). Other disorders such as depression and obsessive compulsive disorder also occur more commonly in the relatives of sufferers of eating disorders, indicating the presence of genetic factors that may be passed to offspring (Strober, 1992).

Intervention

In recent years a small number of studies have appeared which offer suggestions on the management of children with varied problems whose mothers have eating disorders (Griffiths *et al.*, 1995; Russell *et al.*, 1998; Woolley *et al.*, 1998). A number of general principles have emerged from this work. First, it is important to bear in mind that sufferers of eating disorders may be very sensitive about the welfare of their children. They can feel guilty and blame themselves, worrying that their children are being harmed by their disorder or associated relationship difficulties, including marital conflict. They may fear that social services could become involved and remove their children. Second, in view of the complex needs of the children, a multi-disciplinary approach may be required. The range of health professionals that might need to be involved includes general practitioners and health visitors, child and adolescent mental health professionals, and paediatricians. Third, there may be conflicts of responsibility to the parent and child when both are significantly impaired or distressed. Good clinical judgement and expert knowledge are required to determine initial priorities for intervention. Such conflicts may be more easily addressed and managed when child and adult mental health professionals are able to have a dialogue and agree on treatment priorities for the family.

In extreme circumstances when there is maltreatment because of failure to provide an adequate diet or other forms of abuse that cause significant harm, child protection concerns may require consultation with the social services department. Significant harm can always be said to have occurred when the children are stunted in growth or wasted because of the failure to provide an adequate diet. However, significant harm may also occur with less severe growth abnormalities, or because of the children's psychological distress caused by unhealthy parental eating attitudes and behaviours that involve the child. Fortunately, the direct involvement of social services with the families can often be avoided because of the ability of therapists to manage the children's and mothers' difficulties by explanation, influencing parental attitudes by various therapeutic techniques including persuasion, and judicious parental separation, perhaps by hospital admission (Russell *et al.*, 1998).

Since the children of mothers with eating disorders may have varied difficulties, a range of interventions will be needed. The choice of interventions can be guided by the usual therapeutic principles regarding efficacy, acceptability to parents and children, resource implications and availability. However, some useful suggestions for intervention have been made with respect to three types of problems that show some specificity in occurring amongst this group of children.

Stein and his colleagues have built on their research regarding infant development and maternal–infant interaction and made suggestions for intervention. Their suggestions are aimed at reversing the interactional processes associated with the onset of problems (Stein *et al.*, 1994; 1996; Stein and Woolley, 1996; Woolley *et al.*, 1998). Parents are helped to recognise their infant's cues during feeding, and given advice regarding the type and range of foods that are appropriate. Intervention also aims to reduce disputes during feeding often triggered by their concern about the mess involved.

Some elements of the management of underfed children of mothers who have anorexia nervosa have been described by Russell and his colleagues (1998). The need to form relationships with the mother-patient as well as the husband or other involved relatives is emphasised. The involved adults should receive nutritional counselling regarding the children's dietary needs, which may also need to be a focus of therapy. If the mother is significantly underweight it is best for her to be admitted for her own treatment. This facilitates the task for the father or other family members of helping the children to consume a healthy diet, and may also reduce family tensions. Effective treatment should lead to weight gain in the children within 2–4 weeks but it is recommended that the children be weighed and measured over two years.

Some suggestions for treatment have been provided regarding adolescent girls suffering from anorexia nervosa whose mothers have the same disorder (Griffiths *et al.*, 1995). The study of eight mother and daughter pairs clearly describes how maternal eating attitudes may reinforce the daughters' fat-phobic attitudes and unhealthy eating behaviours. Maternal attitudes may undermine treatment endeavours, including hospitalisation. Suggestions for helping in these difficult situations include intervention for all the family, such as nutritional counselling. The mothers may need hospitalisation in their own right, and this separation can be helpful to the daughters. This study (Griffiths *et al.*, 1995), as well as clinical experience, suggests that maternal eating disorders reduce the effectiveness of family therapy for adolescent anorexia nervosa that relies on active parental participation. The crucial first stage requires parents to regulate and supervise their starving children's eating to increase weight (Dare *et al.*, 1990; Dare and Eisler, 1995). This task is very difficult to achieve when mothers themselves are fat-phobic, and may even admire or envy their daughter's slimness.

Accounts regarding intervention for children of mothers with eating disorders are descriptive and controlled trials have not been carried out with this group. Intervention needs to be based on a judicious combination of an understanding of mechanisms regarding the development of difficulties and evidence-based approaches to treatment.

A case vignette that illustrates some of these treatment principles follows.

Case B

A professional woman in her thirties and her 6-month-old daughter were referred because of the mother's various difficulties including many symptoms related to anorexia nervosa. The mother had not recovered fully from an episode of anorexia nervosa in adolescence and a second episode lasting 4–5 years occurring in her twenties. She had a history of depression, and had contact with a general psychiatrist who provided supportive psychotherapy and anti-depressants. Background difficulties included sexual abuse in childhood by her grandfather. The referral by the mother's group therapist was prompted by the mother's difficulty in introducing solid foods to her daughter who had been fed by breast.

The initial assessment family interviews revealed that the mother and her husband and their child lived together. The father was supportive towards the mother and tried to help with childcare. They agreed that the problems that concerned them were the mother's worry that introducing solid food would make the child overweight. The mother had introduced solids but was concerned about the infant's weight gain. This had led her on a couple of occasions to add bran to the baby's food to induce diarrhoea and reduce her weight. By contrast, the father thought the baby should be allowed to eat the age-appropriate food that she wanted. He had found it hard to influence the food offered to the baby because the mother would get up very early in the morning and prepare the food for the day, and want him to give the same food. He was very involved with the baby when he was not working, and frequently played with her, and was more relaxed towards her than the mother.

From the interviews it was clear that the mother had abnormal eating attitudes with a high level of concern about her own body shape, exercised regularly to control her weight and persistently dieted. Her body mass index was 18.4 (indicating that she was underweight) and she had amenorrhoea (caused by her low weight and breast-feeding). Discussing the child's development with the health visitor, and examining the growth charts, which revealed that she followed the 50th centile for weight and length, completed the assessment. There was also communication with the group therapist, general psychiatrist and general practitioner regarding the psychiatric treatment of the mother and the infant's development.

Therapy consisted of psychoeducation regarding the infant's nutritional and emotional needs and reassurance that she was growing healthily. Disagreement between the parents focused on feeding, especially as the mother who was rigid in her attitudes wanted help because she was tired by getting up at 4–5 a.m. to prepare the child's food. Various interventions using family therapy principles, including structural and strategic approaches, to help the parents with their different views of their child's dietary and other needs were necessary. There was one joint meeting with a dietician, which did not resolve their conflicts but was useful in clarifying from an 'expert' outside the therapy situation the infant's dietary needs. Subsequent discussions addressed how to deal with the mess that the child made during mealtimes or how to set limits on her sometimes active and exploratory behaviour. Sessions were held approximately every 6–8 weeks, and attendance ceased after about 18 months.

The family re-established contact a few months later. The concern was that their second child, also a girl, now aged 6 months, was waking early. The mother was also concerned about introducing solid foods and the possibility of obesity. Similar discussions to those held previously were held regarding the children's dietary needs. New issues were the need to establish the older daughter in a nursery and the great anxiety this separation caused the mother. Over a number of months the family adjusted to the birth of the second child, and the parents very slowly began to establish their own life – for example, going out together in the evenings – although the mother found this exhausting as she continued to wake early. The mother's abnormal eating attitudes and behaviours continued and so there was discussion about the possibility of referral to a specialist eating disorder service, but she did not wish to pursue this option.

A crisis occurred about one year later when the parents decided to separate, associated with the father developing another relationship. Mediation was recommended regarding the financial and legal implications of separation, especially in view of the strong feelings associated with the marital breakdown. There were discussions about how the disruptive effect of the parents' separation could be minimised for the children. This included exploration of the older daughter's knowledge and fears regarding the parental situation (by this time she was 5 years old). The mother became more depressed, withdrawn and lost some weight, and re-established contact with the general psychiatrist who saw her for a number of sessions and restarted an anti-depressant that helped her mood. The mother's attitudes towards her daughters' eating and weight became somewhat more flexible, related to an acceptance that when staying at their father's flat at weekends they might have a different diet that would include chocolate and also what she regarded as 'junk' foods. At this time the mother expressed concern about the daughters possibly being at risk of sexual abuse by the father (there was nothing to suggest this had happened), although the parents realised this was mirroring the mother's own past. Regular communication with the children's general practitioner and mother's psychiatrist continued.

Screening

Since the children of mothers with eating disorders appear to be at high risk for disorders, it is important to consider whether early detection and intervention for this group are possible. Given the current state of knowledge it is not possible to say whether primary prevention (intervening to prevent the children's difficulties arising) is more cost-effective than secondary prevention (intervention for those with disorders at an early stage before help has been sought). However, the development in the UK and other countries of specialist eating disorder services (Robinson, 1993) means that access to many of the children of mothers with more severe eating disorders is facilitated. It is appropriate to consider the opportunities for secondary prevention.

Screening to achieve secondary prevention is appropriate if three conditions are met (Stewart-Brown, 1995). The disorders under consideration must be serious, which has already been demonstrated. Second, there must be reliable ways of detecting the difficulties, which will be discussed further below. Third, there must be effective interventions when those with disorders are detected. With regard to problems that show some specificity with maternal eating disorders – that is, feeding and eating disorders – there is only scanty evidence, as outlined in the previous section, that intervention is helpful. However, some of the children of mothers with eating disorders have difficulties not specific to the maternal disorder, such as oppositional defiant disorder, enuresis or other problems, and general management principles can be drawn on.

Screening can be thought about in three stages. The first is clarification of patients' family circumstances and whether they have children, their ages, place where they live and main carers. Even this information is not obtained routinely by adult psychiatrists (Berg and Hodes, 1997). If there are children in the care of the patients, the second stage is identification of emotional and behavioural deviance. Enquiry should be made about the children's growth, current weight and height, and menstrual status where appropriate. These first two stages could be carried out using brief questionnaires, completed by sufferers and their partners, and this can minimise the time demands on mental health professionals.

Following these stages, if there is concern about the children they should be directly assessed by a child mental health professional. This would require negotiation with parents and perhaps with other professionals such as health visitors or general practitioners who might have additional information about the children. If the children's difficulties are related to eating and weight it is important to weigh them and measure their height. It could be useful to view family meals in the home, especially when younger children are involved. For older children and adolescents, full psychiatric assessment may be necessary. Following assessment, the necessary intervention can be planned.

Proposals for screening such as those just described have not yet been adequately researched, nor is it even known whether mothers would welcome such intervention. This area should be further investigated.

Conclusions

There is an accumulating body of evidence that the children of mothers with eating disorders are at increased risk for abnormalities of growth, psychiatric disorders including eating disorders, and involvement in discordant family relationships. Eating disorders may significantly interfere with the ability of mothers to care adequately for their offspring and they may require help with this task. The rapid growth in the number of specialist eating disorder clinics in the UK and other countries makes possible early intervention for this group of children. Further research is needed to investigate in clinical and community populations the significance of maternal eating disorders for child development and psychopathology, and the effectiveness of intervention.

References

American Psychiatric Association (1994) *Diagnostic and Statistical Manual of Mental Disorders*, 4th edn. Washington, DC: American Psychiatric Association.

Beglin, S.J. and Fairburn, C.G. (1992) Women who choose not to participate in surveys on eating disorders. *International Journal of Eating Disorders*, 12, 113–116.

Berg, B. and Hodes, M. (1997) Adult psychiatrists' knowledge of the adjustment of children whose mothers have eating disorders. *European Eating Disorders Review*, 5, 25–32.

Brinch, M., Isager, T. and Tolstrup, K. (1988) Anorexia nervosa and motherhood: reproductional pattern and mothering behavior of 50 women. *Acta Psychiatrica Scandinavica*, 77, 98–104.

Cooper, P.J. (1995) Eating disorders and their relationship to mood and anxiety disorders. In: K.D. Brownell and C.G. Fairburn (eds) *Eating Disorders and Obesity. A Comprehensive Handbook*. New York: Guilford.

Dare, C. and Eisler, I. (1995) Family therapy and eating disorders. In: K.D. Brownell and C.G. Fairburn (eds) *Eating Disorders and Obesity. A Comprehensive Handbook*. New York: Guilford.

Dare, C., Eisler, I., Russell, G.F.M. and Szmukler, G.I. (1990) The clinical and theoretical impact of a controlled trial of family therapy in anorexia nervosa. *Journal of Marital and Family Therapy*, 16, 39–57.

Fahy, T. and Treasure, J. (1989) Children of mothers with bulimia nervosa (letter). *British Medical Journal*, 299, 1031.

Fairburn, C.G. and Wilson, G.T. (1993) *Binge Eating*. New York: Guilford.

Franko, D.L. and Walton, B.E. (1993) Pregnancy and eating disorders: a review and clinical implications. *International Journal of Eating Disorders*, 13, 41–47.

Garfinkel, P. (1992) Classification and diagnosis. In: K.A. Halmi (ed.) *Psychobiology and Treatment of Anorexia Nervosa and Bulimia Nervosa*. Washington, DC: American Psychiatric Association.

Garmezy, N. and Masten, A. (1994) Chronic adversities. In: M. Rutter, E. Taylor, and L. Hersov (eds) *Child and Adolescent Psychiatry: Modern Approaches*. 3rd edn. Oxford: Blackwell.

Griffiths, R.A., Beumont, P.J.V., Beumont, D., Touyz, S.W., Williams, H. and Lowinger, K. (1995) Anorexia *á deux*: an ominous sign for recovery. *European Eating Disorders Review*, 3, 2–14.

Harter, S. (1985) Manual for the self-perception profile for children. Denver: University of Denver.

Hill, A.J., Weaver, C. and Blundell, J.E. (1990) Dieting concerns of 10 year old girls and their mothers. *British Journal of Clinical Psychology*, 29, 346–348.

Hoare, P., Elton, R., Greer, A. and Kerley, S. (1993) The modification and standard-isation of the Harter Self-esteem questionnaire with Scottish school children. *European Child and Adolescent Psychiatry*, 2, 19–33.

Hodes, M., Timimi, S. and Robinson, P. (1997) Children of mothers with eating disorders: a preliminary study. *European Eating Disorders Review*, 5, 11–24.

Kumar, R.C. and Hipwell, A.E. (1994) Implications for the infant of maternal puerperal psychiatric disorders. In: M. Rutter, E. Taylor and L. Hersov (eds) *Child and Adolescent Psychiatry: Modern Approaches*. 3rd edn. Oxford: Blackwell.

Lacey, J.H. and Smith, G. (1987) Bulimia nervosa: the impact on mother and baby. *British Journal of Psychiatry*, 150, 777–781.

Lunt, P., Carosella, N. and Yager, J. (1989) Daughters whose mothers have anorexia nervosa: a pilot study of three adolescents. *Psychiatric Medicine*, 7, 101–110.

Maloney, M.J., McGuire, J., Daniels, S.R. and Specker, B. (1989) Dieting behaviour and eating attitudes in children. *Pediatrics*, 84, 482–489.

Morgan, H.G. and Hayward, A.E. (1988) Clinical assessment of anorexia nervosa. The Morgan-Russell Assessment Schedule. *British Journal of Psychiatry*, 152, 367–371.

Morgan, H.G. and Russell, G.F.M. (1975) Value of family background and clinical features as predictors of long-term outcome in anorexia nervosa: four-year follow-up study of 41 patients. *Psychological Medicine*, 5, 355–371.

Pike, K.M. and Rodin, J. (1991) Mothers, daughters, and disordered eating. *Journal of Abnormal Psychology*, 100, 198–204.

Richman, N., Graham, P. and Stevenson, J. (1982) *Preschool to School: A Behavioural Study*. London: Academic Press.

Robinson, P.H. (1993) Treatment of eating disorders in the Health Service. What is available and where? *International Review of Psychiatry*, 5, 19–22.

Russell, G.F.M., Treasure, J. and Eisler, I. (1998) Mothers with anorexia nervosa who underfeed their children: recognition and management. *Psychological Medicine*, 28, 93–108.

Rutter, M. and Quinton, D. (1984) Parental psychiatric disorder: effects on children. *Psychological Medicine*, 14, 853–880.

Rutter, M., Tizard, J. and Whitmore, K. (eds) (1970) *Education, Health and Behaviour*. London: Longman.

Stein, A. and Fairburn, C.G. (1989) Children of mothers with bulimia nervosa. *British Medical Journal*, 299, 777–778.

Stein, A. and Woolley, H. (1996) The influence of parental eating disorders on young children: implications of recent research for some clinical interventions. *Eating Disorders*, 4, 139–146.

Stein, A., Woolley, H., Cooper, S.D. and Fairburn, C.G. (1994) An observational study of mothers with eating disorders and their infants. *Journal of Child Psychology and Psychiatry*, 35, 733–748.

Stein, A., Murray, L., Cooper, P. and Fairburn, C.G. (1996) Infant growth in the context of maternal eating disorders and maternal depression: a comparative study. *Psychological Medicine*, 26, 569–574.

Stewart, D.E., Raskin, J., Garfinkel, P.E., MacDonald, O.L. and Robinson, G.E. (1987) Anorexia nervosa, bulimia and pregnancy. *American Journal of Obstetrics and Gynecology*, 157, 1194–1198.

Stewart-Brown, S. (1995) Screening. In: D. Harvey, M. Miles and D. Smyth (eds) *Community Child Health and Paediatrics*. Oxford: Butterworth-Heinemann.

Strober, M. (1992) Family-genetic studies. In: K.A. Halmi (ed.) *Psychobiology and Treatment of Anorexia Nervosa and Bulimia Nervosa*. Washington, DC: American Psychiatric Association.

Strober, M. (1995) Family-genetic perspectives on anorexia nervosa and bulimia nervosa. In: K.D. Brownell and C.G. Fairburn (eds) *Eating Disorders and Obesity. A Comprehensive Handbook*. New York: Guilford.

Treasure, J.L. and Holland, A. (1990) Genetic vulnerability to eating disorders: evidence from twin and family studies. In: H. Remschmidt and M.H. Schmidt (eds) *Child and Youth Psychiatry: European Perspectives. Volume I. Anorexia Nervosa*. Toronto: Hogrefe & Huber.

Treasure, J.L. and Russell, G.F.M. (1988) Intrauterine growth and neonatal weight gain in babies of women with anorexia nervosa. *British Medical Journal*, 296, 1038.

van Wezel-Meijler, G. and Wit, J.M. (1989) The offspring of mothers with anorexia nervosa: a high risk group for undernutrition and stunting. *European Journal of Paediatrics*, 149, 130–135.

Wonderlich, S.A. (1995) Personality and eating disorders. In: K.D. Brownell and C.G. Fairburn (eds) *Eating Disorders and Obesity. A Comprehensive Handbook*. New York: Guilford.

Woodside, D. and Shekter-Wolfson, L.F. (1990) Parenting by patients with anorexia nervosa and bulimia nervosa. *International Journal of Eating Disorders*, 9, 303–309.

Woolley, H., Wheatcroft, R. and Stein, A. (1998) Influence of parental eating disorders on children. *Advances in Psychiatric Treatment*, 4, 144–150.

World Health Organization (1992) *The ICD-10 Classification of Mental and Behavioural Disorders*. Geneva: World Health Organization.

Chapter 9

The links between somatisation in children and in adults

M. Elena Garralda

Functional symptoms, somatisation and somatoform disorders in children and adolescents

Unexplained somatic symptoms are common amongst children and adolescents in the general population. In Garber *et al.*'s (1991) survey, children and adolescents reported a mean of nearly two somatic complaints in the previous two weeks. Most common symptoms were headaches and low energy – present in about a quarter – sore muscles, nausea and upset stomach, back and stomach pains. About one in ten children has 'functional' aches and pains for which a medical cause is not found (Goodman and McGrath, 1991). The term *somatisation* is used to indicate functional symptoms which are an expression of psychological difficulty or distress but which are ascribed by the sufferer to physical illness and lead to medical help-seeking.

It cannot be assumed that the majority of unexplained or functional physical symptoms of children are – as in somatisation – an expression of psychological distress and lead to increased medical help-seeking. But it seems likely that in many cases they are. For example, Benjamin and Eminson (1992) have described positive associations between physical symptoms and affective disorders, particularly in girls, in the general population. In nearly one in five symptomatic children they identified high levels of worry about health symptoms, preventing school attendance. These health attitudes were significantly and positively correlated with an inclination to consult (Eminson *et al.*, 1996). Kramer and Garralda (1998), in a study of adolescents with psychiatric disorders attending primary care, have documented increased physical symptoms and a connection between these and stress and handicap in young people.

Somatisation is at the basis of a number of ICD and DSM defined psychiatric disorders. Abdominal pains and headaches are often the main symptoms of ICD-10's *somatoform pain disorder*, where the pain is severe, persistent and distressing. In *dissociate (conversion) disorders* there is partial or complete loss of bodily sensations or movement or reduction of the normal integration between memories of the past. In *chronic fatigue syndrome* (*neurasthenia* in ICD-10) the main complaint is marked fatigue after mental effort associated with physical fatiguability and other physical symptoms.

Associated features of somatisation

The risk factors for somatisation appear to be comparable in mild cases seen in primary care and in severe problems leading to attendance at tertiary medical services (Garralda, 1992). It is common for functional symptoms to be brought about by physical problems: for example, unusual gait after a broken leg and plaster immobilisation. Psycho-social stresses are also known to contribute to their continuation. The effects of stressful events are probably mediated by problems in the child's sense of social competence (Walker *et al.*, 1994).

Although most children with somatisation do not have psychiatric comorbidity, a third to a half do. Emotional disorders (anxiety and depressive disorders) are the most common association and there are indications that certain personality features may contribute to the development or continuation of somatisation-related disorders (Garralda, 1996; Rangel *et al.*, 1999a).

Child and adolescent mental health is closely linked to parental and family health and function. This review will focus on the associations between somatic symptoms in children and in adults. It will examine parental somatic symptoms in child somatisation and the influence of parental symptoms on the outcome of children's physical complaints. It will address the long-term outcome of child somatisation and links between somatisation in adult sufferers and in their children. It will consider possible factors accounting for the links found.

Do children with unexplained physical symptoms have family histories of ill-health and of similar symptoms in other family members?

There is evidence that children with functional somatic symptoms have an excess of parents and relatives with physical health problems. This has been shown to be the case in pre-school children as much as in schoolchildren and adolescents, in children in the general population as well as in those attending tertiary paediatric clinics. Although there is some synergy between types of symptoms in children and parents, there are also links across types of symptoms and there are also associations with parental mental health problems. This may be related to the fact that children with somatisation have an increased risk for psychopathology themselves.

Recurrent stomach aches or abdominal pains in pre-school children in the general population are associated with health problems and depressive feelings in their mothers. Zuckerman *et al.* (1987) studied 308 3-year-old children of mothers randomised to a postnatal mothers' group: 3 per cent had recurrent headaches and 9 per cent recurrent stomach aches (i.e. pains were present in the preceding month and also prior to this). Mothers of children with stomach aches and headaches reported an excess of serious health problems in themselves, and more visits to the general practitioner and depressed feelings than other mothers. They also described their children more frequently as having behaviour problems and being 'dependent'.

Similar associations are found in older children seen in paediatric clinics with probably more severe somatic symptoms. This is therefore a robust and pervasive finding. Walker and Greene (1989) compared 41 children aged 8–17 years with recurrent abdominal pain (of at least one-month duration) attending as paediatric outpatients at a university centre, with 28 children with organic abdominal conditions (i.e. gastritis, duodenitis, thought to be more likely to reflect tissue pathology) and with 41 well patients. High levels by mothers on the somatisation scores of the Hopkins Symptom Checklist were comparably present in the groups of children with functional and with 'organic' problems and they were increased in both groups when compared with healthy controls. High levels of anxiety and depressive symptoms, however, were exclusively present in the functional group. This suggests that biological susceptibility to abdominal symptoms may cluster in these families but that the combination of parental mood changes and somatisation may be specific to children with *functional* abdominal pain.

In children severely handicapped with chronic fatigue syndrome, Garralda *et al.* (1999b) have documented more extended family and maternal chronic health problems than in healthy matched controls.

Are the physical symptoms similar in parents and children? Perhaps, but the evidence is not strong. Stone and Barbero (1970) studied 102 children hospitalised because of recurrent abdominal pain: half the children had mothers with gastrointestinal problems. Volkmar *et al.* (1984) described 30 children with conversion hysteria: models of relatives with similar symptoms were reported for 50 per cent (and only 20 per cent in those with adjustment disorders).

However, it is possible that these children's parents also had other physical symptoms. There is work indicating that the family risk is not just for similar but for a variety of symptoms, as implied by somatisation disorder (which requires the presence of many different symptoms). This work has also shown links, as for adults, with anti-social disorders in the family. Routh and Ernst (1984) studied 20 children with recurrent abdominal pain and compared them with 20 with acute organic problems such as appendicitis. They enquired about health problems in their first- and second-degree relatives using the family history method (i.e. from reports, not interviewing the extended family relatives). Anti-social and attention deficit disorders were about twice as common in the relatives of children with functional symptoms as in those with organic problems. The largest increase in the functional group, however, was in relatives with somatisation disorder.

Are somatic symptoms in parents linked to short-term prognosis for children's symptoms?

There is intriguing evidence indicating that the presence of somatic symptoms in parents may be associated with poor prognosis for the children's somatic symptoms and that this may be a mediating factor for the association between continuation of physical symptoms and stressful life events. Walker and Greene (1991) had shown that negative life events are associated with anxiety and depression in children with functional recurrent abdominal pain and in controls with pain of organic origin. More events predicted poor resolution of pain in children with functional symptoms only (not in those with organic abdominal pain). In a subsequent report Walker *et al.* (1994) examined parental somatic symptoms and gender as potential moderator variables for the continuation of child somatic complaints (one year after the index clinic visit). Having fathers with high levels of child somatic symptoms predicted more child somatic symptoms at follow-up, regardless of the presence of associated life stresses. Although boys did not appear more vulnerable to life events for the continuation of symptoms, boys of mothers with high levels of somatic symptoms had more somatic symptoms at follow-up. This would seem to indicate that symptoms in fathers have a particularly strong influence. The presence of symptoms in mothers appears to modulate boys' responses to stressful life events by making it more likely that only those exposed to stressful events will show higher continuation of symptoms.

This raises a number of issues. For example, why is the presence of symptoms in fathers more powerful than symptoms in mothers? Is the effect of maternal somatisation due to mothers having difficulty in helping boys with somatic symptoms to cope with stressful events? Why can they help their daughters better? Or are the effects biologically mediated?

Do children of adults with somatisation have high rates of somatic complaints?

The scarce evidence available indicates high levels of somatic symptoms in children of adults with somatisation. Livingston (1993) compared 35 children with a parent with somatisation disorder, 41 children with a somatising parent (i.e. complaints *not* severe enough to obtain a diagnosis of somatisation disorder) and 30 paediatric controls. Children of parents with somatisation disorder had the highest level of psychiatric disorders (particularly over-anxious disorder) but the rates of psychiatric disorder overall in the three groups were so high that it is difficult to reach any clear conclusions. Of particular interest for this review were the increased number of children with unexplained medical symptoms, hospital admissions and school days missed in the parent somatisation disorder group compared with those in the soma-tising parents group, suggesting the importance of the severity of the parent's condition for the child's symptoms.

These findings gain some support from Christensen and Mortensen's (1975) follow-up into adulthood of children with a history of recurrent abdominal pains. Adults with abdominal symptoms at the time of follow-up were more likely than those without contemporary pains to have children with abdominal symptoms (28 per cent v. 7 per cent).

Do most children with unexplained somatic symptoms become adults with unexplained somatic symptoms?

There is considerable continuity between child and adult symptoms. When considering generation transmission the current presence of symptoms in adults seems to be of more importance than the *history* of symptoms in parents. Stickler and Murphy (1979) carried out a five-year follow-up of 161 children with recurrent abdominal pain: most (56 per cent) had recovered within weeks and by five years 75 per cent had recovered. However, this also means that a quarter remained ill: 18 per cent had developed other psychosomatic symptoms, and 3 children had Crohn's dis-ease, whilst 33 had had psychiatric consultation (though this was not linked to prognosis).

Christensen and Mortensen (1975) followed up into adulthood 34 subjects with a history of recurrent abdominal pain in childhood and compared them with 45 controls. At follow-up half of those in the pain group had gastro-intestinal symptoms (28 per cent of controls), 11 had complaints of irritable colon, and other physical symptoms were present in a third (13 per cent of controls). Abdominal pains in their children were present in 19 per cent and 12 per cent respectively.

Walker *et al.* (1995b), in a five-year follow-up of 31 children with former recurrent abdominal pain and 31 well patients, found that former symptom-atic patients reported significantly higher levels of abdominal pain, and of other somatic symptoms and functional disability (including school and work absence) than well patients. Mothers of former symptomatic patients reported more emotional symptoms than mothers of well children. Although these studies indicate recovery for most child sufferers in the short term, a considerable number continue to have symptoms into adulthood.

In Christensen and Mortensen's study (1975) abdominal pains were not increased in the children of parents with a *history* of recurrent abdominal pain but they were in those with *concurrent* symptoms. This suggests that modelling and/or persistence/severity of symptoms in parents is more important than simply susceptibility for the transmission of somatic pains from adults to children.

There are, however, indications that a history of recurrent physical symptoms in childhood may have stronger associations with adult mood disorder than with adult somatisation. The significant primary factor for the continuation of the physical symptoms, therefore, might be the original association with mood changes in childhood and the continuation of the latter into adulthood.

This was suggested from the follow-up study by Hotopf et al. (1998) of children in the Medical Research Council's 1946 birth cohort national survey of health and development. Children who had reported abdominal pains at three points in time in childhood (2 per cent of the sample) when assessed at 36 years of age were more likely than other subjects to suffer psychiatric disorders, but they were not especially prone to physical symptoms once psychiatric disorder was controlled for. Of the whole sample of over 2,500 subjects, as adults 8 per cent had physical symptoms and 6 per cent psychiatric disorders. The odds ratios for problems in adulthood as a function of recurrent abdominal pain in childhood were 2.72 for psychiatric disorder (1.64 to 4.49 – 95 per cent confidence intervals), but only 1.39 (0.83 to 2.36 confidence intervals) for physical symptoms in adulthood when adjusted for psychiatric disorder.

Because of the loss of subjects at follow-up and the very cursory fashion in which the presence of somatic symptoms was ascertained in adulthood it is difficult to be conclusive from this study. But the findings are intriguing and in line with those from Rangel et al.'s (1999b) 3-year follow-up study of 25 children with chronic fatigue syndrome: 2 out of 3 had recovered, though 1 in 3 of these continued to have some symptoms. There were indications of an excess of anxiety and psychosomatic disorders (including anorexia nervosa) amongst recovered children.

Reports from adults suggest that in only a minority do psychosomatic problems start in childhood. For example, 12 per cent of adults with irritable bowel syndrome (v. 3 per cent of controls) give a history of abdominal pain in childhood (Jones and Lydeard, 1992). However, it is possible that milder or different types of childhood somatic symptoms may have been present earlier.

Summarising so far:

1   About a third to a half of the children with recurrent somatic symptoms may have parents with health problems.

2   A combination of a somatic and a psychological diathesis in families may be characteristic.

3   There is continuity of childhood abdominal pains into adulthood and, in many cases, this may be mediated by an increased risk for psychiatric disorder in adulthood.

4   Children of parents with somatisation have been reported to have increased rates of somatic symptoms and more days off school, but this

is probably linked to having ill parents rather than to having had parents with somatic symptoms in childhood.

Mechanisms for the family aggregation of somatic symptoms

No firm conclusions can be drawn on whether the family aggregation of somatic symptoms reflects genetic or environmental influences (Campo and Fritsch, 1994; Fritz *et al.*, 1997) since the empirical evidence is lacking. There may be an enhanced family biological susceptibility to experience certain physical symptoms or conditions (for example, migraine and headaches, ulcer and abdominal pains). There may be a genetic contribution to personality traits that may predispose to somatisation and anti-social disorders. Functional symptoms in children may be genetically related to anxiety and depressive disorders.

There are a number of ways in which environmental factors may explain the child and adult associations and continuities. It is possible that children with somatic symptoms *model* their behaviour on that of other family members. It is also possible that the presence of unexplained or functional somatic symptoms in parents leads to *health attitudes and behaviours* that over-emphasise physical symptoms and a somatic focus, to enhanced 'disease conviction' and reinforcing attention to symptoms. *Characteristic family interactions* described in both children and adults with functional somatic symptoms may represent risk factors for their development/continuation and for intergeneration transmission. Awareness of these mechanisms may be helpful for treatment.

Learned behaviour: family modelling and reinforcement of illness

More *models for symptoms* are reported by children with functional disorders (i.e. recurrent abdominal pains) than by those with organic disorders (namely sickle cell anaemia) (Bennett Osborne *et al.*, 1989). In this particular study, children with functional pains perceived the frequency and intensity of their pain as similar to their model's, whilst their parents failed to report such a relationship. Together with the increased family somatic symptoms in children with functional symptoms, this suggests learning through modelling in children.

Parental reinforcement of symptoms (encouragement of illness behaviour and more positive consequences for symptoms) and discouragement of coping have been noted in children with physical symptoms (both functional and organic) to a larger extent than in well children or in those with emotional symptoms (Walker *et al.*, 1993; Bennett Osborne *et al.*, 1989; Dunn-Geier *et al.*, 1986). It seems plausible that the presence of functional somatic symptoms in parents makes them more tolerant, nurturing and 'reinforcing' of similar symptoms in their children.

Parents report that they are likely to respond to children with unexplained medical symptoms – as opposed to children with explained medical symptoms or with depression – with less anger, disappointment and punishment than to well children (Walker *et al.*, 1995a). *Relief of parental expectations* and *reduced punishment* of the child may be an additional relevant factor.

Cognitive aspects: disease conviction and hypochondriac preoccupation

A firm belief by parents in the primary biological nature of the child's somatic predicament has been consistently reported in parents of children with somatoform disorders (Garralda and Rangel, 1999). It may also be relevant where the somatic concerns are an expression of emotional disorders. In a study of schoolchildren who were frequent attenders to primary care, those with psychiatric (mostly emotional) disorders had both more stress-related somatic symptoms and handicap and more mothers with 'disease conviction' (i.e. a preoccupation with physical symptoms and a belief that they imply disease) (Garralda *et al.*, 1999a). These beliefs can be deeply ingrained and not readily amenable to medical explanation and assurance. However, it is not clear whether the disease conviction is a consequence of having medically unexplained and therefore uncertainty-inducing symptoms or whether it is a primary factor leading to somatisation. The fact that disease conviction is also seen in adults who are frequent attendees to medical services and who have functional symptoms suggests family transmission (Pilowsky *et al.*, 1987; Kellner, 1986).

Hypochondriac health attitudes may be relevant in children with frequent somatic symptoms. In a general population sample of children and adolescents Eminson *et al.* (1996) found that children with multiple symptoms had more concerns about illness and death, more bodily preoccupations, and they reported more effects of the symptoms and more treatment experience than other children. This indicates a general hypochondriac tendency in them. Work on adults attending pain clinics has found a combination of disease conviction and hypochondriac and somatic concerns (Kellner, 1986). The latter, however, have not been found in adolescents with severe chronic fatigue states or in their parents (Garralda and Rangel, 1999). Different attitudes may therefore be of relevance to the manifestation of somatisation depending on the severity and type of symptom.

Family interactive styles: reduced warmth and criticism, affective inhibition

Reduced warmth in family relationships, together with possibly compensatory enhanced care and togetherness over physical symptoms and reduced expectations from the child, may be characteristic. Some of these features are described in both children and adults with unexplained somatic symptoms and/or somatisation and may therefore mediate generation transmission.

Hodes *et al.* (1999) have reported an association between *reduced maternal warmth and positive comments* about the child and more headaches and stomach aches in children with epilepsy. Enhanced *affective inhibition* (i.e. difficulty expressing negative feelings) has been reported by mothers of children with emotional disorders and reduced sense of physical well-being who are frequent attenders to general practice (Garralda *et al.*, 1999a).

Adult patients with somatisation attending primary care are more likely than other groups of patients with psychological problems to report a childhood pattern of parental *lack of care* (Craig *et al.*, 1993). A combination of reduced parental care and illness in childhood could lead to the development of inadequate strategies to neutralise the effects of threatening crisis and to somatisation in adulthood (Craig *et al.*, 1994). Work comparing adult patients with somatic hypochondriac symptoms and depression, and patients with depression but not pronounced physical symptoms, has shown more disharmonious marriages and sexual maladjustment in the former. Moreover, high levels of agreement between patients with chronic pains and their families on details of the pain were linked to more management problems and ultimately poorer outcome. In addition, patients with a solicitous spouse reported marginally higher levels of pain than those with non-solicitous spouses (Roy, 1982). While it is difficult to know what is cause and effect, the results are suggestive of reduced warmth/care with compensatory togetherness around health issues.

The above may underlie some features traditionally described in families of children with somatic symptoms (i.e. family enmeshment, over-protectiveness, rigidity, and lack of conflict resolution – see Minuchin *et al.*, 1975) for which there is as yet no firm empirical evidence.

Child maltreatment and fabricated illness

Fabricated illness – also called Munchausen by proxy – indicates repeated presentations of children by parents, or those *in loco parentis*, for medical assessment and treatment. This may result in multiple medical procedures. The symptoms are, however, fabricated by parents. The perpetrator denies the aetiology of the child's illness and the symptoms and signs cease when the child is separated from him or her (Bools *et al.*, 1993). Physical danger to the child may be immediate, as with smothering, which is usually presented as apnoeic episodes or fits, or with poisoning, which may be presented as drowsiness or fits. Fabricated illness is associated with psychiatric morbidity in the child but somatisation has not been described as prominent sequelae (Bools *et al.*, 1993).

This parental behaviour may be regarded as an extreme example of the enhanced somatic focus and help-seeking that can be seen in children and families with prominent somatisation (Eminson and Postlethwaite, 1992). It has been characterised by:

1   Gross discrepancy between parental and professional views about the appropriateness of the parents' desire to consult.
2   Parents being unable to distinguish their own needs from their child's needs and satisfying their own needs first.
3   Risk factors in parents, including mothers with a history of abusive experiences in their own childhood, who have abnormal illness behaviour themselves, unusual personality traits, who are single or in non-supportive relationships.

In as far as harm is induced intentionally by the parent on the child, the condition is more appropriately regarded as a manifestation of child abuse than as somatisation *per se*.

Associations have been described between problems such as pelvic pain and abdominal functional symptoms in women and a history of sexual abuse in childhood (Mayou *et al.*, 1995), and sexual abuse may be a risk factor for functional somatic symptoms in some children too. However, there is not clear evidence to indicate how frequently somatisation is a primary presentation in these cases.

In summary, there is suggestive evidence that certain mechanisms may mediate family influences in children with unexplained symptoms. These include: family modelling, reinforcement of illness and reduced punishment of or expectations from the child; health beliefs characterised by disease conviction or hypochondriac concerns; reduced warmth, emotional expressiveness or care in family interactions, with compensatory care and togetherness over physical symptoms. These factors may well play a part in the development or continuation of children's symptoms and in family transmission. Some may be usefully addressed in treatment. Further work needs to clarify to what extent they are a consequence of, rather than contribute to, physical symptoms and help delineate those factors that will turn out to be more susceptible to modification and effective in therapeutic interventions. In some cases fabricated illness may be seen as an extreme expression of parental abusive somatisation by proxy. The role of sexual abuse for somatisation requires further exploration.

References

Benjamin, S. and Eminson, D.M. (1992) Abnormal illness behaviour: childhood experiences and long term consequences. *International Review of Psychiatry*, 4, 55–70.

Bennett Osborne, R., Hatcher, J.W. and Richtsmeier, A.J. (1989) The role of social modeling in unexplained pediatric pain. *Journal of Pediatric Psychology*, 14, 43–61.

Bools, C.N., Neale, B.A. and Meadow, S.R. (1993) Follow-up of victims of fabricated illness (Munchausen Syndrome by Proxy). *Archives of Disease in Childhood*, 69, 625–630.

Campo, J.V. and Fritsch S.L. (1994) Somatization in children and adolescents. *Journal of the American Academy of Child and Adolescent Psychiatry*, 33, 1223–1235.

Christensen, M.F. and Mortensen, O. (1975) Long-term prognosis in children with recurrent abdominal pain. *Archives of Disease in Childhood*, 50, 110–114.

Craig, T.K.J., Boardman, A.P., Mills, K., Daly-Jones, O. and Drake, H. (1993) The South London somatisation study I: longitudinal course and the influence of early life experiences. *British Journal of Psychiatry*, 163, 579–588.

Craig, T.K.J., Drake, H., Mills, K. and Boardman, A.P. (1994) The South London somatisation study II: influence of stressful life events and secondary gain. *British Journal of Psychiatry*, 165, 248–258.

Dunn-Geier, J., McGrath, P.J., Rouke, B.P., Latter, J. and D'Astous, D. (1986) Adolescent chronic pain: the ability to cope. *Pain*, 26, 23–32.

Eminson, D.M. and Postlethwaite, R.J. (1992) Factitious illness: recognition and management. *Archives of Disease in Childhood*, 67, 1510–1516.

Eminson, M., Benjamin, S., Shortall, A., Woods, T. and Faragher, B. (1996) Physical symptoms and illness attitudes in adolescents: an epidemiological study. *Journal of Child Psychological and Psychiatry*, 37, 519–528.

Fritz, G.K., Fritsch, S. and Hagino, O. (1997) Somatoform disorders in children and adolescents: a review of the past 10 years. *Journal of the American Academy of Child and Adolescent Psychiatry*, 36, 1329–1338.

Garber, J., Walker, L.S. and Zeman, J. (1991) Somatisation symptoms in a community sample of children and adolescents: further validation of the Children's Somatisation Inventory. *Journal of Consulting and Clinical Psychology*, 3, 588–595.

Garralda, M.E. (1992) A selective review of child psychiatric syndromes with a somatic presentation. *British Journal of Psychiatry*, 161, 759–773.

Garralda, M.E. (1996) Somatisation in children. *Journal of Child Psychology and Psychiatry*, 37, 13–33.

Garralda, M.E. and Rangel, L.A. (1999) Health attitudes in childhood Chronic Fatigue Syndrome. (*Submitted*).

Garralda, M.E., Bowman, F.M. and Mandalia, S. (1999a) Children with psychiatric disorders who are frequent attenders to primary care. *European Child and Adolescent Psychiatry*, 8, 34–44.

Garralda, M.E., Rangel, L.A., Levin, M. and Roberts, H. (1999b) Psychiatric adjustment in adolescents with a history of Chronic Fatigue Syndrome. *Journal of the American Academy of Child and Adolescent Psychiatry*, 38, 1515–1521.

Goodman, J.E. and McGrath, P.J. (1991) The epidemiology of pain in children and adolescents: a review. *Pain*, 46, 247–264.

Hodes, M., Garralda, M.E., Rose, G. and Schwartz, R. (1999) Maternal Expressed Emotion and adjustment in children with epilepsy. *Journal of Child Psychology and Psychiatry*, 40, 1083–1093.

Hotopf, M., Carr, S., Mayou, R., Wadsworth, M. and Wessely, S. (1998) Why do children have chronic abdominal pain, and what happens to them when they grow up? Population based cohort study. *British Medical Journal*, 316, 1196–1200.

Jones, R. and Lydeard, S. (1992) Irritable bowel syndrome in the general population. *British Medical Journal*, 304, 87–90.

Kellner, R. (1986) *Somatization and Hypochondriasis*. New York: Praeger.

Kramer, T. and Garralda, M.E. (1998) Psychiatric disorders in adolescents in primary care. *British Journal of Psychiatry*, 173, 508–513.

Livingston, R. (1993) Children of people with somatization disorder. *Journal of the American Academy of Child and Adolescent Psychiatry*, 32, 536–544.

Mayou, R., Bass, C. and Sharpe, M. (1995) *Treatment of Functional Somatic Symptoms*. Oxford: Oxford University Press.

Minuchin, S., Baker, I.M., Rosman, B.L., Liebman, R., Milman, L. and Todd, T.C. (1975) A conceptual model of psychosomatic illness in children. *Archives of General Psychiatry*, 32, 1031–1038.

Pilowsky, I., Smith, Q.P. and Katsikitis, M. (1987) Illness behaviour and general practice utilisation: a prospective study. *Journal of Psychosomatic Research*, 31, 177–183.

Rangel, L., Garralda, M.E., Levin, M. and Roberts, H. (1999a) The course of chronic fatigue syndrome. *European Child and Adolescent Psychiatry*. (*In press*).

Rangel, L., Garralda, M.E., Levin, M. and Roberts, H. (1999b) Personality in childhood Chronic Fatigue Syndrome. *Journal of the Royal Society of Medicine*. (*In press*).

Routh, D.K. and Ernst, R. (1984) Somatization disorder in relatives of children and adolescents with functional abdominal pain. *Journal of Pediatric Psychology*, 9, 427–437.

Roy, R. (1982) Marital and family issues in patients with chronic pain: a review. *Psychotherapy and Psychosomatics*, 37, 1–12.

Stickler, G.B. and Murphy, D.B. (1979) Recurrent abdominal pain. *American Journal of Diseases of Children*, 133, 486–489.

Stone, R.T. and Barbero, G.J. (1970) Recurrent abdominal pain in childhood. *Pediatrics*, 45, 732–738.

Volkmar, R.R., Poll, J. and Lewis, M. (1984) Conversion reactions in childhood and adolescence. *Journal of the American Academy of Child Psychiatry*, 23, 424–430.

Walker L.S. and Greene, J.W. (1989) Children with recurrent abdominal pain and their parents: more somatic complaints, anxiety, and depression than other patient families? *Journal of Pediatric Psychology*, 14, 231–243.

Walker, L.S. and Greene, J.W. (1991) Negative life events and symptom resolution in pediatric abdominal pain patients. *Journal of Pediatric Psychology*, 16, 341–360.

Walker, L.S., Garber, J. and Greene, J.W. (1993) Psychosocial correlates of recurrent childhood pain: a comparison of pediatric patients with recurrent abdominal pain, organic illness and psychiatric disorders. *Journal of Abnormal Psychology*, 102, 248–258.

Walker, L.S., Garber, J. and Greene, J.W. (1994) Somatic complaints in pediatric patients: a prospective study of the role of negative life events, child social and academic competence and parental somatic symptoms. *Journal of Consulting and Clinical Psychology*, 62, 1213–1221.

Walker, L.S., Garber, J. and van Slyke, D.A. (1995a) Do parents excuse the misbehavior of children with physical or emotional symptoms? An investigation of the pediatric sick role. *Journal of Pediatric Psychology*, 20, 329–345.

Walker, L.S., Garber, J., van Slyke, D.A. and Greene, J.W. (1995b) Long-term health outcomes in patients with recurrent abdominal pain. *Journal of Pediatric Psychology*, 20, 233–245.

Zuckerman, B., Stevenson, J. and Bailey, V. (1987) Stomach aches and head aches in a community sample of preschool children. *Pediatrics*, 79, 677–682.

Chapter 10

Children of substance-misusing parents

D. Colin Drummond and Geraldine Fitzpatrick

In this chapter, we shall consider parental substance misuse from the dual perspectives of its impact on children in the family and the contributions of different specialists if child care proceedings should arise. Our purpose is to illustrate how parental substance misuse has an effect on the abuser and their family and that there is the need for liaison between child and adult psychiatrists in order to ensure that a coherent opinion is presented to courts.

Impact on children

Many studies show that it is difficult to separate out a direct causal link between children's emotional and behavioural disorders and parental substance misuse or factors associated with that misuse – for example, poverty, domestic violence, and child abuse. There appears to have been little work studying families where substance misuse occurs but is not associated with other evidence of family dysfunction. The issue of dual diagnosis, in which parents use alcohol as self-medication for depression or anxiety, or where chronic substance misuse leads to hallucinations or psychosis, also needs further attention in research. Furthermore, the cases which are referred to mental health services or become the subject of child care proceedings tend to be at the extreme end of the spectrum.

Hence, there is a danger of taking an overly pessimistic view of children's experience in families where the parents misuse alcohol or drugs. In order to maintain a balanced approach, it is important to remain aware that the issue is not that the parent misuses substances, but how that misuse interferes with their functioning as an individual, as a family member and as a parent. For instance, not all children from alcoholic families become alcoholics or show psychiatric disorders. A longitudinal study of resilience in children of alcoholics followed from birth to 18 years indicated that the majority appear to cope well. This was associated with an affectionate temperament in infancy, average or above-average intellect, positive self-esteem and a more internalised locus of control. The children had also received more attention from their primary carer in their first year of life and had not experienced any long separation from their caregiver (Werner, 1986).

Drinking more than a generally-regarded 'safe' level of alcohol (21 units per week in men or 14 units per week in women) does not necessarily result in adverse consequences for the individual (Royal College of Psychiatrists, 1986). Similarly, occasional drug use may not result in serious adverse affects. However, with increasing consumption goes an increasing risk of health, social, or psychological problems; and, in men, drinking more than 50 units per week, and, in women, more than 35 units, carries with it significant risk of harm. Further, the combination of different drugs can produce higher levels of impairment and, at times, unpredictable psychotropic effects. The development of drug or alcohol dependence contributes to the occurrence of increasingly serious problems (Drummond, 1990).

From the child's perspective, it is important to focus on both the immediate behavioural consequences of parents' substance misuse and its impact on their general lifestyle, since both may impair the adult's parenting role and the child's development. Many adults use alcohol or other substances recreationally, with no significant effect on their parenting ability or the welfare of the child. However, for those who are dependent on substances and whose lifestyle is determined by this abuse, impairment of parenting occurs to such an extent that their children suffer neglect, physical, emotional or sexual abuse, or psychological disturbances.

Impact through parental behaviour

Different substances have different effects on the adult's level of consciousness and emotional state. Alcohol within a social context may facilitate social interaction and an increased sense of well-being. However, as an individual becomes drunk there is an interference with their coordination, judgement, verbal performance, memory and problem-solving behaviour. They might become depressed, or the disinhibiting effects of alcohol may result in aggressive behaviour. Drunkenness, with impaired consciousness, means an inability to look after themselves or those who are dependent on them.

In the long term, chronic excessive drinking results in physical changes in the individual: delirium tremens, cirrhosis of the liver and personality changes. The mortality rate amongst alcoholic men over a 20-year period has been shown to be 3.6 times the expected rate (Marshall *et al.*, 1994), and death may be due to aspiration of vomit, epileptic seizures, liver failure, massive bleeding from internal blood vessels, or intentional suicide.

The most commonly used substances other than alcohol are the opiates, cocaine, amphetamines, barbiturates, cannabis and glue. The effect on the individual's emotional state will depend on the type of substance used, the frequency of use and the dosage. Many users take more than one substance concurrently, such as amphetamines and barbiturates, heroin and cocaine, or drugs in combination with alcohol. Any chemical substance which alters an individual's mood will also lead to some impairment of performance. Cannabis acts as a euphoriant, and the use of amphetamines, also a stimulant, may result in agitation or impulsive behaviour. High levels of cocaine and amphetamines can result in aggression and psychotic phenomena, including paranoid delusions and hallucinations. Heroin and barbiturates have a sedative effect, reducing emotional responsiveness, and, in larger doses, impairing consciousness.

Dependence on a drug includes the development of increasing tolerance to it, requiring ever greater amounts to achieve the same effects (Edwards and Gross, 1976). Dependence develops because there is an emotional reliance on the effects in order to feel good. The 'need' is not based on a physical addiction but on emotional factors. Addiction results when continuing use of the substance is required in order to avoid withdrawal symptoms, which include irritability, hyperarousal, anxiety, depression and unpleasant physical side-effects.

The immediate effects of the substances are superimposed on the underlying personality traits that drug misusers in particular tend to share, since these traits have contributed in the first place to their chemical dependency. They include low frustration tolerance, impulsivity, self-centredness, emotional isolation, and feelings of inadequacy, emotional deprivation and depression. Reder and Duncan (1999) refer to this pattern as adult relationships based on 'unresolved care and control conflicts' that originated in adverse experiences in childhood. These characteristics also lead them to form relationships with other drug users or to involve their partner in similar habits and they develop relationships of co-dependency and a social group of other substance misusers. This means that an adult seeking to give up the use of drugs has the task of not only dealing with their dependency but also altering their lifestyle and establishing a social network among non-drug users.

Impact through the family's lifestyle

The use of alcohol or substances may not only result in a significant impairment of an individual's functioning, but also dysfunctional patterns of family dynamics. Such families show increased rates of domestic violence, poverty and unemployment, as well as neglect, emotional abuse or physical abuse of children (e.g. Hampton *et al.*, 1998). Children growing up in such families may be severely disadvantaged but the effect on their development will depend on their age, the length of time exposed to pathogenic family influences, their personal vulnerability and other protective mechanisms (Rutter, 1979).

Although there are many similarities in the family environments of children of alcohol and substance misusers, there are also significant differences. Families where there is illicit drug use by parents, especially use of opiates, tend to show a more chaotic lifestyle. If untreated, their drug misuse is more likely to be associated with criminal activity and even imprisonment. There is increased risk to their children from the activity of drug dealers and other drug abusers who frequent the family home. Intravenous drug use carries the danger of hepatitis and HIV infection and the increased hazard of accidental overdose. On the other hand, in families where one parent binge drinks, periods of disruptive care may alternate with episodes where the parent provides a stable and loving environment for the child.

Again, if drugs are the problem, there is a greater tendency for both parents to be misusers, whereas problematic drinking may be confined to one of the parents, allowing the child to have a more stable relationship with the other caretaker.

From the child's perspective, the adverse impact of illicit drug misuse by parents appears to be qualitatively different from the effects of parental alcoholism. This may well be because alcohol excess is frequently episodic, with intervening periods of sobriety and competence, while the consequences of drug misuse often intrude into the parent's functioning on a daily basis, with their lifestyle increasingly centred around drug procurement and use (Swadi, 1994).

The association between substance misuse and domestic violence is well documented (e.g. Pernanen, 1991; Frude, 1994); 60 per cent of the partners of battered women have been shown to have an alcohol problem and 21 per cent a drug problem (Roberts, 1987). Some families contain a constellation of problems in which substance misuse, partner abuse, parental mental health problems and child abuse co-exist (Browne and Hamilton, in press), so that any two known features should raise concern that the others will also be found. Even if child maltreatment is not occurring, exposure of children to domestic violence is itself a risk factor for later development of anxiety, conduct disorders, criminal behaviour and problems with alcohol (Fergusson and Horwood, 1998).

Impact on children's psychological and physical health

A number of literature reviews have been published in recent years (e.g. Deren, 1986; von Knorring, 1991; Coleman and Cassell, 1995; Rydelius, 1997; Hogan, 1998; Jones Harden, 1998) out of which particular themes consistently emerge. The reviewers make clear the need to separate out effects on the child's physical health, the impact on their emotional development and the risk of child maltreatment.

Physical health risks to children of substance misusers include the development of intra-uterine abnormalities, infection with HIV or hepatitis, exposure to accidents, or development of illnesses.

The psychological symptoms reported to be shown by children of alcohol and drug misusers are remarkably similar. Both environments are associated with an unusually high risk of the child developing mental health problems generally, and behavioural problems, overactivity and short attention spans, anxiety, depression, psychosomatic complaints and difficulties relating to peers and adults, in particular. Not surprisingly, all of these adversities also influence their school performance. The effects are liable to continue into early adult life, increasing the risk of delinquency, criminality, substance misuse and suicidal attempts.

As regards child abuse, there is evidence that parental substance misuse figures disproportionately in the circumstances of children who have suffered maltreatment, of all types and severity, but that parents who comply with drug treatment programmes appear to demonstrate better child-caring capacities than those who default (Reder and Duncan, 1999). Theoretical models used to explain the genesis of child sexual abuse, for example, emphasise the relevance of parental alcohol misuse. Finkelhor (1984) described four mechanisms underlying child sexual abuse: (i) the adult entertains sexual feelings towards a child; (ii) the adult's internal inhibitors are reduced; (iii) external constraints against him acting upon his impulses are reduced; and (iv) the child is less able to avoid the adult's coercion. The effects of alcohol are considered a particularly significant factor in reducing the adult's internal inhibitors.

These general themes can be discussed more fully according to the different developmental age of the child: pregnancy and the perinatal period; infancy and early childhood; middle childhood; and adolescence.

Pregnancy and the perinatal period

Many female drug users are of child-bearing age and, during pregnancy, alcohol and other drugs cross the placenta and can cause abnormalities of the developing foetus (Dixon, 1989). The most serious is foetal alcohol syndrome, the prevalence of which is said to be between 1 and 3 per 1,000 live births (von Knorring, 1991): these children have a low IQ, specific facial characteristics and defects in various other systems. Alcohol intake is also related to increased risk of foetal growth retardation and complications of pregnancy and labour (Rosett, 1980). Studies have also suggested that hyperactivity later in childhood is associated with exposure to alcohol *in utero* (Cantwell, 1972; Steinhausen *et al.*, 1982).

Narcotics abuse is associated with obstetric complications and increased incidence of stillbirth or low birth-weight, and the babies are at risk of suffering drug withdrawal symptoms and fits. Many clinicians reporting withdrawal symptoms of the newborn note that the mother may herself be depressed or anxious because of the complications of labour itself or increases in her requirement of the drug brought about by the physiological changes of birth. The babies themselves tend to be very irritable, cry frequently, have feeding difficulties, and are difficult to cuddle. The combination of the baby's and the mother's irritability interferes with early mother–infant bonding and, potentially, with adequacy of attachment.

Infancy and early childhood

Children require a stable environment in which their physical and emotional needs are consistently met if they are to reach their developmental potential. Alcoholic families are less cohesive, less organised and more conflict-ridden (Clair and Genest, 1987), and abuse and neglect are known risks for young children of substance misusers. During infancy and early childhood there are more accidental injuries reported (Chafetz et al., 1971). There is an increased risk of physical abuse and infants may be exposed to irregular feeding routines leading to failure to thrive. They also show evidence of developmental delay due to lack of age-appropriate stimulation.

The absence of regular routines, with little limit-setting on normal toddler behaviour, may result in such children being perceived as out of control and subjected to inappropriate disciplinary measures and physical abuse. Even young children can become highly attuned to changes in the emotional relationship between the parents, and to parents' altered mental states, and may develop the same frozen watchfulness that was originally described in severely physically abused children (Ounsted, 1972).

An association that is under-recognised is that parents sometimes use their own substances to quieten a crying child or a toddler with normal challenging behaviour. In a few instances, this can lead to the child's death, which may remain undetected as a child abuse fatality, and it is possible that this may account for a number of deaths attributed to the Sudden Infant Death Syndrome, which is known to be more common amongst substance-misusing families (Davidson Ward et al., 1990; Hobbs and Wynne, 1996).

Middle childhood

In middle childhood, children of substance-misusing parents show a higher frequency of emotional and behavioural disorders (Deren, 1986), hyperactivity, attention disorders and aggression (West and Prinz, 1987). There is an increased risk of school adjustment problems, poor academic achievement, poor peer relationships, exclusion from school and truancy (Sowder and Burt, 1980; Coles and Platzman, 1993).

Children at this age become more aware of the pattern of parental substance misuse and the lifestyle associated with it. They may be introduced to criminal behaviour at a young age: for example, shoplifting to finance their parent's habit, or acting as a courier to procure the drugs. Such behaviour puts them at risk of physical or sexual abuse by other adults within the drug community (Moncrieff et al., 1997). The child may also take on the role of carer to their parent who is regularly drunk or unwell; and children of alcoholics are more likely than children of non-alcoholic families to describe their childhood as unhappy (Callan and Jackson, 1986). At this age, a small but significant number of children will suffer a pattern of disruptive care due to removal from their family because of inadequate care or because of their parent's hospitalisation for treatment. A number of children will experience the sudden loss of a parent from death due to an accidental drug overdose.

One of the most distressing parental behaviours for the child to tolerate is unpredictability, in which the child does not know from one day to the next whether their parent will be angry, violent, affectionate, helpless, or even conscious. Their unreliability at timekeeping may mean that the child is not picked up from school, or that contact meetings are failed without warning. Such children may resort instead to compulsive self-reliance, perhaps together with an increasingly parentified role in the family in which it is they who worry about their parent's well-being, instead of the other way round, and assume responsibility for ensuring that their parent is physically safe when under the influence of the substances.

Adolescence

There is undoubtedly an intergenerational continuity of alcohol and illicit drug use, in which offspring of substance-misusing parents have a significantly higher likelihood of becoming substance misusers themselves, beginning in teenage years (Deren, 1986; von Knorring, 1991; Rydelius, 1997). Schuckit and Sweeney's study (1987) showed that adolescents were four times more likely to become alcoholics if they had an alcoholic parent. Both genetic and 'social inheritance' factors are involved, in which the parents model and normalise excessive use of alcohol or drugs as well as provide inadequate general care. Teenage boys are also more likely to show anti-social and criminal behaviour. However, it is also possible for adolescents brought up in such families to develop an excessively moralistic and judgemental over-reaction, avoiding situations in which they perceive there is the risk of loss of personal control. A common problem in many substance-misusing families in which the parents are providing inadequate care is that the eldest child becomes parentified and assumes increasing responsibility for looking after the younger siblings, the result being that they drop out of education prematurely.

Teenage girls may try to escape from the family environment through early sexualised liaisons and pregnancies. However, another reason for their sexualised behaviour or attempts to leave home may be that they are suffering sexual abuse for a first time during adolescence. The onset of abuse at this time would be linked to their alcoholic father's sexual interest in post-pubertal girls, rather than younger ones.

Collaborative assessments in child care court cases

Because substance misuse by parents can adversely affect their children's welfare, some families will come to the attention of statutory services and, ultimately, child care courts. Child mental health and addiction specialists are often asked to provide assessments for child care proceedings of families in which a parent misuses substances, and we believe it is essential for there to be a collaborative understanding between the experts.

Our approach is to clarify the different areas that each professional will address, followed by separate assessments. The child specialist is able to consider issues from the child's perspective and assess the impact of the parental drug or alcohol misuse on the child and whether he or she has suffered, or is likely to suffer, significant harm. The substance misuse specialist's contribution, from the adult's perspective, is to assess the relevance of the parent's substance misuse for their level of functioning, what intervention is possible and the longer-term prognosis. The adult specialist may also offer treatment and then review whether changes have occurred in the parent's addiction and functioning. However, neither of these separate assessments can in itself provide the overall picture, and recommendations to the court must arise out of an on-going conversation between the specialists, which bridges their different perspectives. This collaboration should allow them to draw inferences that highlight the adult's behaviour as a parent, the child's experiences of being parented in that way, and the likelihood of the parent's behaviour changing.

We can represent that conversation by posing the common questions asked by courts in such cases, which are also the ones that need to be discussed between the assessors.

Is the parent currently misusing drugs or alcohol?

Substance-misusing parents in care proceedings may not view their use of drugs or alcohol as a problem and may seek to minimise their level of use. Admitting to having a substance misuse problem still carries a high degree of social stigma (particularly so in women) and brings with it a known risk of losing one's children into the care system (Miller, 1983). This can lead to an understandable degree of 'denial'. Careful enquiry is required, including from other families and through social services and police reports, concerning past and current use and its impact on their health and social functioning. Biochemical and other investigations can be particularly helpful (Drummond and Ghodse, 1999), especially liver function tests and the newer test, carbohydrate deficient transferrin, which is up to 90 per cent specific for alcohol misuse. In the case of drug misuse, urine drug testing provides the main objective evidence of recent use (Wolff et al., 1999), while hair testing allows for the analysis of most illicit drug use over the previous several months. Even so, when the parent is actively attempting to conceal a drug or alcohol problem, diagnosis can be extremely difficult and the conclusions of the assessment must be based on a balance of probabilities.

What is the pattern of the parent's substance misuse?

Substance misusers whose parenting has given rise to concern show a gradually increasing pattern of drug or alcohol intake, often over many years. As the quantity and frequency of use rise, so do the financial cost and the amount of time spent obtaining and consuming the drug. A pattern of drinking will become increasingly stereotypic, so that the individual will drink the same high amount of alcohol during weekdays as they used to drink only at weekends, and when they have child care responsibilities as much as when they do not. Therefore, with progressive dependence comes an increased risk of being intoxicated with the drug at times which are socially unacceptable or likely to involve risks to themselves or their children. For example, they may start to arrive for work or drive to school to collect the child in an intoxicated state. The onset of withdrawal symptoms may encourage the individual to drink early in the morning and an overwhelming craving may lead them to drink in highly inappropriate situations.

A drug user may switch from smoking heroin to injecting in order to compensate for their increasing level of tolerance, opening the way to blood-borne infections, such as hepatitis or HIV, and the risk of heroin overdose (Farrell, 1991; Rhodes *et al.*, 1996).

Does the parent's drug or alcohol misuse have an impact on parenting?

The issues to be considered here are those already discussed above, particularly the parent's behaviour whilst intoxicated and their general lifestyle. These include whether there is domestic violence, ambivalent relationships with other drug misusers, accompanying psychiatric disorders, self-harming episodes, neglect of the child, exposure to danger, or unreliability.

What impact has the parent's behaviour had on the child?

For a court to make an Order under the Children Act, it must be satisfied that the child has suffered, or is likely to suffer, from 'significant harm' which resulted from the parenting they have received (Reder and Lucey, 1995). The harm could be to their physical or psychological welfare. It is assessed through collation of information about the child derived from a number of sources, especially social workers' records of the history of child care concerns, other involved professionals such as paediatrician, health visitor and schoolteachers, and direct assessment in the child and adolescent mental health team, including interviews with the child individually and observing them with their parent(s). Fitzpatrick *et al.* (1995) have suggested that the assessment should consider whether there is disturbance to the child's developmental pathways along the following dimensions: physical development; attachment; socialisation; moral sense; awareness of an inner emotional life; language; and learning. Significant disruption to the child's development and well-being might suggest the need for therapeutic help and/or alternative placement.

Even young children can offer relevant views about the care they have received and about their future placement, but their opinions may be influenced by the emotional and interpersonal conflicts they are experiencing as a result of the family disharmony and disruption (Reder and Fitzpatrick, 1998).

What is the prognosis for the parent's substance misuse?

Generally, prognosis is similar across a range of different substances (Hunt *et al.*, 1971). Complete abstinence from drugs during the year following an episode of treatment is generally low: around 10 per cent. However, this is a very strict criterion for success and, using less stringent criteria, approximately 30 per cent will have a 'favourable' outcome, with few or no episodes of uncontrolled use, and approximately 30 per cent will have a 'poor' outcome, with continued problematic use. The remaining 30 per cent will have an 'intermediate' outcome, with some episodes of problematic use during a one-year follow-up (Edwards *et al.*, 1997). Over a longer-term follow-up of 10–20 years, a similar 'favourable' outcome of 30 per cent has been found (Vaillant, 1983; 1995; Edwards *et al.*, 1983). However, there is also typically a much higher mortality rate than in the non-substance-misusing population among the remainder who have continued substance-related problems.

Several factors need to be taken into account in assessing prognosis, and the following are negative prognostic factors (Vaillant, 1995; Edwards *et al.*, 1988; Moos *et al.*, 1990).

Family history

A positive family history of substance misuse, particularly in first-degree relatives, is associated with a worse prognosis. This may be related to constitutional factors that lead, for example, to early onset or a more severe course. Alternatively, the early life experiences of a child being cared for by a substance misuser may influence social adjustment or social learning.

Social adjustment

A disrupted childhood (for example, the early loss of a parent or growing up in the care of the local authority) and childhood behaviour or psychiatric disorders can influence a range of adjustment difficulties in adulthood. Severe child abuse is associated with an early onset of substance misuse problems and is often accompanied by personal difficulties or disorders in later life.

Social stability and support

Severe and prolonged substance misuse is associated with a loss of social stability and positive support, and the substance misusers who become socially isolated have a poorer prognosis. Being involved in a relationship with another substance misuser, in a violent or abusive relationship or in a social network that supports continued substance misuse is also associated with a poor outcome.

Multiple unsuccessful attempts to engage in treatment

Sometimes, recovery from substance misuse can occur without professional help, typically when a person undergoes a significant change in their lifestyle (for example, meeting a new sexual partner, getting a job, having a child). However, prognosis is inversely related to the number of unsuccessful treatment attempts. Sometimes, this is an indication of the individual's ambivalence in effecting change in their substance use. Alternatively, it may reflect the severity of the problem.

Comorbidity

The presence of psychiatric comorbidity, including depression, suicide attempts, personality disorders or severe mental illness, is not uncommon in substance-misusing parents involved in care proceedings (Reiger *et al.*, 1990; Marshall and Alam, 1997; Weaver *et al.*, 1999), and is a poor prognostic factor. Further, polydrug misuse is associated with a worse prognosis.

Ambivalence and motivation

Motivation to engage in treatment is an important predictor of ultimate success (Prochaska and Di Clemente, 1986). Individuals who already recognise that they have a problem and need treatment are considered to be in a 'contemplation' stage of the change process. Where a degree of coercion from others has brought the individual to treatment, they are more likely to be in a stage of 'pre-contemplation' and, if they do not recognise their substance use as a problem, they are unlikely to engage with or make effective use of treatment options. More often, a substance misuser will be ambivalent about the need for treatment and will show an approach–avoidance conflict with treatment agencies.

What kind of treatment does the parent need?

Thorough assessment and clear feedback are crucial in helping substance-misusing parents to engage in treatment (Miller and Rollnick, 1991). It is also important to note that motivation can be enhanced by therapy and substance misusers can benefit from treatment even when they enter under a degree of coercion (Weisner, 1993). Symptoms of dependency can have a bearing on the appropriate choice of treatment goal, since for those patients with a history of severe dependence, a goal of controlled (or moderate) use may be difficult to achieve (Edwards *et al.*, 1997).

The main modalities of treatment are available through the NHS, in the voluntary sector or through self-help organisations (Drummond, in press). They include: counselling agencies (most effective with individuals with mild or moderate problems, using a 'controlled drinking' goal); self-help organisations (such as Alcoholics Anonymous and Narcotics Anonymous, although one is dependent on the individual's self-reported progress); day programmes (following detoxification and achievement of some stability); specialist drug and alcohol services (with facilities for detoxification, counselling, support, medication and management of any co-existing mental health problems in the more severely dependent patients); and residential rehabilitation programmes (providing intensive assessment and treatment for severely dependent substance misusers).

How should progress be monitored?

As in the case of initial assessment, the self-reported substance use by the individual cannot always be relied upon and evidence of progress needs to be from a variety of sources. The most objective and reliable data come from blood and urine investigations (Drummond and Ghodse, 1999) but, as the blood measures for alcohol misuse take 1–2 months to recover following a drinking episode, there is little to be gained by testing more frequently than monthly. Saliva alcohol tests are relatively inexpensive and could find increasing use in detecting intoxication where an individual denies they have been drinking. Urine testing for drugs should usually be weekly or random.

The final opinion to the court should arise out of an appraisal of how all these themes interrelate. In care proceedings, the welfare of the child is paramount and the impact of the parent's problems must be considered primarily from the child's perspective. However, the nature of the parent's difficulties, the way that they manifest, the likelihood of therapeutic interventions being successful, and the long-term prognosis for the parent, are crucial factors in determining the child's future welfare. It requires close collaboration between substance misuse and child and adolescent specialists in order for the assessment and recommended interventions to be helpful.

References

Browne, K.D. and Hamilton, C.E. (in press) Police recognition of links between spouse abuse and child abuse. *Child Maltreatment*.

Callan, V.J. and Jackson, D. (1986) Children of alcoholic fathers and recovered alcoholic fathers: personal and family functioning. *Journal of Studies on Alcohol*, 47, 180–182.

Cantwell, D.P. (1972) Psychiatric illness in the families of hyperactive children. *Archives of General Psychiatry*, 27, 414–417.

Chafetz, M.E., Blane, H.T. and Hill, M.J. (1971) Children of alcoholics: observations in a child guidance clinic. *Quarterly Journal of Studies on Alcohol*, 32, 687–698.

Clair, D. and Genest, M. (1987) Variables associated with the adjustment of offspring of alcoholic fathers. *Journal of Studies on Alcohol*, 48, 345–355.

Coleman, R. and Cassell, D. (1995) Parents who misuse drugs and alcohol. In: P. Reder and C. Lucey (eds) *Assessment of Parenting: Psychiatric and Psychological Contributions*. London: Routledge.

Coles, C.D. and Platzman, K.A. (1993) Behavioral development in children prenatally exposed to drugs and alcohol. *International Journal of the Addictions*, 28, 1393–1433.

Davidson Ward, S.L., Bautista, D., Chan, L., Derry, M., Lisbin, A., Durfee, M.J., Mills, K.S.C. and Keens, T.G. (1990) Sudden infant death syndrome in infants of substance-abusing mothers. *Journal of Pediatrics*, 117, 876–881.

Deren, S. (1986) Children of substance abusers: a review of the literature. *Journal of Substance Abuse Treatment*, 3, 77–94.

Dixon, S.D. (1989) Effects of transplacental exposure to cocaine and methamphetamine on the neonate. *Western Journal of Medicine*, 150, 436–442.

Drummond, D.C. (1990) The relationship between alcohol dependence and alcohol-related problems in a clinical population. *British Journal of Addiction*, 85, 357–366.

Drummond, D.C. (in press) Services for alcohol use disorders. In: M.G. Gelder, J.J. Lopez-Ibor and N.C. Andreasen (eds) *The New Oxford Textbook of Psychiatry*. London: Oxford University Press.

Drummond, D.C. and Ghodse, A.H. (1999) Use of investigations in the diagnosis and management of alcohol use disorders. *Advances in Psychiatric Treatment*, 5, 366–375.

Edwards, G. and Gross, M.M. (1976) Alcohol dependence: provisional description of a clinical syndrome. *British Medical Journal*, i, 1058–1061.

Edwards, G., Oppenheimer, E., Duckitt, A., Sheehan, M. and Taylor, C. (1983) What happens to alcoholics? *Lancet*, ii, 269–271.

Edwards, G., Brown, D., Oppenheimer, E., Sheehan, M., Taylor, C. and Duckitt, A. (1988) Long term outcome for patients with drinking problems: the search for predictors. *British Journal of Addiction*, 83, 917–927.

Edwards, G., Marshall, E.J. and Cook, C.C.H. (1997) *The Treatment of Drinking Problems: A Guide for the Helping Professions*, 3rd edn. Cambridge: Cambridge University Press.

Farrell, M. (1991) Physical complications of drug use. In: I.B. Glass (ed.) *International Handbook of Addiction Behaviour*. London: Routledge.

Fergusson, D.M. and Horwood, L.J. (1998) Exposure to interparental violence in childhood and psychosocial adjustment in young adulthood. *Child Abuse and Neglect*, 22, 339–357.

Finkelhor, D. (1984) *Child Sexual Abuse: New Theory and Research*. New York: Free Press.

Fitzpatrick, G., Reder, P. and Lucey, C. (1995) The child's perspective. In: P. Reder and C. Lucey (eds) *Assessment of Parenting: Psychiatric and Psychological Contributions*. London: Routledge.

Frude, N. (1994) Marital violence: an interactional perspective. In: J. Archer (ed.) *Male Violence*. London: Routledge.

Hampton, R.L., Senatore, V. and Gullotta, T.P. (eds) (1998) *Substance Abuse, Family Violence, and Child Welfare: Bridging Perspectives*. Thousand Oaks, Calif.: Sage.

Hobbs, C.J. and Wynne, J.M. (1996) Child abuse and sudden infant death. *Child Abuse Review*, 5, 155–169.

Hogan, D.M. (1998) The psychological development and welfare of children of opiate and cocaine users: review and research needs. *Journal of Child Psychology and Psychiatry*, 39, 609–620.

Hunt, W.A., Barnett, L.W. and Branch, L.G. (1971) Relapse rates in addiction programs. *Journal of Clinical Psychology*, 27, 455–456.

Jones Harden, B. (1998) Building bridges for children: addressing the consequences of exposure to drugs and to the child welfare system. In: R.L. Hampton, V. Senatore and T.P. Gullotta (eds) *Substance Abuse, Family Violence, and Child Welfare: Bridging Perspectives*. Thousand Oaks, Calif.: Sage.

Marshall, E.J. and Alam, F. (1997) Psychiatric problems associated with alcohol misuse and dependence. *British Journal of Hospital Medicine*, 58, 44–46.

Marshall, E.J., Edwards, G. and Taylor, C. (1994) Mortality in men with drinking problems: a 20-year follow-up. *Addiction*, 89, 1293–1298.

Miller, W.R. (1983) Motivational interviewing with problem drinkers. *Behavioural Psychotherapy*, 1, 147–172.

Miller, W.R. and Rollnick, S. (1991) *Motivational Interviewing: Preparing People to Change Addictive Behaviour*. London: Guilford.

Moncrieff, J., Drummond, D.C., Candy, B., Checinski, K. and Farmer, R. (1997) Sexual abuse in people with alcohol problems: a study of the prevalence of sexual abuse and its relationship to drinking behaviour. *British Journal of Psychiatry*, 169, 355–360.

Moos, R.H., Finney, J. and Cronkite, R. (1990) *Alcoholism Treatment: Context, Process and Outcome*. New York: Oxford University Press.

Ounsted, C. (1972) Biographical science: an essay on developmental medicine. In: B. Mandelbrote and M.C. Gelder (eds) *Psychiatric Aspects of Medical Practice*. London: Staples.

Pernanen, K. (1991) *Alcohol in Human Violence*. London: Guilford.

Prochaska, J.O. and Di Clemente, C.C. (1986) Toward a comprehensive model of change. In: W.R. Miller and N. Heather (eds) *Treating Addictive Behaviours: Processes of Change*. New York: Plenum.

Reder, P. and Duncan, S. (1999) *Lost Innocents: A Follow-Up Study of Fatal Child Abuse*. London: Routledge.

Reder, P. and Fitzpatrick, G. (1998) What is sufficient understanding? *Clinical Child Psychology and Psychiatry*, 3, 103–113.

Reder, P. and Lucey, C. (eds) (1995) *Assessment of Parenting: Psychiatric and Psychological Contributions*. London: Routledge.

Reiger, D.A., Farmer, M.E., Rae, D.S., Locke, B.Z., Keith, S.J., Judd, L.L. and Goodwin, F.K. (1990) Comorbidity of mental disorder with alcohol and other drug abuse. Results from the Epidemiological Catchment Area (ECA) study. *Journal of the American Medical Association*, 264, 2511–2518.

Rhodes, T., Hunter, G.M., Stimson, G.V., Donoghoe, M.C., Noble, A., Parry, J. and Chalmers, C. (1996) Prevalence of markers for hepatitis B virus and HIV-1 among drug injectors in London: injecting careers, positivity and risk behaviour. *Addiction*, 91, 1457–1467.

Roberts, A.R. (1987) Psycho-social characteristics of batterers: a study of 234 men charged with domestic violence offences. *Journal of Family Violence*, 2, 81–94.

Rosett, H.L. (1980) A clinical perspective of fetal alcohol syndrome. *Alcoholism: Clinical and Experimental Research*, 4, 119–122.

Royal College of Psychiatrists (1986) *Alcohol: Our Favourite Drug*. London: Tavistock.

Rutter, M. (1979) Protective factors in children's responses to stress and disadvantage. In: M.W. Kent and J.E. Rolf (eds) *Social Competence in Children*. Hanover, NH: University Press of New England.

Rydelius, P.-A. (1997) Are children of alcoholics a clinical concern for child and adolescent psychiatrists of today? *Journal of Child Psychology and Psychiatry*, 38, 615–624.

Schuckit, M.A. and Sweeney, S. (1987) Substance use and mental health problems among sons of alcoholics and controls. *Journal of Studies on Alcohol*, 48, 528–534.

Sowder, B.J and Burt, M.R. (1980) *Children of Heroin Addicts: An Assessment of Health, Learning, Behavioral, and Adjustment Problems*. New York: Praeger.

Steinhausen, H.C., Nestler, V. and Huth, H. (1982) Psychopathology and mental functions in the offspring of alcoholic and epileptic mothers. *Journal of the American Academy of Child Psychiatry*, 21, 268–273.

Swadi, H. (1994) Parenting capacity and substance misuse: an assessment scheme. *ACPP Review and Newsletter*, 16, 237–244.

Vaillant, G.E. (1983) *The Natural History of Alcoholism: Causes, Patterns, and Paths to Recovery*. Cambridge, Mass.: Harvard University Press.

Vaillant, G.E. (1995) *The Natural History of Alcoholism Revisited*. Cambridge, Mass.: Harvard University Press.

von Knorring, A.-L. (1991) Children of alcoholics. *Journal of Child Psychology and Psychiatry*, 32, 411–421.

Weaver, T., Renton, A., Stimson, G. and Tyrer, P. (1999) Severe mental illness and substance misuse. *British Medical Journal*, 318, 137–138.

Weisner, C. (1993) Toward an alcohol treatment entry model: a comparison of problem drinkers in the general population and in treatment. *Alcoholism: Clinical and Experimental Research*, 17, 746–752.

Werner, E.E. (1986) Resilient offspring of alcoholics: a longitudinal study from birth to age 18. *Journal of Studies on Alcohol*, 47, 34–40.

West, M.O. and Prinz, R.J. (1987) Parental alcoholism and childhood psychopathology. *Psychological Bulletin*, 102, 204–218.

Wolff, K., Farrell, M., Marsden, J., Monteiro, M.G., Ali, R., Welch, S. and Strang, J. (1999) A review of biological indicators of illicit drug use: practical considerations and clinical usefulness. *Addiction*, 94, 1279–1298.

Chapter 11

The problem of parental personality

Alison Westman

The parent or alternative carer is crucial in shaping the context and quality of the child's environment, and the impact of the carer's functioning on the child, both directly and indirectly, will be determined to a great extent by their personality. When families present, whether in clinical practice or in the legal arena, assessment should include consideration of the influence of parental personality on the emergence of difficulties, the nature of the presentation at that point in time and the likelihood of successful engagement in a therapeutic endeavour, with resolution of the problems.

Personality disorder remains a controversial diagnosis in adult mental heath practice. In the context of the mental health assessment of children and adolescents, it is often thought to be an inappropriate diagnosis given the developmental stage of the clinical population. Furthermore, an emphasis on family-focused intervention may not lend itself to consideration of whether the parent has underlying abnormalities of personality or merits such a diagnosis. However, it is necessary to consider whether there is a range of parental behaviour that is pathological in terms of the child's emotional and behavioural development. If so, assessment of this aspect of the parent's functioning will be important in the appraisal of risks to the child, the likely outcome of the child's psychological problems, and a reassessment of the roles of mental health professionals and other agencies in promoting and protecting the child's welfare.

This chapter reviews the definition of personality, the concept of personality disorder and the utility of the diagnosis of personality disorder for mental health professionals working with parents of dependent children.

Personality and disorders of personality

Personality is a concept familiar to people from all backgrounds and across cultures. There have been attempts at definition and classification since ancient times (reviewed in Tyrer *et al.*, 1991). However, definition of personality depends on observation of behaviours, attitudes and social adjustment, and on what the individual can explain about their experience of their inner world and their understanding of their thoughts, feelings and motivations (de Girolamo and Reich, 1993; Wolff, 1989). Personality traits are thus difficult to define and measure objectively. None the less, they form reasonably stable patterns of behaviour, which distinguish between individuals and account for consistent responses across diverse situations.

From earliest times, it has been apparent that there are individuals whose behaviours (and, by inference, their personalities) are abnormal in comparison with the wider population. From a psychiatric perspective, personality disorder is diagnosed when adults present with abnormal patterns of behaviour, which do not reflect the presence of a mental illness and are distinguishable from any comorbid process (Tyrer et al., 1991). Loranger et al. (1991) found that the presence of comorbid mental illness did not affect the stability of the diagnosis, although it might influence the accuracy of reporting of symptoms. The maladaptive behaviour may or may not cause distress to the individual but usually causes distress in intimate interpersonal relationships and in the individual's relationship with society (Tyrer et al., 1991; de Girolamo and Reich, 1993). The patterns of behaviour are recurrent and persistent, and the major international classification systems require that they have been characteristic not only of recent but also long-term functioning, usually from childhood or adolescence. As with measurement of traits in the normal population, and unlike the symptoms and signs of mental illness, personality dysfunction can only be inferred from maladaptive behaviour. Reliability of diagnosis in clinical practice is poor and it has been difficult to establish reliable estimates of prevalence of personality disorders. However, four community surveys, which used specific assessment methods to make diagnoses of unspecified personality disorders, gave prevalence rates of 10.3–13.5 per cent (reviewed by de Girolamo and Reich, 1993; Casey and Tyrer, 1986; Maier et al., 1992; Reich, 1988; Reich et al., 1989; Zimmerman and Coryell, 1990).

Personality disorders are divided into different types by grouping clusters of the most prominent maladaptive traits. Recent developments have brought the international systems of classification closer in terms of common categories (Sara et al., 1996), which include anti-social/dissocial, histrionic, obsessive-compulsive/anankastic, borderline/emotionally unstable. None the less, the validity of categories has not been established and they should be viewed as hypothesised rather than empirically established syndromes (Casey, 1997). Tyrer et al. (1991) note that the different categories of personality disorders have their origins in different areas of clinical and theoretical practice and are a heterogeneous group.

Longitudinal studies of personality in normal adults have demonstrated that traits are reasonably stable during 2 to 30 years (Costa and McCrae, 1986). There is also fair to good temporal reliability for personality disorders, although there is better agreement for the presence or absence of a personality disorder, with individual types being less stable (Tyrer et *al.*, 1983). Two broad groups of personality disorders can be identified: immature personality disorders that will improve over time, and mature personality disorders that tend to persist into late-middle or old age (Tyrer and Sievewright, 1988).

Notwithstanding problems with establishing validity and its poorer status compared with diagnosis of mental illness, personality disorder continues to be considered a useful diagnosis by most general psychiatrists as it offers a means to categorise those individuals whose behaviour reflects seriously abnormal personality function (Tyrer and Alexander, 1979). However, the categorical approach to diagnosis may be particularly criticised as individuals with significant pathology may be omitted – for example, because they lie at the boundaries of different categories, do not meet specific criteria, or are milder cases of the less common disorders (Gorton and Akhtar, 1990; Kass *et al.*, 1985; de Girolamo and Reich, 1993). It is not uncommonly the experience of professionals outside adult mental health, especially in the context of child care proceedings, to find that use of the categorical approach to parental personality assessment leads to a failure to identify and describe significant levels of psychopathology and parenting problems, with a consequent minimisation of the risk the individual presents to a child in their care (Meadow, 1985; Reder and Duncan, 1999).

The controversy that surrounds personality disorder reflects not only the problem of validity and reliability of diagnosis, but also its use in clinical practice. The presence of maladaptive behaviour in individuals without a comorbid mental illness can lead to critical clinical judgements being made, as they are considered to be responsible for controlling such behaviour. Some clinicians may minimise the patient's difficulties, even in the presence of comorbid illness, and attribute negative connotations to their presentation, such as being attention-seeking or manipulative (Lewis and Appleby, 1988), and feel pessimistic about the possibility of a positive and prompt response to therapeutic interventions (Holmes, 1999).

Holmes (1999) discusses recent conceptual developments which have assisted the psychiatrist in taking a simplified but clearer approach to the issue of personality disorder. The use of Axes 1 and 2 in DSM-IV (American Psychiatric Association, 1994) provides the clinician with a structure to consider the relative contributions of personality and mental illness in the patient's presentation. The concept of severe personality disorder allows the consideration of that group of individuals with severe dysfunction who are likely to be at risk and in need of intervention. Deliberate self-harm, interpersonal conflict and domestic violence are common forms of presentation for these individuals, many of whom are parents. These problems are therefore particularly pertinent in the consideration of the quality of child care provided.

Personality disorder and parenting

The tasks and responsibilities of a parent involve a complex interrelated matrix of behaviours to meet the child's needs – physical, emotional, cognitive and social (summarised by Duncan and Reder in Chapter 6). It is apparent that this process is an interpersonal one, determined by an adult being in a relationship with a child. Since personality disorder can be considered to be a disorder of interpersonal functioning (Holmes, 1999), its presence in a parent who experiences pervasive and persistent symptoms, associated with chronic psychiatric problems and social and interpersonal impairment, is bound to impact upon child care. Indeed Rutter and Quinton (1984) have shown that the increased rates of emotional and behavioural disturbance found in the children of parents with mental illness are especially associated with parental personality disorder.

Assessment of the disruptive impact of personality dysfunction on parenting and child development is assisted by the use of a detailed framework, such as that synthesised by Reder and Lucey (1995), which permits further deconstruction of the role of a parent. Their framework is divided into five main headings: the parent's relationship to the role of parenting; the parent's relationship to the child; family influences; the parent's interaction with the external world; and the potential for change.

The parent's relationship to parenting

The children of a parent with a personality disorder are at increased risk of maladjustment, exposure to a range of associated psycho-social adversities being of particular relevance (Rutter and Quinton, 1984). At the most practical level, if an individual's personality disorder significantly disrupts their ability to sustain employment or to organise themselves to provide financial support from benefits and stable housing, they will not be able to provide physical care in terms of a secure and stable home environment, regular food, attention to hygiene, and so on.

Their capacity to manage the care of their children may be further compromised by increased vulnerability to develop comorbid mental illness (Tyrer *et al.*, 1991; Holmes, 1999) and a poorer response to treatment, both in the short and long term, which is probably related to greater mental state pathology at presentation and increased vulnerability to relapse (Tyrer *et al.*, 1993; 1994; Zimmerman *et al.*, 1986). An increased prevalence of personality disorder is found in populations of individuals making suicidal attempts, engaging in deliberate self-harm, abusing substances, and in the general and forensic psychiatric populations (the anti-social type predominating in the latter) (Tyrer *et al.*, 1991). Individuals who are prone to frequent acute episodes of mental illness will not be able to provide optimal child care if such difficulties cause recurrent periods of absence and introduce insecurity and inconsistency in the provision of physical and emotional care. Their children may also be exposed to parental behaviour that causes extreme anxiety, such as repeated losses or threats of loss, or uncontrolled or aggressive outbursts. Recent examples, from the author's own medico-legal work, of distressing parental behaviour witnessed by children have included the cutting of wrists, dangling off a balcony, and overdosing.

Such difficulties will also affect the parent's ability to give age-appropriate emotional child care. It is essential for parents to facilitate their child's emotional development through consistent, sensitive, reciprocal attention to their psychological needs in order to promote the establishment of well-functioning attachment relationships. In the absence of such experiences, children may find it more difficult to grow in confidence, explore and learn from their environment, and establish satisfying relationships as they move into wider social settings. Parents who by virtue of their own genetic loading and poor early experiences of being parented, and whose emotional functioning is further compromised by episodes of intercurrent mental illness and other stressful life events, will have problems delivering consistent positive parenting. They may have a diminished capacity to model pro-social behaviours themselves and fail to notice and affirm pro-social behaviours in their children. According to Patterson and Capaldi (1991), anti-social mothers are more likely to find difficulties monitoring their child's behaviour and administering discipline. The process of teaching their child, whether by modelling or instruction, to anticipate consequences or problem-solve may be very difficult for personality-disordered parents who struggle to reflect on and control their own impulsive responses. An absence of early models of good-quality parenting may also compromise their understanding of their child's age-appropriate physical and emotional needs and the level of protection required.

Secondary maladaptive behavioural responses by the child will pose on-going and escalating challenges to the parent, provoking further inappropriate responses by the parent with the establishment of 'coercive cycles' of anti-social behaviour and ineffective and punitive discipline (Patterson, 1982).

The socialisation of children is facilitated by introduction into appropriate social contexts to allow the gradual development of interaction with others. Parents with abnormal personality traits and maladaptive patterns of behaviour are likely to be socially marginalised and less able to provide such positive examples. For children whose parents are unable to provide adequate care, a significant relationship with another supportive and caring adult may support the child's development but this will not be available if the parent cannot access other social or professional assistance or sustain relationships with partners.

To be able to understand the tasks of parenting, adults need to be able to make links with their own childhood experiences and reflect on the parenting they received. Such reflection, if it can lead to positive change, can be protective for the child. However, thinking about inadequate, neglectful, abusive or rejecting parenting is likely to be difficult for emotionally needy individuals with personality disorder, particularly as their capacity to form helpful, supportive relationships will be low.

The parent's relationship with the child

A parent who has had emotionally impoverished or abusive early experiences is likely to find it difficult to establish and sustain a positive and appropriate parental relationship. For example, it may be difficult for that person to recognise their child as an individual with a separate identity and differing needs. Unacceptable personal attributes in the carer or another associated individual (for example, an absent and abusive father) may be located in the child by the parent. An emotionally needy and vulnerable parent may not have the capacity to take a child-centred perspective and prioritise the child's needs. They may be insensitive to, and intolerant of, negative or rejecting responses from the child and may have difficulty coping with envy arising from the child apparently functioning as a more contented and successful individual.

The emotional vulnerability of a parent, coupled with a limited capacity to model appropriate adult behaviours and establish appropriate structures to support child care, may lead to the loss of the parent–child hierarchy and a skewing of family relationships. A child may respond to the perceived threat of loss of a vulnerable parent by trying to take responsibility not only for the physical care of the adult and the home but also for the emotional well-being of the parent. Barnett and Parker (1998) discuss the pathological effect of such role reversal if it is intense or prolonged, as it may limit the child's development and also establish a pattern of intergenerational transmission. This response in a child suggests that there is an underlying disorder of attachment, that the emotional needs of the child are not being met, and predicts later difficulties in emotional adjustment. None the less, Hetherington (1989) found that experience of parental role reversal enhances the competence of some girls following parental divorce, but only if the level of stress is moderate (not low or high) and if supported by close and caring adults. However, girls encountering excessive parentification post-divorce, who are overburdened and without a supportive and caring adult, are at increased risk of developing depressive symptoms and low self-worth.

Post-divorce situations are also likely to be time-limited and it is highly unlikely that the identified protective factors would be present for a girl caught in a parentified relationship with a personality-disordered parent.

Family influences

Children grow up in a context in which they are dependent and cannot select their own environment. When home life is disturbed by tension and conflict, they will be unable to choose to separate themselves from it effectively and will be less able to modify emotional or behavioural pressures placed upon them. The principal family influences affecting children of parents with personality disorder are exposure to: domestic violence, abuse, and losses.

Domestic violence

Exposure to hostile parental behaviour such as irritability, aggression and violence, whether direct or witnessed between the parents, is disturbing to children (Rutter and Quinton, 1984; Jaffe *et al.*, 1986; Moffitt and Caspi, 1998). Those exposed to domestic violence have been shown to have lowered self-esteem and empathy with others, and a raised prevalence of emotional, conduct and psychosomatic disorders (Black and Newman, 1996; Rutter and Quinton, 1984). The increased psychiatric risks to children of parents with mental disorders are not a direct function of the parent's symptoms but arise from a combination of psycho-social adversities, with the greatest risk factors being family discord and hostility. It is the pervasive nature of impaired interpersonal functioning rather than the particular category of personality disorder, whether anti-social or non-anti-social, which predicts a worse outcome for the child (Rutter and Quinton, 1984).

Moffitt and Caspi (1998) review hypothetical models and supporting research for the adverse effect of exposure to interparental conflict on children. Partner violence may disrupt the quality of parenting, with poor parenting mediating the link between partner violence and children's behaviour problems. Emotional stress may mediate the link between interparental violence and children's behaviour problems as their security is threatened. Children may also imitate adult partner violence, adopting cognitive beliefs about violence as a means to resolve conflict. Research has not proven these to be causative associations and an alternative hypothesis suggests that a heritable liability to aggression increases the likelihood of the emergence of conduct problems. However, the introduction of a genetic aetiological model leads on to consideration of a more complex model of gene–environment interaction. The study by Hetherington *et al.* (1994) shows that the emergence of anti-social behaviour is influenced by the environmental aspects of family life.

When exposed to interparental violence, boys tend to show more symptoms of externalising disorders, whereas girls show more symptoms of internalising disorders. The overall adjustment of boys is associated with the degree of violence to which they are exposed, but both genders show lower levels of social competence (Jaffe *et al.*, 1986). There is a consistent

association between greater intensity of conflict and worse behavioural problem outcomes, with physical violence being worse than mental and verbal
conflict (Grych and Fincham, 1990).

Other mediating variables discussed by Melzack (1997) include the child's
age, the relationship between the child and perpetrator, the nature, extent and
meaning of the conflict between parents, the extent to which the experience
of violence is connected with loss and change, the effect upon the child's
understanding of their world, and their ability to cope. Vulnerability may be
increased by exposure to violence when the perpetrator is in a relationship
with the child, identification with the perpetrator, loss, insecurity and the
non-availability of emotional support. A resilient response may be mediated
through having an active problem-solving approach to difficulties and stress,
being able to explain and integrate past and present social and personal
experiences, being connected to the community, and having a parent who can
contain anxieties. The presence of an adult who can be used by the child as a
secure relationship is an essential factor.

Ferguson and Horwood (1998) reviewed the impact of domestic violence
on children's adjustment into young adulthood. They found that children
exposed to domestic violence also experience a wide range of adverse social
and contextual factors associated with interparental violence, such as social
and economic disadvantage, parental separation, impaired family functioning, parental alcoholism, criminality, and physical and sexual abuse. Exposure
to domestic violence is associated with adverse outcomes in young adulthood, such as depression, anxiety, suicide attempts, alcohol or substance
abuse, nicotine dependence, and criminal activity. There is evidence of a differential response to mother- or father-initiated violence, with the latter having an increased number of outcomes including anxiety, conduct disorder
and property crime, whilst the former is associated with alcohol abuse and
dependence.

Abuse

The risk of physical abuse to children living with parents who are violent
towards each other is reviewed by Moffitt and Caspi (1998). Of particular
note is the 1975 National Family Violence Survey which studied over 2,000
American families (Straus, 1990). Among parents who engaged in serious
spouse abuse, half of the fathers and a quarter of the mothers said they had
engaged in serious child abuse (compared with less than 10 per cent of parents in relationships without serious spouse abuse). Less severe interparental
violence – for example, pushing, slapping, throwing objects – increased the
risk of abuse by more than double (which may be an underestimate as this
study looked at intact families). Overall, the research reviewed indicated that
the risk of child abuse is between three and nine times greater in homes where
there is interparental violence.

Losses

The likelihood of marital disharmony and disruption is increased in the families of individuals with personality disorder who, by definition, have significant interpersonal difficulties and difficulties establishing and sustaining positive relationships (Rutter and Quinton, 1984). Such adults commonly have chosen a spouse with mental disturbance (Rutter and Quinton, 1984), and anti-social mothers are more likely to separate from the child's father (Patterson and Capaldi, 1991).

Unstable parental relationships increase children's experiences of loss. Such losses may take the form of separations, with or without on-going contact, temporary or permanent loss through injury or death, and the repeated loss of emotional care and support. Discordant parental relationships and repeated separations are linked to a range of emotional, conduct and anti-social problems in children (Wolkind and Rutter, 1985). Research points to the absence of the father being significant in the emergence of behavioural problems and anti-social behaviour in boys (reviewed by Lykken, 1995) but also in increased rates of teenage pregnancy in girls (Kristol, 1994; Lykken, 1995). These maladaptive outcomes may result from the mother becoming overwhelmed by the demands of coping alone, the absence of a role model and the emergence of coercive interactions between divorced mothers and sons with loss of effective control (Hetherington and Stanley-Hagan, 1999). Consistent, positive parenting and the elimination of conflict are difficult for divorcing parents (Hetherington and Stanley-Hagan, 1999). In such circumstances, the presence of a personality disorder will exacerbate difficulties, as the individual's capacity to manage adaptively is already compromised, and their children will be at increased risk of the emergence of emotional or behavioural disorders, or will already be presenting these.

A study of young people convicted for serious crimes, including violent offending, found that 57 per cent had experienced the loss of a significant figure (Boswell, 1997). Farrington (1989) found that the best predictors of violence in boys aged 8–10 years were mediated by parents and included physical neglect, harsh and erratic discipline, and separation from parents, principally because of parental conflict. Bailey (1997) suggests a model for the emergence of anti-social behaviour in childhood. Threats of loss or rejection have an impact on the child and chronically inconsistent and rejecting parental responses may lead to insecure attachment (Bowlby, 1973). Such parental behaviours are likely to cause a state of perpetual uncertainty about the physical or emotional availability of the parent. If the child's emotional response is anger, a model is gradually learnt in which anger, uncertainty and insecurity become core features, increasing the risk of the development of anti-social behaviour.

The parent's interaction with the external world

The presence of a support network through extended family and friends is an important factor in protecting children from the risk of abuse. Again, parents with personality disorder are less likely to have such networks, with links being further jeopardised by comorbid mental illness (Tyrer et al., 1994).

With few relational or informal social supports, a network of support from professionals becomes increasingly important, to assist the parent and monitor the child's well-being. Parents with personality disorder are likely to be difficult to engage in cooperative relationships with professionals, and previous attempts by mental health services may have been frustrating and unsuccessful (Tyrer et al., 1994; Holmes, 1999). The pessimistic opinions of professionals working with the family may impede further attempts at effective work and complicate inter-professional liaison and joint approaches to intervention.

The likelihood of neglect of the child's health care needs is also increased as clinic appointments may be failed and help-seeking behaviour is unlikely.

The potential for change

If child care problems are identified, the parent must be able to grasp the need to change and start to work towards achieving agreed goals. However, as discussed, the potential for change may already be considered poor. Within psychiatry, patients with diagnoses of personality disorder are a notoriously difficult group to engage in treatment. The impact of the dysfunctional aspects of the patient's interpersonal functioning upon the psychiatrist may influence attitudes of therapeutic pessimism, making it difficult for the clinician to remain objective in the formulation of management plans which adequately address the patient's needs (Holmes, 1999). Despite evidence to demonstrate the increased likelihood of such patients responding to inpatient and intensive interventions, diagnosis of personality disorder may reduce the chances of effective treatment being offered within adult psychiatry (Tyrer et al., 1994). Indeed, as the responsibility for change is considered to rest with the individual, and decisions regarding their capacity to engage are guided by professional opinions about their insight into their situation and motivation (Cassell and Coleman, 1995), the possibility of effective change may be low.

However, it must also be acknowledged that treatment to ameliorate the disturbance of an adult with severe personality dysfunction will be a long endeavour, and the circumstances and time-scale may not be commensurate with the needs of a developing child. Parents with personality disorders can find it particularly difficult to engage in family-focused therapeutic work which shifts from perceiving the child as the problem to exploring the parental role and need to change. They are likely to disengage from treatment with difficulties unresolved.

Parent, child and environment – genetic and behavioural considerations

The causes of maladaptive personality traits are difficult to determine since problematic behaviours emerge over the course of development, arising from the complex interaction between the predominantly genetically determined constitutional make-up of the person and their environment (Wolff, 1989), particularly the emotional environment (Tyrer *et al.*, 1991). This is a dynamic process, with the gene–environment interaction leading to alterations in the individual's constitution, with subsequent on-going changes in the interaction between the individual and the environment.

The early physical, emotional and social environment experienced by the child is significantly affected by the parent's personality traits (with their heritable components). These also influence exposure to the wider environment beyond the home as the child grows up. Parenting of good quality will facilitate the child's development by recognising 'the strengths, qualities and potential difficulties in genetically different children' (Lykken, 1995). Consistent and predictable responses will enhance attachment and emotional development. However, care given by parents with abnormal personality traits may compromise the emotional environment. Parenting which cannot identify the child's needs and is inconsistent and unpredictable will cause confusion and uncertainty which may disrupt developmental pathways.

However, the temperamental attributes of children will themselves modify the care environment and may increase their vulnerability and risk. The New York Longitudinal Study (Thomas *et al.*, 1963; Chess and Thomas, 1984), which studied 133 3-year-olds and followed them up for 20 years, identified three subdivisions of temperamental groupings – the 'easy', 'difficult' and 'slow to warm up' child syndromes. The rating of temperament and global adjustment at 3 years predicted adult adjustment and temperamental style, with those with a difficult temperament having the most problems.

Nevertheless, Chess and Thomas (1984) found that the most harmful factor in the later emergence of adjustment difficulties was conflict between the parents at entry into the study. This is consistent with other studies exploring the impact of parental conflict on children. The majority of children are resilient. However, certain children will be more vulnerable to environmental stresses, genetic influences being important in their susceptibility (Paris, 1998). Paris (p.151) summarises the gene–environment interaction thus: 'Biological factors as reflected in trait profiles, determine vulnerability. Psychological and social factors function as precipitants for psychopathology.'

Children who are most resilient have personality traits which increase their likelihood of forming secure attachments and persisting in their goals. Children with a difficult temperament are challenging as they are impulsive, excitable and unresponsive and have difficulties adapting. They are often experienced as emotionally unrewarding children. They are more difficult to manage and to socialise (Lykken, 1995), and having a difficult temperament increases the probability of the child becoming the focus of negative parental attention (Rutter and Quinton, 1984). Problems in socialisation will also cause difficulties as the child's environment expands and problems are encountered in establishing peer relationships or fitting into the structures at school.

Conclusions

The diagnosis of personality disorder does present the clinician with difficulties, including its validity, reliability and its impact on clinical care. There will continue to be mental health practitioners who do not find it beneficial. From the child mental health perspective, not relying on a categorical diagnosis in the assessment of parental competence may allow a more discriminating approach to describing parental strengths, difficulties and risks. It may help to avoid the potentially dangerous situation that can arise when adult mental-state psychiatric assessment fails to reveal symptoms meeting criteria for a personality disorder, leading to an erroneous assumption that the individual's parenting ability is adequate.

However, if it is accepted that diagnosis of personality disorder is imperfect, but that confirmation of parental personality disorder at least highlights the possibility of parenting difficulties and child protection concerns (whether or not the primary clinical focus is the child), it has value. Community surveys indicate a considerable prevalence of personality disorders, and many of these individuals will have dependent children. They are at increased risk of comorbid mental illness, have poor social networks, find it more difficult to establish stable adult relationships or to facilitate the development of emotional relationships with their children, and are at increased risk of forensic problems such as anti-social behaviour, drug and alcohol abuse. All of these problems exacerbate parenting difficulties and indicate a group of children at increased risk for a range of mental health problems. The emergence of such problems will increase the stresses within the family and cause further decompensation in the functioning of the parent and child.

General psychiatrists are likely to be treating significant numbers of such parents. However, Barnett and Parker (1998) note that adult services often fail to respond to the knowledge that their patients have dependent children, perhaps because they consider that they do not have the necessary expertise in child development to identify difficulties or understand how to take their concerns forward. They may also fear additional demands being made upon their resources and that there may be a conflict of interest and responsibility between their primary role with the parent and the needs of the child. A diagnosis of personality disorder may also make adult practitioners wary of becoming too actively involved.

Identification of these patients as parents does have implications for management, across adult and child mental health services, involving the resources of both and requiring close professional liaison, flexible and intensive intervention and considerable professional tolerance and patience – with the patients and each other! The task therefore appears to be one of increasing and improving the quality of liaison between the adult and child mental health services at a local level. Improved liaison will facilitate communication about worrying cases. Suspicions about inappropriate demands being made upon adult resources could be addressed at an early stage, and child mental health practitioners' anxieties about the use of the diagnosis of personality disorder could be considered in the context of case work. Education about clinical issues for clinicians in the 'opposite camp' could helpfully cross-fertilise practice and support developments in assessment and interventions.

It would be idealistic indeed to assume that a different pattern of working together would prove to be the panacea for the difficulties of these parents and their children. However, if more comprehensive mental health responses could prevent or ameliorate the suffering of one generation of children and modify the intergenerational transmission of maladaptive behaviours, the effort would seem to be justified.

References

American Psychiatric Association (1994) *Diagnostic and Statistical Manual of Mental Disorders*. 4th edn. Washington, DC: American Psychiatric Association.

Bailey, S. (1997) Psychiatric assessment of the violent child and adolescent towards understanding and safe intervention. In: V. Varma (ed.) *Violence in Children and Adolescents*. London: Jessica Kingsley.

Barnett, B. and Parker, G. (1998) The parentified child: early competence or childhood deprivation. *Child Psychology and Psychiatry Review*, 4, 146–155.

Black, D. and Newman, M. (1996) Children and domestic violence. *Clinical Child Psychology and Psychiatry*, 1, 79–88.

Boswell, G. (1997) The backgrounds of violent young offenders: the present picture. In: V. Varma (ed.) *Violence in Children and Adolescents*. London: Jessica Kingsley.

Bowlby, J. (1973) *Attachment and Loss. Vol. 2: Separation: Anxiety and Anger*. London: Hogarth Press.

Casey, P.R. (1997) Clinical assessment of personality. *Advances in Psychiatric Treatment*, 3, 182–187.

Casey, P.R. and Tyrer, P.J. (1986) Personality, functioning and symptomatology. *Journal of Psychiatric Research*, 20, 363–374.

Cassell, D. and Coleman, R. (1995) Parents with psychiatric problems. In: P. Reder and C. Lucey (eds) *Assessment of Parenting: Psychiatric and Psychological Contributions*. London: Routledge.

Chess, S. and Thomas, A. (1984) *Origins and Evolution of Behavior Disorders*. New York: Raven Press.

Costa, P.T. and McCrae, R.R. (1986) Personality stability and its implications for clinical psychology. *Clinical Psychology Review*, 6, 407–423.

de Girolamo, G. and Reich, J.H. (1993) *Personality Disorders*. Geneva: World Health Organization.

Farrington, D.P. (1989) Early predictors of adolescent aggression and adult violence. *Violence and Victims*, 4, 79–100.

Ferguson, D.M. and Horwood, L.J. (1998) Exposure to inter-parental violence in childhood and psychosocial adjustment in young adulthood. *Child Abuse and Neglect*, 22, 339–357.

Gorton, G. and Akhtar, S. (1990) The literature on personality disorders, 1985–88: trends, issues and controversies. *Hospital and Community Psychiatry*, 41, 39–51.

Grych, J.H. and Fincham, D. (1990) Marital conflict and children's adjustment: a cognitive contextual framework. *Psychological Bulletin*, 108, 267–290.

Hetherington, E.M. (1989) Coping with family transitions: winners, losers and survivors. *Child Development*, 60, 1–14.

Hetherington, E.M. and Stanley-Hagan, M. (1999) The adjustment of children with divorced parents: a risk and resiliency perspective. *Journal of Child Psychology and Psychiatry*, 40, 129–140.

Hetherington, E.M., Reiss, D. and Plomin, R. (eds) (1994) *Separate Social Worlds of Siblings: The Impact of Non-shared Environment on Development*. Hillsdale, NJ: Lawrence Erlbaum Associates.

Holmes, J. (1999) Psychotherapeutic approaches to the management of severe personality disorder in general psychiatric settings. *CPD Bulletin Psychiatry*, 1, 35–41.

Jaffe, P., Wolfe, D., Wilson, S.K. and Zak, L. (1986) Family violence and child adjustment: a comparative analysis of girls' and boys' behavioral symptoms. *American Journal of Psychiatry*, 143, 74–77.

Kass, F., Skodol, A.E., Charles, E., Spitzer, R.L. and Williams, J.B.W. (1985) Scaled ratings of DSM-III personality disorders. *American Journal of Psychiatry*, 142, 627–630.

Kristol, I. (1994) Children need their fathers. *New York Times*, 3 November.

Lewis, G. and Appleby, L. (1988) Personality disorder: the patients psychiatrists dislike. *British Journal of Psychiatry* 153, 44–49.

Loranger, A.W., Lenzenweger, M.F., Gartner, A.F., Lehmann Susman, V., Herzig, J., Zammit, G.K., Gartner, J.D., Abrams, R.C. and Young, R.C. (1991) Trait-state artefacts and the diagnosis of personality disorders. *Archives of General Psychiatry*, 48, 720–728.

Lykken, D.T. (1995) *The Antisocial Personalities*. Hillsdale, NJ: Lawrence Erlbaum Associates.

Maier, W., Lichtermann, D., Klingler, T. and Heun, R. (1992) Prevalences of personality disorders (DSM-III-R) in the community. *Journal of Personality Disorders*, 6, 187–196.

Meadow, R. (1985) Management of Munchausen syndrome by proxy. *Archives of Disease in Childhood*, 60, 385–393.

Melzack, S. (1997) The emotional impact of violence on children. In: V. Varma (ed.) *Violence in Children and Adolescents*. London: Jessica Kingsley.

Moffitt, T.E. and Caspi, A. (1998) Implications of violence between intimate partners for child psychologists and psychiatrists. *Journal of Child Psychology and Psychiatry*, 39, 137–144.

Paris, J. (1998) Does childhood trauma cause personality disorders in adults? *Canadian Journal of Psychiatry*, 39, 137–144.

Patterson, G.R. (1982) *Coercive Family Process*. Eugene, Oreg.: Castalia.

Patterson, G.R. and Capaldi, D.M. (1991) Antisocial parents: unskilled and vulnerable. In: P.A. Cowan and M. Hetherington (eds) *Family Transitions*. Hillsdale, NJ: Lawrence Erlbaum Associates.

Reder, P. and Duncan, S. (1999) Conflictual relationships and risks of child abuse. *Journal of Child Centred Practice*, 6, 127–145.

Reder, P. and Lucey, C. (1995) Significant issues in the assessment of parenting. In: P. Reder and C. Lucey (eds) *Assessment of Parenting: Psychiatric and Psychological Contributions*. London: Routledge.

Reich, J.H. (1988) A family history method for DSM-III anxiety and personality disorders. *Psychiatry Research*, 26, 131–139.

Reich, J.H., Yates, W. and Nduguba, M. (1989) Prevalence of DSM-III personality disorders in the community. *Social Psychology*, 24, 12–16.

Rutter, M. and Quinton, D. (1984) Parental psychiatric disorder: effects on children. *Psychological Medicine*, 14, 853–880.

Sara, G., Raven, P. and Mann, A. (1996) A comparison of DSM-III-R and ICD 10 personality disorder criteria in an outpatient population. *Psychological Medicine*, 26, 151–160.

Straus, M.A. (1990) Ordinary violence, child abuse, and wife beating: what do they have in common? In: M.A. Straus and R.J. Gelles (eds) *Physical Violence in American Families: Risk Factors and Adaptations to Violence in 8,145 Families*. New Brunswick, NJ: Transaction.

Thomas, A., Chess, S., Birch, H.G., Hertzig, M. and Korn, S. (1963) *Behavioral Individuality in Early Childhood*. New York: New York University Press.

Tyrer, P. and Alexander, J. (1979) Classification of personality disorder. *British Journal of Psychiatry*, 135, 163–167.

Tyrer, P. and Sievewright, H. (1988) Studies of outcome. In: P. Tyrer (ed.) *Personality Disorders: Diagnosis, Treatment and Course*. London: Wright.

Tyrer, P., Strauss, J. and Cicchetti, D. (1983) Temporal reliability of personality in psychiatric patients. *Psychological Medicine*, 13, 393–398.

Tyrer, P., Casey, P. and Ferguson, B. (1991) Personality disorder in perspective. *British Journal of Psychiatry*, 159, 463–471.

Tyrer, P., Seivewright, N., Ferguson, B., Murphy, S. and Johnson, A.L. (1993) The Nottingham study of neurotic disorder: impact of personality status on response to drug treatment, cognitive therapy and self-help over two years. *British Journal of Psychiatry*, 162, 219–226.

Tyrer, P., Merson, S., Onyett, S. and Johnson, T. (1994) The effect of personality disorder on clinical outcome, social networks and adjustment: a controlled clinical trial of psychiatric emergencies. *Psychological Medicine*, 24, 731–740.

Wolff, S. (1989) *Childhood and Human Nature: The Development of Personality*. London: Routledge.

Wolkind, S. and Rutter, M. (1985) Separation, loss and family relationships. In: M. Rutter and L. Hersov (eds) *Child and Adolescent Psychiatry: Modern Approaches*. 2nd edn. Oxford: Blackwell.

Zimmerman, M. and Coryell, W.H. (1990) Diagnosing personality disorders in the community. *Archives of General Psychiatry*, 47, 527–531.

Zimmerman, M., Coryell, W., Pfohl, B., Corenthal, C. and Stangl, D. (1986) ECT response in depressed patients with and without a DSM-II personality disorder. *American Journal of Psychiatry*, 143, 1030–1032.

Chapter 12

Child abuse and parental mental health

Peter Reder and Sylvia Duncan

The physical abuse of children was 'rediscovered' by physicians over fifty years ago (Caffey, 1946; Woolley and Evans, 1955). Since then, some observers have expressed concern at the continuing 'medicalisation' of what they consider to be essentially a social problem (e.g. Parton, 1985). A widely-held view emerged from the ensuing debate that child physical abuse and neglect occurred through an interaction between parents, children and their social environment. The model described parents with emotional conflicts, caring for vulnerable children, while living in circumstances of social stress (e.g. Steele, 1980; Schmitt and Krugman, 1992). In the context of this model, parents who maltreated their children were not generally considered to be suffering from a psychiatric disorder.

However, recent research into child abuse and neglect has not fully supported this assumption. In particular, reviews of child deaths have shown significant associations with parental mental health problems. This chapter summarises current knowledge derived from reports into non-fatal and fatal abuse, including a study that we have undertaken.

Research in this area has been hampered by problems of definition. The notion of 'child abuse' is best considered as a social construction in which parameters for acceptable parental behaviour change over time and vary from culture to culture (Reder *et al.*, 1993). This has allowed some studies to use the existence of a single bruise as their index of 'abuse', while others have focused on whether courts had removed a child from parental care. In addition, researchers do not always distinguish between the different forms of child abuse and neglect. Difficulties also arise with psychiatric diagnoses, and arguments continue as to whether substance misuse or personality disorder, for example, constitute a psychiatric disorder. In our view, the former does, because it may lead to disturbances of consciousness, thought and mood, while the latter does not, because it primarily describes long-standing problems with relationships that originated in adverse childhood experiences (Reder and Duncan, 1999a). Our preference is to use the more general term 'mental health problems'.

Non-fatal abuse

Many commentators are at pains to point out that most psychiatric patients can and do parent adequately (e.g. Cassell and Coleman, 1995; Burns *et al.*, 1996; Oates, 1997). None the less, when compared with controls, parents who maltreat their children are often shown to be depressed (Falkov, 1997) or to have a history of attempted suicide (Hawton *et al.*, 1985). Sheppard (1997) used the Beck Depression Inventory to examine mothers whose families made up child and family social work caseloads: he found a significant association between maternal depression and recorded child maltreatment, especially physical and sexual abuse. Glaser and Prior (1997) reviewed the cases of all children whose names were on the Child Protection Registers of four English local authorities. Parental mental illness, including suicidal attempts, anorexia nervosa, depressive psychosis and schizophrenia, was present in 31 per cent of cases and substance misuse in 26 per cent. These compare with prevalence estimates in the general population for depression of 15 per cent (Kandal *et al.*, 1991) and for schizophrenia of just under 1 per cent (Bamrah *et al.*, 1991), and the calculation by Brisby *et al.* (1997) that 7 per cent of parents drink harmful levels of alcohol (see Cleaver *et al.*, 1999).

In an extensive project, Oliver (1985) reviewed the histories of families living in an area of southern England which contained successive generations of child maltreatment. He concluded that, 'In the parents and antecedents, mental and personality disorders, suicidal attempts, mental handicap, dependence on drugs (mothers) or on alcohol (fathers), epilepsy and criminality were conspicuous features' (p. 484).

In the United States, Taylor *et al.* (1991) and Murphy *et al.* (1991) examined the records of 206 serious physical abuse and neglect cases brought before the Boston Juvenile Court. They found clear evidence of a severe affective disorder in one or both of the parents in 14 per cent of cases and a psychotic disorder in 13 per cent.

Parental mental health problems also feature on a number of research-based risk checklists. For example, Browne and colleagues evolved protocols for predicting which parents are most likely to abuse and/or neglect their children (Browne and Saqi, 1988; Browne and Herbert, 1997; Agathonos-Georgopoulou and Browne, 1997). The relative importance of risk characteristics was determined by discriminant function analysis, and a history of parental 'mental illness, drug or alcohol addiction' was found to be a significant predictor of later child maltreatment.

Parental substance misuse has been particularly identified as a risk factor for child abuse and is also included on many other high-risk checklists (e.g. Greenland, 1987; Armstrong and Wood, 1991). Follow-up studies of children exposed to illicit drugs *in utero* have demonstrated a significant association with subsequent child maltreatment of sufficient seriousness to necessitate removal of the children from their parents by child protection agencies

(Olofsson *et al.*, 1983; Kelley, 1992; Jaudes *et al.*, 1995). A number of projects have examined cases of serious child abuse or neglect brought before the courts. Famularo *et al.* (1986) found that 52 per cent of such families had at least one parent with a history of alcoholism. Murphy *et al.* (1991) report that a documented problem with either alcohol or drugs in at least one parent was present in 43 per cent of such cases (this figure rose to 50 per cent if suspicions of substance misuse were included) and the children of these parents were significantly more likely to be removed into permanent alternative care. In Famularo *et al.*'s investigation (1992), 70 per cent of the physically abusing parents whose children were removed from their care by courts abused alcohol and 51 per cent abused cocaine.

However, most studies of substance-misusing parents who remain in treatment programmes have suggested a better outlook (e.g. Lawson and Wilson, 1980; Wilson, 1989; Burns *et al.*, 1996). Although substance misuse was said to be 'rampant' in Murphy *et al.*'s sample of parents brought before the juvenile court for serious child maltreatment, the authors offer their clinical experience that 'parents who do stop abusing substances are likely to go on to other success in caring for their children' (1991, p. 209).

Children's vulnerability

A prospective study by Rutter and Quinton (1984) on the effects of parental psychiatric disorder on children's psychological welfare and development provides a useful link to our understanding of the increased risk of child abuse and neglect by such parents. They found that the impact was not disorder-specific but was more determined by the social and relational consequences of the parents' disorders. In other words, the children were primarily affected by their parents' general functioning and behaviour.

We believe that this translates well to problems of child abuse and neglect, in which it is the manifestation of the parents' problems through their *behaviour* that best describes the risk to their children. For example, parents who are self-preoccupied and emotionally and practically unavailable (as the result of depression, psychosis or substance misuse) are more likely to neglect their children, as are those who show unpredictable or chaotic forward planning due to psychosis, depression or substance misuse. The frequent separations that are the consequence of repeated hospital admissions may also lead to emotional or physical neglect. Physical abuse is more likely to result from parental irritability or over-reaction to stress that sometimes accompanies anxiety, depression or psychosis, as well as the parent's distorted beliefs or aggressive behaviour during psychotic episodes. Unusual parental preoccupations as part of obsessive conditions or phobias may also lead to physical abuse of the children. It is the disinhibition and boundary-blurring of substance misuse that can raise the risk of child sexual abuse.

Fatal child abuse

Numerous reports from different countries link parental mental health problems and fatal child abuse. Through a review of world literature on parents
who murder their children, Resnick (1969) concluded that 67 per cent of the
murdering mothers and 44 per cent of the fathers had been psychotic, while
depression was evident in 71 per cent of the mothers and 33 per cent of the
fathers. In the UK, d'Orban (1979) considered that 27 per cent of women
imprisoned for actual or attempted murder of their children were mentally ill.
Alfaro (1988) reviewed fatal child abuse reports furnished by nine states of
the USA and found that up to 36 per cent of perpetrators suffered from a
mental illness and up to 43 per cent misused substances. Crimmins *et al.*
(1997) found that 59 per cent of women convicted of murdering their children
reported a history of mental health problems, and 31 per cent of the killings
were said to be drug-related. In Australia, 36 per cent of parents who
had killed their children were found to suffer from a psychiatric disorder
(Wilczynski, 1997). Substance misusers who failed to comply with treatment
figured highly among the perpetrators of fatal abuse in a number of studies
(see Deren, 1986; Bays, 1990).

The literature indicates, however, that neonaticide (the murder of a baby on
its first day of life) is a phenomenon distinct from other forms of child killing
(Resnick, 1970). It tends to involve young mothers who, although suffering
from considerable emotional turmoil which usually leads to denial of the
pregnancy (e.g. Bonnet, 1993; Fitzpatrick, 1995), do not show evidence of a
formal psychiatric disorder.

More recent studies in the UK have continued to show an association
between child abuse deaths and parental mental health problems. Wilczynski
(1997) reviewed 48 children's deaths in England which had been referred by
the police to the Director of Public Prosecutions as likely homicides. Extrapo-
lating from her figures, 50 per cent of the suspects suffered from a current
psychiatric disorder, 48 per cent had previously received psychiatric treatment, 31 per cent had made a prior suicide attempt, 60 per cent had previously 'used' substances and 33 per cent had 'used' substances immediately
before the crime. Twenty-four per cent of the suspects were diagnosed as
depressed and a similar number as psychotic at the time of the killing.

In the UK, whenever a child has died or been severely injured as a result of
maltreatment, or when abuse is suspected, a local case review must be conducted by all involved agencies in order to identify practice lessons. An overview report is then submitted to the Department of Health. The procedures
for conducting these reviews are specified in Part 8 of the document *Working
Together* (Home Office *et al.*, 1991). In an analysis of 100 such 'Part 8'
Reviews, Falkov (1996) concluded that there was clear evidence of psychiatric
morbidity in at least 25 per cent of the perpetrators of the child's death.
The primary diagnoses were: psychosis (in ten cases), depression (in five),

'personality disorder' (five), drug-dependency (two), and Munchausen syndrome by proxy (two). The diagnosis was unknown in one instance. Alcohol abuse was an associated problem in five cases. Overall, psychiatric morbidity in one or other caretaker was evident in 32 per cent of the families but there was insufficient information available to form a judgement in another 23 per cent, so that the actual figure could have been somewhat higher.

Falkov found it more difficult to elicit information from the files about the nature of general psychiatrists' involvement in the child protection process but there was a strong impression that few of them recognised risks to their patients' children or actively informed statutory agencies about any concerns for a child's safety.

A one-year cohort of 'Part 8' Reviews

Coincidentally with Falkov's study, we had set out to review a one-year cohort of 'Part 8' Reviews in order to identify general patterns which might have implications for practice. This was a follow-up of an earlier study based on 35 fatal child abuse inquiry reports (Reder *et al.*, 1993) but using a more representative group of cases. The Department of Health gave us access to the 'Part 8' Review files, together with a grant to assist the study.

We chose to consider those child deaths notified under the 'Part 8' procedures during the twelve months up to March 1994, which were mostly a different cohort from that studied by Falkov. Our approach with each case was to draw a genogram of the child's family, identify which professionals had been involved with them and then compile a detailed chronology of events as the case had unfolded. We then read through each chronology, pausing regularly to hypothesise why the family or professionals had behaved in that particular way and what factors had influenced decisions and interventions. Our theoretical framework for making sense of the complex cases was based in family systems theory, but we were also interested to record factual and demographic information. We then looked for common themes across all the cases.

Our detailed analysis focused on 49 cases, 35 in which physical abuse or neglect was already confirmed as the cause of the child's death, and a further 14 in which we were highly suspicious that the death was abuse-related, even though a different diagnosis had been given, such as Sudden Infant Death Syndrome. The full project and findings are reported in Reder and Duncan (1999b) and here we shall focus on one aspect of the study, which considered whether the presence of mental health problems in the children's caretakers was a conspicuous feature.

We found that the material contained in the 'Part 8' Review files was of variable quality. Some case files did not accurately record psychiatric symptoms or signs and did not contain details of a psychiatric assessment and we had to make informed judgements about what did constitute a 'mental health problem'. For example, we decided to use the category of 'substance misuse' for caretakers who had been described as showing significant and prolonged problems of excessive alcohol or drug use which had a major impact on their lifestyle, but we chose to omit any reference to 'personality disorder'.

Mental health problems

We found a substantial association with parental mental health problems. Among the 35 'confirmed' cases, in which the caretaker responsible for the child's death had been identified, 15 (43 per cent) of the perpetrators had been suffering from an active mental health problem at the time that they killed the child. Three were showing evidence of a paranoid psychosis and this was a probable diagnosis with a fourth. Two had a depressive disorder and a further two postnatal depression. For the remaining seven, the problem was significant substance misuse. Furthermore, two of the four parents with a paranoid psychosis also significantly abused drugs and/or alcohol. Two other perpetrators had a previous psychiatric history.

Considering all 49 cases, which include the 'suspicious' as well as 'confirmed' deaths, requires us to look for an active mental health problem in *either* of the current caretakers, since no perpetrator was identified as responsible for killing the child in the 'suspicious' cases. In the 35 'confirmed' cases, 2 partners of the perpetrators had shown evidence of a current mental health problem, which was substance misuse in both instances. In the 14 'suspicious' cases, 4 caretakers in 3 families had had an active mental health problem, one being depression with somatic complaints and the remaining three being substance misuse.

Children's vulnerability

Some clues as to the nature of the risk to the children did emerge from our study, although detailed information was not always available in the Review reports. We formed the impression that the caretakers with mental health problems had become absorbed with their own preoccupations and personal needs in a variety of ways that impacted on the children. For the substance-misusing parents, their lifestyle was very self-centred, so that their children's safety and welfare were neglected. Many of these children appeared to have died from an avoidable accident or an assault when they asserted their own needs.

In one case, the child's father regularly abused drugs and the mother was a chronic heroin addict. The couple's relationship was unstable and characterised by violence and repeated separations. There were at least two referrals to social services expressing concern about the parents' drug taking and its effect on the child and, when she was aged 2½ years, she was taken to hospital, having ingested methadone. Over the next 16 months, the mother repeatedly moved with her daughter to a refuge, temporary homes and squats and then to a caravan. During that time, there was evidence that the mother spent most of her money on drugs and her life was chaotic. The child may have been sexually abused by a stranger in a toilet and was noted to be bruised, while her mother increasingly left her with different people. The child died aged 3 years 7 months after ingesting her mother's methadone.

Children of depressed parents seemed to be at risk of harm when they intruded more actively into their parent's preoccupations by crying or making other demands.

A 51-year-old father of three children had experienced recurrent depression which featured self-blame. During one of his depressive episodes, he was found spinning and shaking one of the children and this led to another brief informal hospital admission. The couple's third son was born two months later and, when he was aged 6 weeks, the father threw him downstairs after shouting at another of the children for crying. He told police that he had experienced an uncontrollable urge to get the children out of his way. He was convicted of manslaughter and detained at a special hospital.

Children of a psychotic parent appeared to intrude into their preoccupations in a different way. The case histories suggest that they had become episodically incorporated into their parent's delusional thinking and the final assault was an attempt by the parent to rid themselves of the perceived threat from the child.

One mother began talking to her infant as though the child had become her own mother – in other words, as though she had turned into the grandmother, who was already dead. The mother went on to make overt threats to kill her child and she eventually strangled her when she was 20 months old.

Another mother, with a prolonged postnatal depressive psychosis, eventually killed her child when 20 months old. Her delusions included a belief that the daughter was a reincarnation of her own mother and she repeatedly threatened to kill the child.

The father in another family was diagnosed as suffering from an alcohol-induced paranoid illness four years before he killed two of his children. During this time, he experienced auditory hallucinations telling him to sexually molest his children. However, he aggressively shunned all attempts at treatment.

Other authors have also pointed out the severe risk to a child when incorporated into their parent's psychotic ideation (Husain and Daniel, 1984; Cassell and Coleman, 1995) – a process which we believe can be understood as a change in the psychological meaning that the child has for their parent. We have discussed elsewhere (Reder *et al.*, 1993; Reder and Duncan, 1995) how a parent may unwittingly invest their child with particular psychological significance, such as a wish that they could provide the love that the parent never received in their own childhood, and then lash out in frustration when they fail in that role. A disturbed parent can also invest their child with a new significance as the result of delusional thoughts or psychotic hallucinations, and it is the changed meaning that renders them vulnerable to serious abuse.

Warnings

Some of the caretakers in the cases we studied appeared to give covert warning signs of the impending harm to their child by persistently approaching professionals with displaced concerns. We have identified numerous examples in both our fatal abuse studies, although it could be argued that this was only apparent in hindsight.

> *The day before a father with alcoholic hallucinosis killed two of his children, he took the eldest daughter to the GP with stomach pains, went to the practice of a child psychologist to apologise for being drunk and aggressive in her office 6 months previously and asked to have an appointment with a psychiatrist. The next day, he visited his GP's surgery and asked for an appointment later in the day.*

> *In another example, a few weeks before a mother threw her baby out of the window whilst suffering from postnatal depression, she told her community psychiatric nurse about her strong fears that the child would be removed if she was deemed not to be coping. Some days later she anxiously asked the health visitor to watch her bathe the baby.*

In one case, there appeared to be both overt and covert warnings.

> *The mother had delusions that the social worker had come to take her daughter away, and threatened to kill anyone who removed her. Over the four years of the child's life, the mother made 11 requests for rehousing, 14 attendances at her GP complaining that the child had a minor ailment, and a further 32 GP visits with her own minor ailments. She made repeated requests for day-care, a nursery place, accommodation or full care because she was finding the child a handful and volunteered that, when she felt depressed, she wanted to harm her and that she had previously tried to strangle another child of hers. She made another threat to kill her daughter, and her mother, six months before she committed the act and, perhaps when*

no professional recognised the danger, the mother sent the police and fire brigade to her mother's home.

Assessment paralysis

A particularly striking process issue arose from our study. The presence of parental mental health problems appeared to have a major impact on the functioning of members of the child protection networks involved with the families, which we have termed 'assessment paralysis'. We mean by this an apparent impasse in the professional network which interfered with thinking about the needs of the child alongside those of the parent. This usually occurred when the parent showed delusional thinking with irrational behaviour, or evidence of a depressive illness. Professional concern became focused on whether the parent did, or did not, have a diagnosable psychiatric disorder. While this concern was clearly relevant, because it determined whether that parent needed admission to a psychiatric hospital, if necessary under a Section of the Mental Health Act, it became the factor which decided whether *any* intervention was possible. Once the general practitioner or psychiatrist considered that the parent was not showing evidence of a formal psychiatric disorder, members of the child protection network seemed unable to assert that the parent's behaviour was so bizarre or so dangerous that, no matter what label was put to it, the child needed protection from it.

> *In one example, there had been long-standing concerns about the mental state of a mother, who eventually drowned her daughter when she was 4 years old. This mother had a history of school non-attendance, anorexia nervosa and stealing during childhood, was physically abused by her own mother and had been taken into care as a 15-year-old after setting fire to her parents' home. She became pregnant the following year and went on to have four children, but the three eldest were placed with other caretakers. Her adult psychiatric history began when she was aged 23 with deliberate self-harm, attempting to set fire to her flat and admitting that she wanted to smother her child. Over the next eight years, the mother presented repeatedly with depression, paranoid ideas and threats to kill her children, herself, her parents or professionals. She was observed breaking down her front door, throwing household items and rubbish over the balcony, shouting and screaming incoherently and claiming that people were following her and coming to cut her head off. She twice locked herself and her daughter in the flat and on one of these occasions was seen at a window brandishing a knife. During this time, there were five referrals for domiciliary psychiatric assessments but each one concluded that she was not showing evidence at the time of a formal psychiatric disorder and there were no grounds for invoking the Mental Health Act. This conclusion was accompanied by a decision that no further action could be taken.*

In our view, two parallel assessments are necessary in such cases: one of the parent's psychiatric state and one of the safety of the child. The essential point is that an adult's capacity to parent is not determined by whatever diagnosis is, or is not, used to explain their behaviour. Risk of harm to a child comes from the parent's *behaviour* itself, not from their psychiatric *diagnosis* as such. The diagnosis may guide the choice of treatment offered to the adult and may indicate their long-term prognosis and liability to behave in a similar way in the future. It does not determine the immediate risk of harm to the child. A child's safety should be determined by the nature of the parent's *behaviour*, and this in itself should be sufficient to indicate whether protective action is necessary. Assessments need to consider issues from the perspectives of the adult and the child, and the differing needs of each may require different decisions and interventions.

Implications

In summary, then, parental mental health problems do seem to increase the risk of child maltreatment in general, with substance misuse particularly associated with non-fatal and fatal child abuse. It appears to be the lifestyle that often accompanies illicit drug use that impacts so adversely on child care (e.g. Swadi, 1994). However, successful treatment can be a significant protective factor.

Clearly, clinicians need to be sensitive to the welfare of children of psychiatric patients. This is well illustrated by the three patients discussed by Mogielnicki *et al.* (1977), who had presented to a casualty department with psychosomatic complaints such as chest pain, limb weakness, headaches and visual blurring. Psychiatric interviews revealed that they feared being violent to their children or were already inflicting harm on them. Instead of presenting disguised warnings of risk to their children, parents may occasionally express obsessional preoccupations with harming their child. Anthony and Kreitman (1970) and Button and Reivich (1972) describe successful psychotherapeutic treatment of such mothers, none of whom acted upon their murderous thoughts. However, no references were made to child protection measures during treatment, which we would consider essential.

These findings must have important implications for the training of professionals and the organisation of clinical services, particularly in the light of Oates's (1997) summary that 25 per cent of all new female psychiatric patients have a child under 5 years of age, 25 per cent of women with a serious chronic mental illness have children under the age of 5, 26 per cent of adults with schizophrenia live in households with a child under the age of 16 years, and 60 per cent of women with a serious chronic mental illness have children under 16 years of age (see also Oppenheimer, 1981). Increased trends towards care in the community imply that children will be more frequently exposed to the behavioural and interactional consequences of parental mental health problems.

We would characterise the core implication as the need for everyone to 'think family' and to consider the mutual influence between children and parents. Adult mental health and substance misuse specialists should not focus exclusively on their patients as individuals and need to be more sensitive about risks to children in the family. It may only require a few simple questions about the number of children, how they are and how the parent is getting on with them. Health professionals may need to overcome dilemmas about confidentiality when considering whether to inform statutory agencies about suspected risk to the children (Department of Health *et al.*, 1994; Reder, 1996a) and can be helped in this by discussion with their Trust's Named Professionals for Child Protection (Department of Health and Welsh Office, 1995; Reder, 1996b; Reder and Duncan, 1997).

In turn, children's services have a responsibility to keep colleagues working with adults informed and aware of child protection issues and to refer to them at an early stage parents whose mental health is causing concern. All services need to liaise regularly together and need to be prepared to undertake parallel assessments, from the parent's perspective and from the child's, as well as consider the overlap and distinctions between them.

> *This was underlined by a telephone referral from a psychotherapist in private practice to a child psychiatrist. The psychotherapist had been treating a single mother for manic-depression, because she had not wanted to take medication, but the mother had returned from a holiday depressed, saying that she felt like killing her 11-year-old daughter and herself. The psychotherapist had spoken to the family's GP, who said that she did not believe that there was any danger and, in any case, the mother was 'not sectionable'. However, it was unclear what risk assessment had guided the GP towards this opinion. The child psychiatrist urged the psychotherapist also to consider the case from the child protection perspective, not merely from the aspect of the mother's mental state. Whether the mother was, or was not, 'sectionable' was marginal to a concern for the child's safety and it was this that needed an informed assessment, probably from social services. If necessary, this could lead to a protective intervention, such as the child living elsewhere temporarily. Interventions for the mother could then be considered from an adult perspective.*

References

Agathonos-Georgopoulou, H. and Browne, K.D. (1997) The prediction of child maltreatment in Greek families. *Child Abuse and Neglect*, 21, 721–735.

Alfaro, J. (1988) What can we learn from child abuse fatalities? A synthesis of nine studies. In: D.J. Besharov (ed.) *Protecting Children from Abuse and Neglect: Policy and Practice.* Springfield, Ill.: Charles C. Thomas.

Anthony, E.J. and Kreitman, N. (1970) Murderous obsessions in mothers toward their children. In: E.J. Anthony and T. Benedek (eds) *Parenthood: Its Psychology and Psychopathology*. Boston, Mass.: Little, Brown & Co.

Armstrong, K.L. and Wood, D. (1991) Can infant death from abuse be prevented? *The Medical Journal of Australia*, 155, 593–596.

Bamrah, J.S., Freeman, H.L. and Goldberg, D.P. (1991) Epidemiology of schizophrenia in Salford, 1974–84: changes in a urban community over ten years. *British Journal of Psychiatry*, 159, 802–810.

Bays, J. (1990) Substance abuse and child abuse: impact of addiction on the child. *Pediatric Clinics of North America*, 37, 881–904.

Bonnet, C. (1993) Adoption at birth: prevention against abandonment or neonaticide. *Child Abuse and Neglect*, 17, 501–513.

Brisby, T., Baker, S. and Hedderwick, T. (1997) *Under the Influence: Coping with Parents Who Drink Too Much*. London: Alcohol Concern.

Browne, K. and Herbert, M. (1997) *Preventing Family Violence*. Chichester: John Wiley & Sons.

Browne, K. and Saqi, S. (1988) Approaches to screening for child abuse and neglect. In: K. Browne, C. Davies and P. Stratton (eds) *Early Prediction and Prevention of Child Abuse*. Chichester: John Wiley & Sons.

Burns, E.C., O'Driscoll, M. and Wasson, G. (1996) The health and development of children whose mothers are on methadone maintenance. *Child Abuse Review*, 5, 113–122.

Button, J.H. and Reivich, R.S. (1972) Obsessions of infanticide: a review of 42 cases. *Archives of General Psychiatry*, 27, 235–240.

Caffey, F. (1946) Multiple fractures in the long bones of children suffering from chronic subdural haematoma. *American Journal of Roentgenology and Radium Therapy*, 56, 163–173.

Cassell, D. and Coleman, R. (1995) Parents with psychiatric problems. In: P. Reder and C. Lucey (eds) *Assessment of Parenting: Psychiatric and Psychological Contributions*. London: Routledge.

Cleaver, H., Unell, I. and Aldgate, J. (1999) *Children's Needs – Parenting Capacity: The Impact of Parental Mental Illness, Problem Alcohol and Drug Use, and Domestic Violence on Children's Development*. London: The Stationery Office.

Crimmins, S., Langley, S., Brownstein, H.H. and Spunt, B.J. (1997) Convicted women who have killed children: a self-psychology perspective. *Journal of Interpersonal Violence*, 12, 49–69.

Department of Health, British Medical Association and Conferences of Medical Royal Colleges (1994) *Child Protection: Medical Responsibilities*. London: HMSO.

Department of Health and Welsh Office (1995) *Child Protection: Clarification of Arrangements between the NHS and Other Agencies*. Department of Health.

Deren, S. (1986) Children of substance abusers: a review of the literature. *Journal of Substance Abuse Treatment*, 3, 77–94.

d'Orban, P.T. (1979) Women who kill their children. *British Journal of Psychiatry*, 134, 560–571.

Falkov, A. (1996) *Study of Working Together 'Part 8' Reports. Fatal Child Abuse and Parental Psychiatric Disorder: An Analysis of 100 Area Child Protection Committee Case Reviews Conducted under the Terms of Part 8 of Working Together under the Children Act 1989*. Department of Health.

Falkov, A. (1997) Parental psychiatric disorder and child maltreatment. Part II: Extent and nature of the association. National Children's Bureau Highlight No. 149.

Famularo, R., Stone, K., Barnum, R. and Wharton, R. (1986) Alcoholism and severe child maltreatment. *American Journal of Orthopsychiatry*, 56, 481–485.

Famularo, R., Kinscherff, R. and Fenton, T. (1992) Parental substance abuse and the nature of child maltreatment. *Child Abuse and Neglect*, 16, 475–483.

Fitzpatrick, G. (1995) Assessing treatability. In: P. Reder and C. Lucey (eds) *Assessment of Parenting: Psychiatric and Psychological Contributions*. London: Routledge.

Glaser, D. and Prior, V. (1997) Is the term child protection applicable to emotional abuse? *Child Abuse Review*, 6, 315–329.

Greenland, C. (1987) *Preventing CAN Deaths: An International Study of Deaths Due to Child Abuse and Neglect*. London: Tavistock.

Hawton, K., Roberts, J. and Goodwin, G. (1985) The risk of child abuse among mothers who attempt suicide. *British Journal of Psychiatry*, 146, 486–489.

Home Office, Department of Health, Department of Education and Science and Welsh Office (1991) *Working Together under the Children Act 1989: A Guide to Arrangements for Inter-agency Co-operation for the Protection of Children from Abuse*. London: HMSO.

Husain, A. and Daniel, A. (1984) A comparative study of filicidal and abusive mothers. *Canadian Journal of Psychiatry*, 29, 596–598.

Jaudes, P.K., Ekwo, E. and van Voorhis, J. (1995) Association of drug abuse and child abuse. *Child Abuse and Neglect*, 19, 1065–1075.

Kandal, E.R., Schwartz, J.H. and Jessell, T.M. (1991) *Principles of Neural Science*, 3rd edn. London: Prentice-Hall.

Kelley, S.J. (1992) Parenting stress and child maltreatment in drug-exposed children. *Child Abuse and Neglect*, 16, 317–328.

Lawson, M.S. and Wilson, G.S. (1980) Parenting among women addicted to narcotics. *Child Welfare*, 59, 67–79.

Mogielnicki, R.P., Mogielnicki, N.P., Chandler, J.E. and Weissberg, M.P. (1977) Impending child abuse: psychosomatic symptoms in adults as a clue. *Journal of the American Medical Association*, 237, 1109–1111.

Murphy, J.M., Jellinek, M., Quinn, D., Smith, G., Poitrast, F.G. and Goshko, M. (1991) Substance abuse and serious child mistreatment: prevalence, risk, and outcome in a court sample. *Child Abuse and Neglect*, 15, 197–211.

Oates, M. (1997) Patients as parents: the risk to children. *British Journal of Psychiatry*, 170 (suppl. 32), 22–27.

Oliver, J.E. (1985) Successive generations of child maltreatment: social and medical disorders in the parents. *British Journal of Psychiatry*, 147, 484–490.

Olofsson, M., Buckley, W., Anderson, G.E. and Friis-Hansen, B. (1983) Investigation of 89 children born by drug dependent mothers: II. Follow-up 1–10 years after birth. *Acta Paediatrica Scandinavica*, 72, 407–410.

Oppenheimer, R. (1981) At risk: children of female psychiatric patients. *Child Abuse and Neglect*, 5, 117–122.

Parton, N. (1985) *The Politics of Child Abuse*. London: Macmillan.

Reder, P. (1996a) Child protection: medical responsibilities. *Child Abuse Review*, 5, 64–66.

Reder, P. (1996b) Revised child protection arrangements for the health service. *Child Abuse Review*, 5, 128–132.

Reder, P. and Duncan, S. (1995) The meaning of the child. In: P. Reder and C. Lucey (eds) *Assessment of Parenting: Psychiatric and Psychological Contributions*. London: Routledge.

Reder, P. and Duncan, S. (1997) Adult psychiatry – a missing link in the child protection network: Comments on Falkov's 'Fatal Child Abuse and Parental Psychiatric Disorder' (DOH, 1996). *Child Abuse Review*, 6, 35–40.

Reder, P. and Duncan, S. (1999a) Conflictual relationships and risks of child abuse. *Journal of Child Centred Practice*, 6, 127–145.

Reder, P. and Duncan, S. (1999b) *Lost Innocents: A Follow-Up Study of Fatal Child Abuse*. London: Routledge.

Reder, P., Duncan, S. and Gray, M. (1993) *Beyond Blame: Child Abuse Tragedies Revisited*. London: Routledge.

Resnick, P.J. (1969) Child murder by parents: a psychiatric review of filicide. *American Journal of Psychiatry*, 126, 325–334.

Resnick, P.J. (1970) Murder of the newborn: a psychiatric review of neonaticide. *American Journal of Psychiatry*, 126, 1414–1420.

Rutter, M. and Quinton, D. (1984) Parental psychiatric disorder: effects on children. *Psychological Medicine*, 14, 853–880.

Schmitt, B.D. and Krugman, R.D. (1992) Abuse and neglect of children. In: R.E. Behrman (ed.) *Nelson Textbook of Pediatrics*, 14th edn. Philadelphia: Saunders.

Sheppard, M. (1997) Double jeopardy: the link between child abuse and maternal depression in child and family social work. *Child and Family Social Work*, 2, 91–107.

Steele, B. (1980) Psychodynamic factors in child abuse. In: C.H. Kempe and R.E. Helfer (eds) *The Battered Child*, 3rd edn. Chicago: University of Chicago Press.

Swadi, H. (1994) Parenting capacity and substance misuse: an assessment scheme. *ACPP Review and Newsletter*, 16, 237–244.

Taylor, C.G., Norman, D.K., Murphy, J.M., Jellinek, M., Quinn, D., Poitrast, F.G. and Goshko, M. (1991) Diagnosed intellectual and emotional impairment among parents who seriously mistreat their children: prevalence, type, and outcome in a court sample. *Child Abuse and Neglect*, 15, 389–401.

Wilczynski, A. (1997) *Child Homicide*. London: Greenwich Medical Media.

Wilson, G.S. (1989) Clinical studies of infants and children exposed prenatally to heroin. *Annals of New York Academy of Sciences*, 562, 183–194.

Woolley, P.V. and Evans, W.A. (1955) Significance of skeletal lesions in infants resembling those of traumatic origin. *Journal of the American Medical Association*, 158, 539–543.

Chapter 13

Health visitors, children and parental mental health problems

Renuka Jeyarajah Dent and Colleen McIntyre

Parenting is a complicated role involving a series of responsibilities and tasks performed within an on-going relationship. Parents must meet both the physical and psychological needs of their children and must protect them from physical harm, excessive distress and inappropriate social demands or exploitation (Hill, 1986). Parenting is not a quality that someone does or does not have but is a relationship which responds to fluctuations in other relationships (Reder and Lucey, 1995).

In the United Kingdom the National Health Service offers health professionals the opportunity to prepare and support parents in the care of their children. Health visiting began in 1867 with the Manchester and Salford Ladies Sanatory Reform Association employing 'respectable' women to go from door to door giving advice on health and hygiene (Hale *et al.*, 1968). The profession is much changed since then, especially with the establishment of the NHS in 1946, since when every family receives home visits, free of charge, for the first five years of each child's life. The health visitors' role is unique because, as fully qualified nurses, they offer unsolicited home visits to families with young children. The aim is for health visitors to recognise and assess health and relationship problems within the family as a whole and to initiate, at an early stage, the necessary actions on behalf of 'children in need' as described in the Children Act 1989. The health visitor seeks to encourage and empower adults in their role as parents but also to ensure that the children's well-being is not being jeopardised. The Department of Health suggests that this approach may reduce the chances of child maltreatment in the family (Home Office *et al.*, 1991) and has issued guidelines (Department of Health, 1997) on the responsibility of community nurses in relation to the recognition and referral of families under stress and of families where child maltreatment is suspected.

Although the main business of health visiting remains the one-to-one relationship with families, health visitors also have a role to play within the emphasis on public health in current government policy. In the last 150 years, there have been four distinct phases of public health, culminating in the present 'new public health' approach. This amalgamates strategies directed at

environmental change, personal preventive measures and therapeutic intervention – approaches which separately characterised the first three phases of
public health (Ashton and Seymour, 1988). The Community Practitioners
and Health Visitors Association (CPHVA, 1997) report four principles
underpinning the practice of their membership. These are: the search for
health needs; the stimulation of awareness of health needs; the influence on
policies affecting health; and the facilitation of health-enhancing activities.
Their more general perspective is informed by contact with a client caseload.
It is crucial that these principles are debated and adequately resourced during
the formulation of service level agreements. As primary health care professionals, they will require smooth and efficient referral routes to secondary
and tertiary services, such as child or adult mental health teams, and support
from these teams through liaison and consultation, in order to function
optimally in their role. This is especially important if health visitors are going
to work cost-effectively in the face of conflicting priorities and reducing
numbers. The CPHVA (1999) report that there is an urgent need to train new
health visitors but also to encourage those already in the profession to
remain. There are particular shortages in the profession amongst ethnic
minority groups (especially Asians) and men.

There is little doubt that health visiting has limited the amount of physical
neglect and malnutrition suffered by children in the UK (Browne, 1995).
However, child maltreatment is still one of the top five most common causes
of death to young children, with children under 5 being at particular risk of
death (Creighton, 1995) and, more generally, with 5 in every 1,000 of this age
group listed on Child Protection Registers nationally (Browne, 1995). Abuse,
while not always resulting in death, can present very serious danger to children in other ways, and, in England, 32 children in 10,000 require protection from maltreatment (Department of Health, 1995a). Reviews on the
causes of maltreatment have emphasised a growing recognition that child
abuse and neglect are products of a poor parent–child relationship (Browne,
1995), and interventions based on strengthening this relationship will be
most effective. Parental mental illness will in all probability have a negative
effect on this relationship and the health visitor will need to decide when
interventions provided by that service alone are not enough.

Assessing the impact of psychiatric problems on the on-going task of parenting is complex, especially because the effects on the child are often subtle
and concern the potential for emotional or physical harm rather than proven
abuse (Cassell and Coleman, 1995). There is a considerable literature on the
influence of parental psychiatric disorder on children (e.g. Beardslee *et al.*,
1983; Murray, 1992; Cummings and Davies, 1994). Psychiatric problems will
inevitably add additional stress to the already complex task of parenting. At
the very least, preoccupation with their own feelings will reduce the parent's
appropriate availability to the child and, at the other end of the spectrum,
distortions of reality involving the child can put the child in more immediate

danger. However, whether the parent's psychiatric problems are having psychological effects on the child to the level of 'significant harm' is often difficult to define. Similarly, little has been written about the risks of physical abuse or neglect when a child is living with a disturbed parent (Cassell and Coleman, 1995). However, parental mental health problems are often revealed in child abuse investigations (Farmer and Owen, 1995). Risk is frequently contextual and therefore focusing solely on the parent's psychiatric problems is likely to miss key indications of danger or, alternatively, lead to a lack of recognition of benefits in the care provided to the child. The child, parent and context within which they live will need careful analysis (Jeyarajah Dent, 1998). Falkov's (1996) study of parental psychiatric disorder and child deaths highlighted both the absence of adult psychiatric services' participation in child protection procedures and the failure of child agencies routinely to consider the implications of adult mental health problems for children (Falkov, 1997). The danger to children can only be assessed if all relevant information is brought together in one place.

In our discussion of the role of health visitors, we shall describe a survey undertaken in that part of central west London covered by the Riverside Community Healthcare (RCHC) NHS Trust to ascertain the prevalence of perceived parental psychiatric problems, the impact of these problems on parenting and the support available from other health and social services.

We describe the characteristics of the locality in which the study took place, the aims of the survey, its process and the main findings. We conclude with a discussion of the issues raised by the survey in terms of future good practice and ways forward, highlighting the pivotal role of health visitors at the interface between children's and adults' concerns, especially in the light of the current government's reported intention to support families through a preventive and evidence-based approach, with the swift delivery of multi-professional resources as defined by a family's need.

The survey

The RCHC Trust covers an area served by two health authorities – Ealing, Hammersmith and Hounslow (Jarman score 24.7) and Kensington, Chelsea and South Westminster (Jarman score 28.7, where the Jarman underprivileged areas score is a composite indicator of deprivation derived from a number of key variables – a high score indicates greater deprivation, poorer health and greater health care demands). The population covered by the Trust is ethnically diverse and contains a broad range of social class. The overall Jarman score for these areas is low in comparison to some other inner-city London boroughs (e.g. Camden and Islington) which should indicate decreased health care demands. However, there is considerable variation in scores within the areas: for example, Fulham scores 10.1 whilst White City scores 50 and, within South Westminster, which has an overall Jarman score of 24.5, there are both households lacking the basic amenities and those at the other end of the spectrum. An audit into 'failure to thrive' by the Trust's health visitors in 1995 identified that 9.4 per cent of under-5s had a growth pattern that required a health management plan (McIntyre and Collinson, 1997).

On average each health visitor participating in the survey had a caseload of 235 families, where the London average ranges between 200 and 400. In keeping with national trends, the Trust is currently changing its working practices from caseloads including all families to targeting particular families. Therefore, families become 'active' for an 'episode of care', or 'non-active', in which case there is no intervention. At the time of the survey, the total number of children on the Child Protection Register within the Trust was 202: 14 in South Westminster, 14 in South Kensington and Chelsea, whilst Hammersmith had 174. This probably reflects differences in local practice as the former boroughs intentionally have a higher threshold for registration, preferring to emphasise family support.

An initial informal examination of health visitor reports to child protection conferences had indicated that parental mental health problems were an important issue throughout the Trust. This survey was undertaken with the aim of quantifying the problem in order to improve the quality of the service offered to these families.

The aim of the survey was to establish:

- the prevalence of parental mental health problems within the population served by RCHC Trust's health visitors;
- the numbers of these parents whose parenting skills were, in the opinion of health visitors, adversely affected by their mental ill-health;
- the extent and effectiveness of multi-agency work.

The process involved training health visitors to increase their knowledge of what constitutes a mental health problem and the importance of their role in relation to this, and the completion of a three-part questionnaire by 46 health visitors under the supervision of clinical facilitators. The process ran from February to April 1998. Information from Pringle and Thompson (1986) was used to agree a shared understanding of the parameters of mental health problems in relation to neurotic and psychotic disorders.

The findings were that the 46 health visitors completed questionnaires on 10,800 families, all of whom had children under 5 years in order to qualify for health visitor intervention. In the opinion of the health visitors, 645 (6 per cent) of these families included a parent (in the majority of cases the mother) with mental health problems. Estimates of the prevalence of mental health problems in the general population vary considerably and should be treated with caution as studies use different definitions which are not necessarily comparable (Bird, 1999). An example is that 10–25 per cent of the general population annually present with mental health problems, usually in the primary care setting, and within this figure 2–4 per cent will have a severe mental illness, with a smaller number suffering a severe and enduring mental illness.

Further analysis of these 645 families was undertaken. Health visitors considered that in 264 (42 per cent) of these families parenting was adversely affected by mental health problems. In other words, they considered at least one child in the family to be a child 'in need' or requiring 'protection' as defined by the Children Act (1989). This constituted 2 per cent of the original sample of 10,800 studied. Interestingly, 153 (24 per cent) of the sample of 645 had been referred to a general psychiatrist. This allowed the health visitors' analysis of the parental mental health problem to be compared with the diagnosis obtained from a mental health specialist. The overall diagnostic profiles given by both the specialists and health visitors were similar. Depression was considered to be by far the most common problem identified by both, occurring in some form in 67 per cent of those parents deemed to be suffering from a mental health problem.

What was clear was that a relevant number of parents were considered by health visitors to be suffering mental ill-health (only some of whom had been referred to a general psychiatrist) and for one-third of them this was thought to be adversely affecting parenting. There was a variation between the boroughs in the numbers of families thought to have a parent with mental ill-health; Westminster had the largest numbers, with 247 out of 1,638 (15 per cent) families studied said to be affected, in 83 (5 per cent) of which, parenting was thought to be adversely affected.

Each health visitor taking part in the survey was also asked to fill in more detail on one family from their recent caseload, in which they thought parenting ability was adversely affected by mental ill-health. Parental depression and domestic violence figured highly in these cases and around half of the children in the families were considered to be at risk of suffering significant harm. Although the health visitors had attended inter-agency meetings on the majority of these families, few of these had included adult mental health professionals. By contrast, in most instances it had been the health visitors who had initiated contact with the family's GP, social services or adult mental health services.

Despite the high level of inter-agency activity required by the 41 families, health visitors reported feelings that they were working in isolation, without support from other agencies, and had inadequate knowledge in their work more generally with parents suffering mental ill-health. Health visitors were asked to list their main concerns about working with families containing adults with mental health problems, to give examples of both successful and unsuccessful inter-agency work and to suggest ways in which inter-agency work could be improved. Answers to these 'free-flow' questions were not easy to analyse as similar themes often appeared in all questions and many more respondents answered questions relating to problems than to successes with inter-agency working.

However, a number of common themes could be identified, which are given below as negative or positive themes.

Negative themes

- Lack of personal knowledge and experience of adult mental health conditions and lack of support from mental health services – for example, sometimes having to encourage parents to engage with medication regimes or other interventions without enough information.
- GP's reluctance to refer on to adult mental health services, and health visitors being unable to do this without their agreement.
- Difficulties with assessing risk to the child, especially when the parents do not seem to be coping.
- Lack of being listened to by other agencies and general difficulties in engaging social services.
- Lack of support in working with those families with parental mental health problems that are not serious enough to warrant referral to psychiatrists, even when feeling out of their depth.
- A lack of resources in general – for example, difficulty finding the time for the work required with the families and a long waiting list in the local child and family mental health service.
- Lack of feedback from other agencies – for example, the need for a diagnosis of the parent's problem and details of the appropriate treatment.
- Fears for personal safety.
- A child's safety not taking precedence over confidentiality in the work of some professionals.
- Depressed adults who sometimes lacked motivation to seek help, so the family did not get the required help.
- Parental problems seen in isolation from those of the children by, for example, information being held in different agencies and remaining unintegrated.

Positive themes

In a sense these themes related to the flip side of the negative themes. In other words, there were examples of successful liaison with specific agencies – for example, a child and family consultation service, child psychologists, the perinatal team and the psychotherapist who attends the child health clinic. The advice and joint work offered by community psychiatric nurses were also appreciated.

Health visitors said that inter-agency work could be improved by regular planning meetings with adult mental health specialists; by sharing of information, including that relating to successful and unsuccessful intervention and parental illness; and by joint training and case presentations. Respecting and valuing each other's roles and opinions were also mentioned.

The four most common themes in answers to the free-flow questions were:

- the role of the GP which was perceived as unsupportive;
- a general lack of resources to draw on in supporting the families;
- the need for more training;
- the need for more time to work effectively with the families.

Discussion

Limitations in resources make it essential for health visitors to prioritise families according to need. The pattern of contact with families where parents suffer mental ill-health will of necessity be increased and health visitors will have to consider if enough support is available from child care agencies. This is especially the case now that the Department of Health is encouraging a wide spectrum of family support to be offered by a variety of agencies, as required and often before the involvement of social services. This survey highlighted the demands made on one particular health visiting service by families with parental mental ill-health, and the health visitors' perception of inadequate support in their work with these families. It should be noted that the figures quoted in this survey are likely to be an underestimate of the prevalence of mental health problems in parents of children and adolescents in the general population as families were only included if they had children under the age of 5 years. In the course of routine primary care a substantial proportion of mothers experiencing depression, for example, go undetected and receive no additional help from the health service (Seeley et al., 1996).

This survey highlighted depression as the most prevalent mental illness in those families with young children. Downey and Coyne (1990) give a useful review of the literature in relation to parental depression and its effects on children. They cite evidence from research which shows that depression is highly prevalent among women of child-bearing age, with approximately 8 per cent of mothers being clinically depressed at any given time, and rising to 12 per cent in mothers who have recently given birth. Downey and Coyne conclude that there is a high rate of serious psychological problems in children of depressed parents but warn against simplistic notions of the nature of this link. There may be contextual factors that produce spurious relations between parenting provided by depressed parents and the difficulties experienced by their children. In our survey, for example, there was a high number of families in the sample studied in depth for whom domestic violence was a reality, and the effect that this has on children both materially and psychologically is likely to be considerable.

Anecdotal evidence points to health visitors working almost exclusively with mothers, excepting circumstances where the father is the single parent. This reflects societal attitudes which place parenting as the primary responsibility of the mother and thus present the health visitor with little opportunity to assess the parenting skills of the father. O'Hagan (1993) has even suggested that not working with fathers and concentrating on the mother can amount to the institutional abuse of women. This is perhaps most relevant in depression where feelings of powerlessness are common. All professionals working to protect children should recognise the importance of assessing the child and carer in the context in which they live: in other words, taking account of all the caretakers, their relationship to the child and their relationships with each other.

Mentally ill parents present a complex challenge to health visitors. A common complaint by those participating in this survey was the lack of information from other agencies, particularly in relation to the parental illness. Several reviews of child abuse deaths have also shown the lack of information shared by adult mental health services (Falkov, 1996). However, this survey also showed that health visitors had great difficulty obtaining referral of parents to adult mental health services, with the GP being seen as particularly unresponsive to the health visitors' concerns, and it would seem to us that the perceived lack of support by GPs is an important factor to be remedied for future good practice, especially with the inception of 'primary care groups'.

There are many possible implications for practice but in this chapter we will concentrate on six.

First, health visitors work with families on an assigned GP practice list and it is important that they meet frequently with the GP in order to discuss cases that are causing concern, including mothers receiving antenatal care. In this way, information and responsibility are shared.

Second, care planning meetings are held by adult mental health specialists in relation to individual patients. To ensure consideration of the whole family we recommend that health visitors be invited to all meetings for patients in families where there are children under 5 years. Indeed, health visitors within the RCHC Trust are now beginning to meet regularly in their localities with multi-professional teams which include adult mental health specialists. If community psychiatric nurses were attached to primary care teams, this would further increase links between adult mental health and child welfare services.

Third, health visitors reported a wish for more training. Indeed, Seeley *et al.* (1996) have shown that, with the provision of modest resources, health visitors can be trained in the detection and management of, for example, postnatal depression and associated difficulties in the mother–infant relationship, and can deliver an intervention that is both effective and highly acceptable to depressed mothers. In our opinion this 'training' should include both the opportunity to update knowledge on psychiatric conditions and treatment regimes *and* regular case consultancy with a professional such as a child psychologist or psychiatrist. This could provide the opportunity to look at cases with the child's welfare as the primary focus; aid in formulating the right questions to adult mental health specialists; and address the impact of parenting on the child. This would add a different professional perspective to supervision.

Fourth, health visitors complained that they lacked time to do the work required. This is a frequent complaint nationally. Browne (1995) reports that health visitors are now forced to undertake fewer home visits because the profession is not being adequately resourced or developed; and Collinson and Cowley (1998) write about the difficulty of assessing need and prioritising families after just one visit following the birth of a baby, as is recommended by the Audit Commission (1994). Central government appears keen to strengthen the role of health visitors and, clearly, resource issues will need to be addressed.

Fifth, this survey identified the need in one Trust for health visitors to exchange information with adult psychiatric services and thus better identify the impact of mental illness on the family, particularly in relation to parenting. The study could be developed further by auditing a selection of files in order to analyse how much time these families actually demand and at what points in the cases' history additional resources may have been required by health visitors. We suggest that this is an important issue as health visitors are inevitably working with possible risk to children and are entitled to the protection of a total and systematic managerial approach to risk-taking in the service. The risk strategy should include having an integrated policy and procedure for information sharing and decision making and, critically, should make provision for learning from experience. Carson (1998) explains the various aspects to be considered in such a strategy.

Effectiveness and a primary-care-led health service are two current national policies for the NHS. Data collection and analysis within defined areas of policy and procedure could give direction and support to developments regarding clinical effectiveness and evidence-based practice in the primary care of the families that are identified through this survey. This issue is an important one. Robinson (1999) reports that identified concerns around health visiting have not been systematically researched or addressed through policy action. This survey presents the opportunity to study further the policies required to support a particularly vulnerable group of families, and to consider how child-focused and adult-focused specialists can work together for the benefit of the child.

Sixth, health visitors clearly hold a pivotal position at the interface between children's and parents' concerns. This is demonstrated by the findings of this survey and, more generally, in many current central government publications and initiatives – for example, *Supporting Families* (Home Office Ministerial

Group on the Family, 1998) and *Sure Start* (Department for Education and Employment, 1999). The government has recognised the universal, non-stigmatising, non-judgemental nature of health-visiting work and also the need for other agencies to be involved at the appropriate threshold. Health visitors have the unique opportunity to identify mental health problems in parents, seek appropriate interventions and consider possible threat to the children in the family. In this survey many health visitors in one health trust covering an inner-city area reported a lack of support from other agencies in their work with these parents. Many also reported not having the time or the knowledge to work effectively with them. This has important implications for the implementation of 'Sure Start'. If health visitors, with considerable core qualifications, experience difficulties in working with and empowering this client group, then it is likely that the 'resourceful friend' concept suggested by the initiative will need to consider these difficulties when putting projects into operation. In the survey health visitors reported identifying mental health difficulties faced by parents but feeling powerless to really influence the situation. With the injection of new money and clear emphasis on collaboration detailed by 'Sure Start', parents should be able to get the help they need to give their children a better start in life. Health visitors are in a good position to influence policy and resources.

In ending, we need to acknowledge the frequently-documented problems with multi-agency working together in order to ensure that the best interests of the child prevail (e.g. Department of Health, 1995b). The survey described in this chapter highlighted the difficulties experienced by health visitors in engaging social workers and adult mental health specialists. The Department of Health is advocating a continuum of provision for families, with formal child protection investigations being undertaken only as a last resort. This approach requires close multi-agency planning and our survey identified the need for improvements in liaison between professionals working with mentally ill parents. It would appear that the training of adult mental health specialists needs to address further their role in relation to promoting the welfare of children.

Resource implications have already been acknowledged as an important consideration, but audits of child protection files by the first author of this chapter (RJD) have illustrated the often sequential or parallel (rather than integrated) assessments by different professionals on each file, leading to poor case formulation and planning. This will not benefit the children who most need our support and protection.

Acknowledgements

We are grateful to the 46 health visitors who cooperated with this study in completing questionnaires relating to 10,800 families.

Special thanks to Carol Gayle and Sonia Stewart (Health Visitor Clinical

Facilitators) for their assistance in the planning and preparation required for this survey.

References

Ashton, J. and Seymour, H. (1988) *The New Public Health*. Milton Keynes: Open University Press.

Audit Commission (1994) *Seen But Not Heard*. London: HMSO.

Beardslee, W.R., Bemporad, J., Keller, M.B. and Klerman, G.L. (1983) Children of parents with major affective disorder: a review. *American Journal of Psychiatry*, 140, 825–832.

Bird, L. (1999) *The Fundamental Facts*. London: Mental Health Foundation.

Browne, K. (1995) Preventing child maltreatment through community nursing. *Journal of Advanced Nursing*, 21, 57–63.

Carson, D. (1998) Reducing the riskiness of risk assessment. In: R. Jeyarajah Dent (ed.) *Dangerous Care: Working to Protect Children*. London: The Bridge Child Care Development Service.

Cassell, D. and Coleman, R. (1995) Parents with psychiatric problems. In: P. Reder and C. Lucey (eds) *Assessment of Parenting: Psychiatric and Psychological Contributions*. London: Routledge.

Collinson, S. and Cowley, S. (1998) An exploratory study of demand for the health visiting service within a marketing framework. *Journal of Advanced Nursing*, 28, 499–507.

CPHVA (Community Practitioners and Health Visitors' Association) (1997) Public health: the role of nurses and health visitors. London: CPHVA.

CPHVA (Community Practitioners and Health Visitors' Association) (1999) A CPHVA response to *Supporting Families – A Consultation Document*. London: CPHVA.

Creighton, S.J. (1995) Fatal child abuse: how preventable is it? *Child Abuse Review*, 4, 318–328.

Cummings, E.M. and Davies, P.T. (1994) Maternal depression and child development. *Journal of Child Psychology and Psychiatry*, 35, 73–112.

Department for Education and Employment (1999) *Sure Start: Making a Difference for Children and Families*. London: DfEE.

Department of Health (1995a) *Children and Young Persons on Child Protection Registers – Year Ending 31 March 1995, England*. Personal Social Services Local Authority Statistics. London: HMSO.

Department of Health (1995b) *Messages from Research*. London: HMSO.

Department of Health (1997) *Child Protection: Guidance for Senior Nurses, Health Visitors and Midwives*. London: HMSO.

Downey, G. and Coyne, J.C. (1990) Children of depressed parents: an integrative review. *Psychological Bulletin*, 108, 50–76.

Falkov, A. (1996) *Study of 'Working Together' Part 8 Reports: Fatal Child Abuse and Parental Psychiatric Disorder*. London: HMSO.

Falkov, A. (1997) Adult psychiatry – a missing link in the child protection network: a response to Reder and Duncan. *Child Abuse Review*, 6, 41–45.

Farmer, E. and Owen, M. (1995) *Child Protection Practice: Private Risks and Public Remedies*. London: HMSO.

Hale, R., Loveland, M. and Owen, G. (1968) *Principles and Practice of Health Visiting.* Oxford: Pergamon.

Hill, P. (1986) Child psychiatry. In: P. Hill, R. Murray and A. Thornley (eds) *Essentials of Post Graduate Psychiatry.* London: Harcourt & Stratton.

Home Office, Department of Health, Department of Education and Science and Welsh Office (1991) *Working Together under the Children Act: A Guide to Arrangements for Inter-Agency Co-operation.* London: HMSO.

Home Office Ministerial Group on the Family (1998) *Supporting Families – A Consultation Document.* London: HMSO.

Jeyarajah Dent, R. (1998) BridgeALERT: key information for identifying children in danger. In: R. Jeyarajah Dent (ed.) *Dangerous Care: Working to Protect Children.* London: The Bridge Child Care Development Service.

McIntyre, C. and Collinson, M. (1997) Failure to thrive: a prevalence audit. *Health Visitor Journal,* 70, 254–256.

Murray, L. (1992) The impact of postnatal depression on infant development. *Journal of Child Psychology and Psychiatry,* 33, 543–561.

O'Hagan, K. (1993) *Emotional and Psychological Abuse of Children.* Buckingham: Open University Press.

Pringle, N. and Thompson, P.J. (1986) *Social Work, Psychiatry and the Law.* London: Heinemann.

Reder, P. and Lucey, C. (eds) (1995) *Assessment of Parenting: Psychiatric and Psychological Contributions.* London: Routledge.

Robinson, J. (1999) Domiciliary health visiting. A systematic review. *Community Practitioner,* 72, 15–18.

Seeley, S., Murray, L. and Cooper, P.J. (1996) The outcome for mothers and babies of health visitor intervention. *Health Visitor,* 69, 135–138.

Chapter 14

Needs assessment in the children of parents with major psychiatric illness

Juliet Singer, Sylvia Tang and Mark Berelowitz

The concept of need has gained currency in the planning of modern health and welfare services. For example, the 1989 Children Act promotes a concept of 'children in need', the Care Programme Approach emphasises identifying patients' unmet needs, and purchasers are required to identify priorities of needs so that resources can be targeted. There are considerable methodological difficulties in measuring unmet need, as the definition of need varies according to the perspective of the organisation, discipline or body assessing it. Needs-based purchasing plans for child mental health services, based on epidemiological data, have been attempted (Light and Bailey, 1993). However, the prospect of joint commissioning with other agencies such as social services, education and housing, voluntary bodies and the law enforcement agencies (NHS Health Advisory Service, 1995) will mean that this type of calculation and therefore the tools used to measure need have to take into account differing estimates of need made by different agencies.

In relation to the duties of local authorities to provide for children in need, the Children Act 1989 includes within its definition children who are 'unlikely to achieve or maintain, or have the opportunity of achieving or maintaining, a reasonable standard of healthy development without the provision of services by a local authority'. The Department of Health has nine categories of children in need, including those who have need as a result of: parents' or carers' disability, illness, mental illness or addictions; or, living within an unstable, stressed, conflictual, emotionally or developmentally damaging family (Department of Health, 1997, quoted by Cleaver *et al.*, 1999).

The Medical Research Council defines *need for mental health services* as being present when (a) there is functional impairment, and (b) this is due to some potentially remediable or preventable cause – for example, psychopathology for which there is effective and acceptable treatment (Brewin *et al.*, 1987; Bebbington *et al.*, 1996). This differs from *epidemiology*, which is about the prevalence of specific disorders within the population. Although a great deal is known about child psychiatric epidemiology, little is known about the extent and correlates of unmet need for mental health services in community samples of children and adolescents. One study (Flisher *et al.*, 1997) found that unmet need was significantly associated with indicators of economic disadvantage, parental psychopathology, and poor school grades. They also found parent-reported access barriers, such as concern that the child would want to solve their problems unassisted, would refuse to attend services or would be hospitalised or taken away against the parent's will.

A group of children very much at risk for having significant unmet needs are the children of parents with mental health problems. Indeed, as has been extensively documented, children of parents with major mental illness are at high risk of developing clinically significant psychological disturbances (Rutter and Quinton, 1984; Rutter and Cox, 1985; Beardslee *et al.*, 1983; Cummings and Davies, 1994). The needs of these children are likely to extend beyond mental health services, and input from educational services, social services and other organisations may also be necessary at some point.

However, there may be some structural obstacles to identifying children in need when the origins of the need lie within the parents or adult carers. *Children's Needs – Parenting Capacity* (Cleaver *et al.*, 1999) was commissioned by the Department of Health in recognition of the connections between children's welfare and development and parents' circumstances. It found persistent problems in formal collaboration between services for adults and children, which have come about because of a variety of professional, legislative and structural reasons. The report goes on to state that these create boundaries around adult and children's services which are difficult to permeate and which undermine the achievement of an holistic approach to the needs of patients.

It seems likely that, for such children, the referral, uptake and compliance with services may depend on a variety of factors that are associated with the parental mental illness.

Awareness by professionals of children and their needs

As Oates (1997) has indicated, the prevalence of patients as parents is substantial, at around 25 per cent of all adult psychiatric patients, although adult services may not be aware of a proportion of these. Adult psychiatric case notes of patients who are parents may not contain any information at all about the patient's children (Tamarit and Yin-Har Lau, 1999). In spite of the often harrowing events that attend a parent's hospitalisation, the children usually remain 'invisible' to staff. Even when they are acknowledged, the best of psychiatric care tends to overlook the effects on the child (Shachnow, 1987).

However, it seems that dependent children may be taken into account when assessments under the Mental Health Act are undertaken, although possibly not in a way that meets the best interests of the child. Hatfield *et al.* (1997) looked at 3,554 Mental Health Act assessments, and found that parents of dependent children were significantly less likely to be detained following assessment.

Parental perceptions of child maladjustment

Parents may be inaccurate both in under- and overestimating their children's problems. For example, depressed mothers whose children have high levels of non-compliant behaviour tend to over-rate psychiatric disorder in their children (Brody and Forehand, 1986). Hoberman (1992) attributed the high proportion of unmet need for services among children and adolescents to parents having difficulty in assessing the presence of psychiatric disorder in their children. Stormont et al. (1997) interviewed adult inpatients with psychotic illnesses and found that 26 per cent believed their children had psychological problems, 53 per cent thought their own illness was bad for the children, and 37 per cent thought their children needed help.

Parental mental illness

Aspects of the parental psychopathology, such as paranoid ideation or delusions, phobic or obsessional symptoms, lack of energy and motivation, lack of insight into their own illness and non-engagement, disorganisation and fears over children being taken from them, may all interfere with the child's access to, and appropriate use of, services. Also, some children may be placed with relatives or in foster care when their parent is admitted, thereby losing the link with the service which knows their parent well. Children may have very negative images of services through contact associated with their parent.

The study

We therefore decided to attempt one form of needs assessment in children of a community sample of mothers with major mental illness. The intention was to assess their lifetime qualitative and quantitative disturbances and to establish what input these children had received from psychiatric services, social services, education and other agencies. It was hoped that this study would give more understanding of what treatment was needed for these children, how it could be provided, and how links between child and adult services could be strengthened.

A further aspect of this study was to assess the children's perceptions and beliefs regarding the parental illness and how these correlated with the mothers' knowledge about their children's understanding.

The study was conducted in stages. Initially an audit was undertaken of the psychiatric morbidity in children of psychiatric patients attending a hospital, along with an evaluation of the children's understanding of their parent's disorder and their service utilisation. The next stage, to be reported elsewhere, will be to compare these findings with a relevant control group. The project was developed jointly between the Child and Adolescent Department and the Adult Psychiatry service at the Royal Free Hospital in London.

Method

To collect our audit sample we approached all the adult psychiatrists in the service, who gave us names from their outpatient list of female patients who had children. Over a six-month period senior house officers and registrars completed forms in their outpatient clinics documenting the patients they saw who fitted our criteria. Community psychiatric nurses and social workers also identified appropriate patients from their caseloads. We gained consent from all the consultant adult psychiatrists to approach their patients directly.

The subjects were mothers who met the following criteria:

1   having children between the ages of 6 and 16 years living at home;
2   *and* having had at least one hospital admission since the age of 18 years and currently attending the outpatient clinic.

Where there was more than one child in a family, up to two children were interviewed. These were chosen according to their age, the two who were closest to 12 years being identified.

A major concern we had was whether these mothers would allow us to interview their children. We felt it was extremely important to interview the children directly in order to access accurately their psychopathology and level of functioning. Many studies have reported variable diagnostic agreement between parent and child (Orvaschel *et al.*, 1981; Barrett *et al.*, 1991) and, although mothers were generally more capable than children of providing information on factual or time-related material, children had to be interviewed in order to obtain valid information about their own internal states, such as mood swings, fears and feelings of guilt.

In order to maximise the numbers of mothers who consented to take part we felt it important to discuss the project with them in person rather than seek their consent via letter. An introductory letter was sent from their consultant explaining in brief that a study was being conducted and that a researcher would contact them. They were then contacted by telephone and an appointment was made to visit them at their home where the project was discussed with them in detail, they were given an information sheet and their formal consent was obtained. They were offered a £10 store voucher as a token of our appreciation of their time.

The following instruments were utilised for the first-stage audit:

KIDDIE-SADS (lifetime version) (K-SADS-PL, version 1.0, based on Puig-Antich and Chambers, 1978) A semi-structured diagnostic interview designed to assess current and past episodes of psychopathology in children and adolescents according to DSM-III-R and DSM-IV criteria. A C-GAS (Children's Global Assessment Scale) score is also generated (Shaffer *et al.*, 1983). This interview is first done with the mother and then the child.

Strengths and Difficulties Questionnaire plus Impact Supplement (Goodman, 1997)   A brief self-report behavioural screening questionnaire that provides balanced coverage of children's behaviours, emotions and relationships. This is completed independently by the child, mother and teacher.

Questions about service utilisation   Mothers were asked whether their child had had contact with any of a wide range of services provided by health, education or social services. Contact with Child Psychiatry was checked in that department. The mother's opinion was sought as to ways the service helped or did not help, or, if offers of assistance were turned down or were terminated by the family, why this was. She was also asked what help she would have liked both in the past and currently with respect to her child(ren).

Questions about children's perceptions and beliefs regarding their mother's illness   A semi-structured interview was developed by the researchers to assess what the children understood was the matter with their mother, why she had to go to hospital, what treatment she was given and why, how they thought the illness happened, and how it affected them. The children were also asked what opportunities they had to talk to others about questions or concerns they may have had. The mothers were given a 'mirror image' of this interview asking them how they thought their child would answer if asked those questions.

Thirty-three patients who potentially met the criteria were identified from the Royal Free Hospital catchment area, but four cases were excluded, one due to chronic physical illness, and three due to poor English. The remaining 29 patients had between them 55 children, including 45 aged 6–16 years. (The total number of adults aged 17–55 years attending the Outpatient Department in a six month period was 625.)

Five mothers, all of whom suffered from psychotic illnesses, refused outright, for the following stated reasons: not wanting school to be contacted; 'Talking about my illness, anything to do with the hospital scares me . . . I'm getting better, I don't want to be reminded of any of it'; '£10 isn't enough' (the patient appeared quite unwell, being thought disordered and agitated); another mother, after she received our first introductory letter, wrote back saying she had been harassed by letters for two years, stated she was not a psychiatric patient and threatened legal action; did not give a reason. In addition, one mother completed interviews but her 15-year-old daughter did not want to take part.

Of the remaining 23, 12 mothers (14 children) were interviewed for the first stage of the audit. A further 11 have proven extremely difficult to contact or complete the assessments with, despite several attempts, including telephone calls, letters and home visits. We shall comment further on the possible relevance of these non-participants when considering the needs of this group of children.

Results

General demographic information

Eleven of the 12 mothers were Caucasian. The number of times, since their child's birth, these mothers had been admitted to hospital ranged between 1 and 9 admissions (mean = 3.8 admissions). The length of time they had spent in hospital, again since their child's birth, varied from 1 week to 9 months (mean = 3.7 months). Seven were single parents and in only three cases was the child's natural father still with the mother. One of the 13 fathers was known to have schizophrenia, one pre-senile dementia, and the rest were said by the mothers not to have any psychiatric disorder. There were three only children. Only one sibling of the research children was in the care of the local authority.

The mean age of the children was 10.9 years, with a range of 8–15 years.

Children's psychiatric state

Table 14.1 summarises the identified mental heath problems of the children. Taking all sources of information into account, 11 out of 14 children (79 per cent) had a lifetime psychiatric diagnosis from at least one source, and 10 out of 14 (71 per cent) had a current diagnosis. In terms of comorbidity, 11 out of 14 (79 per cent) attracted more than one lifetime diagnosis, and 9 out of 14 (64 per cent) more than one current diagnosis. Two children had possible abnormal perceptions (hallucinations), but the common diagnoses were mood disorders, anxiety disorders, and behavioural disorders (oppositional defiant disorder and attention deficit disorder).

The Strengths and Difficulties Questionnaire (SDQ), which was completed by mothers, children aged over 11 years, and teachers, was our only source of information from outside the family. Overall, the SDQ domain scores showed a wide number of affected areas, with the teachers rating the classroom impact (difficulties which distress the children and interfere with daily life) more highly than the parents or children (see Table 14.2).

In terms of Global Assessment Scale scores, most children scored between 40 and 60, which equates with fluctuating or moderate impairment in several areas of daily functioning.

With regard to service utilisation, only two children (siblings) were in current treatment with a child mental health service. Two others had had brief

Table 14.1 Summary of fourteen cases, showing mother's diagnosis, child's diagnosis, services offered and uptake issues

Case no.	Child's age	Child's sex	Mother's diagnosis	Child's K-SADS diagnosis (lifetime)	Services offered (and uptake issues, comments from the mother)
1(a)	14	Male	Recurrent depressive disorder	Major depressive disorder, aged 8 yrs, 10 yrs and currently Social phobia, from aged 5 yrs Generalised anxiety disorder, from aged 12 yrs	Family therapy arranged by adult psychiatrist (attended for 3 weeks, but 'poorly organised and children didn't like it')
1(b)	12	Female	(same mother)	Major depressive disorder, aged 11 yrs Generalised anxiety disorder Bulimia nervosa, from aged 12 yrs	Family therapy (see above) Foster care (mother felt she was not well looked after)
2	13	Male	Recurrent depressive disorder Generalised anxiety disorder	Separation anxiety, long-standing Attention deficit disorder, long-standing Oppositional defiant disorder, since 11 yrs Transient tic disorder, aged 11 yrs	School referred to child psychiatrist aged 3 yrs (attended 'a few months') Attended a special school for 3 weeks (didn't like it and returned to mainstream schooling) Paediatrician advised Ritalin (mother refused it) Currently seeing educational psychologist every 3 weeks
3	15	Male	Borderline personality disorder Substance misuse	No diagnosis	Nil
4	11	Female	Borderline personality disorder Recurrent depressive disorder	No diagnosis	Respite foster care during admissions ('unhappy and lonely there') Child and family social worker Nursery placement and childminder so mother could attend psychiatric day-centre Child psychiatry outpatients (seen three times but this was not mentioned by mother)

Case	Age	Sex	Mother's diagnosis	Child's diagnoses	Services/interventions
5(a)	9	Female	Recurrent depressive disorder	Separation anxiety, long-standing Major depressive disorder, 4–5 yrs	Social services offered childminder (but arranged privately) School tutor (arranged by mother) Family therapy (attending currently, 'might be useful, need to learn about parenting')
5(b)	8	Female	(same mother)	Separation anxiety, long-standing Oppositional defiant disorder, from 4 yrs Post-traumatic stress disorder, aged 6 yrs Obsessive compulsive disorder, from 8 yrs	As above, for 5(a)
6	13	Female	Recurrent depressive disorder	Separation anxiety disorder, aged 7–11 yrs Attention deficit disorder, long-standing Post-traumatic stress disorder, aged 9 yrs Adjustment disorder, aged 10 yrs Oppositional defiant disorder, from 10 yrs Major depressive disorder, aged 12 yrs Specific phobia	GP referred to child psychiatrist (attended for 3 months but 'found it difficult') Educational psychologist After-school club
7	11	Male	Recurrent depressive disorder Generalised anxiety disorder Substance misuse	Enuresis, aged 7 yrs Attention deficit disorder, long-standing	Special educational needs coordinator (classroom assistance) School counsellor (offer not taken up)
8	14	Female	Borderline personality disorder	Post-traumatic stress disorder, aged 5 yrs Major depressive disorder, aged 11 yrs Oppositional defiant disorder, from 11 yrs Anorexia nervosa, aged 12 yrs Bulimia nervosa, current Major depressive disorder, current	Nursery place Play scheme Child Protection Register, up to 10 yrs Special (EBD) school, from aged 11 yrs ('very helpful') Child psychiatry, aged 13 yrs (stopped second appointment, 'they were biased because I am lesbian')

Table 14.1 continued

Case no.	Child's age	Child's sex	Mother's diagnosis	Child's K-SADS diagnosis (lifetime)	Services offered (and uptake issues, comments from the mother)
9	10	Female	Bipolar affective disorder	No diagnosis	Child Protection Register, aged 1–3 yrs Nursery place Child and family social worker Foster care for respite and during mother's admissions After-school club Family therapy (attended for 3 sessions, 'not helpful')
10	8	Female	Paranoid schizophrenia	Enuresis, current Adjustment disorder	Nursery place ('good, learnt to talk') Family therapy, aged 2 yrs ('didn't help') Child Protection Register, current, for third time Play schemes Foster care, for admissions and respite
11	15	Male	Depressive episode	Generalised anxiety disorder, current Attention deficit disorder, current	Play schemes After-school club
12	14	Male	Bipolar affective disorder	Adjustment disorder, aged 11 yrs Major depressive disorder with psychotic features, aged 12 yrs	Foster care Play schemes (offered, child refused) Educational psychologist (saw 3 times until he retired) Special (EBD) school from 13 yrs ('extremely helpful, became happy') Child psychiatry (referred but child refused to attend)

episodes of treatment in the past, and one family had had a substantial period of treatment many years previously. Three had ended treatment prematurely after very few appointments. One was referred but refused to attend. Twenty-three per cent had a child and family social worker, although all 14 might be defined as children in need. Four had had at least one period in foster care, and three were currently or had previously been on the Child Protection Register. Play schemes, nurseries and after-school clubs were all very important for these families. Three children had seen an educational psychologist, and two attended a school for children with emotional or behavioural disturbances (EBD). One boy was referred to an EBD school but refused to attend.

Three mothers believed that their children did not think they had an illness. These children had various views on this. One believed her mother suffered from an 'interphobic evil illness'; one replied 'she's not right in the head'; and one thought her mother had an illness but did not know what it was called.

Eight mothers thought their children would reply 'don't know' if asked how they thought their mother's illness or problem occurred. Only one child did in fact give this answer, the others had varied explanations: 'she can't cope with kids, with everyday life'; 'caused by a dramatic event'; 'everything gets on top of her, like with dad dying and the bills . . .'; 'if me and my brother keep fighting'. One child gave a detailed explanation of what she thought her mother's illness (schizophrenia) was due to, saying 'if someone has a bad dream, the voices in the dream stay in their head for the rest of their life until the hospital gives them medication. The person can do nothing about it . . . it could happen to anyone who had a really bad dream.'

There was almost total agreement between parent and child in terms of how the child would recognise if their mother was not feeling well. Themes such as being tired, moody, shouting and crying emerged strongly. Three mothers did not think that when they were unwell it affected their child, although they reported changes in their own behaviour when unwell. All the children reported experiencing strong negative emotions when their mothers were in hospital, such as confused, upset, angry, lonely, anxious, missing her. A number of mothers recognised that their children were upset when they left to go to hospital, but they did not seem to be aware of how distressed their children felt whilst they were staying in hospital or when they were unwell at home. For example, one mother said her daughter 'got upset when I was taken to hospital', though her daughter told us she felt angry, got into fights at school, and at home would stay in her room and cry a lot during her mother's admission. One mother said that, although her son missed her while she was in hospital, he 'carried on as normal'. He, on the other hand, described feeling unhappy and angry and found himself getting behind with his school work as it was hard to concentrate. All of the children felt the hospital admissions were helpful for their mothers, for various reasons

Table 14.2 Findings from Strengths and Difficulties Questionnaire, as scored by parent, child and teacher

Case no.	Impact score (how much child's difficulties affect day-to-day functioning)			Domains (areas in which child is showing difficulties)			Global Assessment Score (score of 50 indicates moderate degree of interference in functioning; below 50 more severe impairment)
	Parent	Child	Teacher	Parent	Child	Teacher	
1(a)	normal	borderline	abnormal	pro-social emotional	emotional	pro-social emotional peer	50
1(b)	normal	borderline	normal	emotional peer	nil	nil	45
2	borderline	borderline	abnormal	hyperactivity emotional peer	nil	pro-social conduct hyperactivity	41
3	normal	borderline	abnormal	nil	nil	pro-social hyperactivity	60
4	normal	normal	normal	nil	nil	nil	75
5(a)	borderline	n/a	normal	emotional	n/a	nil	50
5(b)	normal	n/a	normal	conduct	n/a	emotional	45
6	borderline	normal	abnormal	conduct emotional hyperactivity	emotional peer hyperactivity	pro-social hyperactivity	45
7	normal	borderline	abnormal	hyperactivity	conduct	pro-social conduct hyperactivity	50

8	normal	abnormal	borderline	conduct emotional peer hyperactivity	conduct emotional hyperactivity	conduct hyperactivity	45
9	normal	n/a	abnormal	conduct	n/a	conduct	65
10	normal	n/a	borderline	conduct	n/a	pro-social conduct	61
11	borderline	normal	abnormal	nil	nil	pro-social conduct emotional peer hyperactivity	45
12	abnormal	borderline	normal	nil	conduct	nil	55

including being away from stress, and two said explicitly that admissions were good for their mother because they gave her a break from them.

We enquired whether these mothers had been given any help in explaining their problems to their children. Only two mothers had been offered such help, one from her social worker, whose offer was taken up, and one from her community psychiatric nurse, whose offer had been turned down. Four mothers stated firmly they did not want help in this area. One mother stated this was because she did not agree with her diagnosis (schizophrenia) but also because she wanted to hide it from her daughter who she felt would not understand. Both mothers with bipolar affective disorder thought their children had concerns due to possible inheritance. One of these mothers wanted professional help to tackle this issue with her daughter, but the other wanted only family members to talk to her son so as not to worry him.

Only three children stated they would like to talk to a doctor or a nurse about their mother's illness. One said he would like to ask why his mother got angry with him and why she went to hospital. One girl said she would like to ask the same questions, but only in secret and would not want her mother to find out. Four children said they would find it too difficult to talk to professionals, that they were shy or embarrassed, though most children said they had talked to someone in their family.

Discussion

The children in this audit had exceptionally high rates of psychiatric disturbance, including potentially treatable problems. Many of the children's problems had started early, and persisted or recurred. There did not seem to be any pattern to the children's diagnoses.

It proved essential to interview both mothers and children, since interviewing only mothers would have missed 27 per cent of the morbidity, and interviewing only children would have missed 33 per cent.

Service utilisation was alarmingly low, despite being in an area of London with very extensive child mental health services. Mothers seemed to find practical assistance more useful than professional help. However, it was clear, even from this small audit, that a large proportion of vulnerable children with significant psychiatric disorders were not receiving help from their local services, and indeed many were not even being referred at all. Our data do not allow us to draw strong conclusions about the low referral rate or the high drop-out rate, but the problem of mismatch between need and utilisation must be addressed if the children's needs are to be met.

The parents selected for our audit appear to fall into two groups – those interested in discussing their children's needs and those reluctant to participate. As regards the first group, the following are the initial responses of the first five mothers approached:

- 'It's a good idea ... children get left out ... my daughter's fine though.'
- 'I'd like to talk to someone about my son ... also the £10 voucher can buy food.'
- A mother who had had one child previously placed in care was initially concerned about participating, asking if 'anything bad will happen if I take part?' She felt that the issues being researched were important and said that she 'wished there was a nurse who was properly trained to talk to my children when they visit me, because it's so disturbed on the ward'.
- 'Since my children were born I've cried all the time. Now they cry all the time ... they've lost their childhood ... they need help but they don't want it.'
- 'My daughter behaves badly ... they referred her for psychotherapy but I missed the appointment because I was too scared to leave the house.' This mother, who suffered from schizophrenia, went on to say about her daughter, 'she's been through a lot and I can't help her'.

As a means of identifying unmet needs, however, the process of conducting the interviews did have its pitfalls. They all took place in the patients' homes and required a variable number of visits, often as many as three. These subjects obviously represent a vulnerable group and appointments made to collect the data were often cancelled for various reasons, such as them not being at home when arranged, not feeling well enough or experiencing an acute social crisis. The interviews, particularly with the mothers, took much longer than anticipated. They seemed to welcome the opportunity to talk about their children and often would talk in great detail. We felt that it was important to be sensitive to this need, especially as many emotive subjects were covered. This did mean that a number of visits were often necessary.

The subjective impression was that the women interviewed were more cooperative than patients recruited for other general psychiatric research. They also seemed more reliable and were better organised regarding running a home, with their homes being in a better state of repair, orderliness and cleanliness. Certainly this may be due to selection bias, as all mothers needed to have children primarily resident with them, and those whose children had been taken away were excluded. The level of cooperation was surprising considering the delicate nature of the questioning and indeed we had expected quite the opposite prior to commencing the project. For some women it seemed particularly welcome to have the opportunity to discuss these issues. However, it appeared that not much thought had previously been given to the specific effects their own mental health problems might be having on their children and many of the women were quite surprised at the questions asked. They seemed to minimise both the interruptions to everyday life during periods of illness and separation, and the psychological, behavioural and emotional effect on the children. They often reported the children to be rather well-behaved, lacking in understanding of mental illness and ignorant of the real implications of the mother's illness. There was no consideration of any effects of the stigma of mental illness on the children's lives.

Regarding services offered, it appeared that many offers had been made, usually through agencies other than mental health, such as school, GP or child and family social worker. However, it seemed that the services taken up were on the whole not related to any therapeutic intervention by psychiatric departments or family or individual psychotherapy, which were often reported as being unhelpful or upsetting. Mothers were very inaccurate regarding when the child or family attended various treatments, what the interventions were and the location of the service. Other services offering practical help were thought to be much more useful, such as after-school clubs and play schemes. Attitudes were quite mixed regarding foster and respite care, some finding it a welcome and necessary resource and others reporting it as interfering. It seemed that this was a group of women who were difficult to engage in treatment for issues relating to the children or family. It may be that their threshold for level of disturbance was higher, or that they were generally suspicious as regards therapeutic intervention. This may be related to their own experiences of mental health services or their fear that professionals might remove the children from their care. With regard to the children's understanding of their mother's illness, they had varied explanations as to its cause but all could clearly describe their mother's behaviour when she was unwell and how this affected them, although their mothers tended to be unaware or to minimise these effects. Most of the mothers interviewed had attempted to offer some explanation to their children regarding their psychiatric problems and were clear about omitting certain details, such as suicidal behaviour, that they acknowledged would upset their children too much. A third of the mothers and most of the children, however, said they would not like a professional to help explain these difficulties with the children.

There was, with the mothers we were able to interview, a curious discrepancy between their tendency to talk at length about their children with an apparent concern for their welfare, and their considerable underestimation of the degree of psychological disturbance the children were displaying, together with recurrent histories of poor compliance with child-focused psychological interventions that had been offered. There was no evidence that they had been uncooperative with their own psychiatric treatment and this contrast is difficult to explain. It may be that some of these mothers were in a dilemma, caught between genuine concern for their children's suffering but wanting to minimise it because they felt guilty about it or feared that they could not face the extra burden of responsibility this placed on them. For others, it might be that their conflict was between being desperate for more help for themselves and allowing their children's needs to be prioritised. Whatever the explanations might be, there is an indication of a barrier to interventions being effectively provided to children in such families, which needs to be addressed by those offering services to them.

By contrast with the group of mothers and children we were able to interview, almost as many again failed to participate, and we were unable to complete interviews with eleven of the women we had identified who met our criteria. Five of these initially gave consent when the project was first discussed with them, but did not attend appointments arranged subsequently or respond to telephone calls or letters. Seven of these mothers suffered from a psychotic illness. We are left to speculate as to whether the children who could not be included represent an even greater pool of unmet need.

The NHS Management Executive (1991) described three main elements of need assessment: (1) epidemiological evidence about the level and types of mental health problems; (2) knowledge of the treatment and management strategies available and their known efficacy and cost-effectiveness; and (3) the views of users on what services they regard as important and their accessibility and acceptability. These issues all raise important questions in the assessment of need in this group of children. The parameters of defining psychiatric need or caseness are debatable. Whether these parameters were drawn up around children with a formal psychiatric disorder, mild disturbance or any evidence of disruption in their family would lead to large differences in practice. The notion of prevention may also be taken into account and hence consideration of their long-term risk for disorder, relationship difficulties and parenting difficulties. The perspectives and views of the wide range of services and agencies that contribute to child and adolescent mental health need to be integrated. We have found a number of difficulties in identifying and assessing this group of children for the study and would presume that engaging these children in treatment is likely to be difficult. The factors affecting the relationship between need and potential and expressed demand are complex. Needs have to be felt as such, perceived, then expressed in demand (Morris, 1967). The mental health needs of these children, from a professional's point of view (though maybe not from the mother's), are not being addressed and hence the risk of long-term difficulties for these children is likely to be accumulating.

Finally, various strategies may be suggested for identifying unmet needs in these children, though these remain to be tested in practice. Adult psychiatrists and social workers could screen the children of the parents on their caseload in the knowledge that they are likely to be experiencing considerable difficulties. The needs of the children could also be explicitly detailed in the parent's Care Programme Approach documentation. Talking to the parents about the impact their illness may have on their children may increase the parents' understanding and ability to access support for their children. For their part, child and adolescent mental health professionals should be aware that children's symptoms may be directly related to psychiatric disturbance in their parents. All practitioners must recognise that the needs of parents and children intertwine.

References

Barrett, M.L., Berney, T.P., Bhate, S., Famuyiwa, O.O., Fundudis, T., Kolvin, I. and Tyrer, S. (1991) Diagnosing childhood depression; who should be interviewed – parent or child? *British Journal of Psychiatry*, 159, 22–27.

Beardslee, W.R., Bemporad, J., Keller, M.B. and Klerman, G.L. (1983) Children of parents with major affective disorder: a review. *American Journal of Psychiatry*, 140, 825–832.

Bebbington, P., Brewin, C.R., Marsden, L. and Lesage, A. (1996) Measuring the need for psychiatric treatment in the general population: the community version or the MRC Needs for Care Assessment. *Psychological Medicine*, 26, 229–236.

Brewin, C.R., Wing, J.K., Mangen, S.P., Brugha, T.S. and MacCarthy, B. (1987) Principles and practice of measuring needs in the long-term mentally ill: the MRC Needs for Care Assessment. *Psychological Medicine*, 17, 971–981.

Brody, G.H. and Forehand, R. (1986) Maternal perceptions of child maladjustment as a function of the combined influence of child behaviour and maternal depression. *Journal of Consulting and Clinical Psychology*, 54, 237–240.

Cleaver, H., Unell, I. and Aldgate, J. (1999) *Children's Needs – Parenting Capacity: The Impact of Parental Mental Illness, Problem Alcohol and Drug Use, and Domestic Violence on Children's Development.* London: The Stationery Office.

Cummings, E.M. and Davies, P.T. (1994) Maternal depression and child development. *Journal of Child Psychology and Psychiatry*, 35, 73–112.

Department of Health (1997) *Children's Services News*, 10. Department of Health.

Flisher, A.J., Kramer, R.A., Grosser, R.C., Alegria, M., Bird, H.R., Bourdon, K.H., Goodman, S.H., Greenwald, S., Horwitz, S.M., Moore, R.E., Narrow, W.E. and Hoven, C.W. (1997) Correlates of unmet need for mental health services by children and adolescents. *Psychological Medicine*, 27, 1145–1154.

Goodman, R. (1997) The Strengths and Difficulties Questionnaire: a research note. *Journal of Child Psychology and Psychiatry*, 38, 581–586.

Hatfield, B., Webster, J. and Mohamad, H. (1997) Psychiatric emergencies: assessing parents of dependent children. *Psychiatric Bulletin*, 21, 19–22.

Hoberman, H.M. (1992) Ethnic minority status and adolescent health services utilization. *Journal of Mental Health Administration*, 19, 246–267.

Light, D. and Bailey, V. (1993) Pound foolish. *Health Service Journal*, 11 February, 16–18.

Morris, J.N. (1967) *Uses of Epidemiology.* Edinburgh: Livingstone.

NHS Health Advisory Service (1995) *Together We Stand.* London: HMSO.

NHS Management Executive (1991) Assessing health care needs. A DHA project discussion paper. London: Department of Health.

Oates, M. (1997) Patients as parents: the risk to children. *British Journal of Psychiatry*, 170 (suppl. 32), 22–27.

Orvaschel, H., Weissman, M.M., Padian, N. and Lowe, T.L. (1981) Assessing psychopathology in children of psychiatrically disturbed parents. *Journal of the American Academy of Child Psychiatry*, 20, 112–122.

Puig-Antich, J. and Chambers, W. (1978) The Schedule for Affective Disorders and Schizophrenia for School-Age Children (KIDDIE-SADS). New York State Psychiatric Institute.

Rutter, M. and Cox, A. (1985) Other family influences. In: M. Rutter and L. Hersov (eds) *Child and Adolescent Psychiatry: Modern Approaches*. 2nd edn. Oxford: Blackwell.

Rutter, M. and Quinton, D. (1984) Parental psychiatric disorder: effects on children. *Psychological Medicine*, 14, 853–880.

Shachnow, J. (1987) Preventive intervention with children of hospitalized psychiatric patients. *American Journal of Orthopsychiatry*, 57, 66–77.

Shaffer, D., Gould, M., Brasic, J., Ambrosini, P., Fischer, P., Bird, H. and Aluwahlia, S. (1983) A children's global assessment scale (CGAS). *Archives of General Psychiatry*, 40, 1228–1231.

Stormont, F., Craig, T., Atakan, Z., Loader, P. and Williams, C. (1997) Concerns about the children of psychiatric in-patients – what the parents say. *Psychiatric Bulletin*, 21, 495–497.

Tamarit, L.M. and Yin-Har Lau, A. (1999) Children's needs when their mothers are admitted to psychiatric units. *Psychiatric Bulletin*, 23, 214–217.

Section 4

Service developments

Chapter 15

Parents with mental health problems

Involving the children

Glenda Fredman and Peter Fuggle

This chapter addresses the involvement of children in family work when their parent presents with mental health problems. Although we are both clinical psychologists, we bring different perspectives to this issue including systemic approaches (Boscolo *et al.*, 1987), communication theory (Pearce, 1989), and developmental and cognitive psychology (Bruner, 1990). We begin by reflecting on how children are commonly excluded from the theory and practice of therapy with parents presenting with mental health problems. We go on to describe an approach to involving children in the work with their parents, using a case example to connect our theoretical perspectives with practice. (The therapeutic work with this family was carried out by GF. Names and biographical details have been changed to ensure anonymity.)

Absence of attention to affected children

Family approaches to adult mental health problems have commonly focused on the adult 'symptom bearer' as the patient. Consequently family treatment approaches have emphasised the needs of the individual diagnosed with the illness and have only considered family members in terms of their contributions to the persistence and management of that index patient's symptoms. Research on Expressed Emotion, for example, showed that persons with schizophrenia whose families were characterised by overinvolvement, hostility and criticism towards the patient had higher rates of relapse than if the family climate was characterised as relatively warm and quiet (Leff and Vaughn, 1985). Psychoeducational family interventions were therefore developed to address the processes by which the family created tension and reinforced the symptomatic behaviour (Berkowitz, 1988; Falloon *et al.*, 1985; 1988). Through an emphasis on the organic basis to the mental illness, the intention was to remove blame from the family for the development of the illness. Although the family was held responsible for ensuring a calm enough emotional atmosphere to prevent relapse, the way that children participated in this endeavour was generally unspecified.

Family therapy approaches to adult mental illness have also construed the

whole family as 'the patient', with therapeutic interventions aimed at relationships and communication between all family members. The focus in these
approaches has shifted from the individual's functioning to family processes
and organisation, in the belief that they have contributed to the origin and/or
the maintenance of the mental health problem. For example, the problem has
been seen not as a psychopathological condition of the individual but as an
indication of communication problems within the family (Bateson *et al.*,
1972; Haley, 1980) or a function of relationship dynamics (Palazzoli and
Prata, 1983). The family has been seen as a critical factor in the successful
management of the problem rather than its cause. Family treatment, therefore, has involved relabelling the individual's psychiatric disorder as a family
problem and focusing on communication and relationship difficulties.
Although children have been included in the systemic formulation and therapeutic tasks in this model, the adult has generally remained the focus of
concern and the problem is rarely formulated in terms of the needs, language
or experience of the child.

Outcome research of family therapy generally reflects this absence of attention to the *affected* child members of the family since it traditionally evaluates
efficacy of family treatments in terms of removal of the symptoms of the
individual diagnosed with the illness (Markus *et al.*, 1990); changes in the
complaints of, or about, the identified patient; and/or systemic or relationship
change in the family as a whole (Carr, 1991). Therefore an emphasis on the
identified patients diagnosed with mental health problems, their presenting
symptoms and the associated systemic and relationship factors in the family
seems to have distracted family therapy practitioners and researchers from
also attending to the consequences of the symptoms for the affected individuals, in particular children, in the family.

As Rutter and Quinton (1984), Hall (1996) and other contributors to this
volume discuss, children of parents with mental health problems are at
increased risk of emotional and behavioural difficulties. Not all of these
children will present with psychiatric problems that meet criteria for diagnosis, yet many are significantly affected by their family circumstances. For
example, a befriending project for children of parents with schizophrenia in
Leeds reported that 73 per cent of the children were significantly affected by
their parent's illness, and the main issues they reported were a sense of being
ignored, a pressure to be good, false maturity and fear of family separation
(Aldridge and Stuart, 1998). Also Gustafsson *et al.* (1995) report behavioural
symptoms of some severity among a significant proportion of the siblings of
children referred with child-psychiatric symptoms in their study.

Although the efficacy of family therapy for the treatment of childhood
disorders has been well documented (Pinsof and Wynne, 1995) we are not
aware of accounts of family work designed specifically with a focus on the
well-being of the *affected* children in the family and we have not come across
any studies that have evaluated family therapy for those children affected by

an *adult's* mental health problems. In a small retrospective study, Engquist (1998) reported the lack of involvement of younger children in the treatment of older, often adult, siblings with a psychiatric illness. None of the children had attended meetings in connection with the onset of psychosis in their sibling and, in half the cases, information about their sibling was given to them up to a year after the onset of the disease. All these affected siblings reported that they would have liked the opportunity to talk with someone to make sense of their sibling's behaviour, to relieve feelings of loneliness and to discuss their concerns about acquiring the illness themselves and their worries about their friends finding out.

This chapter takes the affected child as its focus. It suggests a family approach to working with children where parents or adult siblings show symptoms of mental illness.

> *Nine-year-old Shireen came to the attention of the local child mental health services via her school who were concerned about her poor attendance. Her mother, a lone parent, was finding it increasingly difficult to get Shireen to leave the house. She would cling to the walls when it was time to go and had frequently clawed off huge tracts of wallpaper when her mother tried to 'drag her' off to school. Shireen's mother, Ms J, had been diagnosed with schizophrenia long before Shireen was born. She had been taking medication for many years and had also developed a number of strategies for managing the positive symptoms of her illness, especially auditory hallucinations and agitation. When she heard voices she would listen to her Walkman portable cassette player 'to drown them out'. Generally this method was quite effective but, at times, when she felt the voices overwhelming her or when she found herself becoming especially agitated, she would arrange for Shireen to stay with one of her friends. Shireen was always told that her mother was very tired and needed to rest. Ms J could not predict these episodes, having no idea when she might feel overwhelmed.*

Making sense of the illness experiences

Our approach starts with the assumption that children and adults seek to organise their experiences of events, their thoughts and feelings into some sort of coherence in order to understand significant aspects of their world. A narrative or story offers a way of holding together complex and possibly ambiguous, contradictory or conflicted experiences within a connected pattern of meaning. Bruner (1990) cites research evidence to show that people are naturally predisposed to construct narratives that enable them to make sense of the unusual and unexpected, and that 'children produce and comprehend stories, are comforted and alarmed by them' long before they are able to express simple logic with language. Bruner therefore argues that logical propositions are most easily understood by the child when they are embedded in an on-going story and that children construct their own stories to make meaning out of such propositions. Our clinical experience supports Bruner's observations since we have noted that abstract explanations, such as professional diagnoses or causal explanations, have rarely enhanced children's ability to make sense of their experience of the parent's mental illness and in some cases have restricted their ability to integrate their experience with their own interests and understandings.

Bruner identifies a number of key features of a narrative. A story always comprises a *sequence* of events, actions or states involving *actors* or characters which are connected by a *plot* to give meaning to the events. A narrative can be distinguished from other ways of making sense of the world, such as deductive reasoning, by its indifference to the distinction between 'real' and 'imaginary'. In this sense the story is internal to the discourse, its reality is a linguistic reality (Anderson and Goolishian, 1988). Therefore the use of the word 'story' here in no way implies that people are living a fantasy or that the stories people construct are whimsical. Rather it implies that narratives are constructed to make sense of experiences and that the meaning these stories hold provides a framework for interpreting further experiences and for influencing actions. In this way we live our lives according to the stories we tell ourselves and those we are told by others. Our stories shape our lives, influencing which experiences we pay attention to, give meaning to and continue to incorporate into our constantly evolving narratives (White and Epston, 1990).

Bruner has proposed that narratives often have a function of linking the exceptional to the ordinary and of regulating affect, particularly feelings such as shame, embarrassment and the perception of what is emotionally permissible. Therefore when children witness their parents doing unusual things they construct stories or narratives to give meaning to these events as a way of generating a coherent explanation of their parent's symptomatic behaviour. Bruner reflects on the use of narratives for bringing children into the culture and demonstrates the power of unusual events to trigger narrativising or storying in even very young children.

> *Ms J would spend hours and sometimes the most part of many days wearing her Walkman or lying on the bed in a dark room. Shireen attributed her mother's wearing of the Walkman to 'Oh that's when mummy's sick of me . . . I can be a pest at times.'*
>
> *Although Ms J had frequently called Shireen a pest and had often explained that she had to rest because she was 'sick' or 'tired', it was Shireen who connected 'pest' and 'sick' with her mother's wearing the Walkman to construct the story that her mother wore it because she was sick of her. Shireen went on to interpret her unpredictable stays with her mother's friend in terms of 'mummy gets tired – sick and tired of me – I can*

*be a pest at times – so she sends me to [her friend] Sally – to get better –
have a rest from me'.*

Ms J had told Shireen she was 'sick and tired' of the mess she made, and
Shireen had incorporated this experience into her evolving narrative of self-
blame. Here Shireen had filled in the gaps herself to construct a story to
make sense of her mother's behaviour, whereby she attributed her mother's
being tired and her withdrawal to her own bad behaviour. Her narrative of
self-blame evolved to incorporate her expectation that her mother might
one day leave her at Sally's permanently, which in turn influenced her
behaviour to the extent that she cried and clung on to the walls to avoid
leaving home.

Children and parents need to create a coherent narrative together to
make sense of the parent's symptomatic behaviour and the child and parent's experiences of those symptoms. Below we describe an approach in
which children are included in a conversation with parents so that they
might actively participate in the construction of a story or narrative which
is linked to other meanings in their experiences. The therapeutic aim is to
work with children and parents to construct a story which does not blame
or pathologise self or others and which creates opportunities for adaptive
action and relationships for the children, parents and significant others.
The story needs to help each individual make sense of their experiences
and also fit with the stories of their significant community and professional
helpers.

Shireen was living a story of self-blame and fear of permanent separation.
This story did not fit with her mother's experience of events nor with that of
Sally or her mother's mental health workers. Because Shireen had not told
this story, the adults caring for her could not use it to make sense of her
behaviour. In this way her narrative was neither practical nor adaptive.

Creating a context for making practical sense

Typically children are excluded from the process of their parent's psychiatric
care.

> *Although Shireen's mother had a diagnosis of mental illness before Shireen
> was born, Shireen had never been involved with her mother's mental health
> services. Ms J had always attended hospital appointments on her own and
> Shireen stayed with mother's friends when her mother was admitted as an
> inpatient.*

We suggest an approach which involves the child early in the work. In cases
where a family member is recently diagnosed, all family members can be
invited to a 'planning meeting' to talk about the way forward for everyone in

the family and to discuss how everyone is getting on. The identified patient and other family members can be invited to include anyone else they might think could be of help – for example, friends, relatives, significant professionals. Since families may expect to be seen as responsible for the problem or to be blamed, it is important to frame this initial meeting without attributing fault. Therefore care needs to be taken to avoid causal connections between the family and the problem by pointing out that everyone is affected by the situation and that everyone, including the children, could give some good ideas about how the therapy team might best be of help. The intention is to use this time to begin to construct a coherent narrative of the parent's mental illness with the family. Quite often, the parent identified with the mental illness does not want to involve their child with mental health services. Offers to meet in the premises of children's services or on 'neutral ground' may be more acceptable. This sort of planning meeting necessitates liaison between child and adult mental health services. For example, the parent's key worker might initiate the meeting in consultation and coordination with child mental health services.

> *Ms J initially refused the invitation to bring Shireen with her to a meeting to help clarify what sense she was making of her mother's situation, insisting that Shireen was a 'good child' and had 'no problems'.*

Hence we suggest routinely beginning with a conversation which involves the parent and significant others in establishing a context for talking about the child's experiences with the mental illness (Fredman, 1997). Such a context evolves in relation to the views that each person holds about the parent's symptoms, their ideas about talking with children about the subject, as well as time, place and relationships significant to knowing and telling. It can be helpful to start by exploring what each significant person 'knows' about the parent's experiences and mental health status, their recognition of each other's awarenesses and the beliefs that they hold about people knowing and telling. Such an exploration would include asking about: 'who knows what'; 'who is open to talking about what'; 'who wants who to know what'; and 'who believes what about who knows what'. Establishing a context for making sense of the parent's symptoms therefore involves 'talking about talking' (Fredman, 1997).

Talking about talking

To explore the parent's experiences of talking about their illness one may ask: 'Whom have you discussed your experiences with?'; 'What was that like?'; 'How did it help?' (We refer to the parent's 'experiences' in order to avoid pre-empting or influencing a construction of illness which may not fit with their own narrative.) Questions like 'What are the advantages/disadvantages of talking?' can create opportunities to explore the meanings parents give to talking about their experiences with mental health problems. It can also help to discuss alternative contexts for talking, including relationships, time and place – for example: 'When would it be a good time to talk?'; 'Who else might want to join in?'

Asking Ms J 'What will it be like for you/Shireen if you discuss your experiences with her?' and 'How will it make things between you?' enabled her to address previous or anticipated effects of talking about the mental health problem experience on herself, on others and on relationships.

Ms J had only talked about her experiences with doctors and with her friend Sally who had also spent some time as an inpatient in a psychiatric hospital. She did not think talking with the doctors helped much, and sometimes it made it worse, whereas Sally was sympathetic and also willing to stand in and help. Ms J did not want Shireen to know about her experiences 'No – definitely not – the kids at school will take the mickey – your mum's a nutter.' When it was suggested that Shireen might need help with explaining to the children at school why she was not staying with her mum, Ms J agreed to discuss ways of helping Shireen sort this out, wanted her friend Sally to join in and agreed to have her community psychiatric nurse and social worker along.

Constructing coherent narratives

Stories are not formed in isolation. People construct their stories in relationship with others, including their families and communities, and may draw on many contexts to guide their meanings and actions, for example, their relationships, cultures, genders or religions (Pearce, 1989). Over time much of lived experience goes unstoried and hence is never 'told' or expressed. Many adults with a diagnosis of mental illness have told us that they have never explained their symptoms to themselves or others. Hence they have not worked out a coherent account for themselves of their experiences or behaviour. Having to explain the situation to the child therefore challenges the adults, both parents and professionals, to make overt ideas and beliefs about the parent's symptoms that they may never have articulated before. It is an assumption of this approach that inviting the parent and child to relate their experiences of the parent's mental health problems, in a context relatively protected from threat or blame, enables them to construct a coherence between their lived experience of the symptoms and the meanings they make to account for them. In this way the experiences they live become the stories they tell.

When Ms J was asked what explanation she gave to her feelings of agitation and to the voices which troubled her, she said that she did not really think about it. When asked what the doctors had said, she replied, 'I am ill . . . schizophrenia . . . must take the medicine.' However she did not want to give that explanation to Shireen, 'Definitely not – I don't want her to think her mum's a nutter.'

Here Ms J shared the logical explanation she had been given by her doctors to explain her symptoms. This 'illness' explanation was useful in guiding her actions towards taking medication and attending hospital appointments and ensured her contact with her community psychiatric nurse. However, an 'illness' construction did not fit with her relationship with her daughter nor with her daughter's community (school and peers) since, for Ms J, in those contexts it included her negative self-description of 'nutter' and anticipated teasing or stigmatising of her daughter. Ms J needed help with constructing a narrative which would make sense of her symptoms and experiences for both her and Shireen and which would fit with the stories and explanations of the health professionals, and Shireen's relationship with her school and peers. Shireen needed a story which could make practical and adaptive sense of her mother's behaviour, a story which would enable her to leave the home without fear or self-blame.

We suggest convening meetings with families to construct narratives which give meaning to parents' symptomatic behaviour and which fit for significant members of the family, community and helping professionals. When we pro-posed this sort of meeting to Ms J, she chose to attend initially with her friend Sally, her community psychiatric nurse (CPN) and her social worker and to include Shireen in a second meeting.

The principles guiding this work are informed by the systemic approach (Boscolo *et al.*, 1987) and involve: creating a non-evaluative atmosphere; generating and elaborating a repertoire of stories about the mental illness/symptoms; addressing the fit of stories between people and with different contexts such as place, time, culture; coordinating preferred stories with significant people involved; reflecting on the effects and meanings of new stories for people and relationships; and translating the stories into action (Fredman, 1997).

Creating a non-evaluative atmosphere

Initially the aim is to create many different ideas about the parent's symp-toms, behaviour and experiences, with contributions from all significant members of the system, including the children, the parents, other family members, professionals or agencies involved with the family. The family and professionals should be given the message that all views are relevant and potentially useful; hence dichotomies of agree–disagree or right–wrong are avoided.

Generating explanations and elaborating stories

All people present are asked for their own views about the symptoms and are invited to consider the perspectives of other significant people who are not present. It is important that the views of the children, whether present or absent, are voiced.

> *Ms J's CPN reported that Ms J had a diagnosis of schizophrenia which accounted for her agitation and hearing voices. Sally said Ms J was under a lot of stress and that at times Shireen's behaviour aggravated her mother's agitation. Sally suggested that Shireen probably thought her mother was ill and Ms J added that Shireen was always told that her mother was very tired.*

Inviting people to elaborate their explanations can generate narratives.

> *In the process of elaborating Sally's ideas about 'stress' Ms J related her story of growing up in a children's home from the age of 7, where she was 'maltreated', ran away at 15, and lived rough until she was diagnosed with schizophrenia at 18. Ms J had never told the story of her 'maltreatment' despite presenting at psychiatric services from the age of 10.*

Evaluating preferred stories

Having generated a repertoire of stories and beliefs, each person at the meeting is invited to identify their preferred explanations for the symptoms. Questions like 'Does that [explanation] fit for you?'; 'Which bits do you want to keep/get rid of/change?'; 'Do you have other ideas you would like to add?' enable participants to evaluate the different stories each other has constructed to make sense of their experiences of the symptoms. It is then possible to address which versions of which story would fit most suitably for the children and their contexts.

> *Ms J did not want to discuss her diagnoses (schizophrenia or personality disorder) with Shireen and preferred that Shireen think she was 'ill' or 'tired'. Sally thought it might help Shireen to know that her mother was sometimes troubled because she had had a very sad time in her childhood. The CPN was concerned that Ms J should continue to take her medication which she needed for her schizophrenic illness. The social worker was concerned about burdening Shireen with distressing information about her mother's childhood.*

Co-constructing preferred stories

The aim of this approach is to facilitate the child's participation in the co-construction of a narrative which gives practical meaning to the experience of the parent's symptoms. Hence the process differs from a psychoeducational approach whereby the child might be presented with a logical explanation of the parent's symptoms, or told a story previously constructed by adults to account for their experience, or allowed to be audience to adults' conversations about the illness. In the approach described in this chapter, the child's participation in the co-construction of the narrative is essential and involves sharing their own stories with and evaluating the explanations of other significant people involved in the parent's mental health problems.

> *Shireen's participation at the second meeting created a context for the generation of additional and different explanations and for the co-creation of yet further stories. Thus Ms J and her helping network were able to hear Shireen directly relating her story of 'self-blame' (described above), and Ms J was able to comment on the poor fit of this story with her own meanings. Shireen in turn witnessed her mother reporting that she was 'a good child' and that nothing was her fault and was audience to Sally's reference to her mother's unhappy childhood.*

Reflecting on the effects of new stories

It is not always possible for people to create coherent narratives to make sense of experiences. Certain lived experiences may not be able to be told when the contexts of time, place or relationship do not fit. Asking questions that extend explanations towards a narrative often enables people to construct a story which links with other meanings in their experience. Similarly, inviting associations between participants' preferred explanations can generate narratives never before told, enabling them to make sense of previously unexplained experiences or make new connections between old meanings.

> *Ms J was previously unable to relate her 'maltreatment' in care and therefore never storied these events to create a coherent account of her experiences. Asked whether she had ever made the connection between her experiences in care and the voices and agitation she was currently experiencing, whether Shireen knew she had had such a difficult time as a child growing up and whether there was something about these times she might want her to know one day, Ms J replied that she had never made any connections with her symptoms, had never spoken of these times to anyone and might tell Shireen when she was older. When invited to reflect on new*

narratives which had evolved during the session in this way, Ms J became tearful and spoke with intense emotion of the pledge she had made to keep Shireen out of care whatever happened.

Here the co-construction of a new narrative opened space for new connections between meanings.

Ideally, it is important that all significant professionals and family members participate in the process of co-creating and coordinating narratives with the family. In practice, this may be difficult to achieve and sometimes the effects of new co-created narratives may challenge the narratives of people who have not participated in the original co-constructing conversations.

Ms J's psychiatrist did not attend the two meetings described above. When Ms J later began to refer to her problems as 'stress' and to question her diagnosis of schizophrenia, he warned the community psychiatric nurse that she was at risk of not adhering to her treatment. Fortunately the community psychiatric nurse had attended the meeting and could contextualise Ms J's response in terms of her newly evolving narrative.

Translating stories into action

The meanings stories hold provide a framework for interpreting further experiences and for influencing actions. This approach aims to involve children with parents and professionals in creating practical meanings. We use the word 'practical' here to connote meanings that create opportunities for adaptive action.

Shireen's self-blame story was neither practical nor adaptive since it rendered her fearful and created difficulties in her relationship with her mother and the school. By joining the adults at the second meeting, Shireen was able to identify her preferred explanations of her mother's symptoms and to participate with significant adults in the co-construction of a story which incorporated her mother's symptoms as an expression of stress, Ms J's experiences in care, her pledge to protect her daughter, Shireen's self-blame and the desire of all the adults present to protect Shireen from undue responsibility. This alternative narrative opened opportunities for Ms J to acknowledge that leaving Shireen in the unpredictable care of different friends added to the child's fears of leaving home. Ms J was also able to state her conviction that these unpredictable arrangements were preferable to the fate she believed a children's home might have in store for her daughter. This narrative also provided professionals with new meanings of Ms J's approach to Shireen's care arrangements, thereby creating opportunities for adaptive interactions.

Following the two meetings, Ms J agreed to meet with the social worker to discuss changes in the care system since she had stayed in children's homes. Consequently she was willing to discuss options for respite foster care for her daughter. Ms J and Sally told Shireen that her mother would continue to go away for rests from time to time in order to restore her energy, that her exhaustion was related to her difficult childhood, and that the social worker would arrange for Shireen to stay with a family until her mother returned so that she could be looked after and her mother could know she was safe and well. Shireen resumed attendance at school.

Discussion

In this chapter, we have presented an approach to enable children, parents and their professional networks to create coherent accounts of the family's experiences of the mental illness so that they can go on living together in adaptive interaction. We emphasise that children need to participate in the co-creation of a narrative which makes sense of their experiences and which fits with the meanings of the parents and professionals. To this end it is important that all significant professionals participate in these conversations and continue to validate the adaptive narrative with the family. Certain mental health problems may be more accessible to stories that can be shared and not all difficulties will need professional involvement in the storying of the experiences. Here we have described a case where the parent has a diagnosis of schizophrenia. This approach also lends itself well to the effects of depression on the family.

Involving children is not part of routine clinical practice with adults presenting with mental health difficulties. Hence the children are commonly only considered if they present with problems attracting professional attention, for example in the school. This lack of attention to the children can be explained in part by some parents' reluctance to engage in discourse about the child in the context of an adult mental health service. Our clinical experience includes families who have prohibited children from meeting professionals or, more extremely, where children have been actively silenced by adults to such a degree that professionals have needed to consider following usual procedures for assessing whether the safety of the child is being compromised. We have also encountered professionals who show reluctance to involve the child, with the unfortunate consequence that the needs of the child go unrecognised. This approach needs liaison between adult and child mental health services and joint work requires that both parents' and children's needs and interests are represented.

We have outlined an approach to co-creating narratives with families and we invite the reader to use these principles as guidelines rather than prescribed techniques, and therefore to prioritise the family's feedback and agenda rather than assume this as an established method. For clarity the practices are presented as if they follow a logical progression. The construction of narratives, however, is rarely such an ordered affair. Narratives are created in conversation and in relationship and are continually evolving and changing as the context changes. People may hold several different stories to account for the same experience and how or whether a story is used is influenced by the contexts of relationship, time and place.

Therefore we are not presenting a treatment method here but rather an approach to talking with children and parents about the parent's mental illness. Hence the intention is not to construct a completed narrative as if it were the definitive end-product of the work. In fact it is unusual that a coherent narrative reveals itself in its entirety to the interviewer in the session, since the coherence is constructed as the family goes on to live and tell the story in relationship with each other. In this way Ms J and Shireen continued to evolve their narrative in relationship with each other, friends and professionals long after the meetings were over.

References

Aldridge, S. and Stuart, A. (1998) The Willow Scheme: an innovative project offering befriending support to young carers living with a severely mentally ill relative. Presentation at National Children's Bureau Conference on 'Mentally Ill Parents and their Children', London.

Anderson, H. and Goolishian, H. (1988) Human systems as linguistic systems: preliminary and evolving ideas about the implications for clinical theory. *Family Process*, 27, 371–393.

Bateson, G., Jackson, D.D., Haley, J. and Weakland, J. (1972) Toward a theory of schizophrenia. In: G. Bateson, *Steps to an Ecology of Mind*. New York: Ballantine.

Berkowitz, R. (1988) Family therapy and adult mental illness: schizophrenia and depression. *Journal of Family Therapy*, 10, 339–356.

Boscolo, L., Cecchin, G., Hoffman, L. and Penn, P. (1987) *Milan Systemic Family Therapy*. New York: Basic Books.

Bruner, J. (1990) *Acts of Meaning*. Cambridge, Mass.: Harvard University Press.

Carr, A. (1991) Milan systemic family therapy: a review of ten empirical investigations. *Journal of Family Therapy*, 13, 237–263.

Engquist, M.L. (1998) Siblings of psychotic persons: reactions and influence on their network. *Human Systems*, 9, 15–20.

Falloon, I.R.H., Boyd, J.L., McGill, C.W., Williamson, M., Razani, J., Moss, H.B., Gildreman, A.M. and Simpson, G.M. (1985) Family management in the prevention of morbidity of schizophrenia. *Archives of General Psychiatry*, 42, 887–896.

Falloon, I.R.H., Hole, V., Mulroy, L., Norris, L.J. and Pembleton, T. (1988) Behavioural family therapy. In: J.F. Clarkin, G.L. Haas and I.D. Glick (eds) *Affective Disorders and the Family: Assessment and Treatment*. New York: Guilford.

Fredman, G. (1997) *Death Talk: Conversations with Children and Families*. London: Karnac.

Gustafsson, P.A., Engquist, M. and Karlsson, B. (1995) Siblings in family therapy. *Journal of Family Therapy*, 17, 317–328.

Haley, J. (1980) *Leaving Home*. New York: McGraw-Hill.

Hall, A. (1996) Parental psychiatric disorder and the developing child. In: M. Göpfert, J. Webster and M.V. Seeman (eds) *Parental Psychiatric Disorder*. Cambridge: Cambridge University Press.

Leff, J. and Vaughn, C. (1985) *Expressed Emotion in Families*. New York: Guilford.

Markus, E., Lange, A. and Pettigrew, T.F. (1990) Effectiveness of family therapy: a meta-analysis. *Journal of Family Therapy*, 12, 205–221.

Palazzoli, M. and Prata, G. (1983) A new method for therapy and research in the treatment of schizophrenic families. In: H. Stierlin, L.C. Wynne and M. Wirching (eds) *Psychosocial Intervention in Schizophrenia*. Berlin: Springer-Verlag.

Pearce, W.B. (1989) *Communication and the Human Condition*. Carbondale, Ill.: Southern Illinois University Press.

Pinsof, W.M. and Wynne, L.C. (1995) The efficacy of marital and family therapy: an empirical overview, conclusions, and recommendations. *Journal of Marital and Family Therapy*, 21, 585–613.

Rutter, M. and Quinton, D. (1984) Parental psychiatric disorder: effects on children. *Psychological Medicine*, 14, 853–880.

White, M. and Epston, D. (1990) *Narrative Means to Therapeutic Ends*. New York: W.W. Norton.

Chapter 16

Working with families where there is parenting breakdown

Eia Asen

Principles of systemic work

Child welfare agencies and mental health workers frequently face the dilemma as to whether or not to remove an abused or neglected child from its parent(s). Permanent separation of a child from its parent(s) potentially violates parental rights, but failure to do so can sometimes result in grave injury, death or lasting emotional damage. When professionals are unable to decide whether to let the child remain with its natural family or not, this indecisiveness can be abusive in its own right: it leaves the child in a situation of limbo – which in some cases can last years – further adding to the child's emotional or physical suffering.

The Marlborough Family Service, based in North London, is an NHS resource which has over the years gained considerable expertise in undertaking comprehensive assessments of parenting capacity and working therapeutically with families. The overall approach used by the Marlborough Family Service team is 'systemic'. Problems and problem behaviours – that is, abuse – are viewed in context and there is a specific focus on how individual behaviour affects the immediate contexts (family, professionals) and how the contexts affect individuals and their beliefs and actions. The abused or neglected child is considered as part of a family and the family as part of a wider social context – the neighbourhood and the culture they come from or live in. Child abuse and neglect also tend to generate a professional context: social workers, police, courts, doctors, teachers, health visitors and others enter the scenario and their responses have an effect on the likelihood of resolution or further abuse. The abused or neglected child therefore needs to be assessed in a variety of contexts – the immediate and wider family, the home and the neighbourhood, the wider social setting – and in relation to the professional network that is often powerfully present. Assessment also needs to address the changing culturally- and societally-sanctioned patterns of child-rearing.

Working systemically means addressing each of these layers, both in terms of assessment and intervention. The assessment of parenting capacity therefore needs to include the evaluation of the child and parents, as well as the social context of which the family is part (Wolfe and Wekerle, 1993). The assessment also needs to address the relationship between the family and the professional network. If there are conflicting opinions and actions by individual professionals, this will affect the child and family and cause further disturbance. The family and professionals in turn are very much affected by the social welfare system and fluctuations in child care policies arising from highly publicised cases where children have remained with very disturbed parents. Such fluctuations of public and political opinion may be reflected in conflicting advice from senior management which can render field-workers confused and paralysed.

The assessment process itself is therefore not a simple one-off 'photograph' of parenting capacity at the time of interview, but could be described as the assembly of a 'four-dimensional picture', consisting of:

1   a 'snapshot' of the current child–parent(s) relationship;
2   a 'photo-album' of the family's own history;
3   a 'live sample' of current family interaction;
4   an 'aerial shot' of the family's eco-map.

Assessment and therapy are not two separate entities: a comprehensive family assessment needs to test the parents' and the whole family's ability to change. This can only be done if the assessing team intervenes therapeutically with the aim of bringing about change. Assessing the responses of the family and significant others to such interventions helps to make informed predictions about the various family members' potential for change.

Different phases of family work

The Marlborough Family Service has developed a distinct approach which has been modified repeatedly over the years (Cooklin *et al.*, 1983; Schuff and Asen, 1996) and currently consists of work carried out over a period of 2–3 months. It consists of meetings with the professional network, outreach work with families in their homes and neighbourhood, multi-family work in a day unit for families and work with individual children and their parents. The different phases of the assessment and therapeutic work are described below.

Phase 1: Network phase

Certain families seem to have unique skills to involve a whole range of professionals and they are usually referred to as 'multi-problem' or 'multi-agency' families. It is very common that the more disturbance the family or its individual members present, the more will new professionals be recruited to provide 'help'. Frequently such 'help' further enhances the parents' sense of failure – thus requiring more 'help' which, in turn, leads to an even more helpless posture of the parents. Their children remain at risk despite (and often because of) multiple inputs, particularly when professionals disagree between themselves (Reder, 1986), with the result that the family receives double, treble or quadruple messages. It is not rare to encounter families who have twenty or more different professionals attached to them, raising the question as to whether there is anything left for the parents to do, with all the parenting functions seemingly being carried out by an army of professionals. Characteristically the degree of anxiety among the professionals is greater than that of the family itself; and the more anxious the various workers are, the less anxious the parents tend to be. The term 'dangerous professionals' (Dale with Davies *et al.*, 1986) has been coined to describe such scenarios – dangerous because they may unwittingly maintain or enhance abusive behaviours.

The assessment of the professional network is therefore an essential component in the work with multi-agency families, prior to assessing the family. Network meetings have a number of different aims:

1   To bring together parents and other significant carers of the child and all professionals actively involved with the family, in order to map who is providing what input to whom, when and why (and perhaps even 'how').

2   To provide a forum in which the professionals' concerns and duties can be clearly explained to the family and where all participants have the opportunity to discuss any differences of opinion.

3   To ensure that the parents can define what they want from the various professionals and to enable them to comment on their own concerns, with the aim of helping all to find a joint solution to the presenting problems.

4   To ensure that the child protection agencies can clearly define the minimum standards of child care expected of the parents.

5   To identify an action plan with clearly outlined tasks for each participant within a given time span.

The network meeting is attended not only by the various professionals but also by the parents and whoever they regard as their own significant network, ranging from members of the extended family to neighbours, priests or friendly lawyers. A range of questions are put to professionals and family in order to understand relationships and roles as well as the different views on the quality of parenting. At the end of the meeting an action plan is drafted, specifying which helpers will remain involved and which will not; which tasks are to be carried out by whom and for what purpose; what specific areas of change should be targeted; the likely consequences of 'no change'; and a date for a network review meeting.

Once agreement has been reached for the family to attend the Marlborough, a contract is drawn up which details the questions that need to be answered and the work that needs to be carried out to address these questions, outlining areas of change as well as the consequences of change or no change.

Phase 2: Family Day Unit work I

After an initial home visit which allows us to meet the family in their natural living context and to learn about their issues firsthand, families are invited to attend the Family Day Unit (Asen *et al.*, 1982) for one week, Monday to Friday, from 8.45 to 15.15.

The aim of the Family Day Unit is to provide a setting where emotional intensity can be achieved by re-creating issues that families have to cope with in their ordinary lives. This intended 'hot-house effect' tends to bring out the relationship problems in a dramatic fashion and under relatively controlled and therefore safe conditions. As a result, specific barriers to change, which constrain many of these families, are broken.

The tightly constructed programme consists of different meetings and activities throughout the day, from planning meetings to family activities, from formal therapeutic meetings to informal discussions, from parents' groups to multi-family games. This involves family members in various configurations: as a parental couple, partners, whole family, mothers with children, children by themselves, individual adults, and members of a small community. Different contexts – such as outings, shopping trips, the joint preparation and eating of meals, supervision of children in playgrounds, playing with one's own children, coordinating play activities with other families, discussing events/plans whilst children are around and in need of supervision – all make heavy demands on parents. It requires them to demonstrate their competence and makes overt how parental disturbance may or may not interfere with child-rearing ability.

Studying conflictual family interactions and having problematic behaviours enacted 'live' allow an understanding of how dysfunctional sequences arise. The potential for change can then be tested *in vivo*: families are first encouraged to identify typical pressure points of family life and they are then asked to stage and 'enact' them (Minuchin, 1974). This gives the clinicians the opportunity to study how a sequence evolves, how impasses occur and how solutions can be found.

Constant feedback is essential. Every day ends with an open discussion of the day's events, describing in detail positive and negative behaviours and incidents. All families participate in this activity, commenting about each other as well as discussing the staff's observations. In a formal meeting at the end of the week staff summarise their observations and views of each family in a staff meeting. This staff discussion is videotaped and replayed to the families, who can themselves reflect on the staff's 'reflections'. Commenting on the staff's observations facilitates new perspectives of themselves, of the institution, staff, and other families.

The reasons for carrying out this work in a multi-family setting are as follows:

• to connect socially isolated families with one another;
• to diminish the stigma which many of the families experience;
• to give parents and families the opportunity to contribute constructively to the welfare of other families and support each other when attempting to achieve changes;
• to bring in another observational vantage point which is not a professional one and thus receive feedback about their own problematic or disturbed behaviours from other families (peer criticism can often be better listened to than criticism that comes from professionals).

This multi-family group therapy has as its focus the sharing of common experiences and difficulties, and encourages families to learn from one another and to give help to each other. Each family also receives family therapy sessions in their own right and there is also individual input to specific family members. Moreover, using a systems approach includes seeing the child(ren) by themselves, both for assessment and therapeutic purposes.

Phase 3: Home-based work

Following their attendance at the Family Day Unit, families are then seen in their own homes. The main reason for this is to evaluate the extent to which they are able to 'translate' any changes they may have made to their natural environment. Weekly home visits, each lasting 2–3 hours, are made over a period of four weeks. To see families in their natural environment allows clinicians to study their day-to-day difficulties and how these reflect parental and family disturbance. Much of this work is done by constructing elaborate maps which identify the family's connections with its environment and with significant others: the space, state and location of their flat or house, the immediate neighbourhood and the family's network. This helps parents and children to look at their situation from a different perspective, from outside, and thus reflect and act differently about their living situation.

Phase 4: Family Day Unit work 2

Families usually return for another week to the multi-family setting, usually about one month after their first spell. Home-based work may have revealed particular difficulties that can best be addressed more intensively over the course of a whole day in our Unit. The basic ingredients of the work are identical to those described above.

Phase 5: Follow-up work

At the end of the contracted work a review meeting is held involving the professional and the family's network. Here our views and recommendations are discussed. Families are never surprised about these views as they have heard them in daily feedback sessions. Follow-up varies according to where the family lives. Local families will be followed-up by our team. This is much more difficult for families living in other London boroughs or outside London, and in these cases we may work out a detailed plan together with the local team, or provide on-going consultation.

Subsequent work with local families focuses upon building on any positive changes that have been made. However, in a number of cases our team recommends permanent separation of the child(ren) from the parents, and in such situations the focus of work will be on separating, planning contact visits, and possible individual or couple work with the parents once the children have been placed elsewhere.

Case example

Jane, 37, is a single mother with three children. At the age of 10 she had been referred to the local child psychiatric services because of 'depression' and she received individual psychotherapy for three years. At the age of 14 she took an overdose and spent nine months in an adolescent unit where she disclosed sexual abuse by her stepfather, and was discharged to live with foster carers. Further episodes of 'depression' were diagnosed for which she received a considerable number of different anti-depressants, and she had two further inpatient admissions before the age of 20. Jane went to college but always felt socially isolated. She had a few brief relationships with abusive men, and met John, the father of her children, in her mid-twenties, although they never lived together. Shortly after the birth of her last child Jane discovered that John had previously spent time in prison, having been convicted of sexual abuse of children. She and the children cut off all contact with him and never saw him again.

Some years ago Jane and her three children were referred by their social worker to the Marlborough Family Service, after the local authority had instituted care proceedings. There had been increasing concerns regarding Jane's ability to parent her three children. At the time Bill was 8 years of age, presenting as a disruptive child at school with threats of permanent exclusion. He was described as being either very 'high' or very 'depressed'. He also had started fires both at home and at school. The younger of the two boys, Tom, aged 6, had been diagnosed as suffering from a serious brain disorder (epilepsy, ataxia, learning disability), requiring him to attend a special school. He needed constant supervision as his behaviour could be quite unpredictable, including running into the path of oncoming cars.

Molly, the 3-year-old girl, bright and very lively, presented in her nursery with behavioural problems. She was reported to have bitten other children, particularly when she felt ignored.

The initial network meeting revealed the involvement of a considerable number of workers, some of whom were quite unaware of their colleagues' inputs. All together, 21 different professionals, representing health, education and social services, were working with this family, with relatively little – if any – communication and coordination between the various agencies. There were many different opinions on how this mother and her children could 'best' be helped. Not surprisingly, with so many professionals involved and a whole range of opinions available as to what was 'best', Jane seemed both confused and paralysed, not knowing what her own parenting skills were or should be. At the end of the network meeting an action plan was drawn up, specifying which helpers were remaining involved; which tasks were to be carried out by whom and for what purpose; which specific areas of change were to be targeted (e.g. Bill's disruptiveness, Molly's behavioural problems, Tom's special needs and how these affected family dynamics, etc); and what action was going to be taken by whom if the concerns increased or decreased.

The Marlborough team (two family workers) then met with the whole family in their flat – on the seventh floor of a run-down housing estate. The flat was damp and in a bad state of repair, with two small bedrooms. Jane explained how the physical surroundings were enhancing her own sense of despair and social isolation. The visit also provided an opportunity for studying family interaction in vivo, with mother struggling in the kitchen to prepare a meal whilst the children fought with one another. Jane did not seem to know what tasks to focus on or what to prioritise and she ended up locking herself in the toilet in despair. This seemed to provoke Bill into lighting a small fire in the bedroom. His brother shouted 'fire, fire' and their mother immediately came out of the bathroom and extinguished the flames. She turned to the team and said: 'I'm glad you're here . . . now someone can really understand what I have to deal with every day.' The team then discussed with Jane what particular aspects of her family life she thought might benefit from help (such as creating some individual space for herself; acquiring more authority; getting the children to play more cooperatively). Jane started listing a whole range of problem behaviours of her children, from Molly's biting to Tom's whining, from Bill's provocations to the children's continual fighting. The team and Jane worked out a plan of how to tackle each of these issues with behavioural techniques. Another home visit was arranged to look further at issues of the family's social context and how some of the issues of social isolation and housing might be tackled.

A week later the family started attending the Family Day Unit. Jane was initially very reluctant to make contact with the five other families present at the same time. She sat in a corner as her own children established lively contact with their peers. It was very noticeable that the more her children engaged in play with other families, the more withdrawn and 'switched off' Jane became. It seemed that, at some level, the children deliberately increased their activity level to stimulate their mother into 'waking up' and taking action. It was only when Bill got into a fight with two other children that Jane was asked by one of the fathers to 'wake up' and 'do something'. One of the other mothers challenged Jane on the second day: 'Your kids have to be wild to switch you on.' Jane was shocked, but then started reflecting, with the help of the team and other parents, on how her own state of mind might be affecting her children's responses. Two other mothers in particular made some constructive suggestions and Jane was able to experiment with new ways of responding to her children. Gradually Jane herself made contact with other families, including – on the third day – exchanging telephone numbers with three parents.

An outing to the supermarket – which was filmed with the family's knowledge and permission on a small camcorder – provided more information about Jane's difficulties in keeping each child in mind whilst crossing streets, choosing food and struggling with her children's unruly behaviour in public places. As this shopping trip involved three other familes, there was ample opportunity for 'live' reflection on how things were going – with not only staff but, above all, other parents commenting on what they saw, as well as making suggestions. This required Jane to remain 'switched on' (as she called it) and attempt to use new strategies. Later on, back in the clinic, a video feedback session helped Jane to look at the sequence of events from a different perspective and to identify different ways of dealing with the same scenario in the future.

At the end of the week, in the formal staff review session, Jane and her children received considerable positive feedback, as well as areas of concern and future work being outlined. A plan for the following weeks was drawn up with Jane, involving more home-based work as well as individual sessions for her, to help her to think about her own needs and how these could be balanced with her children's. She started talking about how much she identified with her disabled son and how this revived memories of her being 'damaged' and abused in her family of origin. Two meetings were arranged involving her own mother, exploring transgenerational issues, such as how her own mother's moods had affected Jane during her childhood and how her own mother had dealt with violence in her own family of origin. Jane found this particularly helpful as she had been having very little contact with her mother. Meeting with her mother in the presence of a third person enabled Jane to look at their relationship from a different point of view. These meetings resulted in more frequent contact between the children and their grandmother.

One month later the family returned for another week to the Family Day Unit. Three new families had joined the programme and Jane took it upon herself to make them feel welcome and explain what she had found useful during her last spell in the unit. She seemed much more 'switched on' and this was reflected in her children's behaviour which had become much less attention-seeking. Jane had clearly found ways of engaging with her children in positive interactions rather than 'switching off' and then only responding to mini-crises. Some of the work focused on how Jane could overcome her social isolation: for example, how she could ask her social worker for some child-minding arrangements so that she could go out some evenings. She also started thinking about how she could contribute to changes in her physical environment, and some of this work involved role-plays, with other parents acting as if they were tough officers from the local housing department or unsympathetic social workers. Jane was then coached by other parents on how she could present herself differently so that she would be heard and be taken more seriously, as well as getting help on what arguments to use and what tone of voice to adopt.

At the end of the week Jane and her children had made further progress with the relationship and management issues that had brought them to the unit. They had also begun to make good connections with other families in our unit, resulting in social contacts outside our programme.

Outpatient work with this family continued for another six months, with more home-based work, family sessions in our clinic and further individual work with Jane. There were ten individual sessions in all, helping her to reflect on how her own personal experiences might impact on her children's mental health and what actions she could take to protect them from her own 'moods'. A two-year follow-up showed 'good enough' parenting and family functioning. All the children's names had been removed from the Child Protection Register, but the social services department had remained involved, providing some practical support to the family as well as successfully rehousing the family. Jane had stopped her anti-depressants and reported that her – their – lives had the 'normal ups and downs' but that she was mostly 'fine'.

Conclusion

Much of the work described here takes place within a statutory and legal framework. The children are usually on Care Orders and many will be placed with foster carers. Attending the Marlborough is often seen as the parents' 'last chance' to prove that they are 'good enough' to have the children reunited with them, or that they are able to make sufficient changes so that rehabilitation becomes likely. Many of the families are initially reluctant to attend but quickly engage, particularly once they have met other families in our Family Day Unit with similar experiences to their own. Our unit provides detailed reports for social services and courts and our findings are constantly shared with the parents (for example, 'If we had to write the report on you today, we would say a, b and c and you may think that this is not very positive . . . if you want us to write a different report you have to make a few changes'). This approach is most likely to be successful if all relevant professionals are in agreement from the outset, so that the assessment and therapeutic work are supported by everyone. This also allows our team to coordinate their input with that of other professionals and thus support their work. Families do best when they connect with other families in our multi-family setting, allowing for first steps to be made with learning from other families who 'are all in the same boat', experimenting with forming relationships that could become an important resource in the future.

References

Asen, K., Stein, R., Stevens, A., McHugh, B., Greenwood, J. and Cooklin, A. (1982) A day unit for families. *Journal of Family Therapy*, 4, 345–358.

Cooklin, A., Miller, A. and McHugh, B. (1983) An institution for change: developing a family day unit. *Family Process*, 22, 453–468.

Dale, P. with Davies, M., Morrison, T. and Waters, J. (1986) *Dangerous Families*. London: Tavistock.

Minuchin, S. (1974) *Families and Family Therapy*. London: Tavistock.

Reder, P. (1986) Multi-agency family systems. *Journal of Family Therapy*, 8, 133–152.

Schuff, H. and Asen, K.E. (1996) The disturbed parent and the disturbed family. In: M. Göpfert, J. Webster and M. Seeman (eds) *Parental Psychiatric Disorder*. Cambridge: Cambridge University Press.

Wolfe, D.A. and Wekerle, C. (1993) Treatment strategies for child physical abuse and neglect – a critical progress report. *Clinical Psychology Review*, 13: 473–500.

Chapter 17

Parenting skills interventions

Martin Herbert

Introduction

Parenting skills are multifaceted: often complex, much of the time intuitive –
a repertoire acquired by learning rather than 'instinct', and one that is shaped
(and reshaped), often painfully, on the anvil of firsthand experience. As a
prerequisite for the long-term unconditional commitment they must make,
parents have to learn to love their child. Love at first sight or at preview is a
minority achievement for first-time mothers (Robson and Kumar, 1980).
What follows, as the child grows up, is the acquisition of a vast array of
caregiving skills and behaviour management strategies. Mothers and fathers
provide 'good' or 'good enough' parenting, using a variety of methods
informed by diverse family, social and cultural models.

What is personally learned has its roots in individual experiences of being
parented and grandparented, observations of other parents 'on task', advice
doubtless from many well-wishers, plus contributions from books, magazines
and television. Fine-tuning and more radical modifications of one's child-
rearing 'theories' are likely to emerge in the daily trial and error of actually
raising a child. Unfortunately, perhaps, most children seem blissfully unaware
of the received wisdom to be found in the multitudinous guides on how to
enhance child development or manage fractious behaviour. They frequently
resist being moulded to parents' preconceptions and ideals, not uncommonly
usurp their authority and indulge in wilful parent 'management' and
manipulation (Herbert and Iwaniec, 1977).

The individual differences in behavioural style, as one child succeeds
another in the family, may also bewilder and dismay parents. The fondness
and pride engendered by, for example, a first child of easy temperament may
be transformed into the resentment and embarrassment caused by the sibling
who displays aversive temperamental attributes – one of the so-called
'mother-killers' described by Thomas, Chess and Birch (1968).

Fortunately, most children, particularly those who benefit from good
health and constitutional (e.g. central nervous system) integrity, grow up to
be reasonably 'normal' and 'norm-abiding', despite parents' inexperience or

so-called 'mistakes', and in spite of their failure to attend courses and work-shops on parent-craft. Such resilience, of course, has its limits. Parental mal-treatment and neglect of the child, on one side of the risk equation, and vulnerabilities such as intellectual, physical or temperamental disabilities in the infant, on the other, are likely, over time, to generate serious emotional/behavioural disorders in the child, and daily disciplinary confrontations for the parent.

Rationale for parenting skills interventions

There has been a significant convergence in recent years of four developments which underline the relevance of, and need for, parent-training interventions: the growing demand in the health and social services for evidence-based interventions; increasing awareness at service delivery and national policy-making levels (for example, the Parenting Orders of the Crime and Disorder Act) of the critical role of early parenting in the evolution of serious mental health and forensic problems in early or later life; the growing concern about the costs – individual, social and financial – of mental health problems, notably conduct and delinquent disorders, in children and, as antecedents or consequences of such difficulties, their parents; also the burgeoning reports of well-designed studies indicating high levels of success for what were thought of, in the past, as intractable problems of childhood and adolescence (e.g. Barlow, 1997; Cedar and Levant, 1990; Herbert and Wookey, 1998; Serketich and Dumas, 1996; Todres and Bunston, 1993; Webster-Stratton, 1991).

The point about the empirical evidence is perhaps the most notable one, in bringing parenting interventions to the notice of agencies representing differ-ent disciplines and, indeed, governments (Herbert, 1995; Taylor and Biglan, 1998). These interventions are educative/training/counselling programmes conducted in the home or clinic, individually or in groups, with the purpose of helping parents cope more effectively, and (as a bonus often) enjoyably, with their children and their problems. Whose problems they are – parent's or child's – in any particular case is a moot point, and for most families an unanswerable and unrewarding 'chicken-and-egg' conundrum. It is most profitable to think of one's clients as interdependent members of attachment systems which require analysis as such, alongside consideration of salient individual attributes. There are many approaches to parent training based on a variety of ideological/theoretical models, psychodynamic approaches, Adlerian methods, the non-directive Rogerians or the more directive operant technology of radical behaviourists. These theoretical approaches find expression in a plethora of parenting programmes (see Davis and Spurr, 1998; Henry, 1981; Smith, 1996). It is worth noting that the boundaries between what is termed 'training' and what is called 'therapy' become blurred in the area of work described below.

This chapter, concentrating as it does on skills, will not consider the psychodynamic, Adlerian and Rogerian-style programmes, which are most concerned with attitudes and relationships. I have chosen Behavioural Parent Training (BPT) from the heterogeneous collection of parenting interventions because this approach has far outstripped any other as the target of validational studies (e.g. Barlow, 1997; Brestan and Eyberg, 1998; Kazdin, 1987; Patterson, 1982; Taylor and Biglan, 1998). A further reason for focusing on BPT is the wide range of social, clinical and developmental problems to which it has been applied (Callias, 1994; Herbert, 1993; Howlin, 1998; Wolfe and Wekerle, 1993). A major proportion of the research effort has been on families with developmentally handicapped children (such as those with autistic continuum or learning disabilities), with disruptive/non-compliant youngsters, and with maltreated children. I will not concentrate on the more didactic BPT projects such as (*inter alia*) the Early Intervention Lovaas methods, Portage or EDY (Education of the Developmentally Young), which have proved their worth with developmentally handicapped children (see Howlin, 1998; Lovaas, 1996), but rather projects involving the latter two categories of children.

Behavioural Parent Training (BPT)

To be effective, treatment/training programmes require an explicit conceptual foundation – that is, clear statements about what an intervention is designed to accomplish, and by means of what processes of change. The crucial issue is how the procedures used in therapy or training will influence the processes implicated in the dysfunction or counteract these influences by developing new repertoires. The early attempts to find methods to produce change in family relationships and interactions, sometimes covered by the generic term Behavioural Parent Training, were rooted in a mainly operant theoretical analysis of the contingencies involved in parent–child interactions (Skinner, 1953). Over the years this theory has been supported and elaborated by empirical studies of family interactions by many researchers, notably Gerald Patterson (1982), the seminal influence on BPT developments. Kendall and Hollon (1994) and Bandura (1977), among others, have contributed to the theoretical foundations of cognitive behavioural methodology, an essential element in contemporary programmes. BPT, and Behavioural Family Therapy, of which it is a core component, are based on the rationale that many of the problematic behaviours of childhood are developed and sustained in the home by learning situations enmeshed in dysfunctional parent–child and other intra-familial interactions. These maladaptive interactions, in turn, have their origins on both sides of the parent–child equation, in a host of biological, social and psychological factors.

Social learning theorists suggest that the very processes of learning that help the child adapt to life can, under certain circumstances, contribute to his/

her maladaptation. An immature child who learns by imitating an adult is not necessarily to know when it is deviant behaviour that is being modelled. A parent may unwittingly reinforce deviant behaviour and extinguish pro-social actions. If it is accepted that many deviant behaviours of childhood and adulthood are acquired as a function of faulty learning processes or as a result of the absence of appropriate training, for whatever reason, then there is a case for arguing that problems can most effectively be remedied, indeed prevented, when and where they occur, by applying principles of learning. Inappropriate behaviour and attitudes can be 'unlearned' by changing reinforcement contingencies and reframing cognitions – in other words, modifying the on-going social 'lessons' of life. The emphasis on the social aspect of learning is central to BPT. Learning takes place within a social nexus; events are mediated by human agents and within attachment and social systems (e.g. families, schools) and are not simply the impersonal consequences of behaviour.

As research on the interactions of families progressed it became clear that there was an additional critical feature of the interactions of dysfunctional families, namely coercion. In a coercive interaction, the aversive behaviour of each person is terminated or reduced in frequency by the aversive behaviour of the other person, the long-term effect being to increase the likelihood that original aversive behaviour will occur again. For example, a mother orders a child to do something he doesn't like so he tantrums. If the mother stops insisting that the child do what was asked, the child's tantrum stops, reinforced by getting his way – the removal of the mother's demand. The parent's behaviour – reneging on her demand – is negatively reinforced when the child stops tantruming. Thus, both the tantruming and the removal of parental demands are more likely to occur in future interactions. If left unchanged, these 'successfully' applied coercive patterns of interaction on the part of the child are likely to continue into school life and beyond.

The triadic model

The triadic approach is geared to the only people – parents, caregivers and teachers – who can intervene often enough and long enough to produce the long-term changes in what are often (especially in the case of the chronic or therapy-resistant problems of childhood) matters of faulty socialization, or difficulties in furthering the process of rearing children.

One of the child's major acquisitions on the road to becoming a social being is the development of internal controls over behaviour; the internalisation of standards of conduct and morality implied by the term conscience. There is substantial agreement about the conditions conducive to the acquisition of internalised rule (norm) formation. These include firm moral demands made by parents upon their offspring, the consistent use of sanctions, techniques of punishment that are psychological rather than physical (that is, methods which signify or threaten withdrawal of approval) and an intensive use of inductive methods (providing reasons and explanations).

Social learning theorists suggest that children with potentially serious anti-social problems are at risk because (*inter alia*) their early social learning/conditioning is proving to be ineffective. Youngsters with oppositional, conduct and (later) delinquent disorders demonstrate a fundamental inability or unwillingness to adhere to the rules and codes of conduct prescribed by society at its various levels. Such failures may be related to the lapse of poorly established learned controls, to the failure to learn these controls in the first place, or to the imbibing of deviant standards from anti-social or emotionally disturbed caregivers. A variety of economic, social and family conditions preclude the operation of pro-social influences of the kind described above, and facilitate the dysfunctional tendencies in the lives of some children. Many adults entering parenthood have not enjoyed models of affectional or competent caregiving; some have endured quite the opposite. There may be few opportunities for supportive, compensatory learning; and when hard-won skills are acquired, the time and space (indeed, money) necessary for responsive parenting are outside their reach.

Disharmonious, rejecting or abusive home backgrounds, the breakdown of discipline, parental loss, and broken homes, are but a few examples of *distal* life variables that are linked aetiologically to disruptive and other disorders (Farrington, 1995; Herbert, 1987a). With regard to *proximal* influences, studies of parents who do not experience child management problems and those who have been referred to agencies for a variety of difficulties have identified marked differences in the behaviour-management repertoires – a matter to which we return.

BPT for cases of neglect and maltreatment

Interventions with parents usually involve elements of self-control (e.g. anger management) training, problem-solving and the encouragement of proximity-seeking and attachment behaviour (see Iwaniec *et al.*, 1988, on failure-to-thrive bonding work). Of necessity, they usually need to tackle wider systemic (family) issues. The treatment targets might include the following (Herbert, 1993): characteristics of the parents (e.g. alcohol abuse, deficits in bonding and child-rearing skills, faulty expectations of the child, low self-esteem, ineffective communication, reinforcement skills, punitive attitudes, failure to supervise the child); characteristics of the child (e.g. non-compliant aggressive problems, incontinence, inappropriately inflexible responses to different situations, disability); unique interaction of the child and his/her parents (e.g. coercive/aversive communications, mutual avoidance, inappropriate, inconsistent – perhaps non-contingent – reinforcement/punishment); significant others in the family (interference, subversion of maternal authority by grandparent, sexual/physical abuse by relative/lodger, etc.); environmental factors (poverty, overcrowding, social isolation); and being cared for by a parent with a mental health problem where parenting may be inconsistent.

Specific techniques to implement these goals are detailed in Herbert (1987b; 1993) and Carr (1999). The findings from several studies of BPT in child protection work have indicated improved child care and management, and/or a reduction in the re-occurrence of child abuse (e.g. Crimmins *et al.*, 1984; Gough, 1993; Paley, 1990; Smith and Rachman, 1984; Wolfe *et al.*, 1988).

Wolfe and Wekerle (1993) concluded on the basis of a review of the literature that cognitive-behavioural approaches enjoyed a consistent success rate in helping maltreating parents improve several of the conditions that predispose them to abusive and neglectful treatment of their children. All such programmes produced improvements in parenting skills – for example in parents' ability to interact positively with their children and control behaviour without over-reliance on negative, coercive, physically punitive child management techniques. Reassessment after treatment and at follow-up (generally three months to one year) tended to support the maintenance and generalization of these changes. Abuse or neglect did not recur among treatment families in those studies reporting significant outcome data.

BPT for disruptive behaviour (conduct) disorders

The conduct disorders of childhood and adolescence, which constitute the most common referrals to child and family consultation services, present an immense challenge to parents and professionals alike. Their onset in childhood (and it is often very early childhood) represents a particularly severe pattern of dysfunction, whereas the findings from many longitudinal studies indicate that young people who begin showing conduct problems in adolescence are much less likely to persist in their anti-social behaviour in adulthood (Farrington, 1995). The relatively less serious 'adolescent limited' pattern is considered an exaggeration of a normal developmental process – a developmentally advanced form of Oppositional Defiant Disorder (Frick, 1997).

Aggressive, anti-social children are at increased risk of being rejected by their peers. They are also at risk of developing a veritable litany of problems later in life, such as truancy, alcoholism, drug abuse, juvenile delinquency, adult crime and interpersonal problems (Robins and Price, 1991). It is therefore vital to interrupt the transgenerational trend of anti-social/aggressive behaviour. Research (see Moffitt and Caspi, 1998) indicates that maltreatment and witnessing parental aggression during early childhood are predictive of children developing conduct problems, which, in turn, predict later partner violence. Rates of partner violence double among young couples who move from dating to cohabiting. They tend to bear children at a young age, and thus aggressive behaviour becomes highly stable across the life course of individuals, and is transmitted from generation to generation within families.

Clearly, there is an urgent need to develop and evaluate standardized therapeutic programmes which can be distributed widely for purposes of training practitioners, who in turn train parents, who in turn (hopefully) train their children. Unfortunately, the prevalence of disruptive behavioural disorders (which are increasing) has generated a need for services that far exceeds available resources and personnel (Herbert, 1995). It is estimated that only between 10 and 20 per cent of children with mental health problems reach specialist consultation, and these may not always be the ones most in need of help (Cox, 1993; Offord, 1982; 1987). In the absence of early treatment a substantial proportion of children with early-onset disorders are likely to remain circulating through the revolving doors of the special needs educational and social services, mental health agencies and criminal justice systems.

BPT programmes address themselves to the fact that parents of children with behaviour problems tend (*inter alia*) to flounder because they issue so many commands, provide attention following deviant behaviour, are unlikely to perceive deviant behaviour as deviant, get frequently embroiled in extended coercive hostile interchanges, give vague commands, and are generally ineffectual in bringing their children's deviant behaviour to a halt (Kazdin, 1987; Patterson, 1982). Parents are encouraged and guided to increase their positive interactions with their children through the use of play and other activities, and by looking to the positives in their actions. They are encouraged to reinforce their children's appropriate behaviour with praise, encouragement and other rewards; also to introduce the child to behaviours which are either intrinsically reinforcing, or which make previously unattainable reinforcements available.

Parents are assisted in reducing unnecessary commands, increasing the clarity of their house rules and the limits they set, and increasing the consistency with which they follow through on their limits. To do this they are guided in the implementation of brief, mild, non-violent sanctions such as judicious ignoring, time-out, loss of privileges and logical consequences. They are provided with the means of understanding and analysing problematic behaviour, and ways of negotiating and problem-solving their way out of previously corrosive, confrontational situations. They are also encouraged to monitor their children effectively, and to engage in meaningful communication. Parents' experience of being parented, and of being children themselves, in the past, is related to their attitudes and attributions in their ideologies of child-rearing. This is one of the ways in which parents are encouraged to make connections between their own thoughts, feelings and behaviours, and those of their children.

An example of a BPT programme

The Childwise Parenting Skills Programme (Herbert and Wookey, 1998) which was developed and evaluated at the Paediatric Assessment Centre, Plymouth, and conducted at community centres, is one example of a programme designed for parents of young children (3 to 8 years). Programme curricula can, of course, be tailored to meet the requirements of particular age groups, problems, caregivers (e.g. foster or adoptive parents) and agencies (see Gill, 1998; Herbert and Iwaniec, 1981; Herbert, 1998a; Sutton, 1992). Groups consist of 10 to 15 parents including as many fathers as possible.

The Childwise Parenting Skills Programme

Introductory home visit

Here we:

- Introduce ourselves; explain the nature of the programme and the collaborative philosophy; give time and place of the group; sort out arrangements for getting to the venue; make a contract; complete baseline measures; observe the child interacting with family members; and leave a handout about the programme.

Session 1

This being the first meeting of the group it is important to establish rapport, a set of working rules, and a sense of confidence in what lies ahead. Problems are shared and defined and parents' needs acknowledged. Each session lasts two hours and includes a twenty-minute coffee break. The two group facilitators:

- Introduce themselves and the other parents/exchange children's photographs;
- Explain the nature of the programme; discuss how other parents have similar problems with their children;
- Present a video – one of our training tapes: a family mismanaging a disobedient toddler;
- Discuss the tape and what constitutes a problem;
- Discuss the specific behaviours manifested by their children that cause them concern;
- Explain red, green and amber code with regard to rules;
- Facilitate small subgroups to specify what each parent's priorities are (discipline/child-rearing);

- Fill in parent rating scale individually;
- Invite parents individually to choose two problem behaviours to work on; parents also describe two pro-social behaviours to record.

Homework

Parents are given a recording sheet and are asked to record the frequency of pro-social behaviours and the chosen problem behaviour. Parents are asked to bring the records with them next week. Handouts are provided each week as reminders of the topics discussed. Subsequent sessions are a mixture of group discussion and debate, exposition, video examples, role-play, rehearsal of behavioural strategies and problem-solving on particular management difficulties.

Session 2

Concentrates on children's needs, especially those for 'special' (quality) time, developmental tasks, praise and play. An account of the 'attention rule' (differential attention) is provided.

Session 3

Focuses on parents' own childhood play experiences and the functions of play. Criteria of child-directive and child-centred behaviours are provided for categorizing parent–child play interactions.

Session 4

Deals with effective praise, the ABC functional analysis of antecedents to behaviours/interactions and their consequences, and how behaviour/ misbehaviour is learned.

Session 5

Focuses on tangible and social rewards and the effect on behaviour. A list of suggested reinforcers is provided. Parents are encouraged to make interesting 'reward' charts.

Session 6

Returns in more detail to the ABC of behaviour with emphasis on the B for Beliefs (perceptions, attributions, theories). Parents' own ABCs, particularly with regard to cognition/stress and its management, are discussed.

Session 7

Addresses the issues of discipline and the sensitive subject of punishment – physical and non-physical. Opportunities to debate and role-play limit-setting, formulating rules, making effective requests and commands are provided.

Sessions 8 and 9

Techniques such as judicious ignoring, time-out, response-cost, distractions and logical consequences are described and debated, also role-played. The problems associated with smacking are listed following brain-storming.

Session 10

This is a session on self-care and stress management for parents.

There is a final debriefing and evaluation of the programme. Booster/refresher sessions are arranged.

Questions raised by BPT

1   *Should parents rehearse or practise the skills they learn?*
    In principle the practice of child management skills would seem highly desirable. On balance the safe answer is *yes*, but there is limited evidence to suggest that actual practice is a *necessary* or *sufficient* condition for helping parents develop such skills.
2   *Should parent training focus on specific target problems or develop know-ledge of general behavioural principles?*
    It does seem that the latter is more cost-effective as it facilitates the implementation and generalisation of newly-acquired child management skills in situations.
3   *Should parent training programmes begin with easy or difficult problems?*
    There is no simple answer. Problems are easier:

    a   if they occur under conditions that permit ready observation by parents;
    b   if they occur with relatively high frequency;
    c   if they are maintained by stimuli from parents rather than others;
    d   if they occur naturally at a specified time (i.e. mealtime, bedtime, and so on).

4   *Does early reinforcement arising from success with easy problems increase cooperation?*
    Beginning treatment with more or less difficult behaviour problems does not seem to affect parental cooperation, but there is still some doubt

about this issue. It may, however, increase parents' sense of self-confidence or competence (self-efficacy) if easy problems are tackled first.

5   *How is parental motivation maintained?*
It seems probable that parents will maintain their enthusiasm and interest for the programme as long as they perceive some progress in managing their offspring's actions, regardless of how difficult these behaviours are to deal with in the therapist's opinion.

6   *How can parental cooperation be encouraged?*
Telephone contact and carefully-timed home visits also increase parents' cooperation.

The following factors have been shown to hinder the successful outcome of interventions (e.g. Dumas and Wahler, 1983; Kazdin, 1990; Lobitz and Johnson, 1975): poor parental adjustment, particularly maternal depression; holding rigid child-rearing ideologies; maternal stress and low socio-economic status; repudiation of causal connection between one's own and one's child's behaviour; social isolation of mother; relationship problems; extrafamilial conflict; the problems are particularly severe and/or long-standing; and parental misperception of the deviance of their children's behaviour.

Such obstacles suggest a level of casework complexity which requires broadly conceived interventions.

Experiential influences

In spite of the documented effectiveness of various types of parent-training programmes in terms of content, the literature contains comparatively little discussion of experiential and developmental issues as they affect individuals, or of the actual therapeutic processes utilized by therapists in order to deal with these and other matters, in their intervention programmes. Cognitive-behavioural techniques such as planned ignoring, time-out, beta commands, praise, differential attention, response cost, logical consequences, anger control, perspective-taking, role-taking, cognitive restructuring, and so on, have been explored in detail (e.g. Herbert, 1987b; 1994). Describing the 'technology' alone, however, does not elucidate what happens when therapists try to change or influence parents' behaviours, attitudes, attributions and practices. How can they encourage regular attendance, persuade parents to keep records or ensure that homework is carried out? How do they help them, when well-'defended', to make connections between their own and their child's actions?

Parents often complain that professionals simply do not understand, or attend to, their side of the story. An extensive qualitative analysis by Webster-Stratton of what parents say about these matters (see Webster-Stratton and

Herbert, 1994) has begun to address this issue. Prior to therapy, most parents of conduct-problem children feel as if they are 'under siege'. The child's hyperactivity, distractability, developmental problems, and unpredictability drain the parents and lead to many ripple effects. Their relationships with other family members, friends, and people in the community (notably at school) are quite likely to be adversely affected. Marital discord and depression are common.

Today, there is less emphasis on the contingency management of specific target behaviours, and more on broad principles of child management, the interpersonal interactions of members of the family, the marital relationships (which are often poor in the parents of problematic children), self-control training, and the perceived self-efficacy of parents (e.g. Bandura, 1989; Dadds *et al.*, 1987; Patterson *et al.*, 1982; Wells *et al.*, 1980). These general issues increase the effectiveness of the specific child management skills being attended to.

Collaboration and partnership in BPT

Webster-Stratton and Herbert (1994) have described in detail the collaborative process of working with families. They suggest that the first role of the therapist in the collaborative process is to build a supportive relationship with the parents. This is often achieved through appropriate use of self-disclosure, humour and optimism, as well as actively advocating for parents (such as at the child's school), as appropriate. A second role of the therapist is to empower parents, through reinforcing and validating parents' insights, helping them to modify powerless thoughts, promoting self-empowerment (i.e. knowledge, skills and values), and building family and group supports. A third role of the therapist is to teach by persuading, explaining, suggesting, adapting, giving assignments, reviewing, summarising, ensuring generalisation, using videotape examples, and role-playing. A fourth role of the therapist is to interpret or 'translate' the cognitive, behavioural and developmental concepts into words that the parents can understand and apply. This includes the use of analogies and metaphors, reframing, and making connections between the parents' own childhood or other life experiences and those of the child. A fifth role of the therapist is to lead and challenge, including setting limits (especially in groups), pacing the sessions, and dealing with resistance. A further role of the therapist is to 'prophesy', which means anticipating problems and setbacks such as the escalation of difficult behaviour that often follows the initial attempts to 'extinguish' forced unacceptable activities that have been positively reinforced. It also includes predicting parent resistance to change, and predicting positive change and success.

This partnership between clients and therapist has the effect of giving back dignity, respect, and self-control to parents who are often seeking help at a vulnerable time of low self-confidence and intense feelings of guilt and self-blame. It is hypothesised that a collaborative model, which gives parents responsibility for developing solutions (alongside the therapist), is more likely to empower caregivers and increase their confidence and perceived self-efficacy in treatment, than are models which do not hold them responsible for solutions. Support for the value of this approach comes from the literature on self-efficacy, attribution, helplessness and locus of control (see Bandura, 1989). Bandura has suggested that self-efficacy is the mediating variable between knowledge and behaviour. Therefore, parents who are self-efficacious tend to persist at tasks until success is achieved; if they have determined their own priorities and goals they are more likely to persist in the face of difficulties.

Outcome studies

Specific studies (see Webster-Stratton, 1991) have demonstrated the following: short-term treatment outcome has been verified by significant changes in parents' and children's behaviour, and in parental perceptions of child adjustment; home observations have indicated that parents are successful in reducing children's level of aggression by 20–60 per cent; generalisation of improvements from clinic to the home occur over follow-up periods of 1–4 years; there is generalisation to untreated child behaviours (generalisation from the clinic to school shows less consistent results); high parental ratings of acceptability and consumer satisfaction are expressed.

Comparison studies

- The Patterson and Gullion (1968) BPT approach has been shown to be superior to family-based psychotherapy, attention (discussion) placebo and no-treatment conditions.
- Forehand and McMahon's (1981) programme has been demonstrated to be more effective than family systems therapy. A group version was more effective than a parent discussion group based on the Systematic Training for Effective Parenting (STEP) programme.
- The Webster-Stratton programme – Group Discussion Video Modelling (GDVM) – has been shown to be superior to waiting-list control condition, an individualised 'bug-in-the-ear' approach, and a parent group discussion approach (without videotape modelling methods; or administered videotape modelling approach without therapist feedback or group discussion). This component analysis of the GDVM parent-training methods suggests that parent training that uses videotape modelling plus parent group discussion and support produces more sustained and long-term effects than programmes which do not. Moreover, the group approach represents a cost-effective alternative to the conventional parent-training format of individual therapy with a single family.

- The consultation format, in which parents receive advice and reading material or have contact by phone, has had its successes, as has the individual, training approach (see Gill, 1998; Herbert, 1987a and b; 1994; 1998b; Sutton, 1992).

Reviews

In an important recent review Brestan and Eyberg (1998) examined 82 outcome studies involving 29 years of research and 5,722 children. Two interventions were identified that met stringent criteria for 'well-established' treatments: the video-modelling parent-training programme (see Webster-Stratton, 1996); and Patterson and Gullion's Living with Children (1968) programme.

Barlow (1997) conducted a review covering the years 1970 to 1997 to identify all relevant studies, including writing to all coordinators of parent-training groups registered in the UK. Eighteen out of a total of 255 studies identified met strict inclusion criteria, and formed the basis of her analysis. The heterogeneity of the studies meant that it was not possible to conduct a meta-analysis. Three main forms of programme emerged: skills training (behavioural and social learning-based); educational (Parent Effectiveness Programmes (PET)); and relationship (Adlerian). Barlow found that group-based programmes generally produced superior results to individual programmes; and one study showed that a behavioural programme produced significant changes in child behaviour irrespective of the method of administration (i.e. group or individual; telephone or home visits). Barlow writes that, although the numbers of parents participating in the treatment groups in this trial were small, the result may testify to the robustness of the behavioural method in producing positive changes. Behavioural programmes produced superior results to either Adlerian or PET programmes. While all group-based parent-training programmes produced changes in children's behaviour using both parent-report outcome measures and independent observations of children's behaviour, the behavioural programmes produced greater effect sizes than the remaining programmes.

Reservations and implications

It is important that this approach does not suffer the fate of Social Skills Training and come to be thought of as a panacea. Not all clients benefit from this approach. One of the research challenges for the future is to discover with more precision what it is, and why it is, that we fail with certain parents and certain children. Researchers like Kazdin (1997) and Taylor and Biglan (1998) make the point that outcome research usually involves demonstrations of *efficacy* rather than demonstrations of *effectiveness* or clinical utility. Efficacy studies are directed at establishing whether a particular intervention works (e.g. reduces symptoms, increases adaptive functioning), and they are usually conducted under tightly *controlled conditions*. Effectiveness, or clinical utility, studies are directed at establishing how well a particular intervention works in the environments and under the 'real-life' conditions in which treatment typically takes place. It is clear that the clinical utility (effectiveness) of psycho-social interventions needs to be established. Efficacy is a necessary but not sufficient condition for demonstrating the effectiveness of psycho-social interventions. That is, a treatment that is no more effective than no treatment or an attention placebo is unlikely to be effective in less controlled clinical practice. However, a treatment may have demonstrated efficacy in clinical trials but may fail to be effective in the notoriously unpredictable hurly-burly of clinical practice. This may be the result of difficulty in implementing the intervention in clinical settings, the non-acceptability of the intervention to clients, or the fact of greater heterogeneity of clinical populations and special problems in clinical settings (e.g. comorbidity, high attrition rates) compared to research settings.

There is some evidence that the collaborative process has the multiple advantage of reducing attrition rates, increasing motivation and commitments, reducing resistance, increasing temporal and situational generalisation, and giving both parents and the therapist a stake in the outcome of the intervention efforts (Herbert, 1998b). An access (or return) of self-confidence and self-pride are the recurring and particularly dramatic benefits of the collaborative approach (Herbert and Wookey, 1998).

Some practitioners suggest that failure is sometimes a reflection of great stress (social and economic, marital and personal) undermining parents with exhaustion and despair (see Webster-Stratton and Herbert, 1994). The disappointing results may relate to the parents' own previous experiences of parenting, to ideologies of child care that are rigid, and to attributes that insist on giving children the sole 'ownership' of their difficulties. Although child management strategies are the primary component of behavioural family interventions, they are not the only therapeutic strategies used. Research has demonstrated that other factors, including parent depression, marital conflict, poverty, social isolation, and single-parent status, all influence the caregiving behaviour of parents, which in turn influences the child's behaviour. These factors, as we saw earlier, are now being addressed in the wider spectrum that constitutes Behavioural Family Therapy.

Of course, negative findings may reflect an erroneous clinical formulation, or perhaps a lack of *ability* on the part of the therapist; there may be an inability on the part of the parents to conceptualise learning principles or a resistance to perceiving improvement in their children's behaviour. During therapy, parents can be expected to resist the therapy process over the sessions. It is common for them to report that they 'have tried' all of the strategies and 'none of them work'. Parents may alternate between hope and despair – one week finding a 'quick fix' that solves all their child's problems, and the next week experiencing setbacks and feeling that nothing works.

Dealing with this and other complex group dynamics requires skills and sensitivity. In the field of clinical work, not all programmes are run by appropriately trained therapists. The issue of programme 'integrity' is critical (see Hollin, 1995). Hollin cites an example of one published study in which the majority of those responsible for carrying out the treatment were not themselves convinced that it would affect recidivism, and the group leaders were poorly trained. In Kazdin's view (1997) treatment ought to be operationalised, and he particularly favours putting treatment into the form of a manual where possible, so that the integrity of treatment can be evaluated, the material learned from treatment trials codified, and the treatment procedures replicated. There has to be room for improvisation in treatment programmes. However, we need a balance of clear manual guidelines, possibilities for improvisation, and space for individual therapist differences – a challenging task. Patterson and Gullion's 1968 guide and Webster-Stratton's manuals and videotapes exemplify two such American attempts. Another British example is the author's (see Herbert and Wookey, 1998). These are but a few of available manuals. Only within the last 5 to 10 years has it been recognized that the use of treatment manuals is a requirement in treatment outcome studies (Brestan and Eyberg, 1998), in order to assure accurate implementation and replication of treatments – in fact a basic requirement for meeting the criteria for well-established treatments.

Influencing policy

Short-term rewards are more potent than delayed reinforcers. Funding research into the early years of childhood means an investment (in terms of preventing, for example, delinquency) with a delayed pay-off. This is a problem for those with research and treatment programmes. Social and political contingencies have a profound influence on the work of those who seek to design and evaluate therapeutic programmes. It is administrators who decide on funding of research projects on disruptive children and offenders, and ultimately what the therapist can achieve. Therapeutic contingencies are designed by therapists; social/political contingencies (rules, regulations, policies or laws) are established by administrators. Policy makers need to be aware of the vexed problems that many parents with unmanageable children face, and need to be made aware of the availability of community-based interventions like BPT, in formulating their short- and long-term strategies for disturbed children, remedial and preventive. Extending parent training skills beyond the remit of a small elite group of clinicians is an important consideration in the development of services. Training other professionals – notably nurses, social workers and health visitors – to conduct BPT interventions is paying dividends (e.g. Nicol et al., 1993; Hollin et al., 1987; Sutton, 1992).

Cost-containment

The issue of cost-containment is increasingly an important one in government services. Behavioural interventions tend to be relatively cost-efficient when compared with long-term therapy. At the Oregon Social Learning Centre the average length of therapy for families with young children with serious behaviour problems was just over 20 hours (range: 4–48 hours) (Patterson and Narrett, 1990). For families with delinquent adolescents, it was typically twice that length (Banks *et al.*, 1991). Drop-out rates tended to be low.

Conclusions

One can differentiate among the many treatments in use, based on the status of their evidence. One reason that empirically supported interventions have not been adopted more frequently (in the opinion of Taylor and Biglan, 1998) is that most approaches to therapy claim to be 'process effective'. For example, interventions are often evaluated by asking clients at the end of therapy whether they think that things have improved. Such studies tell us little, because most clients answer 'yes' to the question, even when more careful assessment shows that no improvement has occurred (Patterson and Narrett, 1990). And without appropriate controls (far too common an occurrence), even if things have genuinely improved, the attribution of the positive changes as due to the treatment may be erroneous.

When children come to treatment as victims of abuse or as sufferers from depression, anxiety, conduct problems or ADHD, there are specific individual and/or parent-mediated treatments that would be interventions of choice. There are horses for courses! Not applying one of the treatments identified as well-established would seem to require a very strong justification.

References

Bandura, A. (1977) *Social Learning Theory.* Englewood Cliffs, NJ: Prentice-Hall.

Bandura, A. (1989) Regulation of cognitive processes through perceived self-efficacy. *Developmental Psychology*, 25, 729–735.

Banks, S.L., Marlowe, J.H., Reid, J.B., Patterson, G.R. and Weinrott, M.R. (1991) A comparative evaluation of parent training interventions for families of chronic delinquents. *Journal of Abnormal Child Psychology*, 19, 15–33.

Barlow, J. (1997) *Systematic review of the effectiveness of parent-training programmes in improving behaviour problems in children aged 3–10 years.* Health Services Research Unit, Oxford: University of Oxford.

Brestan, E.V. and Eyberg, S.M. (1998) Effective psychosocial treatments of conduct-disordered children and adolescents: 29 years, 82 studies, and 5,272 kids. *Journal of Clinical Child Psychology*, 27, 180–189.

Callias, M. (1994) Parent training. In: M. Rutter, E. Taylor and L. Hersov (eds)

Child and Adolescent Psychiatry: Modern Approaches, 3rd edn. Oxford: Blackwell.

Carr, A. (1999) *The Handbook of Child and Adolescent Clinical Psychology*. London: Routledge.

Cedar, B. and Levant, R.F. (1990) A meta-analysis of the effects of parent effectiveness training. *American Journal of Family Therapy*, 18, 373–384.

Cox, A. (1993) Preventive aspects of child psychiatry. *Archives of Disease in Childhood*, 68, 691–701.

Crimmins, D.B., Bradlyn, A.S., St Lawrence, J.S. and Kelly, J.A. (1984) A training technique for improving the parent–child interaction skills of an abusive–neglectful mother. *Child Abuse and Neglect*, 8, 533–539.

Dadds, M.R., Schwartz, S. and Sanders, M.R. (1987) Marital discord and treatment outcome in behavioural treatment of child conduct disorder. *Journal of Consulting and Clinical Psychology*, 55, 396–403.

Davis, H. and Spurr, P. (1998) Parent counselling: an evaluation of a community child mental health service. *Journal of Child Psychology and Psychiatry*, 39, 365–376.

Dumas, J.E. and Wahler, R.G. (1983) Predictors of treatment outcome in parent training: mothers' insularity and socioeconomic disadvantage. *Behavior Assessment*, 5, 301–313.

Farrington, D.P. (1995) The development of offending and anti-social behaviours from childhood: key findings from the Cambridge study of delinquent development. *Journal of Child Psychology and Psychiatry*, 36, 929–1064.

Forehand, R. and McMahon, R. (1981) *Helping the Noncompliant Child: A Clinician's Guide to Parent Training*. New York: Guilford.

Frick, P.J. (1997) Conduct disorder. In: T. Ollendick and M. Hersen (eds) *Handbook of Child Psychopathology*, 3rd edn. New York: Plenum.

Gill, A.N. (1998) What makes parent training groups effective? Promoting positive parenting through collaboration. Unpublished Ph.D. thesis. University of Leicester.

Gough, R. (1993) *Child Abuse Interventions*. London: HMSO.

Henry, S.A. (1981) Current dimensions of parent training. *School Psychology Review*, 10, 4–14.

Herbert, M. (1987a) *Conduct Disorders of Childhood and Adolescence*, 2nd edn. Chichester: Wiley.

Herbert, M. (1987b) *Behavioural Treatment of Children with Problems: A Practice Manual*, 2nd edn. London: Academic Press.

Herbert, M. (1993) *Working with Children and the Children Act*. Leicester: BPS Books (British Psychological Society).

Herbert, M. (1994) Behavioural methods. In: M. Rutter, E. Taylor and L. Hersov (eds) *Child and Adolescent Psychiatry: Modern Approaches*, 3rd edn. Oxford: Blackwell.

Herbert, M. (1995). A collaborative model of training for parents of children with disruptive behaviour disorders. *British Journal of Clinical Psychology*, 34, 325–342.

Herbert, M. (1997) Family treatment. In: T.H. Ollendick and M. Hersen (eds) *Handbook of Clinical Child Psychology*, 3rd edn. New York: Plenum.

Herbert, M. (1998a) Adolescent conduct disorders. In: P. Graham (ed.) *Cognitive Behaviour Therapy for Children and Families*. Cambridge: Cambridge University Press.

Herbert, M. (1998b) *Clinical Child Psychology: Social Learning, Behaviour and Development*, 2nd edn. Chichester: John Wiley & Sons.

Herbert, M. and Iwaniec, D. (1977) Children who are hard to love. *New Society*, 40 (759), 111–112.

Herbert, M. and Iwaniec, D. (1981) Behavioural psychotherapy in natural home settings; an empirical study applied to conduct disordered and incontinent children. *Behavioural Psychotherapy*, 9, 55–76.

Herbert, M. and Wookey, J.A. (1998) *Child-Wise Parenting Skills Manual*, revised edn. Exeter: Impact Publications (PO Box 342, Exeter EX6 7ZD).

Hollin, C.R. (1995) The meaning and implications of 'programme integrity'. In: J. McGuire (ed.) *What Works: Effective Methods to Reduce Reoffending*. Chichester: John Wiley & Sons.

Hollin, C.R., Wilkie, J. and Herbert, M. (1987) Behavioural social work: training and application. *Practice*, 1, 297–304.

Howlin, P. (1998) Psychological and educational treatments for autism. *Journal of Child Psychology and Psychiatry*, 39, 307–322.

Iwaniec, D., Herbert, M. and Sluckin, A. (1988) Helping emotionally abused children who fail to thrive. In: K. Browne, C. Davies and P. Stratton (eds) *Early Prediction and Prevention of Child Abuse*. Chichester: John Wiley & Sons.

Kazdin, A.E. (1987) Treatment of antisocial behaviour in children: current status and future directions. *Psychological Bulletin*, 102, 187–203.

Kazdin, A.E. (1990) Premature termination from treatment among children referred for antisocial behaviour. *Journal of Child Psychology and Psychiatry*, 31, 415–425.

Kazdin, A.E. (1997) A model for developing effective treatments: progression and interplay of theory, research and practice. *Journal of Clinical Child Psychology*, 26, 114–129.

Kendall, P.C. and Hollon, S.D. (eds) (1994) *Cognitive-Behavioral Interventions: Theory, Research and Procedures*. New York: Academic Press.

Lobitz, G. and Johnson, S. (1975) Normal versus deviant children. *Journal of Abnormal Child Psychology*, 3, 353–374.

Lovaas, O.I. (1996) The UCLA young autism model of service delivery. In: C. Maurice (ed.) *Behavioral Intervention for Young Children with Autism*. Austin, Tex.: Pro-Ed.

Moffitt, T.E. and Caspi, A. (1998) Implications of violence between intimate partners for child psychologists and psychiatrists. *Journal of Child Psychology and Psychiatry*, 39, 137–144.

Nicol, A., Stretch, D. and Fundudis, R. (1993) *Preschool Children in Troubled Families: Approaches to Intervention and Support*. Chichester: John Wiley & Sons.

Offord, D. (1982) Primary prevention: aspects of program design and evaluation. *Journal of the American Academy of Child Psychiatry*, 21, 225–230.

Offord, D. (1987) Prevention of behavioral and emotional disorders in children. *Journal of Child Psychology and Psychiatry*, 28, 9–19.

Paley, J. (ed.) (1990) *Child Protection Adviser's Resource Pack: A Compendium for Child Protection Advisers in Health and Local Authorities*. London: NSPCC.

Patterson, G. and Narrett, C. (1990) The development of a reliable and valid treatment programme for aggressive young children. *International Journal of Mental Health*, 19, 19–26.

Patterson, G.R. (1982) *A Social Learning Approach to Family Intervention: Coercive Family Process.* Eugene, Oreg.: Castalia Publishing.

Patterson, G.R. and Gullion, M.E. (1968) *Living with Children: New Methods for Parents and Children.* Champaign, Ill.: Research Press.

Patterson, G.R., Chamberlain, P. and Reid, J.B. (1982) A comparative evaluation of a parent training program. *Behavior Therapy*, 13, 638–650.

Robins, L.N. and Price, R.K. (1991) Adult disorders predicted by child epidemiologic catchment and project. *Psychiatry*, 54, 116–132.

Robson, K.M. and Kumar, R. (1980) Delayed onset of maternal affection after childbirth. *British Journal of Psychiatry*, 136, 347–353.

Serketich, W.J. and Dumas, J.E. (1996) The effectiveness of behavioural parent training to modify anti-social behaviour in children: a meta-analysis. *Behavior Therapy*, 27, 171–186.

Skinner, B.F. (1953) *Science and Human Behavior.* New York: Macmillan.

Smith, C. (1996) *Developing Parenting Programmes.* London: National Children's Bureau.

Smith, J.E. and Rachman, S.J. (1984) Non-accidental injury to children: a controlled evaluation of a behavioural management programme. *Behaviour Research and Therapy*, 22, 349–366.

Sutton, C. (1992) Training parents to manage difficult children: a comparison of methods. *Behavioural Psychotherapy*, 20, 115–139.

Taylor, T.K. and Biglan, A. (1998) Behavioral family interventions for improving child-rearing: a review of the literature for clinicians and policy makers. *Clinical Child and Family Psychology Review*, 1, 41–60.

Thomas, A., Chess, S. and Birch, H.G. (1968) *Temperament and Behavior Disorders in Children.* London: University of London Press.

Todres, R. and Bunston, T. (1993) Parent-education programme evaluation: a review of the literature. *Canadian Journal of Community Mental Health*, 12, 225–257.

Webster-Stratton, C. (1991) Annotation: strategies for helping families with conduct disordered children. *Journal of Child Psychology and Psychiatry*, 32, 1047–1062.

Webster-Stratton, C. (1996) Early intervention with videotape modelling: programmes for families with oppositional defiant disorder or conduct disorder. In: E.D. Hibbs and J. Jensen (eds) *Psychological Treatment Research of Child and Adolescent Disorders.* Washington, DC: American Psychological Association.

Webster-Stratton, C. and Herbert, M. (1994) *Troubled Families: Problem Children: Working with Parents – A Collaborative Approach.* Chichester: Wiley.

Wells, R., Griest, D.L. and Forehand, R. (1980) The use of a self-control package to enhance temporal generality of a parent-training program. *Behaviour Research and Therapy*, 18, 347–358.

Wolfe, D.A. and Wekerle, C. (1993) Treatment strategies for child physical abuse and neglect: a critical progress report. *Clinical Psychology Review*, 13, 473–500.

Wolfe, D.A., Edwards, B., Manion, I. and Koverola, C. (1988) Early intervention for parents at risk for child abuse and neglect: a preliminary report. *Journal of Consulting and Clinical Psychology*, 56, 40–47.

Chapter 18

Perinatal mental health

Psychodynamic and psychiatric perspectives

Alicia Etchegoyen

Introduction

Over the last two decades there has been a growing interest in the psychiatric and psychological problems that occur in child-bearing women, with evidence that perinatal disorder in all its range of severity has considerable personal, social and economic implications.

The Royal College of Psychiatrists' Working Party on 'Postnatal Mental Illness' (1992) noted that:

> there is significant unmet need throughout the United Kingdom for women with postnatal mental illness, there are few comprehensive services, large deficits in patient provision and designated day hospital facilities, as well as lack of specific consultant led teams with specialist knowledge of the impact of mental illness on the baby and older siblings, as well as on the infant's father.

The 'Health of the Nation' document (Department of Health, 1993) singles out postnatal illness as an area of particular concern. These reports indicate an awareness of the importance of recognising and treating postnatal illness and, more recently, prenatal conditions. This interest is reflected in the creation of a Specialist Interest Section on Perinatal Psychiatry at the Royal College of Psychiatrists in 1994.

This chapter will look at pregnancy and parenthood from a psychoanalytic and psychiatric perspective. Some epidemiological and research data on the effects of perinatal morbidity on the child and the family will be presented, followed by a discussion on services available. As a conclusion, a case for the development of perinatal mental health services through specialisation will be put forward.

Psychodynamic aspects of pregnancy and parenthood

Pregnancy is considered to be a unique and specific critical transition in a woman's life, which has to be negotiated at the social, interpersonal and emotional level. For the purpose of this chapter, I shall concentrate on the intrapsychic changes and challenges to psychological equilibrium occurring at this stage.

Pines (1972) writes:

> pregnancy is a crisis point in the search for a female identity, for it is a point of no return whether the baby is born at the end of term or whether the pregnancy ends in abortion or miscarriage. It implies the end of the woman as an independent single unit and the beginning of the unalterable and irrevocable mother–child relationship.
>
> (p. 333)

Pregnancy, particularly the first pregnancy, faces the woman with a fundamental intrapsychic task, that of psychological growth and change from being a daughter of her mother to being a mother of her baby. The mother-to-be has to renegotiate her infantile experiences in relation to significant figures, particularly her parents, as well as her other experiences as a baby and as a child.

The internal and external changes brought about by pregnancy involve some degree of mourning, such as the loss of the 'ideal' or 'inside' baby when faced with the real baby outside, or the loss of the woman's identity as an independent adult. The situation becomes more complicated when there are real losses to be mourned, such as the death of a twin *in utero* or when the pregnancy reactivates previous losses such as past perinatal bereavement.

The centrality of the woman's relationship to her own mother is widely recognised because the mother-to-be has to come to terms with the mothering she had. This is a challenging process which may lead to greater maturity and integration if it goes well, or to psychological distress or disturbance if it fails. Psychoanalytic studies have consistently underlined the pathogenic significance of the reactivation during pregnancy and postnatally of archaic feelings and unresolved conflicts in the woman's relationship to her own parents, problems over feminine identity and over-idealisation of motherhood. Some psychoanalytic writers, such as Main (1958) and Pines (1993), have emphasised the reactivation of unresolved hidden guilt and rivalries of the Oedipal situation. Others (Lomas, 1960a; Raphael-Leef, 1991; Lucas, 1994) have stressed the significance of the reawakening of primitive conflicts in relation to the mother.

Whatever the nature of the conflicts may be, there is general agreement that pregnancy brings about a state of emotional turmoil and increased accessibility to unconscious processes. This is particularly relevant in relation to primitive anxieties (about the inside of the body, fears of loss of identity and of annihilation, fears of damaging or being damaged by the foetus or by jealous siblings or an envious mother, etc.).

In the normal course of events, working through and containment of these primitive anxieties and infantile conflicts take place, which help the mother towards a psychological readiness for the birth and the postnatal period. However, this developmental process is not devoid of pitfalls and difficulty, even for the ordinary 'good enough mother', and in some cases the mother may develop more severe and lasting problems. Hence, it is generally accepted that pregnancy and the puerperium may represent a vulnerable period for the mother and the family.

Zachary (1985) argues that childbirth and the puerperium may be traumatic for both the mother and the baby as this is a stage when 'primitive anxieties are stirred up at a time when it is essential to be adult' (p. 71). Lomas (1960b) suggests that the birth of the baby brings about a permanent change in external reality, by which the mother is faced with the on-going instinctual and emotional demands of a helpless and dependent human being. For the ordinary mother to be able to respond appropriately – described by Winnicott as 'primary maternal preoccupation' (1956) or by Bion as 'maternal reverie' (1962) – she needs to be able to identify with the baby's 'raw' emotional states without losing sight of a mature sense of concern and responsibility.

Research on psychopathology and psychiatric disturbance associated with pregnancy and parenthood has focused mainly on motherhood. The impact of child-bearing on the psychiatric state of the expectant father and the psychopathology of fatherhood is becoming an area of growing interest. Marks and Lovestone (1995) found that women admitted to a Mother and Baby Unit were more likely to have partners who were also suffering from symptoms of psychological distress. These partners were also more likely to have had a psychiatric illness in the past and to have had a difficult relationship with their own fathers (but not their mothers). Marks and Lovestone postulate that the experience of childbirth was particularly difficult in these couples because the prenatal marital relationship was based on a system of shared parental constructs involving a denigrated father and an overvalued mother and a concomitant intolerance towards the idea of a creative (Oedipal) couple. It would appear that in these couples both partners had kept a pre-Oedipal tie to their mothers, the father being the excluded party. The arrival of the baby entailed a permanent change from a two- to a three-person configuration. The appearance of a 'third' brought into focus issues of separation, exclusion and sharing which appeared to be particularly difficult for these men and women.

Overall, becoming a parent is an experience of profound personal upheaval, leading to permanent changes in psychic, social and material circumstances. Parenthood brings about an irrevocable change in the essence of primary relationships (a daughter becomes a mother, a mother and father become grandparents, etc.). It involves a renegotiation of current relationships which may reactivate earlier problems and conflicts which need to be reworked and resolved. In most cases a constructive process of adaptation takes place, and becoming a parent brings happiness and a sense of fulfilment. However, for some men and women, contrary to the idealised images of parenthood, the birth of a baby may lead to marital breakdown, psychiatric illness and, very occasionally, infanticide.

Pregnancy-related illness and psychiatric morbidity

There is evidence of significant psychiatric morbidity associated with childbirth. Oates (1994a) reports that at least 10 per cent of women will suffer from a new episode of major depressive illness in the first year following childbirth. One-third of these will be severe enough to warrant psychiatric treatment. The morbidity rises to 30 per cent if less severe conditions, such as minor depressive episodes, are included. Oates's study (1994a) found that 4 in 1,000 delivered women would require psychiatric admission, 2 in 1,000 with the diagnoses of puerperal psychoses. The extent and severity of the morbidity appear to be largely undetected, since only 1.7 per cent of all delivered women are referred to specialist services. Cox (1998) reports similar findings: 15 per cent of women may develop a serious depressive illness within six weeks of childbirth, which, if untreated, may last for several months, with disabling effects on the woman and her family.

In summary, women in the post-partum period have a greater risk of becoming psychotic, of suffering from major depressive illness, of being admitted to psychiatric hospital, and of psychiatric referral in general, than at any other time in their lives.

What are the factors involved in this higher risk and morbidity? A number of sociological studies on depression indicate the importance of life stress, particularly in women. Brown and Harris (1978) refer to four predisposing factors: loss of mother before age 11; lack of close marital relationship; lack of paid employment; and three or more children under 14. These circumstances apply to many postnatally depressed women.

Paykel et al. (1980) found that recent adverse life events, lack of social support and poor marital relationship were determinant factors in postnatal depression. Kumar and Robson's (1984) study noted that marital conflict and severe doubts about having the baby were associated with prenatal or postnatal depression.

Research findings indicate that failure to detect and treat puerperal psychiatric illness may result in major adverse sequelae for the parents, the newborn and the family. Oates (1994a) points out that untreated postnatal illness may persist over a long period: 30 per cent of postnatal depressive illnesses continue into the child's second year. Profound depression may present great risks to the mother's physical health and safety, including suicide. The infant may be at risk of emotional and physical abuse. Research consistently shows that the highest incidence of fatal abuse by a family member takes place within the first year of life (e.g. Falkov, 1996; Reder and Duncan, 1999). Prolonged mental disturbance may affect interpersonal and family relationships, which in turn may contribute to marital and family dysfunction or breakdown (Cox et al., 1982; O'Hara et al., 1990).

If maternal psychological ill-health persists for any length of time, there are recognisable effects on the social, cognitive and emotional development of the infant, which may remain beyond the resolution of the illness. Murray's prospective study of mothers suffering from postnatal depression (Murray, 1988; 1992; Murray et al., 1991) reported considerable difficulties in the mother–baby relationship in the first three months. The infants appeared more passive, less content, less engaged with the mother and more involved in self-directed activity. The author described longer-term effects at 18 months: an increased incidence of insecure attachment and a delay in developing object permanency (a cognitive schema described by Piaget regarding the independent existence of objects, confirmed by the infant's success in finding an object hidden in different locations). Cox et al.'s (1987) study of children aged 2 to 3 years found that those of depressed mothers presented more difficulties in expressive language and in behaviour than those of non-depressed mothers. Stein et al. (1991) found a significant association between maternal depression during the first year and an impaired quality in the mother–child interaction at 19 months. This finding applied both to mothers who were still depressed at 19 months and to those who had recovered. Cogill et al. (1986) described an association between maternal depression in the first three months and poorer performance by the child on the McCarthy scales of cognitive functioning at 4 years of age.

Marks and Lovestone (1995) and Davenport and Adland (1982) also suggest an increased incidence of mental illness for fathers during pregnancy or following childbirth, with consequences for the couple's relationship and care of the child.

Specialist mental health services available

The Royal College of Psychiatrists (1992) recommends a specialist consultant-led team (requiring three to five sessions of consultant time) for each locality with a delivered population of 5,000 babies and a sub-regional or regional Mother and Baby Unit. Although we are a long way from meeting this national target, there is developing interest in perinatal psychiatry, as evidenced by research activity in many academic departments throughout the country and by the development of innovative services. Of particular relevance are specialist services delivered in the community interface, such as those developed by Oates in Nottingham, Cox in Stoke-on-Trent and myself in London.

Oates has written extensively about service provision and service requirements for women with psychiatric disorder associated with childbirth (e.g. 1994a; 1994b; 1994c). She suggests that a specialist postnatal mental illness service should be: comprehensive, offering a range of treatments in a variety of settings, including the patient's home; integrated, providing continuity between inpatient, outpatient and community care; organised as a multidisciplinary team; able to respond quickly; capable of liaising and providing advice to obstetricians, midwives, health visitors and GPs; offering prenatal advice to women considered to be at high risk of developing postnatal disorder; and involved in research and in the education of key professionals (Oates, 1994c).

An innovative feature of Oates's comprehensive service is that of intensive home nursing of some mentally ill mothers, as an alternative to admission (Oates, 1988). The aim is to manage the individual patient 'deploying the resources of the community, the family and the psychiatric team flexibly in order to preserve continuity of the mother–infant relationship and to minimise the effects of the maternal mental illness on other members of the family' (p. 155). Each nursing intervention is individually designed to meet the needs of the particular patient and the family, and the level of nursing and multidisciplinary support is related to the severity of the illness. Oates found that the home treatment was effective in maintaining family cohesiveness and in providing a good clinical recovery. The mothers also thought that home treatment had helped them to regain their self-esteem and autonomous functioning at an earlier stage.

Cox et al. (1993) described the Charles Street Parent and Baby Day Unit. The unit is open Monday to Friday and its multidisciplinary team is consultant-led and nurse-managed. This specialised day hospital operates as a secondary referral service, in close liaison with adult psychiatry and community agencies, such as GPs, social workers and health visitors. An important feature of its work is the interconnection with the health visitors' routine work, in which health visitors are encouraged to detect postnatal depression, to offer 'listening visits' and to refer complex cases which need to be managed jointly.

A range of treatments and activities is available, such as medication, individual, family and couple counselling, and group work including parenting skills, a women's group, assertiveness training and stress management. The treatment programme is tailored to the individual needs and may comprise a range of group and individual sessions attended throughout the week. The focus of the therapeutic work is to address the mother's mental health problems which are affecting her capacity to care for her baby and family. Most of the individual and group activities involve the mothers without the babies, who are looked after at the unit's crèche. There are some mother-and-baby joint activities, like baby massage and the 'breakfast group' for mothers with a baby and older children. Education by way of giving the women information about the symptoms, prevention and treatments available for postnatal depression is a significant feature of the therapeutic programme.

The Perinatal Mental Health Service, Chelsea and Westminster Hospital, London, was created in 1994 following the opening of the new hospital. The move also coincided with the amalgamation and relocation of a range of midwifery and obstetric services into the same building. This provided the initial opportunity to develop an effective liaison service by way of proactive early involvement. It had become increasingly apparent, in our service for 'under fives' in a child psychiatry department, that failure to respond to the mother's psychological disturbance in pregnancy and the puerperium was a significant contributory factor to the children's presenting problems. It was thought that a specialised service, delivered from a Child and Adolescent Directorate, would facilitate work addressing the needs of the mother-to-be, complemented with work on the mother–infant relationship as well as the mother–father–infant interactions.

The Perinatal Team was initially staffed by relocation of existing resources, with two sessions each of consultant child psychiatrist, child psychiatry specialist registrar, and child psychotherapist. Recently the service has been allocated additional resources including a part-time social worker and a full-time perinatal nurse in recognition of the therapeutic needs of vulnerable mothers and their families.

Our guiding principles are to promote mental health and minimise any adverse effects on the baby and the family, through prevention and early therapeutic intervention as part of the overall care of the pregnant woman. There is an emphasis on antenatal detection of vulnerable women and close liaison with obstetric, midwifery and community services including health visitors, GPs, social services and adult psychiatry, who constitute our main referral sources. Approximately half of our cases are referred antenatally and our age limit is to the end of the baby's first year of life.

Referrals are discussed at a weekly multidisciplinary Perinatal Team meeting which is open to any key professional wishing to refer or discuss an on-going case. There is a daytime professionals rota for telephone consultation. Problems referred include significant anxiety or depression during pregnancy, postnatal depression, difficulties with bonding, complex perinatal bereavement such as previous baby loss, still birth or cot death, and other antenatal or postnatal psychiatric disturbance.

Although the Perinatal Team has evolved as an autonomous service, in practice it has a seamless access to the facilities of the local child and family consultation service, in which some of the staff are based at other times. Referrals of mothers with babies aged over a year and other family problems, including other symptomatic children, can be re-routed into that community service.

> *An example is that of a mother referred by her GP after the birth of her second baby, thought to be suffering from postnatal depression. The mother told us that she felt 'numb, unable to cope, disorganised'. We learnt that her own mother had suddenly died on the day of the birth. This was followed by the baby developing a serious infection needing intensive care. The baby had recovered but the mother felt permanently 'on edge'. We suggested that the perinatal nurse would offer a therapeutic space at her home, to help her address her grief over her mother's death as well as to give some practical help and support with the baby. This home-based short-term intervention (four meetings) was effective in resolving the presenting problems. It also highlighted that there were significant difficulties with the older sibling and marital tensions which needed a family approach, which led to referral to the child and family consultation service.*

The perinatal outpatient service is delivered in a variety of hospital and community settings to facilitate acceptability, accessibility and staff liaison. These include the hospital antenatal department, the hospital children's department and the child and family consultation service. The Perinatal Team is a secondary referral service. Urgent referrals are dealt with by the local acute psychiatric services. Mother and baby inpatient facilities have to be organised locally as well. The service has no direct access to in-patient beds, though relationships with the local adult psychiatric teams are close. There is a limited outreach service offering home assessment and treatment in some selected cases. A recent development includes a Mother and Baby Day Programme led by the perinatal nurse, for those vulnerable mothers suffering from mental illness or significant problems in the relationship with the baby. This development has been influenced by the Parent and Baby Unit developed by Cox *et al.* (1993), the difference being that our present resources only allow for the programme to be available once a week, and the mothers are encouraged to attend all the activities of the day. In addition to addressing the mental health needs of the mother there is a therapeutic emphasis on the mother and baby relationship; hence most of the activities involve the mother and baby dyad. Whenever possible the fathers are involved in the treatment plan. Informal consultation with key professionals is available, together with two regular clinical workshops with health visitors in a community clinic and with professionals within the hospital.

The following example illustrates the principle of early detection and liaison, leading to a good outcome.

> *A 28-year-old Chinese Ph.D. student was referred in the last trimester of a first unplanned pregnancy by the midwives who felt very uneasy about her*

*and uncertain about her management. The patient had indicated that she
wanted 'to go to the desert and die in childbirth'. She had made no preparations for the birth. She had precipitously married a North African man,
and there were considerable marital tensions, exacerbated by cultural and
financial difficulties. The psychiatrist and social worker in the Perinatal
Team carried out an initial assessment. On examination the mother gave a
long history of disturbed interpersonal relationships shaped by overvalued,
quasi-delusional ideas. We learnt that she had denied she was pregnant until
she began to show. She then thought she wanted to follow in the steps of a
nineteenth-century writer, the subject of her doctoral thesis, who had withdrawn from the world and died in the desert. Examination did not elicit
current suicidal ideation, signs of clinical depression or psychotic functioning, and the psychiatric diagnosis was of borderline personality disorder. We
considered that there were clear risk factors regarding the mother's mental
health and safety of the baby after childbirth. The midwives and health
visitor expressed relief on hearing about our findings and our proposed
contribution to the therapeutic plan. We organised marital meetings to help
the couple to start addressing their differences and concentrate on the practical and emotional preparations for the arrival of the baby, and a multi-
agency 'Pre-birth' case conference to plan admission to the local Mother
and Baby Unit. The mother was very anxious after the birth and could not
breast-feed for fear of damaging the baby. She was greatly helped at the
Mother and Baby Unit, where she gained confidence and was able to bond
with her baby. She was discharged after several weeks to a supportive network which included the health visitor, social services and individual psychotherapy for herself. Follow-up after a year indicated that improvement had
been maintained.*

The service offers a variety of treatments including medication as
appropriate and a range of psychological therapies to help the new parents
or pregnant women and their partners adjust to the pregnancy or the new
baby. Focal individual counselling, individual psychotherapy, antenatal and
postnatal group therapy are available.

It is often the case that a 'treatment package' is required, involving a
number of professionals and interventions.

*A relevant example is that of a mother with an 11-month-old baby,
referred by her health visitor who was very concerned about the mother's
detachment and inability to care for the baby. The parents and baby were
seen together at the clinic by the psychiatrist and child psychotherapist.
On examination the mother was found to be profoundly depressed, with
suicidal ideas, and feelings of unworthiness and hopelessness about the
future. She wished to be admitted to a psychiatric hospital without the
baby. We noticed that the father was holding the baby and interacting*

with it while the mother made no contact with her child. She told us that she had been adopted as a baby, that family relationships were distant and the adoption was never discussed. She trained to be a nanny and greatly enjoyed her work. She was happily married and felt ready to have a baby. Towards the end of the pregnancy she started to think about her biological mother and the reasons for her adoption. When the baby was born, she felt 'totally drained of capacities and strength'. She took to her bed and her husband and adoptive mother took over looking after her and the baby.

We suggested admission with the baby to a Mother and Baby Unit, for psychiatric treatment of the depression and to encourage the mother to care for her baby. She was discharged significantly improved. An outpatient network of support was arranged, including psychiatric follow-up, regular health visiting and individual psychodynamic psychotherapy to address her emotional issues about adoption and motherhood which had been triggered by the pregnancy. The focus of the work was the mother's unresolved feelings of abandonment and rejection as an infant, which she re-enacted towards her own baby by identifying with both the rejecting biological mother and the emotionally distant adoptive mother. She had also identified her own child with herself as a baby. An understanding of these issues allowed for some differentiation in the mother's mind between her own early experiences as a baby and a child and that of her real baby. She became emotionally stronger and gained confidence in her own mothering capacities.

This type of re-enactment is what Selma Fraiberg (1975) evocatively called 'a ghost in the nursery', namely the repetition of unresolved emotional issues in the parent's past into the present, which may impair the parent–baby relationship.

The hospital-based Antenatal Group is run on the lines described by Elliot *et al.* (1988) and Elliot (1989). There are two mother and baby weekly groups, one based at a health visitor community clinic and the other at the child and family consultation service: an innovative type of intervention described by Campbell and Salo (1997). The work draws on psychoanalytic group theories and parent–infant psychotherapy as described by Fraiberg (1975), Hopkins (1992) and Miller (1992). Both mothers and infants are considered equal partners in the therapeutic endeavour. The theoretical assumption is that the symptomatic infant is being affected by the mother's unconscious projection ('ghosts in the nursery'). The focus of intervention is therefore the mother and baby interactions within the group setting. It is considered that these groups are particularly helpful for prevention and early intervention in mother and baby attachment problems.

An example is that of a mother referred to the group suffering from depres-

*sion and fears of harming her 3-month-old baby who appeared to cry inces-
santly. The mother gave the group an unemotional account of her deprived
and unhappy childhood in foster care and commented in a matter of fact
way, 'I never had a mother, I do not know how to be a mother to my baby.' It
took several weeks before the mother could begin to acknowledge and share
her anger and distress (literally her own tears) over her abandonment and
neglect. This emotional shift in the mother was accompanied by a shift in
the baby, who became calmer. The mother derived additional help from
other members of the group who offered support and practical advice in
managing the baby's moods, including how to use appropriate stimulation
and play.*

A case for specialisation

Oates (1994a) makes a convincing case for specialisation. She argues that the
majority of women referred to secondary services following childbirth will be
seriously ill, with a baby under 3 months old. If admitted with their babies
they will require specialised skills and routines. Those involved with this
patient group need to develop close working relationships with midwives,
obstetricians, health visitors and child care workers. An understanding
of these disciplines is required as well as a sound knowledge of child
development and child care.

Historically, specialised perinatal mental health services in England have
evolved from adult psychiatry. To my knowledge, our service is the only one
developed from a child directorate. Our service shares some similarity with
the Infant Mental Health Teams developed in America which 'work on
behalf of infants at risk of aberrant development' (Balbernie, 1999, p. 13).
The difference is the central importance of the psychiatric contribution to our
team, while the American model appears to rely on a non-medical multidisciplinary team. It seems to me that child psychiatrists are ideally placed to
provide a specialist service because of their dual training in adult and child
psychiatry and their expertise in child development, parenting and child
risk assessment. Moreover, child psychiatrists and their teams are used to
considering wider family interactions.

Nevertheless adult psychiatric expertise, including inpatient facilities, is
required for those mothers suffering from acute psychotic or suicidal decompensation, as well as for those with chronic mental illness, such as schizophrenia, bipolar illness and disabling neuroses, which is beyond the remit of a
child-centred service. Clarification of this boundary between the perinatal
service and the adult services has been important in securing continued
funding for the team through the budget of the Child and Adolescent Directorate. However, it could be argued that perinatal services are, *par excellence*,
developments at the interface between adult and child mental health and
should be planned and budgeted with this premiss in mind. Indeed Cox

(1998) suggests that a specialist perinatal mental health service should encompass child and adult psychiatry, health and social services.

We now have convincing clinical and research evidence of the serious effects of untreated perinatal disturbance in the child and the family. It is therefore essential to give perinatal mental health services priority and adequate resources, to bring about appropriate interventions, at the interface, to help the parents of today and their children – the parents of the future.

References

Balbernie, R. (1999) Infant mental health. *Young Minds Magazine*, 38, 12–15.

Bion, W. (1962) Learning from experience. In: *Seven Servants*. New York: Jason Aronson, 1977.

Brown, G. and Harris, T. (1978) *The Social Origins of Depression*. London: Tavistock.

Campbell, P. and Salo, F. (1997) Infant-led innovations in a mother–baby therapy group. *Journal of Child Psychotherapy*, 23, 219–244 .

Cogill, S., Caplan, H.L., Alexandra, H., Robson, K.M. and Kumar, R. (1986) Impact of postnatal depression on cognitive development in young children. *British Medical Journal*, 292, 1165–1167.

Cox, A.D., Puckering, C., Pound, A. and Mills, M. (1987) The impact of maternal depression on young children. *Journal of Child Psychology and Psychiatry*, 28, 917–928.

Cox, J. (1998) Mental illness after childbirth. *Children UK*, Autumn, 12–13.

Cox, J., Connor, Y. and Kendell, R.E. (1982) Prospective study of the psychiatric disorders of childbirth. *British Journal of Psychiatry*, 140, 111–117.

Cox, J., Gerrard, J., Coookson, D. and Jones, J.M. (1993) Development and audit of Charles Street Parent and Baby Day Unit, Stoke-on-Trent. *Psychiatric Bulletin*, 17, 711–713.

Davenport, Y.B. and Adland, M.I. (1982) Postpartum psychoses in female and male bipolar manic depressive patients. *American Journal of Orthopsychiatry*, 52, 288–297.

Department of Health (1993) *The Health of the Nation*. London: HMSO.

Elliot, S. (1989) Psychological strategies in the prevention and treatment of postnatal depression. *Baillière's Clinical Obstetrics and Gynaecology*, 3, 879–903.

Elliot, S., Sanjack, M. and Leverton, T.J. (1988) Parents groups in pregnancy. In: B.H. Gotlieb (ed.) *Marshalling Social Support*. Newbury Park, Calif.: Sage.

Falkov, A. (1996) *Study of Working Together 'Part 8' Reports. Fatal Child Abuse and Parental Psychiatric Disorder: An Analysis of 100 Area Child Protection Committee Case Reviews Conducted Under the Terms of Part 8 of Working Together Under the Children Act 1989*. London: Department of Health.

Fraiberg, S. (1975) Treatment modalities. In: S. Fraiberg (ed.) *Clinical Studies in Infant Mental Health*. London: Tavistock.

Hopkins, J. (1992) Infant–parent psychotherapy. *Journal of Child Psychotherapy*, 18, 5–18.

Kumar, R. and Robson, K.M. (1984) A prospective study of emotional disorder in child bearing women. *British Journal of Psychiatry*, 144, 35–47.

Lomas, P. (1960a) Dread of envy as an aetiological factor in puerperal breakdown. *British Journal of Medical Psychology*, 33, 105–112.

Lomas, P. (1960b) Defensive organisation and puerperal breakdown. *British Journal of Medical Psychology*, 33, 61–66.

Lucas, R. (1994) Puerperal psychoses: vulnerability and aftermath. *Psychoanalytic Psychotherapy*, 8, 252–272.

Main, T. (1958) A fragment of mothering. In: *The Ailment and Other Psychoanalytic Essays*. London: Free Association Books, 1989.

Marks, M. and Lovestone, S. (1995) The role of the father in parental postnatal mental health. *British Journal of Medical Psychology*, 68, 157–168.

Miller, L. (1992) The relation of infant observation to clinical practice in an under fives counselling service. *Journal of Child Psychotherapy*, 18, 19–32.

Murray, L. (1988) Effects of postnatal depression on infant development: direct studies of early mother–infant interactions. In: R. Kumar and I.F. Brockington (eds) *Motherhood and Mental Illness*, vol. 2. London: Wright.

Murray, L. (1992) The impact of postnatal depression on infant development. *Journal of Child Psychology and Psychiatry*, 33, 543–561.

Murray, L., Cooper, P.J. and Stein, A. (1991) Postnatal depression and infant development. *British Medical Journal*, 302, 978–979.

Oates, M. (1988) The development of an integrated community-oriented service for severe postnatal mental illness. In: R. Kumar and I.F. Brockington (eds) *Motherhood and Mental Illness*, vol. 2. London: Wright.

Oates, M. (1994a) Postnatal mental illness: organisation and function of services. In: J. Cox and J. Holden (eds) *Perinatal Psychiatry*. London: Gaskell.

Oates, M. (1994b) Postnatal mental illness: auditing services. In: J. Cox and J. Holden (eds) *Perinatal Psychiatry*. London: Gaskell.

Oates, M. (1994c) Notes for purchasers of secondary services for women with psychiatric illness associated with childbirth. (Unpublished, presented at the Marce Conference, Cambridge, England, September.)

O'Hara, M.W., Zekoski, E.M., Philipps, L.H. and Wright, E.J. (1990) Controlled prospective study of postpartum mood disorders: comparison of childbearing and non-childbearing women. *Journal of Abnormal Psychology*, 99, 3–15.

Paykel, E.S., Emms, E.M., Fletcher, J. and Rassby, E.S. (1980) Life events and social support in puerperal depression. *British Journal of Psychiatry*, 136, 339–346.

Pines, D. (1972) Pregnancy and motherhood: interaction between fantasy and reality. *British Journal of Medical Psychology*, 45, 333–343.

Pines, D. (1993) *A Woman's Unconscious Use of Her Body*. London: Virago.

Raphael-Leff, J. (1991) *Psychological Processes of Childbearing*. London: Chapman and Hall.

Reder, P. and Duncan, S. (1999) *Lost Innocents: A Follow-Up Study of Fatal Child Abuse*. London: Routledge.

Royal College of Psychiatrists (1992) *Postnatal Mental Illness*. Council Report, March.

Stein, A., Gath, D.H., Bucher, J., Bond, A., Day, A. and Cooper, P.J. (1991) The relationship between post-natal depression and mother–child interaction. *British Journal of Psychiatry*, 148, 46–52.

Winnicott, D. (1956) Primary maternal preoccupation. In: *Through Paediatrics to Psychoanalysis*. London: Hogarth Press, 1982.

Zachary, A. (1985) A new look at the vulnerability of puerperal mothers. A clinical study of two inpatient families at the Cassel Hospital. *Psychoanalytic Psychotherapy*, 1, 71–89.

Chapter 19

Principles of collaboration between child and adolescent and adult substance misuse services

Mike McClure and Brian Wells

Introduction

Substance misuse is a major social and public health problem, with drug misuse increasing dramatically across all age ranges in almost every country (Vienna International Centre, 1994). In Britain, young people's exposure to illicit drugs has increased considerably over the past decade (Wright and Pearl, 1995; NHS Health Advisory Service, 1996; Balding, 1996; 1997; Measham *et al.*, 1998). Forty-eight per cent of 16–24-year-olds have used illegal drugs (Her Majesty's Government, 1998), and the number of addicts has increased by over 50 per cent between 1992 and 1996. In the last decade there has been a fivefold increase in 12–13-year-olds using drugs and an eightfold increase among those aged 14–15 years (SCODA, 1999). More than a third of 15–16-year-olds have smoked cannabis; one in seven has used amphetamine and just under one in ten has taken Ecstasy.

Specialist services responding to substance misuse problems have, to date, evolved independently of each other. Family issues are frequently not appreciated in relation to aetiology, repercussions for other family members and intergenerational continuities. Adult substance misusers attend adult substance misuse services where their own problems are the focus of concern and intervention. The disturbed children of substance misusers, and adolescents who themselves take drugs, are likely to be referred to child and adolescent mental health services. This separation of provision has prevented the interrelationship of problems in adults and young people from being recognised and addressed.

The way in which a problem is construed will determine the way in which solutions are sought. Substance misuse has been seen variously as a criminal activity; a public health problem; an individual psychopathology problem; a social problem; and an educational problem. To construe it as a family problem should lead to family-orientated services for prevention and treatment. Professionals are becoming more aware of the requirement for this to happen, although this has yet to be translated into effective action. The interrelationship between children and parents in relation to substance misuse has been discussed elsewhere in this volume (see Zeitlin, Chapter 2; Drummond and Fitzpatrick, Chapter 10; Reder and Duncan, Chapter 12). Some salient features need to be stressed in order to show the relevance of cooperation between child and adolescent and adult substance misuse services.

Substance misuse within families

Dysfunctional family relationships are recognised as contributing to the presentation of psychological disorder in children. There is now considerable evidence accumulating concerning the dynamics of families in which there is problem drinking or drug use. An alcoholic father, supported by a spouse in a dysfunctional relationship, may affect the children in the family (Hampton *et al.*, 1998). Difficulties may arise indirectly due to a disturbance in parental and family functioning where children may adopt an inappropriate role as the parentified child to inadequate parents. Substance misuse in one member may alter family dynamics to affect other members (Rydelius, 1997). For example, substance-abusing adolescents may alter the marital relationship of the parents. Family dysfunction may be manifested by marital disharmony and violence with consequent parental separation and divorce. Secondary problems of substance misuse in a parent, such as poverty, prostitution, criminality (with absences through imprisonment) and suicide (McClure, 2000) may also have adverse effects upon the family.

Effects of parental substance misuse on children

Children of substance misusers may have increased need of psychiatric referral which is often directly or indirectly a consequence of parental substance misuse (Coleman and Cassell, 1995; Hogan, 1998). Children may be affected by parental risk of illness or death through hepatitis, cirrhosis, or HIV infection. Kelley (1992) and Famularo *et al.* (1992) report a poor outcome for children of substance-misusing parents, although adherence to a treatment programme improves the prognosis (e.g. Wilson, 1989). Children of substance misusers are also at greater risk from social deprivation and neglect, with a higher incidence of sexual and physical abuse. These adverse factors lead to a greater incidence of emotional and behavioural problems (Rydelius, 1997; Fergusson and Horwood, 1998).

Children may be emotionally damaged or their behaviour adversely affected to a degree where they cannot be cared for at home, leading to a greater incidence of reception into care, with its own associated problems. Stress from a substance-misusing parent, combined with the effects of their own substance misuse, may contribute to young people attempting or committing suicide (McClure, 1994). Studies of fatal child abuse also suggest that a significant minority of the caretakers were substance abusers (Wilczynski, 1997; Reder and Duncan, 1999).

Effects of children's substance misuse on parents

Children and adolescents who misuse drugs or alcohol are at risk of psychiatric and psychological disturbance, school failure and social disruption (Farrell and Strang, 1991; Farrell and Taylor, 1994). They become estranged from their parents who feel angry and helpless in the face of excessive drinking and drug taking by their child. The deterioration of the relationship between children and parents is likely to lead to further stress for the parents (Stewart and Brown, 1993), affecting their marital relationship or resulting in stress-related conditions.

Childhood to adult disturbance and intergenerational continuity

Whether or not parents are substance misusers, it has been established that conduct disorder in childhood is a predictor of later substance misuse problems (Robins and McEvoy, 1991). Conduct-disordered children with substance-misusing, dysfunctional parents are at even greater risk of substance misuse (Rydelius, 1997). Children may use their parents as role models and develop similar substance misuse activity through familiarity with a drug-oriented culture (Velleman, 1992). This modelling of behaviour may be enhanced by increased access to substances. Thus, disturbed children may become substance-misusing adolescents (Cloninger *et al.*, 1988) who later become substance misusing adults (Kandel *et al.*, 1986; Swadi, 1992). They, in their own turn, may pass on substance-misusing behaviour to their own children to perpetuate intergenerational continuity.

Strategic policy statements

Several policy documents have been published recently which progressively address these problems.

Tackling Drugs Together (Her Majesty's Government, 1995) provided a coordinated national strategy for reducing the ill-effects of substance misuse in England. The statement of purpose was:

> to take effective action by vigorous law enforcement, accessible treatment and a new emphasis on education and prevention, to increase the safety of communities from drug-related crime, to reduce the acceptability and availability of drugs to young people, and to reduce the health risks and other damage caused by drug misuse.

The strategy contained proposals for multi-agency coordination at both a national and local level, promoting support from communities.

The document proposed the development of a government drugs publicity strategy involving media and private sector interests, with Department of Health coordination. It aimed to improve access to cost-effective drug services for those who need treatment, and for young people seeking advice. In order to achieve this, it advocated the setting-up of Drug Action Teams by chief executives of district health authorities supported by Drug Reference Groups. The strategy also included setting up a national telephone helpline for drug misusers, their families, friends and carers. Clearer guidance on criteria for purchasing effective drug services in local communities was established. Arrangements for the shared care of drug misusers, involving GPs, were encouraged, and the role of primary care was emphasised. Department of Health activity would be coordinated with the Home Office in relation to public health, treatment and rehabilitation services.

Following *Tackling Drugs Together* (Her Majesty's Government, 1995) the government published *Tackling Drugs: To Build a Better Britain* (Her Majesty's Government, 1998), which is the current ten-year strategy for tackling drug misuse. In addition to reducing the availability of illegal drugs, the focus is on helping young people to resist drug misuse, the protection of communities and the provision of appropriate treatment. There is a recognition that social and educational issues contribute to young people becoming involved with drug taking, including school exclusion, truancy and rough sleeping.

The government strategy proposes that prevention should start early, with better-integrated, broad life-skills approaches at primary school. For older children and adolescents, appropriate programmes including peer approaches, training and wider community support are recommended. A key objective is to reduce the number of people under 25 reporting use of illegal drugs in the last month and previous year.

These documents recognise that implementation of this strategy requires attention to the following issues: prevention and early intervention; publicity; strategic planning; professional awareness; and liaison. We shall elaborate on these themes, emphasising the importance of collaboration between child and adolescent and substance misuse mental health services.

Prevention and early intervention

Prediction of future substance misuse is possible (Boyle *et al.*, 1993) and Kumpfer (1989) has stressed the importance of early identification and prevention. In relation to preventive work with young people, the clear objective is to discourage them from taking drugs. Realistically, one must ensure the availability of early intervention services for those who choose to take risks and need help with the consequences. By targeting the family and not just the individual user it is hoped that there will be more effective uptake of early intervention measures. We believe that, as part of the first assessment of attenders at child and adolescent mental health services and substance misuse services, there should be screening for the possible adverse effects of substances on all family members.

Publicity campaigns

The strategy for prevention is intended to focus on motivating young people to resist drug misuse by reducing its acceptability, and increasing public awareness of the risks of taking drugs. The Department of Health has taken the lead in coordinating publicity campaigns and developing materials. Taking this forward is expected to involve private and commercial interests as well as other government departments, national and local voluntary organisations and statutory bodies. In our view, publicity campaigns should be directed at family members in addition to the individual user.

Planning of services

It is proposed that joint planning fora, under the auspices of Drug Action Teams, should include representatives from child and adolescent mental health services and adult substance misuse services in addition to representatives from social services, education, the Probation Service, and other youth services. Within health service provider units, we suggest that there should be appointment of professionals who will take responsibility for planning jointly between child and adolescent and adult services, with identified provision for young people. Services should be planned not only in relation to treatment, but also in relation to prediction (Boyle *et al.*, 1993), early identification and prevention (Kumpfer, 1989). In considering services and resource allocation, it is particularly important to distinguish between dependency and misuse. Whereas many adults seeking help are dependent, most young people are not yet dependent upon drugs. Purchasers, guided by service users and professionals, should suggest a framework within which optimal services may be provided. Reduction of substance misuse in young people should be a 'Health of the Nation' target.

Professional awareness

Staff from different services must be aware of substance misuse issues affecting not only the individual but also other family members. Professional awareness between child and adolescent mental health services, adult substance misuse services and primary care needs to be raised and we believe that this could occur through joint teaching events and liaison initiatives. The links between the services could also be emphasised in Trust publications.

Consultation, liaison and collaboration

In our view, once links are established between services, consultation and liaison should take place regarding relevant families. Staff from different services involved with substance misuse must endeavour to get to know each other well, and links between teams may be forged in staff afternoons and away-days. Ease of cross-referral is essential when problems are reflected in different family members. Knowledge, communication and collaboration are improved through case discussions and consultation. There is also a need for joint clinical work on specific cases, with written clinical guidelines for each service.

The National Strategy (Her Majesty's Government, 1995) was an important first step, but did not go far enough in recognising the importance of the family and did not emphasise sufficiently the collaboration required between the child and adolescent and adult mental health services. The following case examples from our own experiences illustrate the need for collaboration between previously disparate services.

Case example 1

Denise was a 15-year-old with multiple problems. Her family were about to split up and she was mixing with an older peer group. She regularly smoked hash and took Ecstasy at clubs but did not think drugs were a problem. Her family had been stable until three years ago, since when, her parents had argued frequently and were now thinking of divorce. The mother's depression and father's alcoholism had been worsening.

Management included an attempt at improving family relationships, though it was unsuccessful because the parents' relationship was irredeemable. Denise did not want individual work as she thought that it would not be helpful.

Ideal management would have included earlier intervention for marital problems. The adult service could have tried to address father's alcoholism and mother's depression before the marriage was irredeemably damaged. If the parents' problems had been identified earlier, an adult mental health worker could have foreseen that Denise would be at risk, and an earlier referral for her problems could have been made.

Case example 2

Dave was a 16-year-old who was admitted via Casualty in an intoxicated state and referred to the child and adolescent team the next day. He had a history of delinquency and occasional heroin and crack use. Dave was from an unstable family in which his parents were divorced and his father was a substance misuser. His long history of truancy and delinquency had started several years before his parents' divorce and continued thereafter. Following the referral to the child and adolescent service there was consultation with the adult substance misuse service but he was considered too young for that service. There was consultation with social services, who did not consider that there were sufficient grounds for intervention. Dave then discharged himself from hospital and returned home, presumably to continue his delinquent and substance misuse career. He refused follow-up.

Ideal management would have involved much earlier intervention and a closer link between adult substance misuse services and child and adolescent services. There could have been regular liaison and consultation, and specific arrangements for managing adolescent substance misusers, in partnership with social services, education and youth services.

Recognising that the 1995 National Strategy document did not go into sufficient detail in relation to children and families, the Health Advisory Service published a strategy for children and young people (NHS Health Advisory Service, 1996). A four-tier strategic framework was described, involving partnership between commissioners, purchasers and providers. We shall summarise the four tiers, again emphasising where collaborative initiatives could improve mental health services for substance misusers.

Tier 1 services

Tier 1 services, provided by GPs, primary care counsellors, health visitors, social workers and school medical officers, are often the first point of contact for families. It is therefore important that these professionals should be trained to identify drug misuse and the consequences for other family members. They may advise and counsel family members and may be involved in shared care of youngsters or parents with substance misuse. They need to be aware of resources and should be able to refer the individual or whole family to an appropriate agency in Tier 2 or 3 for specialist help.

Tier 2 services

In Tier 2 services, staff have a more specialised understanding of developmental, family and substance misuse issues. They include child and adolescent psychiatrists, clinical psychologists, family therapists, individual psychotherapists, educational psychologists, health promotion workers, youth justice workers and social workers. They should be trained to provide information and advice and to manage substance misuse problems, where possible, in a family context. Specialist child and adolescent mental health services and adult substance misuse services can provide useful input to Tier 2, particularly in relation to training, consultation and supervision.

Tier 3 services

In Tier 3, staff working in multidisciplinary teams can respond to the greater complexity of problems, which may include substance misuse in a parent or child. It seems to us that family and substance misuse issues are best addressed here by services with input from both child and adolescent and adult substance misuse services. A wide range of interventions should be available, and Tier 3 services need to offer outreach work and link with education, social services and youth-orientated special addiction services and other specialist youth services.

In our opinion, a drug and alcohol clinic specifically for young people can be provided by adult substance misuse services, with appropriate assistance and supervision from child and adolescent mental health staff. Alternatively, the child and adolescent service may provide a substance misuse service for youngsters, with advice, training and supervision provided by the adult substance misuse team. Another alternative is to set up new services, jointly financed and staffed by professionals from both child and adolescent and adult substance misuse services. The service should be able to offer full assessment including developmental, psychological and family assessments, drug screening, and physical assessment (including Hepatitis B and C and HIV testing).

Forms of therapy may include: detoxification; drug reduction and maintenance programmes; individual therapy and counselling; group therapy; family therapy; and consultation. In a day-centre setting, involving all family members, problem behaviour affecting relationships may be identified (Feigelman and Jaquith, 1992). Family therapy may be employed, and there is evidence that behavioural family therapy for adolescent substance misuse is effective (Bry and Krinsley, 1992). It has also been shown that adolescent substance misuse treatment results in an improvement in family relationships (Stewart and Brown, 1993). The aim of family therapy should be to mobilise strengths within the family to help them find alternatives to substance misuse behaviour (Reichelt and Christensen, 1990), and to empower children to resist the influence of substance-misusing parents (Moe and Pohlman, 1989).

Tier 4 services

Tier 4 services are those very specialised services which provide inpatient assessment, care and treatment; secure units; highly specialised clinics for young people with two or more comorbid disorders; and specialist rehabilitation centres for substance misusers. It is recognised that it is not appropriate for young substance misusers to be admitted to adult psychiatric wards or secure mental health units, or indeed specialist substance misuse services for adults. They require their own appropriate inpatient services or specialised fostering and residential placements specifically for young substance misusers. At Tier 4 level, adult services can advise regarding inpatient detoxification, withdrawal and substitution, whilst child and adolescent professionals concentrate on adolescent psychiatric disorders and family issues.

Following the NHS Health Advisory Service report (1996), the Standing Conference on Drug Abuse published a document on *Young People and Drugs* (SCODA, 1999). This emphasised the special status of children and young people, with their different requirements from adults. The report recommended consideration of the overall welfare of the child or young person, whose views should always be sought. However, services are also expected to respect parental responsibility and provide education, involvement and support when necessary. Wherever possible, parents should be involved as much as the young person will accept. Where communication between the young person and the family is still viable, parents should be involved in education, health promotion and prevention. Where substance misuse problems are more severe or are associated with other difficulties, parents may be involved in a joint approach to care, including family therapy.

The SCODA report (1999) recommended that protocols for liaison should be established between the local authority and the young people's substance misuse service with multidisciplinary cooperation. Services should be holistic and child-centred, with a comprehensive range of services available. Professionals should be competent to deliver services according to the principles of best practice, particularly in relation to the Children Act 1989 and the UN Convention on the Rights of the Child.

Implementing the strategies

These recent policy statements have important implications for mental health services. Implementation will require attention to diverse issues, some of which we have already discussed. In addition, the following considerations must be addressed.

Legal issues

The NHS Health Advisory Service (1996) and SCODA (1999) recommend that service providers should be aware of legal issues which depend upon the age of the client, particularly in relation to consent and confidentiality as described in the Children Act 1989. This is particularly pertinent in relation to substance misuse, where young people under the age of 18 years have taken decisions into their own hands. Young people of 16 and 17 years may give consent to treatment, including treatment for substance misuse, without parental consent. For children and adolescents under the age of 16 years there may be concern about the prescription of methadone and provision of clean needles and syringes to young addicts without parental consent (Aldridge and Preston, 1997). This is a controversial issue, with some professionals advocating confidentiality, whereas others insist on family involvement. Staff need to be aware of the local framework for children, including Area Child Protection Committees, in relation to children and parents with substance misuse problems. Young people who are involved with both substance misuse and crime may be involved with the criminal justice system or adolescent forensic mental health services. In these cases it is essential that there is coordination between adolescent mental health services, social services, adult substance misuse services and forensic services. Furthermore, issues of clinical responsibility require clarification within substance-misusing families where both parents and children are disturbed and in need of treatment.

Targeting vulnerable groups of children and adolescents

Child and adolescent mental health services and adult substance misuse services will need to develop strategies with other agencies to target especially vulnerable young people. These include the homeless, young offenders, school non-attenders and children in care or leaving care. Other vulnerable groups include young single pregnant girls, young mentally ill people and young people with learning and physical difficulties.

Many of these young people will have experienced chronic family discord, poverty, separation, domestic instability and parental disorder. Some will have experienced physical, emotional or sexual abuse. Interventions provided by child and adolescent mental health services and adult substance misuse services must be more accessible to these youngsters, many of whom will require outreach workers to establish contact. Clearly, joint initiatives between the services are more likely to be effective.

Teaching and training

Teaching regarding the interrelationship between child and adolescent mental health services and substance misuse services should take place at undergraduate and postgraduate level and as part of continuing professional development. The highly trained professionals in child and adolescent mental health services and adult substance misuse services are especially well-qualified to participate in training programmes.

Child and adolescent mental health services can contribute expertise in relation to individual development, developmental psychopathology, family dynamics and related treatment modalities. Adult substance misuse services can contribute their extensive specialised knowledge regarding pharmacology, detoxification, withdrawal, substitution and individual and group treatment methods. There should be training in working with whole families for all professionals. Training will be most beneficial when it is provided jointly by these two services to widen the knowledge base and competence of professionals from both children's and adult health services. It should also be available, in joint teaching, to professionals from other agencies and all tiers of health input, through general and advanced-level training programmes.

Service evaluation and performance management

Quality assurance and audit will be required to ensure that child and adolescent mental health services and adult substance misuse services are working together and in collaboration with other agencies. For example, routine data collection regarding the characteristics of referrals and enquiry regarding family substance misuse can be audited. Consumer satisfaction surveys and outcome evaluation can also be used to assess the effectiveness of collaboration between the services. For child and adolescent mental health services an audit project might include the number of family members (parents and children) involved in substance misuse. For substance misuse services, an audit of children who might be affected by substance-misusing parents would be useful. There is also a need for further funding for research into the dynamics of families with substance-misusing parents or children.

Commissioning services for children and adolescents who misuse substances

Commissioners will need to work closely with Drug Action Teams to ensure that the strategic framework is accepted by all contributing agencies, including child and adolescent and adult substance misuse services. Healthy alliances should be promoted, using joint commissioning involving health authorities, social services educational departments, criminal justice agencies and the voluntary sector. With the transfer of health service purchasing responsibility to primary care groups and subsequently primary care trusts, it is essential that these new purchasers are aware of the family dimension of substance misuse. There should also be recognition of the need for resources in time, personnel and finances for liaison.

Conclusions

There has been a gap in services for adolescent substance misusers. The process of addressing this gap started with the publication of *Tackling Drugs Together* (Her Majesty's Government, 1995). Since then, more consideration has been given to the overlap in services for children and adult substance misusers, with a strategic framework for collaboration in relation to substance misuse. This has been developed by the NHS Health Advisory Service review (1996), in relation to the commissioning and provision of services for children and adolescents who use and misuse substances, and by SCODA

(1999). Child and adolescent mental health services and adult substance misuse services need to collaborate in conjunction with primary care services, social services, education, specialist youth services and the voluntary sector (Social Services Inspectorate, 1997). It is likely that preventive work needs to occur at an earlier age, given the evidence that initiation into substance misuse is occurring in younger children.

The government is committed to a wide-scale public awareness campaign, though it is likely that public information programmes do not help unless there is also a change in public attitudes. Health professionals should be involved in joint awareness-raising strategies in the community. Examples of this include health education in schools, in GP surgeries, and contact with the media.

In addition to health education strategies, various treatment options should be enhanced, including family therapy, counselling and direct interventions in schools. There should be recognition of the need for resources in time, personnel and finances for joint consultation, liaison, audit, teaching and research. With limited funds, developments should take place within existing resources, though further funding may be required for specific projects, such as a liaison project, or clinical audit. Purchasers should take responsibility for insisting upon effective integration of services for families with substance misuse problems by including this issue in quality standards.

The extent of substance misuse in the young is clearly a problem and substantial resources will be required to reverse the recent increase. So far, the process has been started with the publication of strategy documents which recognise the problems and set priorities. Understanding the interrelationships within families of substance misusers should lead to greater cooperation between child and adolescent services and adult substance misuse services.

References

Aldridge, T. and Preston, A. (1997) Guidelines for the provision of needle exchange services for under 16s. London: ISDD.

Balding, J. (1996) Young people and illegal drugs 1989–1995: facts and predictions. Exeter Schools Health Education Unit, University of Exeter.

Balding, J. (1997) Young people and illegal drugs in 1996. Exeter Schools Health Education Unit, University of Exeter.

Boyle, M.H., Offord, D.R., Racine, Y.A., Fleming, J.E., Szatmari, P. and Links, P.S. (1993) Predicting substance use in early adolescence based on parent and teacher assessments of childhood psychiatric disorder: results from the Ontario Child Health Study follow-up. *Journal of Child Psychology and Psychiatry*, 34, 535–544.

Bry, B.H. and Krinsley, K.E. (1992) Booster sessions and long-term effects of behavioural family therapy on adolescent substance use and school performance. *Journal of Behaviour Therapy and Experimental Psychiatry*, 23, 183–189.

Cloninger, C.R., Sigvardsson, S. and Bohman, M. (1988) Childhood personality predicts alcohol abuse in young adults. *The Research Society on Alcoholism*, 12, 494–505.

Coleman, R. and Cassell, D. (1995) Parents who misuse drugs and alcohol. In: P. Reder and C. Lucey (eds) *Assessment of Parenting: Psychiatric and Psychological Contributions.* London: Routledge.

Famularo, R., Kinscherff, R. and Fenton, T. (1992) Parental substance abuse and the nature of child maltreatment. *Child Abuse and Neglect*, 16, 475–483.

Farrell, M. and Strang, J. (1991) Substance use and misuse in childhood and adolescence. *Journal of Child Psychology and Psychiatry*, 32, 109–128.

Farrell, M. and Taylor, E. (1994) Drug and alcohol use and misuse. In: M. Rutter, E. Taylor and L. Hersov (eds) *Child and Adolescent Psychiatry: Modern Approaches*, 3rd edn. Oxford: Blackwell.

Feigelman, B. and Jaquith, P. (1992) Adolescent drug treatment, a family affair: a community day centre approach. *Social Work in Health Care*, 16, 39–52.

Fergusson, D.M. and Horwood, L.J. (1998) Exposure to interparental violence in childhood and psychosocial adjustment in young adulthood. *Child Abuse and Neglect,* 22, 339–357.

Hampton, R.L., Senatore, V. and Gullotta, T.P. (eds) (1998) *Substance Abuse, Family Violence and Child Welfare: Bridging Perspectives.* Thousand Oaks, Calif.: Sage.

Her Majesty's Government (1995) *Tackling Drugs Together: A Consultation Document on a Strategy for England 1995–1998.* London: HMSO.

Her Majesty's Government (1998) *Tackling Drugs: To Build a Better Britain.* London: The Stationery Office.

Hogan, D.M. (1998) The psychological development and welfare of children of opiate and cocaine users: review and research needs. *Journal of Child Psychology and Psychiatry*, 39, 609–620.

Kandel, D., Davies, M., Karus, D. and Yamaguchi, K. (1986) The consequence in young adulthood of adolescent drug involvement. *Archives of General Psychiatry*, 43, 746–754.

Kelley, S.J. (1992) Parenting stress and child maltreatment in drug-exposed children. *Child Abuse and Neglect*, 16, 317–328.

Kumpfer, K. (1989) Prevention of alcohol and drug abuse: a critical review of risk factors and prevention strategies. In: D. Shaffer, I. Philips and N.B. Enzer (eds) *Prevention of Mental Disorders, Alcohol and Other Drug Use in Children and Adolescents.* OSAP Prevention Monograph 2. Rockville, Md.: Office for Substance Abuse Prevention, US Department of Health and Human Services.

McClure, G.M. (1994) Suicide in children and adolescents in England and Wales 1960–1990. *British Journal of Psychiatry*, 165, 510–514.

McClure, G.M. (2000) Suicide in England and Wales 1960–1997. *British Journal of Psychiatry*, 176, 64–67.

Measham, F., Parker, H. and Aldridge, J. (1998) *Starting, Switching, Slowing and Stopping: Report for the Drugs Prevention Initiative Integrated Programme.* London: The Stationery Office.

Moe, J. and Pohlman, D. (1989) *Kids' Power: Healing Games for Children of Alcoholics.* Published by: Health Communications, Inc. Enterprise Center, 3201 SW 15th Street, Deerfield Beach, Florida, 33442.

NHS Health Advisory Service (1996) *Children and Young People – Substance Misuse Services.* London: HMSO.

Reder, P. and Duncan, S. (1999) *Lost Innocents: A Follow-up Study of Fatal Child Abuse*. London: Routledge.

Reichelt, S. and Christensen, B. (1990) Reflections during a study on family therapy with drug addicts. *Family Process*, 29, 273–287.

Robins, L.N. and McEvoy, L. (1991) Conduct problems and substance abuse. In: L.N. Robins and M. Rutter (eds) *Straight and Devious Pathways from Childhood to Adulthood*. Cambridge: Cambridge University Press.

Rydelius, P.A. (1997) Are children of alcoholics a clinical concern for child and adolescent psychiatrists of today? *Journal of Child Psychology and Psychiatry*, 38, 615–624.

SCODA (1999) *Young People and Drugs*. Standing Conference on Drug Abuse.

Social Services Inspectorate (1997) *Young People and Substance Misuse: The Local Authority Response*. London: Department of Health.

Stewart, M.A. and Brown, S.A. (1993) Family functioning following adolescent substance abuse treatment. *Journal of Substance Abuse*, 5, 327–339.

Swadi, H. (1992) A longitudinal perspective on adolescent substance abuse. *European Child and Adolescent Psychiatry*, 1, 156–170.

Velleman, R. (1992) Intergenerational effects – a review of environmentally oriented studies concerning the relationship between parental alcohol problems and family disharmony in the genesis of alcohol and other problems. 1: The intergenerational effects of alcohol problems. *The International Journal of Addiction*, 27, 253–280.

Vienna International Centre (1994) *Report of the International Narcotics Control Board*. Vienna International Centre.

Wilczynski, A. (1997) *Child Homicide*. London: Greenwich Medical Media.

Wilson, G.S. (1989) Clinical studies of infants and children exposed prenatally to heroin. *Annals of New York Academy of Sciences*, 562, 183–194.

Wright, J.D. and Pearl, L. (1995) Knowledge and experience of young people regarding drug misuse, 1969–94. *British Medical Journal*, 309, 20–24.

Chapter 20

Liaison between child and adult psychiatric services

Begum Maitra and Anthony Jolley

Liaison arrangements between adult psychiatric, medical and surgical services have been a well-established part of most district health services for at least two decades. It is perhaps surprising, therefore, that such arrangements within the mental health service, between adult and child psychiatric services, have, in general, been so poorly developed. This chapter begins by looking at the costs of inadequate liaison between these two services by means of a case example. It then proceeds to describe a liaison project initiated by the authors – a child psychiatrist (BM) and an adult psychiatrist (AJ) – and another case example demonstrates a successful piece of liaison work through the project. This is followed by a general discussion of the potential benefits from, and obstacles to, closer liaison between child and adult services.

The costs of inadequate liaison are well demonstrated by the experience of Mr O and his family – a case example from the child psychiatrist's previous experience of working elsewhere in London, and with very limited opportunity to communicate with the local adult service.

Case vignette I

Mr O (aged 46 years) had a history of repeated brief hospitalisation for episodes of floridly disturbed behaviour that resolved in a day or two, with little or no medication. These episodes started fifteen years ago, within a year of his arrival in Britain as a political refugee from a West African state. Mr O had left behind his wife and four adult children, and a job as a lecturer at a university. As the years passed, his plans to establish himself professionally, and to bring his family over, failed to materialise. Although he remained in regular contact with them, Mr O remarried and had four more children (daughters aged 12 and 11, and sons aged 4 and 1) in this second family.

Concerns were first voiced by the school about the quality of Mrs O's physical care of her daughters. Social services' assessment found the home to be dirty, damp and disorganised. The eldest child (Diana) was doing poorly at school. Mr O was angered by the suggestion that she had learning difficulties, and needed 'special education'. As a former teacher himself he disagreed fiercely with education policy and practices at the child's school. Mr O (a practising Catholic) withdrew his daughters to place them in a Catholic school. When Diana (then aged 11 years) showed traces of vaginal bleeding, concerns were raised by the school and the local authority about the possibility of sexual abuse. However, physical examination revealed no abnormal findings, and no further action was taken.

Conflict between the parents and professionals (education and social services departments) escalated; Mr O distrusted them and they found both parents uncooperative. However, Mr O trusted his GP and his psychiatrist; they in turn were strongly in support of him and critical of social services. When his two daughters complained of being bullied at their new school Mr O withdrew them and decided to teach them himself. This seeming withdrawal of the children from the scrutiny of the outer world and into a potentially dangerous home environment caused serious professional concern. As Reder, Duncan and Gray (1993) have shown, such a pattern of events sometimes precedes serious or even fatal child abuse.

Social services obtained an Emergency Protection Order and forcibly entered the home to remove all four children. Mr O was taken to hospital under section of the Mental Health Act. As on other occasions, he was not thought to warrant further detention the following day. Mrs O's sudden and unexpected death due to thyroid cancer three weeks later meant that Mr O became the sole surviving parent.

While in foster care the two girls allegedly reported that they had been sexually abused by their father. In subsequent care proceedings a child psychiatric opinion was sought on the following questions: Had the children suffered significant harm due to long-standing neglect (mainly educational) and due to possible sexual abuse? How did Mr O's mental disorder affect his parenting capacity? Was Mr O, whether due to his disorder or not, a danger to his children? Was Mr O able to function adequately as a parent on his own?

The child psychiatrist's assessment of the children suggested that the older two children suffered some anxiety in relation to their father's behaviour when he was, in their words, 'mad'. Apart from this there was a warm and trusting relationship between father and all four children. In accordance with cultural patterns of parenting Mr O was a loving but 'authoritarian' parent, who undertook a lot of the child care tasks when he was well, and also when his wife was ill. Evidence from the GP, health visitor, the girls and the neighbours supported the notion that, when well, Mr O was a loving and capable father. The allegations of sexual abuse were never repeated and there was some doubt about the initial report. There was no psychological evidence to suggest that the girls had been sexually abused.

Mr O was a large man with an excitable manner that could have appeared intimidating, but was probably unremarkable within his cultural setting. In interviews with the child psychiatrist he spoke with obvious thoughtfulness and sophistication about his children's educational needs, cultural differences in parenting and educational expectations, and his own episodes of disorder and its treatment. Their mother's death made Mr O determined to resume the care of his children.

There was very little detail about how Mr O behaved towards his children during episodes of illness, and what role his wife had played in 'buffering' them from the potential ill-effects of his symptoms. However, records showed that during a previous episode of illness Mr O had been found naked in church with his younger daughter; further detail was sought from the adult psychiatrist. Mr O had few clear memories himself of the episodes that led to his psychiatric admissions. He had no conscious thoughts of a sexual nature about his children, and could not think that he would have sexually abused them. He admitted that his inability to remember what he did during acute episodes prevented a more emphatic denial.

Mr O had great regard for his psychiatrist, and thought it would be disrespectful to question the doctor's expertise and opinions. Despite this, he did not comply with treatment (depot antipsychotics or mood stabilisers). Mr O hoped to re-qualify and re-establish himself professionally in Britain. He had enrolled on a science-related course at a leading British institution and found that the medication interfered with his ability to concentrate.

The adult psychiatrist's assessment was based on knowledge of Mr O through the fifteen years of his illness. Although different diagnoses had been given in the past, the psychiatrist thought that Mr O suffered from a 'schizophrenia-like illness'. Somewhat oddly, and based probably on psychological testing many years earlier, he stated that Mr O had an IQ of around 60. (Mr O spoke two African languages and excellent French, but had been tested in English.) The psychiatrist believed that Mr O was a good and loving father, that he was unlikely to have sexually abused his children because of his Catholic faith, and that any investigation into the allegation of sexual abuse would tip Mr O into a suicidal depression.

The child psychiatrist's attempts to obtain further information about Mr O's illness, and its impact on his functioning, did not succeed. Without dialogue between child and adult services conclusions could not be reached about Mr O's capacity to function safely and adequately as a single parent, and especially within the context of continuing risk of mental disorder. The most pressing questions were about the following issues.

The nature of Mr O's illness

The details of symptomatology during acute episodes are particularly relevant when attempting to understand the impact of parental disorder on children. The literature suggests that features leading to unpredictable behaviour (such as high arousal and impaired judgement), abnormal beliefs, and suicidal potential are especially important. These symptoms interfere with the appropriate planning and delivery of child care, and pose significant risks to the safety and emotional stability of children. The risks are greater in the absence of a second stable and familiar carer. It has been repeatedly suggested (e.g. Rutter and Quinton, 1984) that children are more likely to be harmed if they are directly involved in the delusional beliefs of a mentally ill parent. This makes it important to understand the meaning of unusual behaviours, such as the report that Mr O had been found naked in church with his daughter. Further, despite the absence of a history of suicidal behaviour the adult psychiatrist warned of the risk that Mr O might become suicidal under stress. If Mr O was to be considered as sole carer of his children it would be essential to know what the psychiatrist's assessment of suicidal risk was based on. Finally, the diagnosis of a schizophrenia-like illness raises questions about the interrelated subjects of 'aetiology' and prognosis. Was Mr O's disorder seen as being particularly 'reactive' to stress (such as his immigrant/refugee status, socio-economic disadvantage, and recent bereavement)? What prognostic implications did this have for Mr O's level of function over the following fifteen years (when his youngest child would reach sufficient maturity)?

Mr O's response to treatment

It was known that Mr O's acute episodes remitted with very little medication, and that he had not complied well with medication prescribed to prevent relapse. What were the chances that relapse might be reduced by a combination of better compliance with medication, and increased support to protect against undue stress? What information was available from past relapses that might, with better multi-agency liaison, improve the prediction of relapse, and perhaps reduce its frequency? What safeguards needed to be set in place to 'buffer' the effects of future relapses on the children?

Mr O's compliance with future treatment and monitoring

The opinions of different agencies varied about Mr O's ability to cooperate with them. In order to predict Mr O's future compliance with any programme of monitoring it would be necessary to look at his past relationships (both good and bad) with professional agencies. If the children were to be safe with Mr O in the absence of a second parent, it was essential that such considerations be based on detailed past information.

The role of adult mental health services in monitoring the effects of Mr O's mental state upon his children

From the responses of the adult team (limited to correspondence between the adult psychiatrist and the local authority) it appeared that their interpretation of their role in the children's care proceedings was limited to providing a diagnosis and a cautiously phrased prognostic statement about the high likelihood of future relapse under stress.

Both clinical experience and research evidence point to the benefits of maintaining contact between children and their primary attachment figures as far as is possible, even when rehabilitation to full parental care may not be feasible. In order to plan for contact that would be safe and rewarding to the children (and to Mr O) it was necessary to have a detailed understanding of potential risks. Based on this, a carefully worked-out plan of information exchange and monitoring would then need to be agreed between adult and child (mental health and local authority) services. The failure to obtain vital information on Mr O's condition made it difficult to gauge future risks to the children realistically, and so ruled out the possibility of Mr O resuming the care of his children. In his last session with the child psychiatrist Mr O wept. He had lost two families, one as a consequence of war and political oppression. He was not quite sure why he had lost the second.

Developing liaison

In recent years there has been a substantial impetus to the creation of innovative services that enable closer links between adult and child psychiatric care. Falkov and Davies (1997) and Reder, McClure and Jolley (Chapter 1 of this volume) have identified several factors that have driven these changes. First is the de-institutionalisation of adult mental health care and the consequent increase in the visibility of children whose parents have mental health problems. Second is the resurgence of interest in psycho-social factors in aetiology of major mental illness, and the requirement of the Care Programme Approach that adult services address a broader agenda of both clinical and social functioning. Last, and complementary to the movements in adult services, is the gradual reintegration of the three main streams of interest in the field of child mental health – the psychiatric, the psychoanalytic and the developmental/educational. The growth of newer disciplines (such as family therapy) has led to increasing interdisciplinary dialogue, widening the focus in contemporary child mental health teams to include the biomedical, interpersonal and social contributors to childhood disorder.

With these movements the apparent distance between adult and child psychiatry created by conflicting aetiological and therapeutic perspectives has begun to break down. Adult and child mental health services can now speak a common language – that of an interactional model in which both biological and psycho-social factors are given due regard in the aetiology and treatment of both adult and child psychiatric disorders. It was in this context of a developing common language that the liaison project described in this chapter was conceived.

The authors, working in a socio-economically deprived sector of the London Borough of Hammersmith and Fulham, recognised that there was a conspicuous need for cooperation due to the substantial overlap between their caseloads. That such overlap existed, and was problematic, was also suggested by a survey conducted in 1996/7 in the London Borough of Lambeth, an area with similar demographic characteristics (The Families and Mental Health Initiative, London Borough of Lambeth; Falkov and Davies, 1997). This survey obtained information on 1,008 (63 per cent) of 1,600 known adults with severe mental illness. Of these, 185 (18 per cent), or almost one-fifth, also had dependent children. Two-thirds of those with dependent children were women, 68 (37 per cent) of whom had a current diagnosis of psychosis. Some 46 (25 per cent) had a history of self-harm and 57 (31 per cent) a history of formal admission under the Mental Health Act. Of greatest concern, however, was the fact that in 36 per cent of cases (65 families) no information was provided in the adult psychiatric records about who looked after the children. Also, an American study (Blanch *et al.*, 1994), which looked at the overlap from the child service perspective, found that 16 per cent of children in foster care and 21 per cent of children receiving preventive services (outpatient services designed to prevent unnecessary out-of-home placements) in New York State had at least one parent with a diagnosed serious mental illness.

The liaison project

Both the adult and child services involved in the project were multidisciplinary teams. The adult service included psychiatrists, community psychiatric nurses, a psychologist and an occupational therapist. It was charged with providing a general community psychiatric service, but with a focus upon the long-term mentally ill, for a population of 40,000, aged 16–75 years, in the northern-most sector of the London Borough of Hammersmith and Fulham. The child service included psychiatrists, psychologists, family therapists and child psychotherapists, and provided for a population of 28,200 children, aged 0–16 years, in the entire borough (population estimates for 1997, Office of National Statistics). The area had a high degree of social deprivation (mean Jarman 8 score of 38) and included a high proportion of socially isolated individuals in temporary accommodation, and two of the most deprived large housing estates in London. Ethnic minorities comprised about 20 per cent of the local population. The adult service was a busy, typical inner-London team receiving between 10 and 25 new referrals per week. The social deprivation of the population was similarly reflected in high call upon child psychiatric services (10 referrals per week), high levels of child social work allocation, and large numbers of children on the Child Protection Register (4.95 per 1,000 children in 1997–8, as compared with the average of 3.06 per 1,000 for all London).

All referrals to the adult service were discussed and allocated at a weekly team meeting, which also afforded an opportunity to provide feedback to the whole team on on-going casework, and to recruit other members of the team as co-workers if appropriate. It was agreed that the child psychiatrist would attend this meeting on a monthly basis, and that one hour of the meeting would be dedicated to discussion of casework involving children. Dialogue between the services was conceived of as taking place in both directions. It was envisaged that the child psychiatrist would bring to the meeting cases in which an identified child-patient had a parent or carer with potential mental health problems that required the involvement of the adult team. In turn, it was expected that the adult team would bring cases for consideration by the child psychiatrist in which there was concern that the children of identified adult-patients were actually suffering or potentially at risk of mental health problems.

The following story of Daniel and his mother, Mrs R, provides an example of liaison between the two teams.

Case vignette 2

Mrs R and Daniel, aged 5 years, were referred by the adult specialist registrar to the child psychiatrist. Mrs R was depressed, under treatment with anti-depressants, and attended monthly follow-up with the specialist registrar. She was finding it increasingly difficult to cope with Daniel's 'behaviour'. He was the third of her four children, and her first son.

Mrs R attended the first meeting with the child psychiatrist at the child service base with her daughters, 11 and 9 years old, and sons – Daniel and a toddler of 2 years. During the interview Mrs R was affectionate and atten-tive to the youngest, while her daughters played together or assisted her in caring for the toddler. Daniel was left to his own devices; he was excited and climbed on to furniture, opened doors, and threw toys about. Mrs R looked increasingly fed up and miserable as she tried ineffectually to control him. She apologised repeatedly, adding that she was so tired out by Daniel that she could not sleep at night. She felt alone and helpless, and thoughts of death would come to her; she said that being a 'Christian' prevented her from contemplating suicide. As she spoke Daniel's activity grew more fever-ish, and the cheeky grin he had been wearing gave way to obvious tension. Mrs R did not notice.

A discussion of Mrs R's background and her childhood in West Africa revealed that she had been the eldest of a large family. This had been a

position of ambiguous privilege because, though she had responsibility and
authority over the younger children, she had felt excluded from the indul-
gence and affection that the younger ones got from their mother. Mrs R
trained as a nurse and took great pride in her profession, and in the care of
her own children. However, her husband's departure while she was pregnant
with the youngest was a blow that brought back childhood feelings of hurt
and rejection. As she spoke and wept the children had gathered around their
mother as though to listen to a familiar story. Without Mrs R appearing to
notice, Daniel had managed to place himself within the circle of her free
arm.

Mrs R spoke of feeling overwhelmed by her current practical and finan-
cial difficulties. The gas cooker had broken down. The children shared the
only bed and bedroom, while Mrs R slept uncomfortably on the settee. Lack
of sleep made her irritable and the children were always more disobedient
when she was tired and unhappy. When her husband left, Mrs R had given
up her nursing career to care for the children. She was guilty about her
inability to cope with the children and housework, embarrassed at taking
'charity' (Child Benefit payments) from the state, and ashamed of the
decline in her status and lifestyle. These feelings prevented her from obtain-
ing assistance to which she was entitled. She withdrew from her usual part
in church activities; in turn this provoked more guilt about not 'contributing'
to the community.

Mrs R's history reveals a number of commonly recognised links between
early (childhood) experience and later depression. While Mrs R's preoccupation with the 'deprivation' suffered in childhood – namely, of her mother's
love – may have been an effect of her depressed mood rather than its cause, it
suggests a vulnerability that, with later loss (her husband's departure),
resulted in depression. Mrs R's greater difficulty with Daniel may be understood in the light of his gender, as well as the particular ebullience of the
child's developing personality. More accustomed to looking after her many
younger sisters, Mrs R expected boys to be 'more difficult', and to respond
better to 'a father's hand'.

Equally, it was possible to see in sessions how Daniel was affected by his
mother's mood and behaviour. Mrs R's depression coincided with his developmental need for exploration and autonomy, and made her less tolerant of
his behaviour. Her irritation and attempts to control him added to the
urgency with which Daniel struggled to break free; her apathy and tearfulness also made him anxious. Daniel's agitation, though very likely an inter-
active effect, began to be attributed to him as a characteristic of personality,
or even of pathology – Daniel's teacher wondered whether he might be
'hyperactive'.

In this case the opportunity for liaison achieved benefits for both the
management of Mrs R by adult services, and also for Daniel, as follows.

*Closer and more effective monitoring of Mrs R's depression and
particularly her suicidal preoccupations*

Mrs R had talked readily to the adult psychiatrist about her sleep, appetite,
and practical problems, but was afraid of speaking about her suicidal
thoughts because she thought she would be hospitalised, and that her children would be 'taken away'. In her anxiety about being seen as a bad parent
Mrs R had initially been reluctant to talk openly about her growing inability
to cope with child care, and especially with Daniel. She felt more able to talk
about her suicidal ideas to the child psychiatrist who, she believed, had no
role in this, but who was able to monitor concerns and liaise with the adult
team.

*Closer monitoring of the risks to the children due to Mrs R's
suicidal thoughts*

Mrs R's increasing openness to the child psychiatrist about her suicidal
fantasies proved highly reassuring to both. The child psychiatrist was able to
monitor the potential risks to the children by direct observation of child care,
and was able to rule out risks due to inattention or neglect, or due to
abnormal beliefs accompanying depression. Regular communication between
the adult and child psychiatrists enhanced the parent's and professionals'
confidence and reduced the anxieties about unpredictability that commonly
accompany suicidal patients. It permitted professionals to work with the
'functioning parent' in Mrs R through the worst of her depression; rather
than feeling blamed/criticised she now shared professionals' worries about
the impact of depression/suicide upon her children.

*Treatment could 'legitimately' be aimed at Mrs R's parenting as one of
the areas of dysfunction caused by her depression*

Mrs R responded rapidly to the child psychiatrist's interest in her childhood
experiences and family dynamics, and in the links drawn between these and
her feelings/abilities as a parent in her own right. As she understood this she
blamed herself less for what she could not do. These changes in her own
perceptions of herself had a dramatic impact on how she spoke of Daniel.
Quite suddenly he had ceased to be a problem to her, and his school, when
contacted, reported that he had 'settled'.

Practical assistance

A lack of basic amenities is a particularly important piece of the jigsaw
that underlies family dysfunction. Daniel and Mrs R lived in an economic-
ally deprived inner-London area where resources are scarce and the local

authority is often struggling to identify those most in need. The joint and coordinated approach to the needs of both Daniel and his mother from both child and adult services was effective in securing resources for the family which otherwise may not have been obtained. Mrs R soon had a bed, a cooker, and a nursery placement for the toddler; her sleep improved and she had some free time. She resumed participation in church activities and became a voluntary helper at the local hospital.

Discussion

A key principle of adult community psychiatry, as espoused by Bennett (1978), one of its most distinguished and influential practitioners, is that community psychiatry should not be so much about *where* it is practised (in, for example, a district hospital as opposed to domestic-style premises) as about *how*. By this, he meant that it should extend beyond the individual patient to see the patient in his or her whole social context, and that treatment should be directed not only to the individual but, as much as possible, also to that social context. It is difficult to see a principle which is more salient to the subject of liaison between child and adult mental health services, and it is a principle that underlies all of the benefits of liaison which are listed below.

Some benefits

A higher profile for children within adult services

Although adult services usually employ standardised forms of assessment which incorporate family background, it is all too easy, particularly in a busy inner-London service, to overlook the area of parenting responsibilities and the impact of parental mental illness on child care. This oversight was highlighted by a recent study (Tamarit and Lau, 1999) of 100 consecutive female admissions to acute psychiatric wards in which case notes documented the existence of children in only 25. One of the major benefits of regular liaison between child and adult services is to raise the profile of child-related issues within the adult service, improve social-history taking, and thereby facilitate the identification of children either suffering from or at risk of mental health problems.

Shaping the process of child referral

Child mental health referral can often be perceived by parents as a threat, especially if they are themselves already stigmatised by mental illness. Parents may be afraid of having 'genetically' transmitted the illness to their children, of having harmed them through the influence of their mental illness, of being seen as bad parents, and of losing their children due to state intervention.

They also suffer guilt and loss of self-worth due to their awareness of coping badly with their parental duties and responsibilities. These feelings can lead to a reluctance of parents to sanction such referrals. It is important, therefore, that the adult team's referrals of these children are framed in such a way that such feelings are not aggravated. The skills involved in framing such initial approaches are the territory *par excellence* of the child psychiatrist and his/her team. Regular liaison with a child psychiatrist can enable the adult team to initiate the process of referral to child services in ways best likely to secure intervention.

A forum for informal discussion of children potentially affected by parental illness

Parental mental illness may have obvious or sometimes subtle, but serious and far-reaching negative consequences to the physical well-being, mental health and normal development of children. This is an area in which adult workers feel less skilled at weighing up relative risks and consequences, and where closer liaison between child and adult services can facilitate consult-ation, with early intervention where appropriate (see Case vignette 2, p. 291), or referral to statutory child protection agencies if necessary.

Improved scope for prophylactic work

Adult services are sometimes confronted by situations in which there is no overt disturbance in a child, but where circumstances are such that internal distress, future symptomatology or curtailed life prospects seem a likely effect of severe parental illness, and in which prophylactic interventions for a child may be indicated. For example, the principal caring role for a mentally ill parent may be assumed by the child, interfering with her/his age-appropriate developmental tasks, and leading potentially to problems of attachment and separation, both with the parent and in relationships in later life.

Definitions and frameworks from the legal and social services fields con-strain statutory child protection agencies and lead to the construction of somewhat artificial 'thresholds' of harm or risk. These do not apply to child mental health work where issues of risk are considered more widely within the research and clinical bases of child development, and the consequences of early experience on later mental and physical health. Mental health profes-sionals are experienced at assessing and predicting the likely consequences of adverse experience, and at assessing the power of protective factors that may ameliorate negative experience within the particular context of the child in question. This includes consideration of the child's individual characteristics and the networks of relationships within which he or she lives. Such an assessment of risk differs notably from the focus of statutory child protection agencies in that it concerns itself less with the identification of abusive 'events' and 'perpetrators'. Its focus on contextual meaning allows preventive therapeutic interventions at levels of risk that are psychologically meaningful but may lie below the threshold of statutory child protection agencies.

Joint working

While the belief systems that underlie the separation of adult and child mental health services are no longer quite so disparate, the continued existence of such a separation gives implicit support to the practice of looking at the needs of children and adults as distinct, and even in competition with each other. False dichotomies may be created; of problem parent and child (*victim*), of problem child and (*innocent*) parent, and also of multi-problem family and (*long-suffering*) agencies. While these dichotomies may be useful as theoretical models, problems arise when assessment and/or treatment is based upon them (see Case vignette 1, p. 285). In an American context, Blanch *et al.* (1994) also noted that one of the outcomes of social funding and policies that focused on the individual rather than on families was that they inadvertently drive families apart.

What is perhaps most dramatically illustrated in Mr O's story are the difficulties that may arise from too rigid an interpretation of confidentiality, leading to lack of information-sharing between child and adult services. It is often assumed that information held by adult services will be interpreted or used by other services to the adult patient's disadvantage. This is far from true. Adult teams often have access to qualitative information about their patients: for example, about positive qualities that might be shaped to improve parenting, about contextual circumstances that allow an understanding of inadequate parenting, and realistic estimates of the patient's ability to respond to help. Before permanent removal of children from parents can be justified it is essential to consider what children will lose if separated from their primary attachments. If these losses are significant, consideration needs to be given to the potential costs and benefits of removal, compared with alternative arrangements such as temporary fostering (while the parent receives treatment) and contact programmes that allow the benefits while minimising risks. There are also significant potential benefits to the parent, from a process that sympathetically weighs up the costs and benefits to them, of doing the best they can for their children.

The therapeutic synergy that can be achieved by joint working between adult and child services is well demonstrated in the story of Daniel and Mrs R (Case vignette 2, p. 291). Joint working can also bring unexpected benefits. These may extend beyond the individual child or adult most clearly affected by improving relationships within the family network. The approach also fosters interdisciplinary learning and the extension of existing therapeutic skills in both child and adult services. Finally, there are the satisfactions for workers in both services of preventive therapeutic work.

Obstacles to liaison

Adult patients and ethical dilemmas

It is not uncommon for adult patients (or their relatives) to confide their concerns for the welfare of their children to adult psychiatrists or other adult team staff in the expectation that these, like other matters, will remain confidential. Adult teams are also often contacted by other professionals, for example GPs, who are in a dilemma over confidentiality, and who seek advice. In such situations, adult staff can be concerned that conveying their worries about these children to other agencies will be viewed by their patient as a breach of confidentiality, alienating the patient, and precipitating default from treatment or follow-up. They fear that this may, in turn, further exacerbate an already unstable home situation. However, it is not uncommon for adult workers to breach confidentiality in circumstances where a patient's judgement is impaired. It is also well recognised in adult services that situations may arise where a duty to protect the public from serious harm outweighs the individual patient's right to confidentiality.

In situations where the risk to children is clear, adult staff have the same responsibility to report their concerns to agencies with statutory child protection responsibilities as do all other professionals. For example, if a patient with a history of violence confides that he has murderous impulses towards his children, the duty to take seriously the immediate risks to the children may outweigh the risks of losing the patient to treatment. There are 'grey areas', however, where adult workers must decide whether their professional responsibility to consider the safety of children overrides their responsibility to treat all information about their patient as equally confidential. There is an inevitable tendency for adult services to be focused primarily on the therapeutic objectives for their adult patients, and the perceived need to maintain a therapeutic relationship with the patient may be an impediment to the full consideration of children in such circumstances.

Resources

When the liaison project was first mooted, there was considerable anxiety amongst adult team members that attempts were being made to recruit them as co-therapists on a routine basis in formal interventions for their patients' children. Despite the potential value of such a role, it was one that the already hard-pressed adult team felt unable to offer, at least on a regular basis. Similar anxieties were felt within the child service, particularly in relation to the very large potential demand that might be identified for prophylactic work. Our experience, however, was that much useful joint work could be done without major resource implications. This principally related to the sharing of information and the development of a common agenda for the care of the whole family. It was recognised, however, that the liaison project had only touched the surface of the potential demand for joint working, and that its resources did not allow, for example, for adult workers to fully assume a co-therapist role in family work, or to be involved in the monitoring of child care by their patients. If future liaison ventures are to explore this territory, a substantially greater resource will need to be provided to both adult and child teams.

'Targeting' in adult services

Adult mental health services face increasing pressure, not least from the policy imperatives of the Care Programme Approach, to focus their interventions upon patients with severe and enduring mental illness. In areas of high psychiatric morbidity such as inner London, this often leaves very limited resources available for other categories of patient, including those with chronic neurotic or personality difficulties, in whom mental disorder can potentially have as potent an adverse effect on children as is the case with schizophrenia and other psychotic disorders. Current priorities for targeting the activity of adult services on the severe and enduring mentally ill do not take into account these potential adverse effects. There is a need for the priorities of adult mental health services to be ordered in such a way that greater attention is given to patients whose children may be at risk due to parental mental disorder.

Training

One of the outcomes of the liaison project was the development of a brief questionnaire to be appended to the initial assessment protocol completed on all patients in local adult services. This was designed to enquire about dependent children, the availability of alternative adult carers, and the effects of parental illness on the safety of children. It also required note to be made of any action (e.g. consultation, referral to child services or social services) taken by adult services in view of these concerns. It was anticipated that the information so gathered would provide a database of children in particular need or potentially at risk due to parental mental disorder. For such a procedure to become a practical reality, it was necessary that a regular programme of liaison and/or training in child-related issues be developed for adult teams.

Funding was obtained for the provision of training to all the local adult teams on the effects of parental disorder upon children. The training was undertaken by a child psychiatrist (BM) with a special interest in child protection issues, and emphasised the evidence from mental health research that informed assessment of risks to children. There were considerable difficulties in engaging the interest of the majority of the local adult teams in this training, and of the adult psychiatrists in particular. Adult services, hard-pressed to deliver the rudiments of service to their clientele, may have balked at the prospect of an additional commitment. However, there is also some reluctance within adult services to fully acknowledge child-related issues and the need for an investment in preventive work. This 'cultural bias' is often deep-rooted and may not be amenable to later training. There is a need, therefore, for the consideration of the interface between child and adult services at the level of the basic professional qualifications of the disciplines that comprise adult mental health teams. The recent decision of the Royal College of Psychiatrists to increase the availability of child psychiatric experience within rotational training schemes for psychiatrists is a welcome move in this direction.

Conclusion

Disparate service organisation and different therapeutic perspectives have conspired for too long to separate adult and child mental health services, to the detriment of both. Much can be achieved by good communication between the two services, and this can be obtained without onerous commitment on the part of either. Our experience suggests, however, that such collaboration represents only the tip of an iceberg of possible interactions between the services. A fuller collaboration, including regular joint working, prophylactic interventions for children and the involvement of adult workers as co-therapists in family interventions, carries substantial resource and training implications for both services, which health purchasers must address. Although made by an inter-agency task force in New York State, a number of Blanch et al.'s (1994) recommendations for action are also relevant to British policy and practice. They suggest the development of a master strategy for 'culture change' in the mental health and social services departments; the revision of all regulations, policies and procedures to incorporate *family* concerns; the merging of multiple funding streams to attach money and services to families rather than to the continued separation of adults and children; the need to target public day-care slots, and respite care for children of mentally ill parents; the need to provide training for family courts, and particularly about alternatives to severance of contact between children and their mentally ill parents.

There is also a need for child services to explore closer collaboration with other mental health services with an adult focus – substance misuse teams, adult learning disability services, and adult psychology and psychotherapy services (particularly when these are separate from mainstream adult services). Such ventures are likely to expose further resource and training needs which are similar to those identified in this collaboration.

References

Bennett, D. (1978) Community psychiatry. *British Journal of Psychiatry*, 132, 209–220.

Blanch, A.K., Nicholson, J. and Purcell, J. (1994) Parents with severe mental illness and their children: the need for human services integration. *Journal of Mental Health Administration*, 21, 388–396.

Falkov, A. and Davies, N. (1997) Solutions on the ground: a family mental health service? In: *Report of the 12th Annual Michael Sieff Foundation Conference 'Keeping Children in Mind: Balancing Children's Needs with Parents' Mental Health'*. Michael Sieff Foundation.

Reder, P., Duncan, S. and Gray, M. (1993) *Beyond Blame: Child Abuse Tragedies Revisited*. London: Routledge.

Rutter, M. and Quinton, D. (1984) Parental psychiatric disorder: effects on children. *Psychological Medicine*, 14, 853–880.

Tamarit, L.M. and Lau, A.Y. (1999) Children's needs when their mothers are admitted to psychiatric units. *Psychiatric Bulletin*, 23, 214–217.

Section 5

Future directions

Chapter 21

An integrative ecology

Mike McClure

An integrative ecology describes complex interactions. This will provide a theoretical basis for understanding interpersonal relationships and the genesis of mental health problems. It is relevant to the interfaces between children and their parents because it is useful for formulating health policy, developing child and adolescent mental health services and designing treatment programmes. Former developments in biology, psychology, psychiatry and sociology led to a separation of child and adult mental health through the very nature of the analytic paradigm that was employed. The new paradigm sees connections at many levels in the complex interrelationships between child development and adult mental health. An integrative ecology synthesises developmental, systemic and holistic constructs. We therefore need to consider the contribution of developmental, systemic and holistic theories which interlink in this ecological model.

Developmental models

A developmental model implies a process of growth from a state of immaturity to a more advanced state of maturity, and a progressive increase in the complexity of structure and psychological functioning as the individual matures. For example, the development of neural pathways and structures within the brain is associated with the development of higher levels of cognitive abilities, during which there is a complex relationship between this anatomical process of neural maturation and psychological development of language, emotions and social relationships (Rutter and Rutter, 1993). In addition, the development of biologically-based cognitive abilities is influenced by experience, creating individual differences in a process of individuation (Rutter, 1994a; 1994b). Genetic influences increase with age during childhood and these biologically-based characteristics interact with environmental influences, including the family relationships.

Experiences of formative relationships in infancy are likely to affect later relationships and psychopathology (Nash and Hay, 1993). The implication is that underlying neural structures and psychological processes produced in the interaction between genetic influences and environment may lead to continuities of characteristics which stabilise in the personality of the individual. Later stressful experiences will tend to accentuate pre-existing characteristics (Caspi *et al.*, 1993) as individuals assimilate new experiences (both good and bad) by incorporating them in pre-existing cognitive schemata. Through a process of reflection, however, individuals relate external events to self-concepts in a way which may produce continuity or discontinuity of self-image and behaviour. The developing individual is affected by the environment, but also acts to shape and select the environment (Rutter *et al.*, 1994) and the responses engendered in others. Events brought about by people's own actions may therefore have effects on their subsequent view of themselves and consequent behaviour.

Developmental transitions

Developmental transitions occur when new psychological structures and behaviours emerge. Transitions involve a qualitative rather than quantitative change, which may occur during sensitive periods of development, resulting in a transformation of psychological processes. For example, the process of bonding and acquisition of secure attachment between the parent and infant is part of the developmental process and may be considered a developmental transition. Disturbance in attachment may occur in children aged 1–4 years, inhibiting a transition and leading to the internalisation of these early relationships, which act as a blueprint to affect their adult relationships. Similarly, the acquisition of the ability to understand other people's state of mind and intentions – 'theory of mind' – is a necessary transition to enable socialisation. Later, hormonal changes at puberty induce a transition which incorporates physiological, psychological and social components of adolescence. When a social role transition such as adolescence is associated with a change in predicted life trajectory, it is termed a 'turning point' in development (Pickles and Rutter, 1991). Causal chains of stimuli, which may be internal or external in origin, may result in consequent cognitive change being either adaptive or maladaptive and, if maladaptive, generating psychological distress.

Systemic models

A system is defined as a complex of component parts that are in mutual interaction. Information flows in and out in an open system and is organised by feedback and control mechanisms. Living systems are in continuous change as they develop to higher levels of organisation. Historically, early models used to explain family interaction were based upon cybernetics, which is the science of control and communication in complex systems. Control was seen as being exercised through communication at different levels, consisting of information and feedback, to achieve a state of balance or homeostasis. General systems theory provided a comprehensive model that was relevant to all living systems, including child–adult interaction in families, in different phases of the family life cycle (Gale and Long, 1996).

A structural model of a family system is concerned with its organisation and functional roles. When extended beyond the nuclear family to the wider family and community it has been described as an ecological model. A strategic model identifies sequential interactional patterns of communication, hierarchy and power within the system. Systemic models also describe how intergenerational processes, including unresolved intrapsychic conflicts derived from the family of origin, may be replicated in the current family.

Postmodern developments in systems theory include the concept of autopoiesis, which stresses autonomy rather than control and rejects the cybernetic machine metaphor (Gale and Long, 1996). A further development is radical constructivism, which considers the nervous system as one in which constructs are formed by interaction with the environment. Social constructionism views ideas, concepts and memories as arising from social interchange, mediated by language and embedded within a social and cultural context. Deconstruction may reveal the artificiality of meaning, structures and behaviour, such as traditional gender-role concepts.

An holistic model of development

Complex, multi-determined processes cannot be understood in terms of single separate variables taken out of context. Contributions from the interface of biology, physiology, psychology, sociology and anthropology give a wider understanding and a more comprehensive 'developmental science' (Magnusson and Cairns, 1997). Individual development is viewed as a complex, multi-determined, integrated process in which biological, psychological and behavioural components interact with each other and with social and environmental factors (Magnusson, 1996). The developmental process extends from the cellular level in the biological system to cultural factors, which interact throughout the life span. This holistic perspective can therefore propose an integrated model of human development and society (Magnusson, 1995), in which genetic expression of thought and behaviour interacts with the social and physical environment. Through feedback and feed-forward mechanisms, the individual may change or select the environment with which to react. Epigenesis is the process by which individual development takes place, characterised by increasing complexity of organisation at all levels as a consequence of interaction between the components and the environment (Gottlieb, 1996).

At another level of description, within each system, there are many subsystems. For example, each neuronal cell may be considered a subsystem of the nervous system and the brain may be considered both as another subsystem and as a system in its own right, with functional segregation of parts co-existing with integration of the whole (Edelman and Tononi, 1996). The theory of neuronal group selection considers that brain development is governed by genetically programmed processes of self-organisation. Differences within neuro-anatomical networks produce the wide variation of neuronal activity, thought processes and behaviour which interact with the environment.

Social development

Social development can also be understood as a process of continual reciprocal interaction between an individual and their living context. The biological individual has potential for expression and action which may be used consciously to promote social development and to alter the social environment (Karli, 1996). Biological, psychological and social components may contribute to observable behaviours such as sexual activity and aggression, with the mediating and integrating influence of affective processes. The behavioural interactions involve selective responses by the individual to the environment, assigning meanings, and then changing the environment, which in turn may act on the individual (Hinde, 1996). In interpersonal and social interactions, relationships affect other relationships, so that the social structure is influenced by, and influences, the beliefs and values of individuals and their relationships. Each level, from individual behaviour to society, involves properties not directly pertinent to the level below. Some individual psychological characteristics are developmentally stable, whereas others are labile with respect to the environment. Through processes such as reinforcement, modelling and internalisation of norms, parents, the family, peers and society influence, and are influenced by, the developing individual. A good example is the acquisition (or rejection) of gender differences and stereotypes, which are influenced by biological, psychological and social interactions.

Links can be made between the processes described by attachment theory, object relations theory and theories of cognitive and social development, to encompass the multiple levels involved in social development (Bartholomew, 1993). Within the parent–child relationship, the child acquires an internal working model of the relationship between the self and the principal caregivers, which forms the basis for future behaviour and interactions with others. Interference with the formation of internal working models by defensive mechanisms may modify the intergenerational transmission of relationship style (Bretherton, 1990). As significant relationships develop between the child and mother, father, siblings, extended family, peers and the wider society, the relationship between parents both affects and is affected by the parent–child relationship within the family system (Dunn, 1993). Derivatives of earlier insecure attachment relationships may cause individuals to respond inappropriately to attachment behaviour or to seek inappropriate attachments later in life (Byng-Hall and Stevenson-Hinde, 1991). Further-more, Caspi and Elder (1988) demonstrated that personal instability leads to marital conflict, which produces poor parenting, resulting in a difficult, unstable child in the next generation.

Society and culture

The sociocultural structure is constructed from personal, group and cultural beliefs and values. Through the course of interactional development, the individual acquires a concept of the self in relation to society's norms of behaviour, values, beliefs, roles and institutions (Hinde, 1996). An indi-vidual's beliefs and values are acquired through interaction with other mem-bers of a group through the processes of socialisation and acculturation. Beliefs and values are formed through this process, resulting in attitudes to others and relationships with them. For example, views about divorce, acquired through experience, directly or indirectly, both reflect and influence the stability of marriages. Activities such as suicide, which is culturally influenced, are the end result of an interaction of biological, psychological, social and cultural factors with the availability of lethal methods of self-harm within the environment (McClure, 2000).

The goals and values that parents have for their children are affected by society's norms and values and influence the parental style. This in turn affects the development of the child, who, through shaping and modelling of relationships between parents and peers within a secure attachment relation-ship with parents, will develop a socially acceptable balance between pro-social cooperation and individualism. Insecure attachments, on the other hand, will lead to maladaptive relationships and difficulty in integrating into society.

Developmental psychopathology

Developmental psychopathology integrates neurobiological, psychological and sociocultural perspectives in the pursuit of identifying causal relation-ships (Rutter, 1996). For example, the finding that the ill-effects of parental divorce and separation are greater than the effects of parental death indicates that divorce plays a major part in the effect on the child. Fergusson *et al.* (1992), however, found that the overall psychopathological risks associated with family discord and those associated with family separations and disrup-tions were similar. There was a dose–response relationship between the degree of family discord and the risks to the children, whereas there was no dose–response relationship between the number of changes and the risk to the child. The implication is that the discord associated with divorce is a major contributor to disturbance in the children.

Quinton *et al.* (1993) examined the effects of parental mental disorder and institutional upbringing on individuals. They demonstrated that persistent anti-social behaviour was dependent on a series of influences over time, including family discord, the peer group and eventual choice of marriage partner. There was a strong likelihood that anti-social individuals would marry or cohabit with anti-social partners, which can be understood as a person–environment interaction for both partners. This does not negate the influence of genetic factors, but demonstrates the importance of external influences.

Champion *et al.* (1995) found that individuals with emotional or behavioural disturbance in childhood were more likely to experience severely stressful events and chronic adversity in adult life, which was due to them shaping an adverse environment. Dodge *et al.* (1990) suggest that cognitive processing of adverse experiences such as abuse may constitute one of the mediating mechanisms. Abused children who developed a hostile attributional style were most likely to develop aggressive behaviour. Consequently, children who are aggressive and continue to be aggressive in adolescence and adulthood, come into conflict more frequently with others. Similarly, McClure *et al.* (1995) describe the complex interplay of biological, psychological and social factors within an environment shaped by the individual, family and society, contributing to the development of eating disorder.

Developments in systems theory

Attention has been focused so far on the bio/psycho/social development of the individual within the family and society. It is possible to widen understanding of this process by reference to other concepts and models. These include chaos theory, catastrophe theory, universality and ecology.

Chaos theory

Chaos theory hypothesises connections between different kinds of irregularity (Gleick, 1988). It is a science of the global nature of systems, supplanting the theory of deterministic predictability. Chaos theory describes non-linear relationships which are not strictly proportional, where randomness is re-construed as an 'aperiodic' system. It describes the process of structuring complexity using concepts such as fractals, bifurcations, intermittencies, and periodicities. Small differences in input to systems can produce a massive difference in output, termed 'sensitive dependence on initial conditions' – the so-called 'Butterfly effect'. Chains of events affected by small changes can reach a point of 'crisis' and such 'crises' can occur throughout a complex system. The study of chaos has revolutionised theoretical biology, fusing the expertise of biologists, physicists, ecologists and epidemiologists.

Catastrophe theory

Catastrophe theory is a general systems theory for describing and predicting discontinuous changes in events. Using several control parameters, it is capable of describing the transition from qualitatively different stable states with an intervening period of instability. Catastrophe theory can be applied throughout the biological sciences to describe interactions resulting in qualitatively different states (Deakin, 1990). An ecological example would be the crisis that can occur with small changes in the levels of food to the growth-rate parameter within a complex living system. McClure (1996) has postulated the interaction of biological, psychological, social and environmental parameters which bring about a qualitatively different mental state of an individual, resulting in their suicidal behaviour.

Universality

Deutsch (1997) discusses progress towards a unified theory of all the basic forces known to physics. Unification of the general theory of relativity and quantum theory forms a quantum theory of gravity, linking with 'superstring theory' which describes the elementary substance of matter. Deutsch explains living processes in terms of molecular replicators – genes whose behaviour is governed by the same laws of physics as apply to inanimate matter. There is thus a link between quantum theory of physical interaction and the theory of evolution as it applies to the development of living organisms. All matter, living and non-living, can therefore be understood through the basic forces of physics.

Ecosystems

Ecology has influenced systems thinking with the concepts of community and networks (Capra, 1996). Ecosystems consist of communities of organisms linked together in networks. Each organism is itself a network with organs, which in turn are networks. The biosphere is the system of life surrounding the Earth with a complex structure of networks within networks.

Deep ecology

The new paradigm of deep ecology interconnects organisms, social systems and ecosystems, which has implications for science, philosophy, economics, politics, health care, education and everyday life (Capra, 1996). Deep ecology involves an holistic world view, seeing the integrated whole rather than a dissociated collection of parts. This may be represented by the so-called 'Gaia Hypothesis', which construes the world as an organism with constituent subsystems. Deep ecological awareness recognises the fundamental interdependence of all phenomena within the cyclical processes of nature. Social ecology stresses the current prominence of the hierarchical 'dominator system' of social organisation evident in patriarchy, imperialism, capitalism and racism (Capra, 1996). Ecofeminism views the domination of women by men as being responsible for other forms of domination and exploitation, including political and capitalist exploitation of nature. Capra considers that self-assertion and integration are both essential aspects of all living systems, which in a healthy network of systems achieve a dynamic balance. From the systemic point of view, the only viable relationships are those that are sustainable in healthy balance. In re-constructing relationships, ecology and psychology are linking together to form eco-psychology.

Integrology – an integrative ecology

When considering the development and current functioning of an individual it is important to have a broad-based model. Ideally, this model should be all-inclusive and demonstrate the interaction of various elements in an integrated system. Although Deutsch (1997) warns against a reductionist model, it may be helpful in conceptualising associations. A suitable integrative ecological model integrates components hierarchically in order of complexity – from the least complex 'elemental' factors to the most complex 'universal' factors (see Figure 21.1). Development over time is represented diagrammatically as 'developmental transitions'. Traditionally, most consideration is given to biological, psychological and social aspects of human development. Integrology, using an ecological model, allows wider considerations using holistic, developmental and systemic constructs.

At the lowest level of complexity are elemental factors based literally upon the basic elements of matter, arranged in terms of increasing complexity from the least complex – sub-atomic, atomic, molecular and non-organic matter. At the interface with the second level of complexity – the 'biological' – are the chemical and physical processes that incorporate elemental and non-organic matter into organic, living material. Again, the 'biological' level is arranged in order of complexity from the least complex – genetic, physiological, organ systems, and the whole body. The third level of complexity is the 'psychological', which also has an interface with the previous 'biological' level at the point where brain activity becomes sentience and thought process. At the lowest level of complexity of the 'psychological' level are basic emotions, then complex emotions, and then cognition and self-awareness at the highest level. The interface between the psychological and social levels represents the social behaviour of the individual. The social level itself is subdivided in terms of increasing complexity into the nuclear family, the extended family, friends, neighbourhood and the community. At the interface with the next

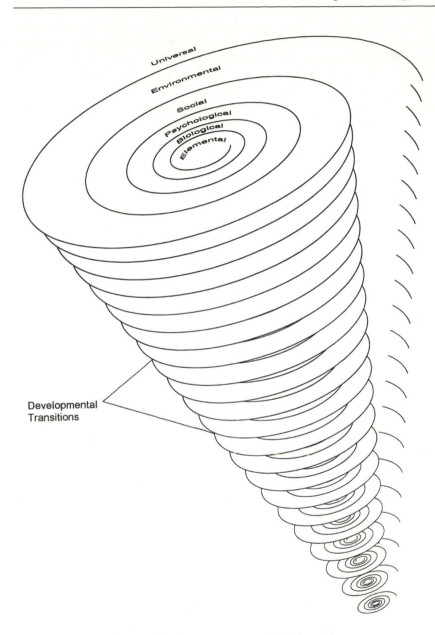

Universal

Environmental

Social

Psychological

Biological

Elemental

Developmental
Transitions

Figure 21.1 Levels of interaction in an integrative ecological model

level of organisation – the environmental – are society, culture, politics and economics. The environment itself consists of the biosphere, the built environment and the natural environment. Beyond the terrestrial environment is our solar system, galaxy and the universe.

This hierarchical integrative ecological model is clearly a simplification (as all models inevitably are) but it demonstrates important principles. All of the levels are interacting dynamically within themselves and with each other according to holistic, developmental and systemic principles. Although there are interactions between them, each level has properties which are not pertinent to other levels. Interactions between individuals or between subsystems within a larger system are shown diagrammatically in Figure 21.2.

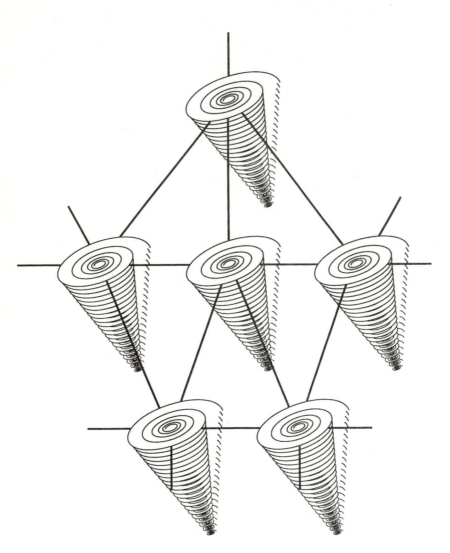

Figure 21.2 Interactions between subsystems in an integrative ecological model

Practical relevance of integrative ecology

Integrative ecology is relevant in relation to the child/adult interfaces at many levels, and it also puts these relationships in context. Specialisation has led to different professionals attributing different principal 'causes' in the production of mental health problems. We can no longer think in a reductionist, Cartesian manner, concentrating on only genetic or biological factors, or only on psychoanalytic defence mechanisms or deprivation. We must be aware of the complex, multi-level interrelationships between factors and be prepared to understand the multiple influences on human thoughts, feelings and behaviour.

At the lowest, elemental level, damage to the foetus, child or adult may occur through elemental deprivation. For example, oxygen or nutrient deprivation to the foetus may have serious and irreversible biological consequences, as may malnutrition or starvation in a child or adult due to famine, neglect or self-starvation. Inadequate intake of essential elements may lead to disease and neurological damage affecting brain development, cognition and behaviour. Furthermore, excessive ingestion of toxic substances, such as lead, alcohol, amphetamine and other drugs, may damage biological tissue, including brain tissue.

At the interface of the elemental and biological levels, developments in microbiology and genetics will continue to clarify the most direct biological relationship between parent and child. Theoretically, genetically inherited mental illness and adverse personality characteristics could be modified at this level, transforming the biological influence of the parent on the child. Pharmacological interventions at the biological level on either parent or child may modify their interactions, decrease expressed emotion and allow for a healthier relationship.

At the psychological level, child–adult interaction can be explained by, for example, attachment theory, psychoanalytic theories and theories of cognitive development. Interventions at the psychological level, through prevention or treatment by counselling or individual psychotherapy, may transform cognition and insight in either parent or child. This would enable better personal integration and improve interpersonal relationships.

At the interface of the psychological and social levels, cognitive and behavioural interventions may decrease behaviours that inhibit interpersonal functioning or increase behaviours that enhance social interaction. Also at the social level, harmony between parent and child may be enhanced by systemic therapies, including group therapy and family therapy and interventions into family networks. At a higher level of complexity, social policy, including health planning, may address resource and organisational problems which have made effective coordination of child and adult services difficult.

At the interface between social and environmental levels, political decisions will dictate the resources available to health and social planners. Economic factors are relevant in terms of resource availability and also the economic cost to society of dependent or destructive families who require resources from social services, health and the penal system. Still within the environmental level, there is an environmental cost, particularly in relation to the built environment, in terms of vandalised, impoverished housing estates, ridden with crime and substance dependency. Individuals in such circumstances are not able readily to access and benefit from the natural environment.

Beyond the terrestrial environment, at the universal level, it should not be forgotten that solar radiation sustains all life. It also has profound effects on our diurnal physiological fluctuations, including sleep patterns. Diurnal mood disturbance, for example, is related to the earth's rotation in relation to the sun. Furthermore, climatic change, such as changes in barometric pressure, affects mood, irritability and even propensity to violence and suicide. Seasonal variation in level of solar radiation, mediated through changes in temperature, climate and environment, is related to Seasonal Affective Disorder.

As a simplistic example, we can take a child born to a mother who has a biologically-based predisposition to depression, and a father with alcoholism, which is both biologically and socially influenced. The mother neglects herself throughout pregnancy, resulting in a difficult labour and slight elemental oxygen deprivation. The child (who has a biological, genetic predisposition to later depression and alcoholism) is irritable following the difficult birth. There are attachment difficulties with the depressed mother, who is unsupported by her alcoholic partner. Lack of a loving relationship and neglect contribute to psychological difficulties in the developing child, who causes more stress for the parents.

The psychological and subsequent behavioural problems bring about difficulties in socialisation, both within the family and in the wider community. As there is a concentration of such families in the neighbourhood, schools and other social facilities are sub-optimal. There is a culture of despondency, with crime, alcoholism and substance misuse commonplace.

Health planning and provision for the child are limited by economic resources which are themselves dependent upon political expediency. The economy, burdened by an unemployable minority in receipt of social security, does not allow sufficient resources for maternal care, schooling or child and family health care. These economic difficulties are related to fluctuations in the world economy, which is itself dependent upon commodity prices of natural resources, such as oil, and climatic change.

Our example child grows up, affected by parents and these other levels of influence, until, in adulthood, the genetic predisposition to depression and alcoholism is expressed, triggered by an episode of psychological stress that follows the father's premature death. Symptoms of hopelessness and despair are accompanied by clinical mood variation, which has some seasonal component. All levels of interaction have influenced the clinical picture, and assessment should therefore understand the interrelationship between the different levels of complexity using the principles of integrative ecology. The levels interact dynamically in ways described by holistic, developmental and systems theory. Once the multi-determined nature of the problem is recognised, interventions can be selected which best address them.

Responding to the interfaces between child and adult mental health requires consideration of many different levels of professional intervention by health and welfare services. It also requires practitioners, trainers and policy makers to take a more integrated approach to mental health problems.

References

Bartholomew, K. (1993), From childhood to adult relationships: attachment theory and research. In: S. Duck (ed.) *Learning about Relationships*. Newbury Park, Calif.: Sage.

Bretherton, I. (1990) Communication patterns, internal working models and the intergenerational transmission of attachment relationships. *Infant Mental Health Journal*, 11, 237–252.

Byng-Hall, J. and Stevenson-Hinde, J. (1991) Attachment relationships within a family system. *Infant Mental Health Journal*, 12, 187–200.

Capra, F. (1996) *The Web of Life: A New Synthesis of Mind and Matter*. New York: HarperCollins.

Caspi, A. and Elder, G. (1988) Emergent family patterns: the intergenerational construction of problem behaviour and relationships. In: R.A. Hinde and J. Stevenson-Hinde (eds) *Relationships within Families: Mutual Influences*. New York: Oxford University Press.

Caspi, A., Lynam, D., Moffin, T.E. and Silva, P.A. (1993) Unravelling girls' delinquency: biological, dispositional, and contextual contributions to adolescent misbehaviour. *Developmental Psychology*, 29, 19–30.

Champion, L.A., Goodall, G.M. and Rutter, M. (1995) Behavioural problems in childhood and stressors in early adult life. 1. A twenty-year follow-up of London school children. *Psychological Medicine*, 25, 231–246.

Deakin, M.A. (1990) Catastrophe modelling in the biological sciences. *Acta Biotheoretica*, 38, 3–22.

Deutsch, D. (1997) *The Fabric of Reality*. Harmondsworth: Penguin.

Dodge, K.A., Bates, J.E. and Pettit, G.S. (1990) Mechanisms in the cycle of violence. *Science*, 250, 1678–1683.

Dunn, J. (1993) *Young Children's Close Relationships*. London: Sage.

Edelman, G.M. and Tononi, G. (1996) Selection and development: the brain as a complex system. In: D. Magnusson (ed.) *The Lifespan Development of Individuals: Behavioural, Neurobiological and Psychosocial Perspectives: A Synthesis*. Cambridge: Cambridge University Press.

Fergusson, D.M., Horwood, L.J. and Lynshey, M.T. (1992) Family change, parental discord and early offending. *Journal of Child Psychology and Psychiatry*, 33, 1059–1075.

Gale, J. and Long, J. (1996) Theoretical foundations of family therapy. In: F. Piercy, D. Sprerkle and J. Wetchler (eds) *Family Therapy Sourcebook*. New York: Guilford.

Gleick, J. (1988) *Chaos*. London: Heinemann.

Gottlieb, G. (1996) A systems view of psychobiological development. In: D. Magnusson (ed.) *The Lifespan Development of Individuals: Behavioural, Neurobiological and Psychosocial Perspectives: A Synthesis*. Cambridge: Cambridge University Press.

Hinde, R.A. (1996) The interpretation of biology and culture. In: D. Magnusson (ed.) *The Lifespan Development of Individuals: Behavioural, Neurobiological and Psychosocial Perspectives: A Synthesis*. Cambridge: Cambridge University Press.

Karli, P. (1996) The brain and socialisation: a two-way mediation across the life course. In: D. Magnusson (ed.) *The Lifespan Development of Individuals: Behavioural, Neurobiological and Psychosocial Perspectives: A Synthesis*. Cambridge: Cambridge University Press.

McClure, G.M. (1996) Catastrophe theory as a model for suicidal behaviour. *Proceedings of the Royal College of Psychiatrists Child and Adolescent Faculty Annual Conference*. Royal College of Psychiatrists.

McClure, G.M. (2000) Suicide in England and Wales 1960–1997. *British Journal of Psychiatry*, 176, 64–67.

McClure, G.M., Timimi, S. and Westman, A. (1995) Anorexia in early adolescence following illness – the importance of the sick role. *Journal of Adolescence*, 18, 359–369.

Magnusson, D. (1995) Individual development: a holistic integrated model. In: *Examining Lives in Context: Perspectives on the Ecology of Human Development*. Washington, DC: American Psychological Association.

Magnusson, D. (ed.) (1996) *The Lifespan Development of Individuals: Behavioural, Neurobiological and Psychosocial Perspectives: A Synthesis*. Cambridge: Cambridge University Press.

Magnusson, D. and Cairns, R.B. (1997) Developmental science: an integrated framework. In: R.B. Cairns, G.H. Elder and E.J. Costello (eds) *Developmental Science*. New York: Cambridge University Press.

Nash, A. and Hay, D.F. (1993) Relationships in infancy as precursors and causes of later relationships and psychopathology. In D.F. Hay and A. Angold (eds) *Precursors and Causes in Development and Psychopathology*. Chichester: John Wiley & Sons.

Pickles, A. and Rutter, M. (1991) Statistical and conceptual models of 'turning points': developmental processes. In: D. Magnusson, L. Bergsmen, G. Rudinger and B. Torested (eds) *Problems and Methods in Longitudinal Research: Stability and Change*. Cambridge: Cambridge University Press.

Quinton, D., Pickles, A., Maughan, B. and Rutter, M. (1993) Partners, peers and pathways: assortative mating and continuities in conduct disorder. *Development and Psychopathology*, 5, 763–783.

Rutter, M. (1994a) Causal concepts and their testing. In: M. Rutter and D. Smith (eds) *Psychosocial Disorders in Young People: Time Trends and their Origins*. Chichester: John Wiley & Sons.

Rutter, M. (1994b) Concepts of causation and implications for interventions. In: A. Petersen and J. Ortimer (eds) *Youth Unemployment and Society*. Cambridge: Cambridge University Press.

Rutter, M. (1996) Developmental psychopathology as an organising research construct. In: D. Magnusson (ed.) *The Lifespan Development of Individuals:*

Behavioural, Neurobiological and Psychosocial Perspectives: A Synthesis. Cambridge: Cambridge University Press.

Rutter, M. and Rutter, M. (1993) *Developing Minds: Challenge and Continuity Across the Lifespan*. New York: Basic Books.

Rutter, M., Champion, L., Quinton, D., Maughan, B. and Pickles, A. (1994) Origins of individual differences in environmental risk exposure. In: P. Moen, G. Elder and K. Luscher (eds) *Perspectives on the Ecology of Human Development*. Ithaca, NY: Cornell University Press.

Chapter 22

Addressing the interfaces

Peter Reder, Mike McClure and Anthony Jolley

This book was conceived out of a realisation that the current organisation of mental health services, together with the highly specialised skills of their staff, preclude an integrated approach to the welfare of adults and children. Despite a growing literature about the effects of parental mental health problems on children, we were not aware of many initiatives to identify and respond to these children's needs. Again, even though it is well known that major psychological problems often occur at transitional phases in people's development (such as around the birth of a child or during adolescence), there remain few specialised services to respond to such problems.

In order to redress these deficiencies, it is first necessary for interface problems to be recognised by professionals – not only those engaged in direct clinical work, but also their managers, trainers, service commissioners and policy makers. Then, willingness must be mobilised at all levels to fill the gaps, even if this implies that professionals may need to widen their knowledge base and repertoire of practice skills and purchasers might need to reprioritise some of their resource allocations. In this final chapter, we shall summarise the practical implications that arise from the research and clinical experiences reported in the previous chapters and also comment on their relevance for professional training.

An agenda for change

It is evident that interface issues will only be recognised if practitioners consider individuals in their wider social, relational and developmental contexts. This might lead some to believe that a revolution in theory and practice is necessary so that, in future, all professionals think in terms of family and wider interactions. However, developments rarely take place in such dramatic fashion, but step by step, and that is what we believe is appropriate with regard to the adult/child interfaces. A few small changes may be all that is necessary to benefit a number of children and parents whose problems are interacting, and these differences may in turn initiate a process that widens the scope of help available to many more.

For example, the long-term goal might be for children's needs to be part of the automatic thinking of adult mental health staff, but this would require careful liaison, personal contacts, cross-referrals, audit and training over time. Small initial changes might include creation of history sheets that prompt the practitioner to compile the family genogram, including ages of the patient's children, and to consider whether there are concerns about the children's welfare. The child and adolescent mental health service (CAMHS) and adult services might collaborate in drawing up a simple list of risk indicators, which could be discussed, for example, at trainee psychiatrists' induction programmes when they joined the service. The value of the history sheet could then be audited and further modified in discussion between the two services.

Beyond these initial steps, the interfaces between child and adult mental health can be recognised through more established liaison, consolidation of certain specialised services, research and training initiatives, and the development of preventive strategies.

Liaison

Staff working in secondary care services have, of necessity, developed their expertise in specific areas and therefore must rely on colleagues in other specialties to complement their skills and broaden the overall picture. The importance of collaboration between services has been underlined by many contributors to this book but it is surprising to reflect that liaison between psychiatric and medical services has a longer history (see Mayou, 1997) than liaison between different elements of mental health trusts. Perhaps this indicates the relentless pressure on funding and resources within mental health services in which the severest end of the spectrum of disorders takes precedence. However, we believe that liaison should not be seen as a low-priority option but as a necessary contribution to effective mental health provision.

In our view, the most crucial liaison initiatives are those that have been discussed in preceding chapters of this book – that is, between CAMHS teams and adult mental health teams in the community and hospitals (including psychotherapy services); between adolescent and substance misuse services; and between mental health and perinatal services.

Once again, these initiatives can start in small ways through personal contacts and arrangements for consultation and cross-referral. Identifying specific liaison staff within respective teams would facilitate the process, since they can act as a 'communication switchboard' between the services. The system of Named Professionals for Child Protection within trusts is a good example of this process (Department of Health and Welsh Office, 1995), whereby a doctor and nurse with recognised expertise and interest in child protection are identified by relevant trusts to offer consultation and advice to colleagues and to oversee their training needs.

Further development of liaison might be towards clinics in which family members are seen together, and the beginnings of such an enterprise have been discussed by Falkov and Davies (1997). In this project, the key worker for patients with psychotic disorders identified their psychological, social and medical needs and this enabled the existence of dependent children to be noted. If the children were having difficulties, it was possible for the whole family to be seen jointly by members of the child and adult mental health teams. However, few provider resources are available which consistently address the whole family. The Marlborough Family Unit in north-west London (see Asen, Chapter 16 in this volume) and the Cassel Hospital in Surrey (Kennedy, 1997; Kennedy *et al.*, 1987) are examples of the small number of family units that have continued to exist within the National Health Service.

While specialist services might need to make deliberate effort over time to bridge the interfaces between children and adults, general practitioners – literally 'family' doctors – are ideally placed to hold both generations in mind and to recruit services that address their overlapping needs. General practitioners could ensure that they include up-to-date genograms in each of their patient's note packs, and budget for the services of family therapists as well as individual counsellors. Regular dialogue between general practitioners and health visitors would also allow them to consider together the welfare of all family members.

Collaborative planning

Communication between the different specialties also has the potential for each to learn from the other's experiences. CAMHS staff have had long years of grappling with the intricacies of multi-professional team work and the controversies it raises about leadership and responsibility. They have also had a considerable history of being based 'in the community'. Furthermore, the various forms of inquiry into children's deaths from abuse have preceded Confidential Inquiries into Homicides and Suicides by Psychiatric Patients by some twenty years (Peay, 1996) and these experiences about children could do much to inform the process undertaken about adults (Reder and Duncan, 1996; Eastman, 1996). On the other hand, CAMHSs are historically much younger than services for adults and continue to borrow from them in such areas as treatment approaches, diagnostic precision, emergency service provision and academic establishment.

Recognition of the interfaces between children and adults clearly has implications beyond mental health services. It involves the need for inter-agency collaboration between health, social services and the voluntary sector. As one example, Falkov (1996; 1997) and Reder and Duncan (1997) point out that, even though we have become progressively more aware of the adverse effects of parental mental health problems on some children, adult mental health services remain a missing link in the child protection network. Very few adult psychiatrists or psychologists sit on Area Child Protection Committees and their capacity to participate in local information-sharing and service planning continues to be underdeveloped. Many general psychiatrists would welcome the opportunity to attend child protection conferences but find that they are rarely given sufficient notice or that the times usually clash with other clinical priorities. If they had a representative on the Area Child Protection Committee, it would be easier to negotiate fixed times for such conferences or other measures to facilitate their input.

In the United States, the New York State Task Force on Mentally Ill Parents with Young Children (Blanch et al., 1994) found that the Office of Mental Health and Department of Social Services rarely engaged in joint planning at the 'systems, program, or client levels', so that clients were exposed to apparently disconnected and uncoordinated services. Their far-sighted recommendations included the development of family services that no longer divided adults from children, the revision of all policies to incorporate family concerns, the provision of education for children of hospitalised adults, and the merging of multiple funding streams in order to attach money to families.

Many initiatives that address the mental and social health of families can only be successful if they are planned and implemented through inter-agency forums. Services for adolescent substance misusers have already been discussed in this book, and there are numerous other examples. The care of children whose parents have been admitted to psychiatric wards as an emergency requires policies that have been thought through between the relevant agencies, while the post-discharge aftercare of all family members needs similar attention. Equivalent collaborative strategies between the voluntary sector, social services and mental health services apply to the needs of mothers and their children who are taking refuge from domestic violence.

Specialised services

Clear management structures for trusts that emerged from the reorganised health service have had many advantages. Service configurations became more tightly defined as trusts were divided into separate Directorates with their own identified budgets and strategic planning responsibilities. However, the drawback has been a greater difficulty in planning for specialised services that cross the Directorate divides, particularly when it is debatable which budget should fund the initiative.

Perinatal mental health services for mothers with psychiatric disturbance are an obvious example of this problem, since it could be contended that the primary patient is the mother and not the child and that treatment needs to focus on the mother's disorder. On that basis, funding for the service should come from an Adult Directorate. However, there are equally cogent arguments that the infant's welfare is as much at stake as the mother's and that knowledge of mother–infant interaction is crucial for the success of such a service. On that basis, the initiative would do well to be based in a Children's Directorate. The most likely consequence of such a polarised debate is the absence of any such service and the obvious solution is for there to be the development of a specialised team with its own identified budget and appropriate skill-mix of staff.

There are many other examples of resource divisions that require imaginative planning in order for them to be solved. For instance, where should the funding for parenting skills work sit? Since it is work primarily focusing on the adult's conflicts and behaviour, does this mean that it should be the province of Adult Directorate staff? But, on the other hand, of course, it is aimed at resolving a problem for the child. Another common question is: who should be responsible for treating a parent's psychological problem that has become apparent during family work in a child mental health service, especially if referral into another department's waiting list runs the risk of treatment drop-out? We are not aware of many services that have managed the creative leap of appointing adult-trained staff into a child and adolescent team, and vice versa, a theme to which we shall return later.

Similar issues face the development of services for adolescents. CAMHSs have traditionally catered for younger people, with the higher age cut-off being in mid-adolescence, either at age 16 or 18, or when the person has left full-time education. There is no doubt that the adolescent process continues beyond those arbitrary cut-off points and that the slightly older adolescent also shows specific problems that require specialised and experienced professional skills. The special requirements of young people during this transitional stage in their lives have been under-resourced for too long. Working with such adolescents is a specific skill that should be trained for in its own right, and specialised services need to be established so that these skills can be applied and targeted. Recent strategic reports (e.g. NHS Health Advisory Service, 1995) describe services for older adolescents within the brief of CAMHSs, thereby extending their upper age limit to the nineteenth or twentieth year. There could be considerable merit in this proposal if it ensured that adolescent services were recognised as a mental health sub-specialty that bridged the transitional phase between childhood and adulthood. However, the work of that sub-specialty would need to be resourced by staff trained to work with that age group and who had fully funded back-up facilities to cater for all their specific mental health needs.

Research

The research studies reported in previous chapters have highlighted the significant impact of parental psychological disturbance on children. Previously, commentators had tended to be defensive about psychiatric patients, emphasising how capable they were of providing satisfactory care of their children. While this is undoubtedly so in many cases, these research findings offer a more balanced and realistic overall picture and thereby allow appropriate monitoring, preventive, liaison and intervention strategies to be developed, to mutual benefit.

Clearly, there remain numerous aspects of the interfaces between child and adult mental health worthy of research. In our view, there is a need for both quantitative and qualitative research, and project topics might include:

- preventive approaches in childhood to reduce the risk of children's mental health disorders or consequences of abuse continuing into adult life;
- intergenerational reverberations of the attachment relationship;
- the role played by children in the generation or course of parental psychiatric disturbance;
- assessing the risk of psychiatric patients maltreating their children;
- links between parental expressed emotion and emotional abuse of children;
- the cost-effectiveness of liaison projects;
- the efficacy of conjoint family work.

In order to recognise the clinical importance of such projects, trusts should be encouraged to prioritise research about the child/adult interfaces in their Research and Development strategies.

Training

Significant training implications emerge from the papers collected together in this book, with relevance for psychiatrists, psychologists, nurses, health visitors, therapists and general practitioners, among others. All undergraduate and postgraduate programmes would need to contain modules that taught about the issues across the child/adult boundaries, such as intergenerational influences and developmental processes. At the postgraduate level, training posts could be created that refined these skills and provided opportunities for research, such as jointly-appointed psychiatry senior house officers or liaison specialist registrars, liaison family therapists or clinical psychologists. In a sense, we are recommending that those intending to work in either the child or the adult specialties would also have undertaken a *family* mental health training.

We are best able to comment more specifically on the training of our own profession and have introduced in Chapter 1 some reflections on the undergraduate and post-qualifying training of doctors and psychiatrists. It is likely that these remarks have equivalent application within the other professions. For psychiatrists, the training implications go beyond the detailed contents of undergraduate and postgraduate schemes and concern the mind-set that is imparted to trainees. In our view, the importance of clarifying a diagnostic formulation needs to be balanced with a curiosity about the social, inter-actional and psychological contributions to the presenting problem. In a sense, the diagnosis should not be regarded as the end of the paragraph but the beginning of a new one.

There are many ways that this attention to process as well as to detail can be learned by trainee psychiatrists, and time spent talking to children during specialist placements and talking to adults during psychotherapy experience are obvious examples. Conversance with family interactional processes and experience at interviewing whole families should be seen as essential skills for all psychiatrists. Introductory family therapy courses should be included in postgraduate programmes. Furthermore, if the different services have already established regular communication arrangements, then trainees should participate in them in order to develop their consultation and liaison skills.

In addition, the value of inter-service academic conferences should not be underestimated. We have found that allocating responsibility for overseeing continuing professional development to one senior member of staff has provided the opportunity for interfaces between various elements of the trust to be addressed through whole-day conferences and the inclusion of presentations at weekly academic meetings. At a national level, academic bodies, such as the Royal College of Psychiatrists and the British Psychological Society, could play a vital role by supporting conference initiatives and continuing professional development programmes that address the child/adult interfaces.

Prevention

Prevention – a cherished ambition of the modern NHS – is usually discussed as strategies at the primary, secondary and tertiary levels. Primary prevention aims to prevent a problem before it starts and involves the identification of members of the population who are at higher risk of developing a disorder, so that preventive interventions can be offered. It is the most difficult to accomplish and to measure in mental health where the risk groups are so large. Secondary prevention focuses on selected groups identified as most at risk of developing a condition and, in the field of mental health, is equally challenging because of the multi-determined nature of disorders and the complexity of most efficacy measures. Tertiary prevention involves providing interventions for those already showing evidence of a disorder in order to lessen its adverse consequences. Most attention has been focused on this aspect, through the application of, for example, treatment outcome measures.

A particular problem about separating out prevention in this way when discussing overlaps between children's and adults' concerns is that tertiary prevention for, say, the parent can be a primary preventive measure for their child. Hence, it is more practical for us to merge our consideration of prevention into more composite themes.

Overall, it seems likely that successful recognition of those children who are the most likely to suffer from psychological, psychiatric or relationship problems in adult life could pay enormous dividends in the long term. Not only might it be possible to prevent personal suffering, but also the traumatic impact of such difficulties on other people and on society in general. If childhood problems, especially those of children who are suffering as a result of their parent's mental health difficulties, could be recognised and treated early, it is possible that their development into chronic disorders could be avoided.

One approach might be for adult services to develop the facility to recognise which of their patients are experiencing parenting problems because of mental health problems. Alternatively, as authors of some of the previous chapters propose, all children of adult psychiatric patients could be screened for early signs of dysfunction. This would require practitioners to develop simple, yet sensitive, screening tools and overcome problems of access to the children. Again, the repetition of child maltreatment one generation on may be prevented by timely recognition in the community of parenting deficiencies and the provision of effective parenting skills programmes. Appropriate perinatal interventions are also likely to impact on mothers' abilities to care for their infants and young children, and prevent prolonged disorders of attachment or care.

At a different level, evidence that psychotherapy for parents who were maltreated as children is an effective measure against repetition of abusive parenting with their own children (Egeland *et al.*, 1988) points to the value of providing appropriate psychotherapy resources as a preventive intervention. The demonstration that many patients of adult mental health services have experienced childhood maltreatment, and that such histories worsen their prognosis, is further argument for psychotherapeutic approaches as a preventive measure. The provision of specialised adolescent mental health facilities could also enable strategies to be developed to prevent risk-taking, anti-social behaviour or substance misuse becoming an established way of life for some young people.

Resources, priorities and longer-term aspirations

It is not unusual for busy clinicians to react to the mention of the adult/child interfaces with comments such as: 'Not another initiative and priority!'; 'I have enough trouble dealing with my own patients' problems!'; and 'Where will the resources come from for us to do more liaising, auditing, family interviewing and training?' A number of contributors to this book have commented on the prioritising and resourcing implications of their recommendations. Certainly, if addressing the child/adult interfaces can be understood as an essential exercise in prevention, then the need to target the limited resources currently available must be addressed.

There is no doubt that providing quality services makes demands on time and resources, especially at the outset when extra effort is needed to plan and organise initiatives. It would be wrong to suggest that liaison between services can operate in the absence of dedicated resources and support from purchasers and trusts. Liaison needs to have a high profile in the trust's business plans and to be funded appropriately. If the Department of Health's and health authorities' priorities make unrealistic demands on inadequately funded providers, then liaison and other measures to address the child/adult interfaces are bound to be seen as the soft option and relegated in importance. This would be short-sighted and regrettable.

We believe that effort to address the parent/child interfaces would pay enormous dividends in the medium to long term. If it became automatic for practitioners to think about other family members, and they were skilled at asking the relevant questions at interview, little time would be wasted in the outpatient clinic or on the ward. Once it is clear that the effectiveness of treatments can be enhanced when the patient's living and relationship circumstances are taken into account, then services are likely to be more efficient, recovery times shortened and relapse rates reduced. Good lines of communication between teams might mean that more cases are discussed and cross-referred but, in all likelihood, more timely responses could be given and severe or chronic developments prevented. Furthermore, adding a relationship perspective to one's areas of enquiry can be extraordinarily interesting, creative and enjoyable.

Our proposals for improved liaison and training across the specialties would not require revolutions in the way that services are thought about and organised. They would make a start by identifying, for example, those symptomatic children who were suffering as a result of their parent's mental health problems, and providing interventions tailored to their needs. But the logical next step might require a shift in focus, since it would entail creating formal structures that recognised the importance of interactional processes to the welfare of all family members. Special initiatives would be required to target preventive strategies towards other family members whose difficulties had not yet come to the attention of existing services.

Before arguments can be mounted for increased clinical resources, it is first necessary to consider whether developments might come about through reprioritisation. We believe that the creation of preventive services for children is so important that it should be prioritised above many problems historically deemed to be the province of CAMHSs, such as anti-social behaviour or school-based problems. However, this does not mean that we are being constrained in the current debate about the future role of child and adolescent psychiatrists by those who advocate a narrow restriction to problems of organic aetiology (Goodman, 1997). We prefer the vision for the profession discussed by Kraemer (1999), in which child psychiatrists (and, by extension, child psychologists and others in CAMHSs) acquire skills in a range of areas so that they can assess and treat children's problems that have a biological, psychological and social contribution. Working at the interfaces between child and adult mental health problems should be seen as a highly skilled enterprise that requires an understanding of many interwoven processes, including: child development; the attachment dynamic; defences against anxiety; family interactional patterns; parenting relationships; genetic predispositions; and adult psychopathology. Such expertise is unlikely to be found outside of specialist multidisciplinary CAMHS teams and it makes good sense to optimise their use.

In adult mental health services, relentless pressure to focus on those people with the severest disorders is limiting the resources available to treat inter-relational and other psychological distress. Left unrecognised and untreated, these problems have huge economic and social cost in lost work days, anti-social behaviour, family disharmony and break-up, and disturbance in children of the family before they become parents in their own right. For those parents whose difficulties are coming to the attention of specialist services, it is clear that the interventions offered must also address the welfare of other family members and that mentally ill adults with children need to receive additional resources because of their crucial parenting role. This, too, should be seen as a priority for a forward-looking NHS.

However, it seems unrealistic to expect severely stretched adult mental health services to be able to make significant changes in their priorities in order to cater for the needs of the children. Hence, the initiatives would need to come from CAMHSs, both for the initial reprioritising of resources and then the seeking of additional funding. Although in the short term some initiatives could be provided by reprioritisation, in the longer term staff sessions would need to be costed appropriately and written into service specifications as *additional* to current establishment.

In order to place the interfaces between children and adults firmly on the map of service provisions, we believe that sessions should be established within all mental health teams for family-focused work. Although CAMHSs already employ family therapists as team members, their work tends to remain child-oriented and the teams would also need to contain one or more practitioners who are able to work therapeutically with parents on interface issues. Similarly, adult mental health teams should employ practitioners who are experienced at recognising and addressing concerns of the children of their adult patients. Only in this way could preventive measures be widely applied, because children's needs would be recognised before they became translated into symptoms or impaired their development.

One means of achieving this provision within adult mental health teams could be for CAMHS staff to provide sessions within those teams, not in a liaison role but as a formal team member with a specific brief for children.

Alternatively, special family clinics, staffed primarily by members of CAMHS teams, could be established that truly bridged the two services because their brief was to address the needs of children of adult patients, whether symptomatic or not. The likely benefits of investing in specialist adolescent and perinatal services, as well as parenting skills programmes, have already been mentioned.

Such changes would need dedicated funding. Short-term funding opportunities do arise from time to time, such as through joint-funded projects, priority services developments or regional training and development resources, and these can be used to initiate a liaison scheme which, if well audited, can be put forward for continuing funding. From the evidence collected in this volume, there are strong arguments for recurring *increased* investment in child and family mental health services.

Our long-term vision, then, is for changes in the mind-set of those planning and providing mental health services. Although adults and young people present with different problems that demand different responses, they clearly also have overlapping needs. The problems of one both affect and reflect problems of the other. While individual mental health professionals cannot be expected to be experts at treating disorder in all age groups, they should be able to recognise and respond to the interface components of problems presenting to them. Service organisation should facilitate this process. Inflexible funding, managerial and planning barriers between child and adult services must become more permeable, both within mental health trusts and between health and other welfare services. As a result, creative initiatives could be conceived and implemented with wide support.

These initiatives would recognise that, when one person presents with psychological problems, each other member of their family matters.

References

Blanch, A.K., Nicholson, J. and Purcell, J. (1994) Parents with severe mental illness and their children: the need for human services integration. *Journal of Mental Health Administration*, 21, 388–396.

Department of Health and Welsh Office (1995) *Child Protection: Clarification of Arrangements between the NHS and Other Agencies*. Department of Health.

Eastman, N. (1996) Inquiry into homicides by psychiatric patients: systemic audit should replace mandatory inquiries. *British Medical Journal*, 313, 1069–1071.

Egeland, B., Jacobvitz, D. and Sroufe, L.A. (1988) Breaking the cycle of abuse. *Child Development*, 59, 1080–1088.

Falkov, A. (1996) *Study of Working Together 'Part 8' Reports. Fatal Child Abuse and Parental Psychiatric Disorder: An Analysis of 100 Area Child Protection Committee Case Reviews Conducted under the Terms of Part 8 of Working Together under the Children Act 1989*. Department of Health.

Falkov, A. (1997) Adult psychiatry – a missing link in the child protection network: a response to Reder and Duncan. *Child Abuse Review*, 6, 41–45.

Falkov, A. and Davies, N. (1997) Solutions on the ground: a family mental health service? In: *Report of the 12th Annual Michael Sieff Foundation Conference 'Keeping Children in Mind: Balancing Children's Needs with Parents' Mental Health'*. Michael Sieff Foundation.

Goodman, R. (1997) Who needs child psychiatrists? *Child Psychology and Psychiatry Review*, 2, 15–19.

Kennedy, R. (1997) *Child Abuse, Psychotherapy and the Law*. London: Free Association Books.

Kennedy, R., Heyman, A. and Tischler, L. (1987) *The Family as In-Patient*. London: Free Association Books.

Kraemer, S. (1999) Who needs child and adolescent psychiatrists? *Clinical Child Psychology and Psychiatry*, 4, 121–127.

Mayou, R. (1997) Psychiatry, medicine and consultation-liaison. *British Journal of Psychiatry*, 171, 203–204.

NHS Health Advisory Service (1995) *Together We Stand: The Commissioning, Role and Management of Child and Adolescent Mental Health Services*. London: HMSO.

Peay, J. (ed.) (1996) *Inquiries after Homicide*. London: Duckworth.

Reder, P. and Duncan, S. (1996) Reflections on child abuse inquiries. In: J. Peay (ed.) *Inquiries after Homicide*. London: Duckworth.

Reder, P. and Duncan, S. (1997) Adult psychiatry – a missing link in the child protection network: comments on Falkov's 'Fatal Child Abuse and Parental Psychiatric Disorder' (DOH, 1996). *Child Abuse Review*, 6, 35–40.

Name index

Adland, M.I. 261
Agathonos-Georgopoulou, H. 167
Akhtar, S. 152
Alam, F. 145
Albridge, S. 214
Aldridge, T. 280
Alexander, J. 152
Alfaro, J. 169
Allen, J. 46
Anastopoulos, A.D. 65
Anderson, H. 216
Angold, A. 25, 70
Anthony, E.J. 91, 175
Appleby, L. 152
Arellano, C.M. 41
Armstrong, K.L. 167
Arnold, R.P. 44
Asarnow, J.R. 12, 23
Asen, E. 228, 230, 320
Ashton, J. 181

Babiker, I. 45
Bailey, S. 158
Bailey, V. 192
Baker, T.W. 39, 41
Balbernie, R. 267
Balding, J. 271
Bandura, A. 239, 248
Banks, S.L. 253
Barber, B.L. 72
Barbero, G.J. 124
Barkley, R.A. 30
Barlow, J. 238, 239, 250
Barnett, B. 155, 161
Barrett, M.L. 195
Barrett, P.M. 96, 99
Bartholomew, K. 306
Bateson, G. 214

Bays, J. 169
Beardslee, W.R. 84, 87, 181, 193
Bebbington, P. 192
Beck, J. 42, 44
Beglin, S.J. 112
Beitchman, J.H. 39
Benjamin, S. 122
Bennett, D. 294
Bennett-Osborne, R. 128
Berg, B. 118
Berger, M. 64
Berkowitz, R. 213
Berndt, T.J. 71
Bewley, S. 59
Biederman, J. 30, 32
Bifulco, A. 41
Biglan, A. 238, 239, 250, 253
Bion, W.R. 259
Birch, H.G. 237
Bird, L. 183
Black, D. 156
Blanch, A.K. 83, 290, 296, 299, 321
Bonnet, C. 169
Bools, C.N. 130, 131
Boscolo, L. 213, 220
Bosma, H.A. 71
Boston, M. 64
Boswell, G. 158
Bowlby, J. 46, 64, 98, 158
Boyle, M.H. 274, 275
Brandon, S. 46
Brestan, E.V. 239, 250, 252
Bretherton, I. 306
Brewin, C.R. 46, 192
Briere, J.N. 39, 40–1, 41, 42
Brinch, M. 109, 110
Brisby, T. 167
Brody, G.H. 194

Subject index